I0824276

Pinch Your Pottery

THE ART & CRAFT OF MAKING PINCH POTS

35 BEAUTIFUL PROJECTS
TO HAND-FORM FROM CLAY

Jacqui Atkin

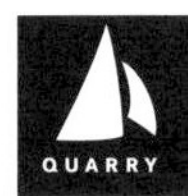

Quarto

First published in 2021 by Quarry Books,
an imprint of The Quarto Group,
100 Cummings Center, Suite 265-D,
Beverly, MA 01915, USA.
T (978) 282-9590 F (978) 283-2742
www.Quarto.com

10 9 8 7 6 5 4 3

ISBN: 978-1-58923-974-6

Library of Congress Cataloging-in-Publication Data is available.

Conceived, edited, and designed by
Quarto Publishing plc, an imprint of
The Quarto Group
1 Triptych Place,
London, SE1 9SH,
United Kingdom

QUAR.325956

Project editor: Anna Galkina
Copy editor: Katie Hardwicke
Photographer: Phil Wilkins
Designer: Rachel Cross
Deputy art director: Martina Calvio
Art director: Gemma Wilson
Associate publisher: Eszter Karpati
Publisher: Samantha Warrington

Printed in China

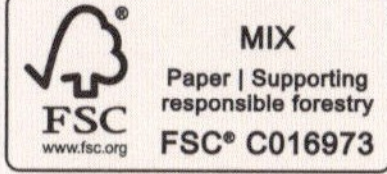

CAUTION

Some materials used in pottery as colorants for clays and glazes can be harmful if breathed in or ingested—studies suggest that some can even be absorbed through the skin. For best practice, be sure to wear the appropriate protection when handling these materials which **ALWAYS** includes a dust mask and rubber or latex gloves.

Slip and glaze materials must be handled and prepared with caution. Pottery suppliers should always supply the relevant health and safety data for their products and information relating to each material will be printed on its container—**be sure to read it.**

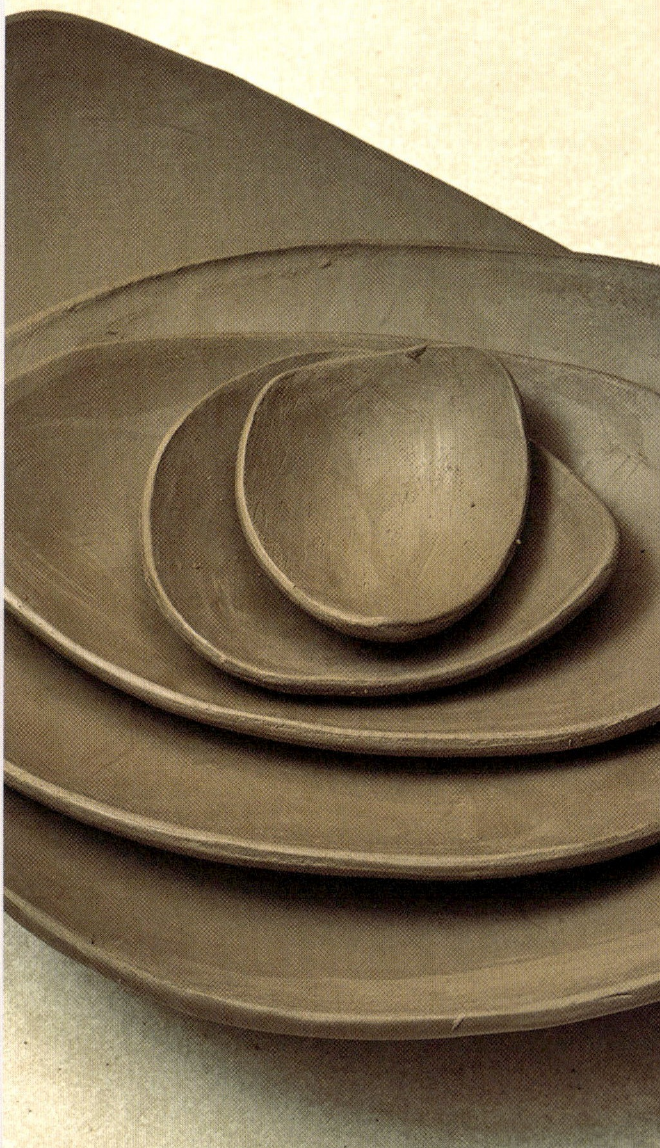

CONTENTS

INTRODUCTION

My sincere hope in producing this book is to dispel any misconceptions about pinching and demonstrate its versatility as a method for making practical and imaginative forms, whether small or large, using mostly your hands, just a few tools, and an electric kiln.

Pinching is the most basic and direct method there is for interacting with clay; its malleable quality instantly makes the handler want to shape it and, in fact, if you give a child a lump of clay without telling them what it is, they will naturally pinch it into something like a bowl or an animal. Do you remember your own first encounter with clay at school? Those lumpen attempts that made your mother so proud. I still have my own children's early clay artworks, which I treasure for their naivety and the wonderful way they were created without the constraints of technical know-how—they contain much of the character of the child.

In historical terms, pinch pots dating back over 17,000 years have been discovered in China. Their original use was no doubt purely practical, to hold food and water, but at some point their making evolved to produce ornate vessels for wider domestic use and as decorative art forms. This was a technique that laid the foundations for forming clay in other ways and coiling was quickly discovered as a way of extending the size of vessels, but millennia passed before the introduction of the pottery wheel in around 4000 bce, so the pinching technique served humans well for a considerably long time.

In contemporary terms, pinching seems to be a making method that's less well-regarded than others. Maybe this is because of its association with early learning, or possibly that it is seen as a rudimentary technique from which you graduate to other, more technical methods with outcomes of greater sophistication. However, in my experience as a teacher, I have found that many people struggle with the complexities of pinching; they assume it is the simplest method but soon find it has challenges like any other. What I usually say is that mastering pinching will teach the best tactile sensitivity of all the making methods. It is a methodical way of working that allows the individual to make adjustments but gives the best control over the clay. Of course, it takes practice to make something of refinement, but once mastered it is possible to make wonderful, innovative forms for practical or decorative use that rival anything made by other methods, even those on the wheel.

Of course, the process does not end with the making; there is always surface decoration to contend with, an element of ceramics that many find daunting, but again, using just a few basic techniques this book will show there is great scope for individual creativity, including using ready-to-use products for those who don't have the time or space to prepare their own.

Happy Potting.

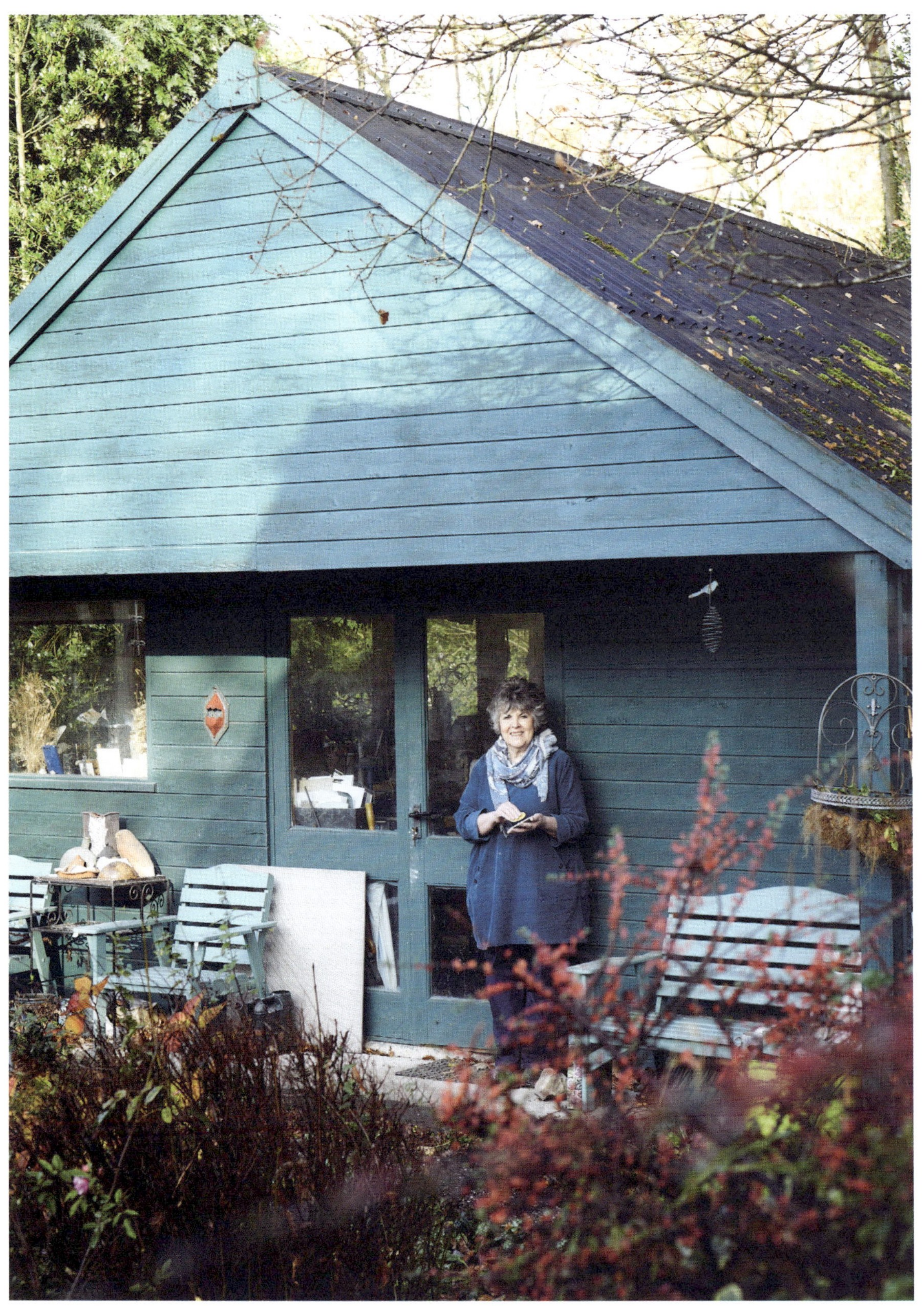

CLAYS

Any clay can be used to make pinched forms with practice but some are much easier to work with than others. Traditionally, there are three main categories of clay: earthenware, stoneware, and porcelain, which are differentiated by their fired density and strength. However, more broadly, there are also clays available with wide firing ranges that fall between categories. This alone can complicate the choice, but in addition within each group there are also variables of colours and textures to exacerbate the dilemma. For pinching, the most important factor to consider is the plasticity of the clay, as this will directly influence its handling ability.

POINTS TO CONSIDER WHEN CHOOSING CLAY FOR PINCHING

Firstly, what color clay? It is imperative that you have an idea of what the finished item will look like and this will include how it will be decorated and/or glazed. This decision will determine the color of clay you should use. For example, brightly colored decoration will work far better on a white or pale-colored clay than it would on a dark clay, although the problem can be overcome by applying a layer of white slip.

Secondly, is the form for domestic use or decorative? All clays can be used for domestic wares but earthenware will need to be glazed to make it waterproof. Stoneware clay vitrifies in firing, making it impervious to water; therefore, in theory, any surface treatment is purely decorative.

Thirdly, firing temperature is a serious consideration if firing often: earthenware clays use less energy to fire than stoneware, with porcelain using the greatest amount.

TIP

To test for plasticity and working quality, roll a short, fat coil, then bend it into a tight loop. A clay with good plasticity will show no signs of splitting along the bend, but a clay with low plasticity will.

Finally, which type of firing? The projects in this book are fired in an electric kiln, but if at any point the maker wanted to experiment with extreme firing methods like raku or pit, the choice of clay type would be critical as these methods require a grogged, open clay body with good thermal-shock properties for successful outcomes.

EARTHENWARE CLAYS

These are low-firing clay bodies that generally fire in the range of 1,830–2,156°F (1,000–1,180°C).

The most familiar of the earthenware clays is red earthenware, or terra-cotta as it is otherwise known. It is a heavily iron-bearing clay, which gives it its earthy color when raw. It fires to a warm, toasted orange at bisque and brown when covered with transparent glaze. This is a great hand-building clay with good plasticity that can be purchased in smooth or grogged form.

White or off-white earthenware clays are formulated from careful blending of ball clays, china clay (kaolin), and fluxes (materials that influence the melting point of a product). Many are highly plastic and again available in smooth or grogged form, the latter being best for pinching because it has more tooth for joining parts together.

These clays are a good choice for colorful surface decoration and inlay work.

STONEWARE CLAYS

Stoneware clays generally fire in the range of 2,190–2,380°F (1,200–1,300°C), and are so called because when fired the clay vitrifies, becoming dense, hard, and impervious like stone.

The range of stoneware clays is the broadest, being available in a whole host of colors, including white, gray, buff, pink, brown, and black, and a wide range of textures. A typical body can be composed of fire clay and ball clay, with varying feldspar content to influence the maturing temperature. Higher feldspar content lowers the required temperature but low-temperature stonewares are often made by substituting the feldspar with a frit. White bodies are made by substituting the fire clay with a lighter version and replacing some of the content with china clay. Stonewares generally have good working properties and plasticity, and many are formulated specifically for use in particular kilns, for oxidized or reduction atmospheres. When buying clay of this type, be sure to check that it is suitable to fire in your kiln.

In recent years there have been great developments in low-temperature stoneware glazes which fire at the lower end of the range in cone 5–6 (2,205–2,269°F/1,207–1,243°C), and clay manufacturers have developed clays to complement them. Do ensure you are choosing the right clay for your decorating and firing requirements when making your choice.

PORCELAIN

This is the highest firing of all the clays at 2,340–2,370°F (1,280–1,300°C) and is renowned for its clarity and translucency. It is an ultra-smooth, fine clay, usually white when fired, although it can also be purchased in colored form, including black.

Points to consider when working with porcelain:

1. You either love porcelain or hate it! It is a tricky clay to pinch and is not recommended for a first attempt because it can be very temperamental, quickly moving from floppy to an unworkable firmness.
2. Porcelain needs to be pinched to a thin, wafer-like section to achieve a translucent, glass-like finish when fired. This requires a delicate touch.
3. It is difficult to join parts if they are even fractionally different in their state of firmness and gauging this accurately is hard. Handles can ping off if a soft one is attached to a firm body, and two sections of different firmness joined to make a hollow form will crack open.
4. This is a clay you will have to persevere with to be successful; it takes a lot of practice to understand how best to handle it and how far you can push it.

PAPER CLAY

Available in all three forms, the handling properties of paper clay are very different to other clays. If you want to try your hand at working with porcelain, a paper clay version is a good place to start because it is much easier to handle, with fewer of the inherent problems of a general porcelain body.

Commercially produced paper clays contain finely chopped fibers of flax and/or cellulose, which produce a very forgiving clay that can be formed in many different ways. The addition of flax gives a body strength and flexibility with the added bonus of making it lightweight and resistant to mold, unlike other paper clay bodies. The fibers add a strong but flexible internal structure to the clay, creating a capillary system that transfers moisture evenly. Paper clays are also available to buy in grogged forms and most have a wide firing range.

The most fantastic quality of paper clay is that sections can be joined at any stage of dryness—even bone-dry—and the structure is incredibly strong, making it easy to transport where required.

The downsides to paper clay are that surfaces can be difficult to refine in the normal way, but potters who use these clays find a way around this problem by working on the surface at different stages. Secondly, they can produce a lot of fumes when firing, so the kiln area must be really well ventilated.

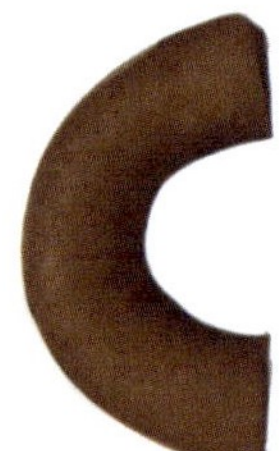
Earthenware clay (red earthenware or terra-cotta)

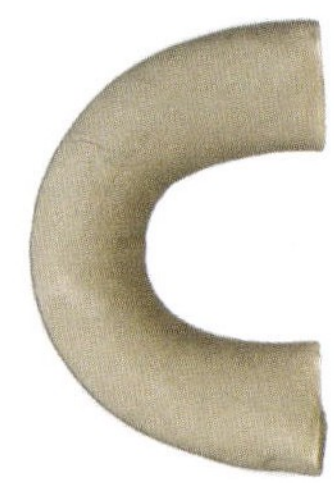
Stoneware clay (buff stoneware clay)

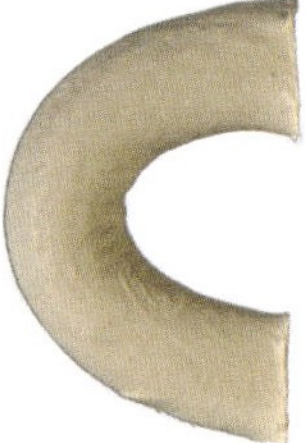
Stoneware clay (smooth white stoneware clay)

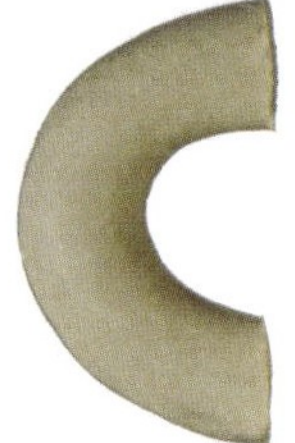
Porcelain

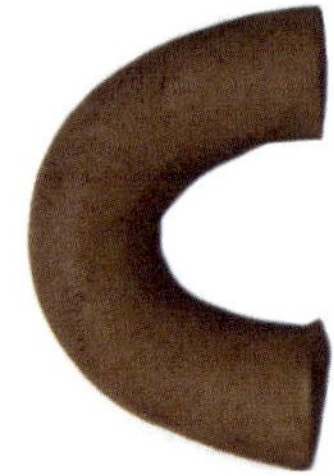
Paper clay (grogged red earthenware)

TOOLS AND EQUIPMENT

One of the reasons pinching is such a great making method is that so few tools or items of equipment are required for successful outcomes. Your best tool is your hands, but listed here are just a few extras that will help you achieve excellent results. Not all are essential, but those that are, are noted.

FORMING TOOLS

CUTTING WIRE: *Essential*
A wire is required to cut clay from the bag and generally for kneading and wedging, which are the methods of preparing clay for use. Unless your clay has a lot of obvious air in it, for the pinching technique it can be used directly from the bag without the need for wedging.

Wires are usually about 18in (45cm) long with toggles at each end. They can be made at home from coat toggle buttons, or wooden curtain rings, and fishing wire of a suitable thickness.

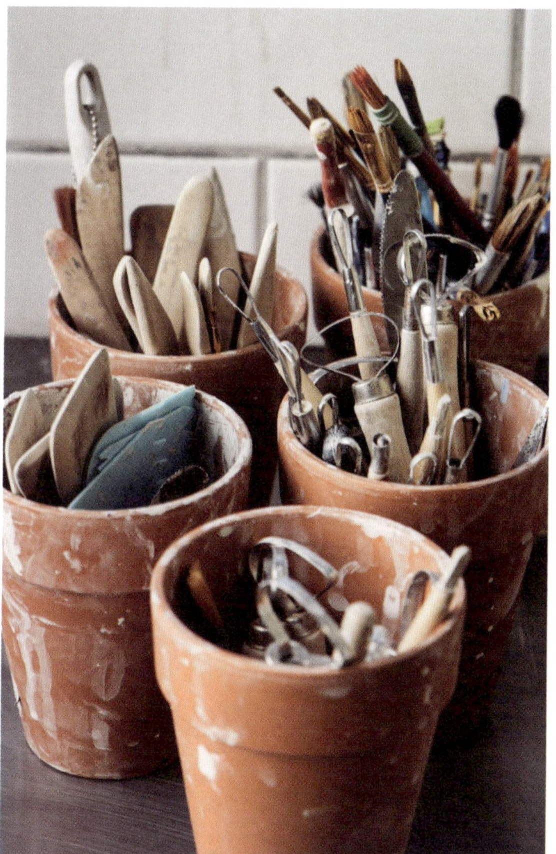

POTTER'S KNIFE: *Can be replaced by a simple craft knife*
Potter's knives have long, pointed blades to make the cutting of wet clay easier but a hacksaw blade, sharpened at one end, works equally well and the serrated edge makes a handy extra tool.

SURFORM OR RASP BLADE: *Useful but not essential*
This is a tool that is used to pare down clay surfaces and level rims. The marks created by the blade can also be used to create decorative surface texture. The blades are available in different sizes.

METAL KIDNEY (PLAIN AND SERRATED): *Essential*
Perhaps the most useful tool of all and generally available in several different sizes, grades, and shapes, from oval to square. Used to refine the clay surface, they are also available with serrated edges for paring down rough surfaces but are most useful for scoring edges to be joined.

RUBBER KIDNEY: *Useful but not essential*
A flexible kidney used for the very fine smoothing and compacting of clay surfaces.

POTTER'S NEEDLE: *Essential*
Useful for marking levels on rims while the work is rotating on a banding wheel prior to cutting. Also useful for piercing holes or releasing air. A good alternative is a bodkin needle fixed into the end of a bottle cork.

HOLE CUTTER: *Essential for some projects in this book*
Available in a variety of sizes, usually with a tapering metal blade, the cutter is rotated as it is pushed through the clay to make holes of different sizes. It is possible to replace a cutter with a drill bit if careful.

LOOP OR RIBBON TOOL: *Useful but not essential*
Mostly used to trim the bases of wheel-thrown pots but are also useful for forming foot rings on pinched forms.

BANDING WHEEL OR TURNTABLE: *Useful*
A banding wheel or turntable is not strictly essential but it does make most tasks easier because it allows the work to be rotated and viewed from all sides, which is especially useful when pinching.

WOODEN MODELING TOOLS: *Essential*
Available from pottery suppliers in a vast variety of shapes but you will probably find you will only need a few—those shown in the projects are the most useful when pinching.

WOODEN SPATULA: *Very useful*
Easily sourced from your kitchen, a spatula is a highly versatile tool for beating, smoothing, and texturing pinched forms.

RIBS: *Essential*
Commercially bought varieties can be made from wood, metal, plastic, and silicon but they can easily be made at home from old store or bank cards. Ribs are mostly used for smoothing and refining, and are generally available in shapes to suit any kind of work.

DECORATING TOOLS

BRUSHES: *Essential*
Good brushes are essential and should include soft fan varieties for applying slips and glazes, and small detail fine liners for underglazes and fine decoration. Toothbrushes are useful for scoring and slipping joints in the clay and for spattering slip decoration. Soft mop brushes are very useful for brushing away residue clay when incising or scoring surfaces.

SLIP TRAILER WITH FINE NOZZLE: *Essential for some of the surface decoration techniques in this book*
These are commercially available in different sizes but can be made from other items, like the bottles in hair-dye kits.

SPONGES: *Essential*
A selection of both natural and man-made sponges are essential when pinching, for smoothing surfaces, cleaning around joins, and applying slip and glaze decoration.

SGRAFFITO TOOLS: *Useful but not essential*
A set of sgraffito tools makes a good addition to the toolbox and are available in various shapes and styles. However, you can use something as simple as a pencil.

HEALTH AND SAFETY

The health and safety issues arising from making pinch pots are few and really no different from other studio work. For safe practice generally, a few basic rules should be observed when working with clay and other related materials.

1. Never eat, drink, or smoke in the workshop.

2. Always work in a suitably ventilated room with easy-to-clean, impermeable work surfaces and facilities for washing close by.

3. Avoid generating airborne dust—it is better to prevent dust than try to control it. To minimize dust hazards:
- Clean up spillages when they occur. This applies to liquids as well as powders because all materials become dust when they have dried. Spillage on the floor can also cause the risk of slipping.
- Clean all tools and equipment at the end of the working day.
- Use a vacuum cleaner with a filter for fine dust, not a brush, to clean all surfaces. After vacuuming wash all surfaces.

4. Wear gloves when handling any coloring agents or oxides.

5. Wear a respirator (face mask) when handling powders.

6. Wear protective clothing but try not to wipe dirty hands on aprons to avoid creating dust as it dries. Wash work clothing regularly.

7. Store dry materials in airtight plastic containers to avoid the possibility of bags breaking open and spilling dust into the atmosphere.

9. When sanding or fettling (trimming or cleaning) dry or bisque-fired pots, wear a respirator and goggles to protect the eyes.

10. Check that your tetanus immunization is up to date. Remember that clay is essentially dug from the ground and may carry bacteria that can cause infection in open wounds.

11. Keep a first aid kit in the workshop and protect cuts and scratches from contact with any ceramic materials.

CORE MAKING TECHNIQUES

The pinching techniques demonstrated in this section form all the basic methods used to make the projects. There are many more ways of working but you will find your pinching method will evolve with practice to ultimately develop your own unique style. These basic techniques will get you started.

CLASSIC PINCH POT

The basic method demonstrated here forms the starting point for almost all of the projects in this book and is worth taking the time to perfect before attempting anything more challenging; you will find that it doesn't take long to master.

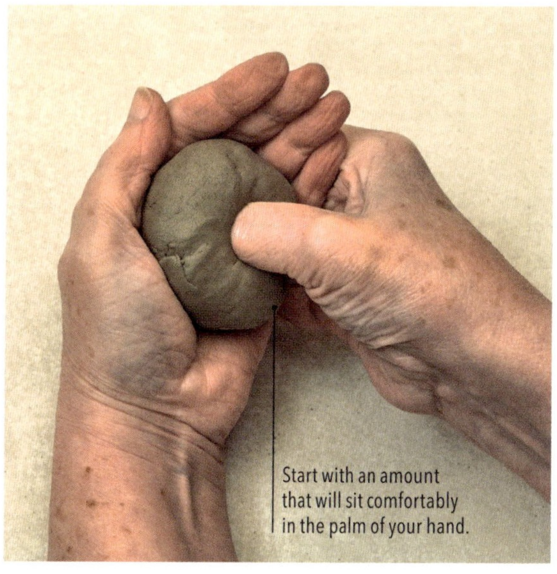

Start with an amount that will sit comfortably in the palm of your hand.

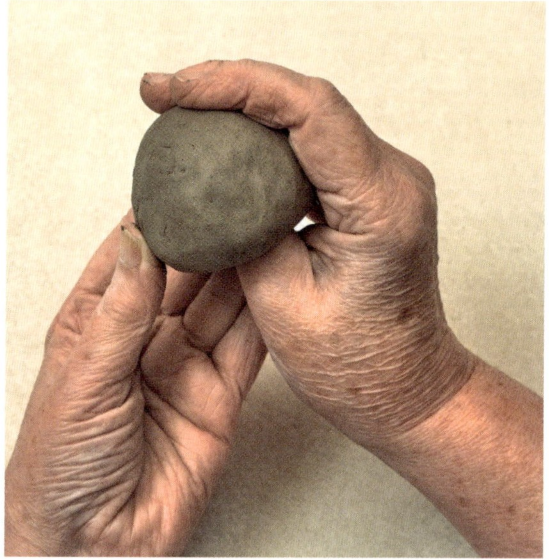

1 Weigh your clay—8oz (225g) is a good weight to begin with. Form the clay into a ball, then, holding it in your palm, press down into the center with the thumb of your other hand until you can feel some pressure in your palm.

2 Pinch out the base of the pot first because it becomes difficult to reach as the shape grows. Work in small pinches between fingers and thumb held in a crooked position, around the wall for even thickness. Work up to, but not including, the rim at this stage to avoid it flaring outward too soon.

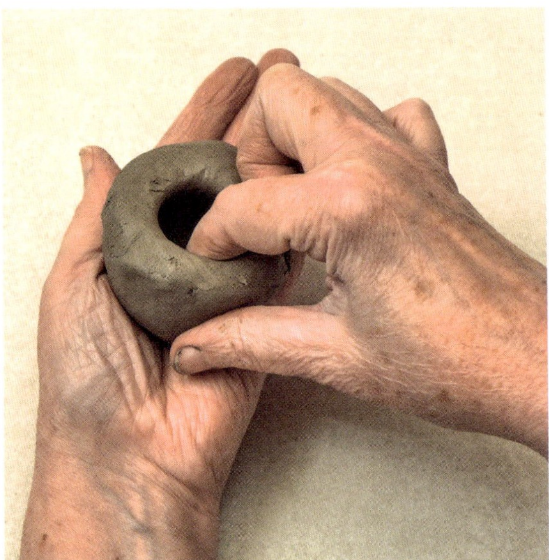

3 Turn the bowl over to rest in the palm of your hand, then pinch the wall in small stages, working rhythmically around the circumference and turning the pot continuously. Maintain control of the rim—it is important to keep it closed until you have almost finished pinching the body.

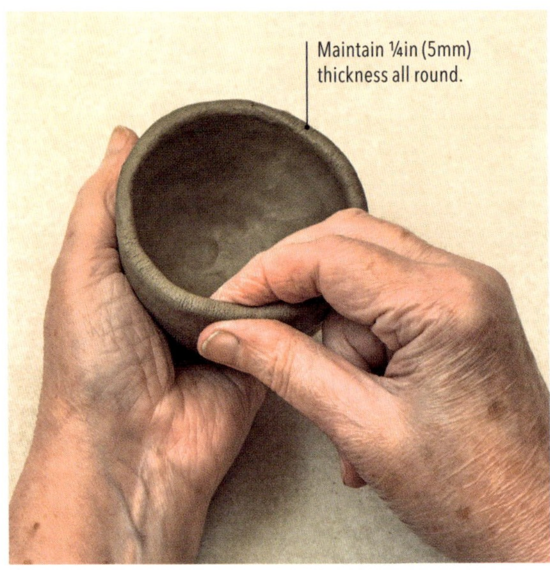

4 Continue to pinch the wall until it is an even ¼in (5mm) thick and cup-shaped, with straight walls and a round base. Now pinch the rim to the same thickness as the wall, then smooth over the surface inside and out with a kidney to remove lumps and bumps. From this stage you can progress to specific projects.

SOME PRACTICAL TIPS TO GET STARTED

- You can pinch almost any clay body, even porcelain can be mastered with practice, but for the best chance of early success start with a basic red or white earthenware.
- Softer clay is easier to pinch than hard clay.
- For beginners, start with grogged clay; it has greater strength to hold its shape without cracking. As you gain experience, you can progress to smoother samples with finer particles that will pinch out to a thinner section.
- If you don't like the feel of grogged clay, try mixing it half and half with a smooth clay that fires to the same temperature; it will retain its strength for building but have a better surface quality and pinch out a little thinner.
- You can't pinch clay with long nails as they get in the way by cutting into the clay.
- Hot hands dry clay quickly and cause cracking; the problem worsens the longer you work on a piece. Cool your hands under cold water regularly and work as quickly as possible.
- You can increase the starting weight of clay as you gain experience but forms can be enlarged in other ways. Start with an amount that will sit comfortably in your palm.
- For repeat forms, weigh the clay before pinching so that you always start with the same amount for each piece.

Adapting the basic shape to pinch a sphere

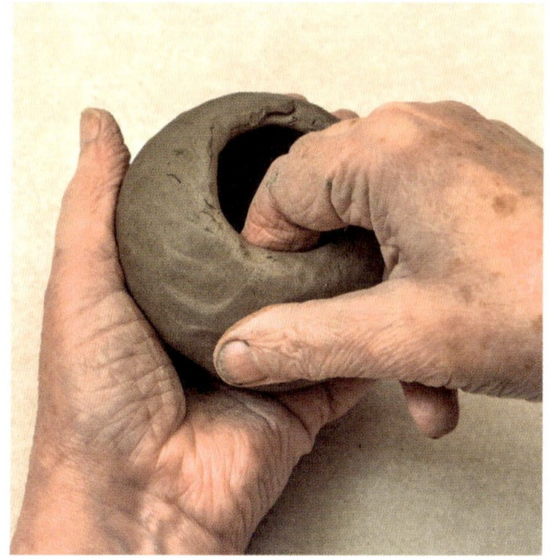

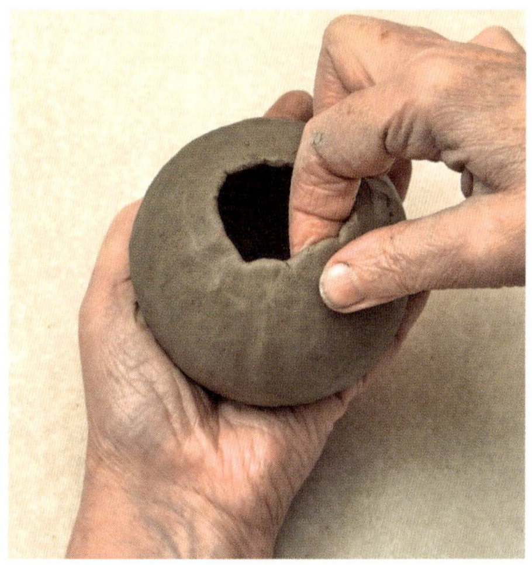

1 Follow steps 1 to 3 of the basic shape but continue to keep your finger crooked on the inside, gently pushing the clay outward to maintain a rounded shape as you ease toward the rim.

2 Change pressure from the inside to the outside, to round the shape over toward the opening, thus closing it in. Some pushing and gentle tugging is required in addition to pinching, to get the correct shape.

COMPOSITE FORMS—JOINING PINCHED SECTIONS

Hollow forms made from joined pinched sections form the base shape for several of the projects.

The principle is that you make a second identical form to the first, with the same thickness and circumference at the rim, then join the halves together to make a hollow form that can then be manipulated into a particular shape, or added to with other pinched sections.

To make identical halves for a form successfully, weigh the clay beforehand.

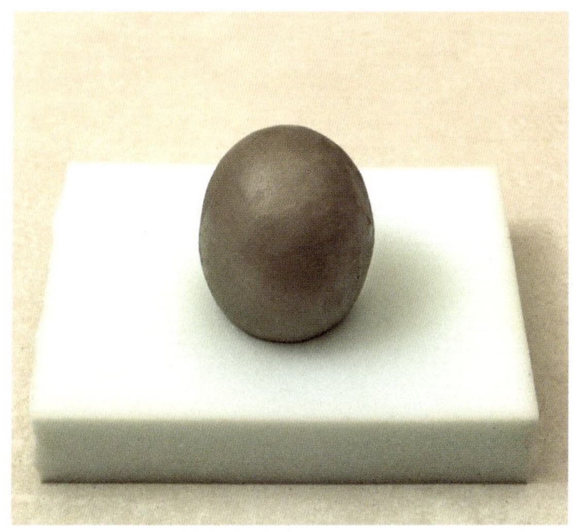

TIP: *Old bits of foam are really useful for sitting a section on when working on the other half and to support the shape as it dries. Cut a hole at the center of a block of foam to support larger items in construction.*

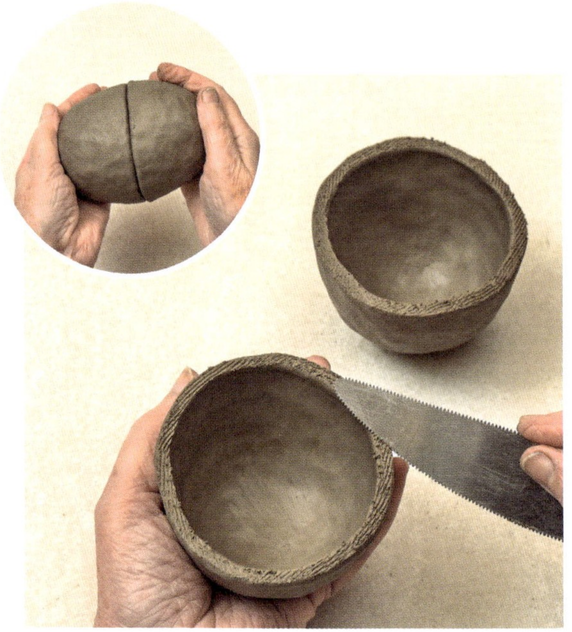

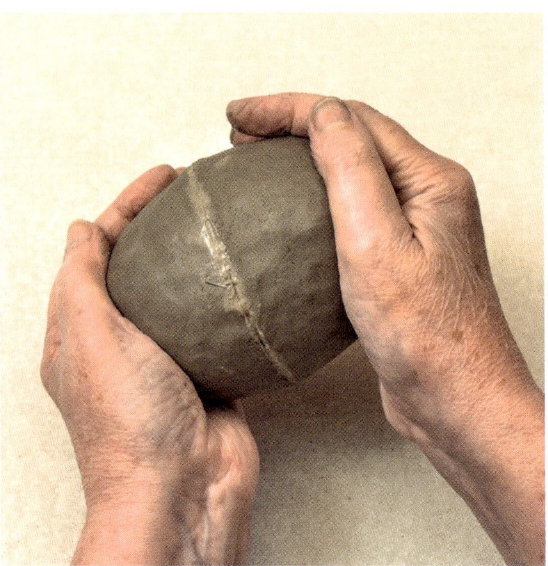

1 When making the second half of a composite form you must test the size of it periodically until it fits exactly, rim to rim, with the first half. When this has been achieved, score the rim of each half using a serrated kidney.

2 Add slip to the rim of each pinched section and carefully join them together, making sure the fit is perfect. Hold the halves together for a few seconds until you are sure they are not going to come apart.

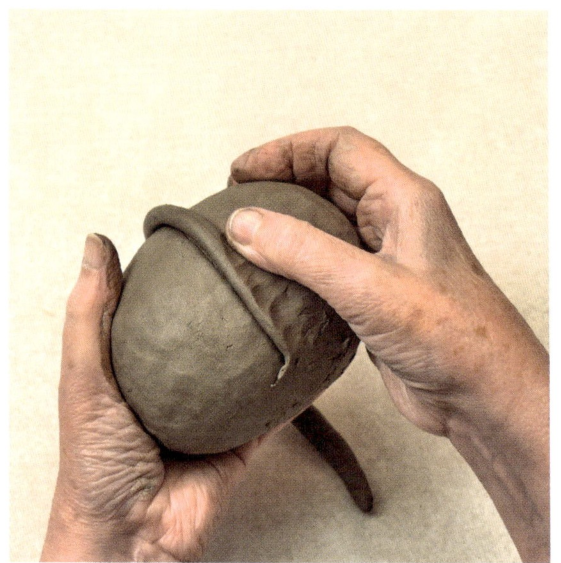

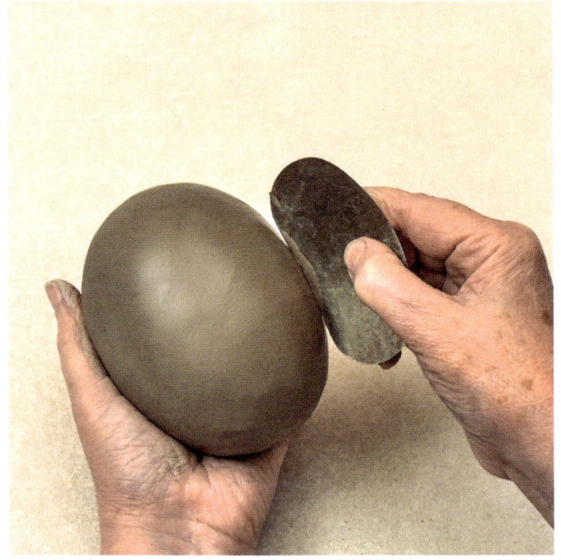

3 Roll a coil of soft clay and place it over the join. Blend it in carefully until the join is obscured. Don't press too hard because the join will open up—this is why it is important that the reinforcing clay is soft.

4 When the coil has been blended over the join, carefully scrape away any lumps and bumps with a kidney and smooth the surface thoroughly. The form should now look roughly egg-shaped.

ALTERING THE SHAPE OF JOINED SECTIONS

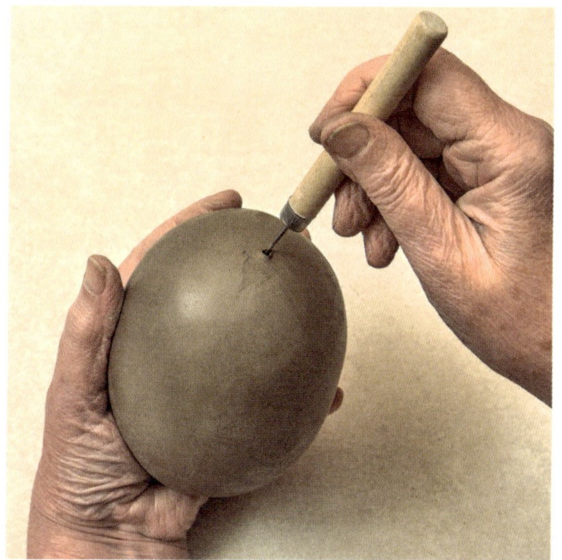

5 When two sections are sealed together, a vacuum is formed inside which maintains the shape. To alter the shape, a hole must be made in some part of the form to allow for the release of air as the shape is manipulated.

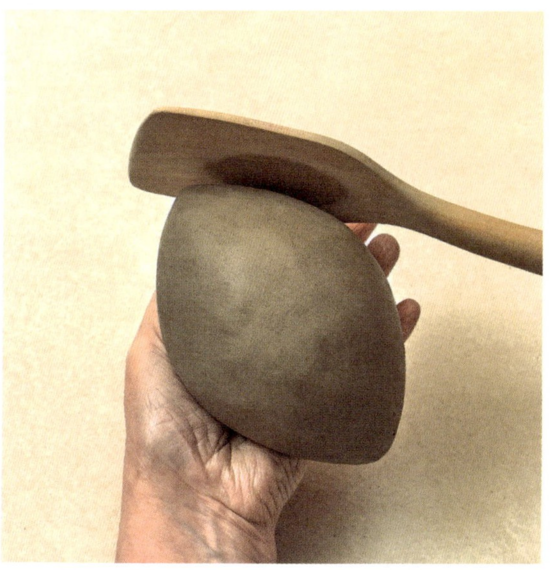

6 Manipulate the shape into the desired form with your fingers, or by beating the surface with a wooden spatula.

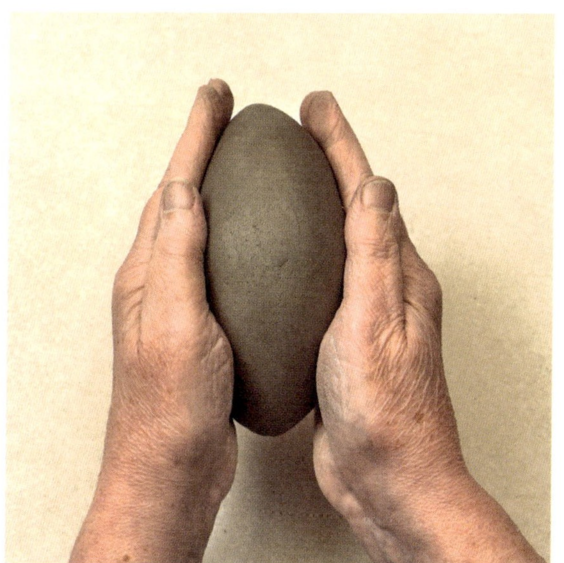

7 Considerable character can be formed providing the hole remains open as you work. For example, the altered outline shape can be adapted further by squeezing it between both hands to flatten it slightly.

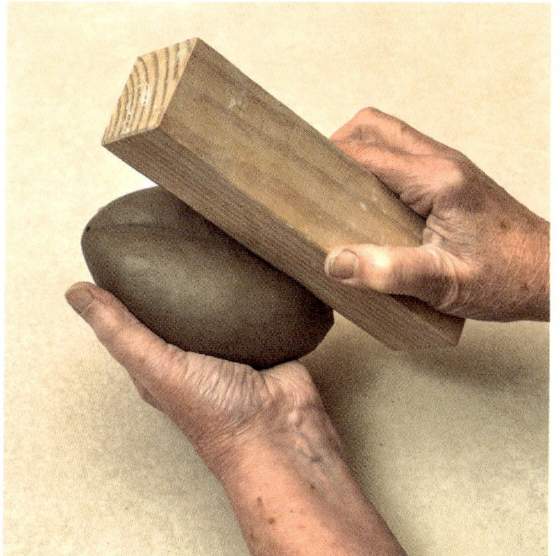

8 Work around the entire circumference of the form to add lines or valleys, if desired, using wooden blocks or tools. Seal the hole when happy with the shape and leave to firm to leather-hard before reintroducing the hole to allow for the release of air in firing.

OPEN-ENDED SECTIONS

Sections like these are used throughout the book to extend the size of forms, or make feature parts such as foot rings, spouts, necks, stems for bowls, and even handles. They can, of course, make forms in their own right.

BASIC CYLINDER

Useful to make small, bud-type vases, as the starting shape for larger forms, or parts for other uses, like handles or feet.

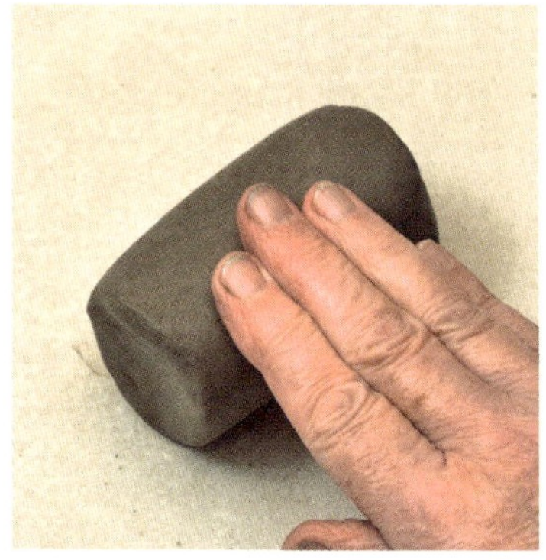

1 Roll and pat a ball of clay into a log shape (the amount of clay required will depend on what you are making).

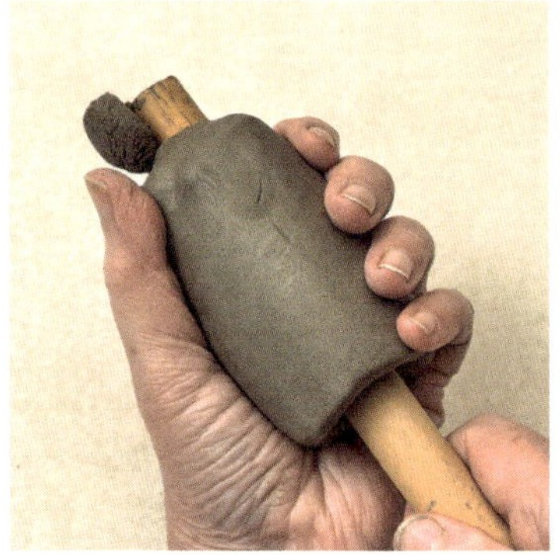

2 Extend a finger through the center of the clay and out the other end. If the log is too long to get a finger through, use a short length of dowel or a pencil to open up the center first.

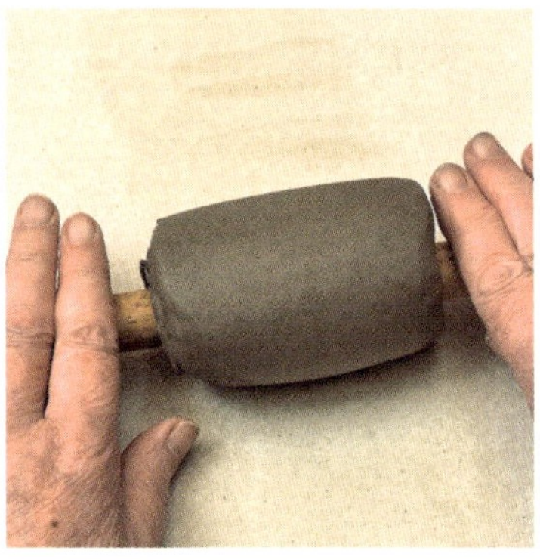

3 Roll the dowel back and forth on the work surface to extend the size of the opening sufficiently to get your fingers inside.

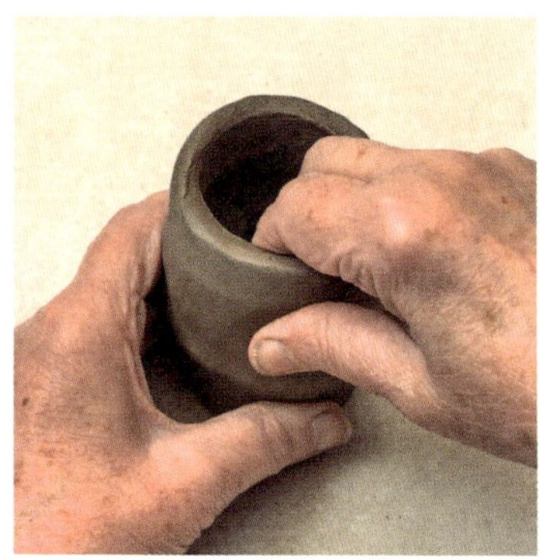

4 Pinch out the wall in small stages, rotating the form the whole time and applying even pressure between finger and thumb.

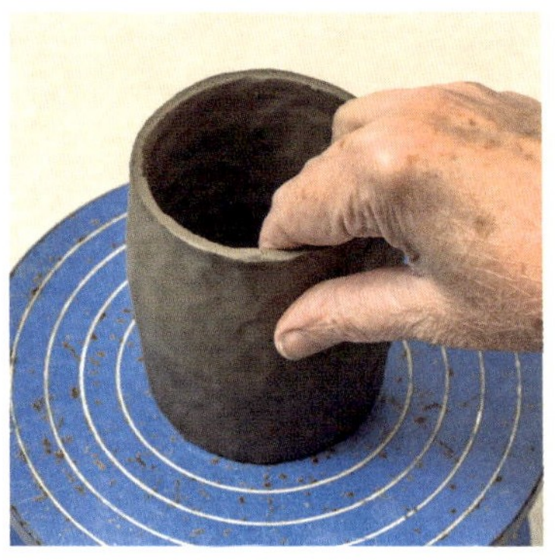

5 Work on one end of the cylinder first, then the opposite end, changing between both regularly to ensure an evenly pinched wall.

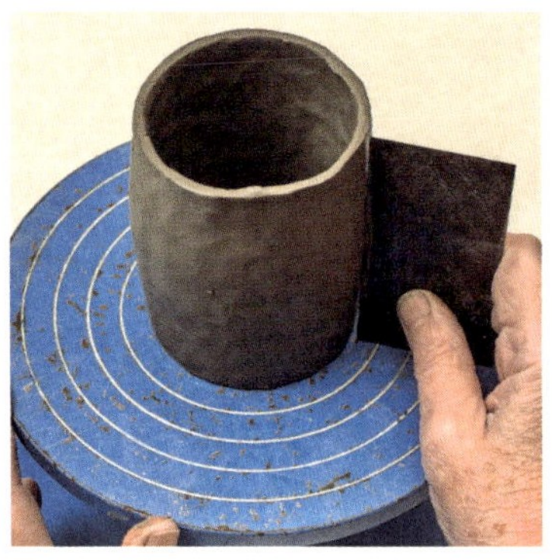

6 When the cylinder is an even thickness, smooth any lumps and bumps inside and out with a metal kidney.

WIDE CYLINDER

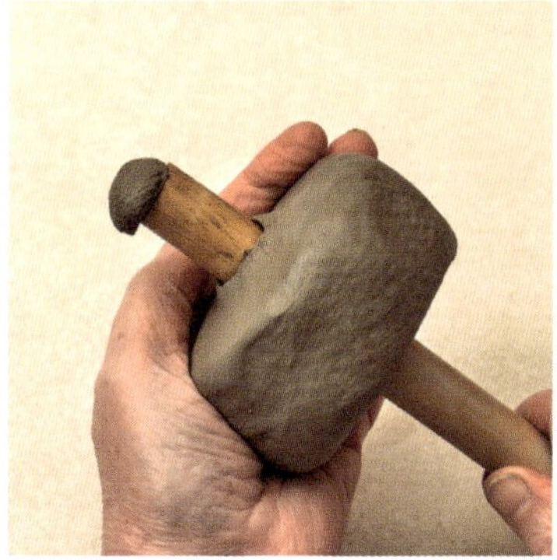

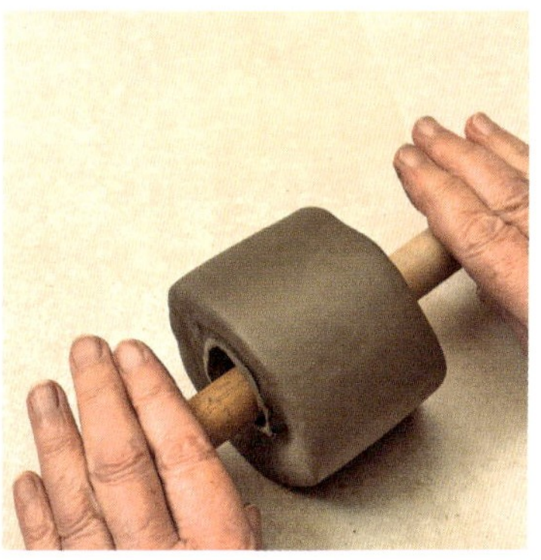

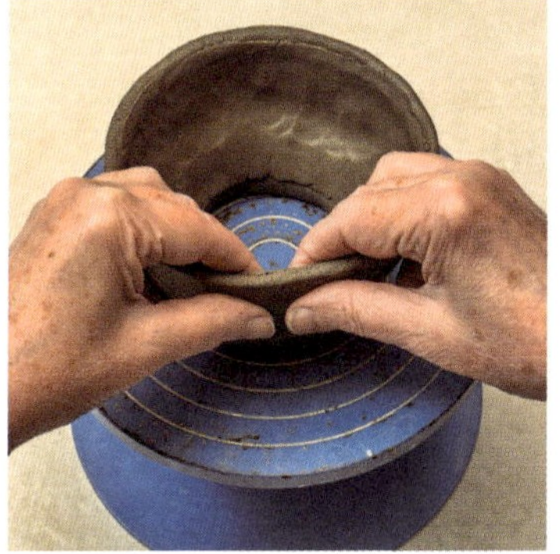

1 Depending on the intended use for this section—an extension to the size or neck—prepare a ball of clay, then roll and pat it into a shallow, wide log. Open the shape up by pushing a thick dowel rod through the center.

2 As for the smaller cylinder, roll the dowel back and forth over the work surface to extend the size of the opening.

3 Pinch the shape out from the middle in small steps, between a straight finger and thumb, to maintain an even thickness and vertical sides. Turn the shape periodically as it enlarges; work on the upper half first, then the lower half. Maintain equal pressure from inside and out to prevent distortion.

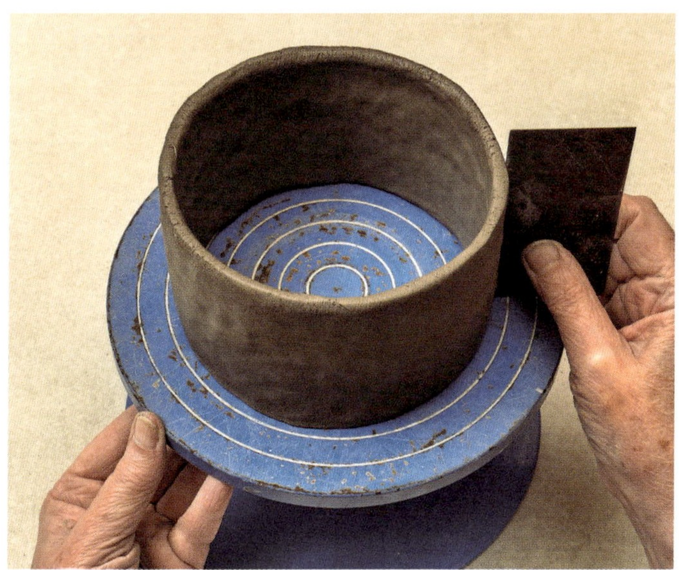

4 Turn the banding wheel and work a palette rib around the exterior wall to ensure it is vertical and refine the surface.

CYLINDERS FOR FOOT RINGS

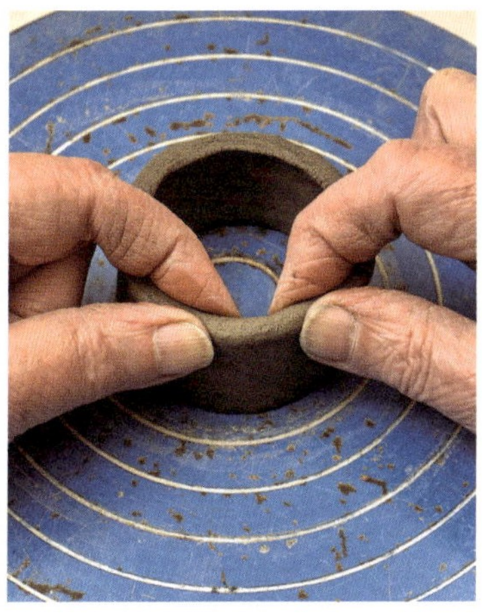

The same basic technique is used on a very small scale to make foot rings for bowls, cups, and other similar items.

CONICAL TUBES

A conical tube is the fundamental shape for most pouring spouts and is therefore an important pinching skill to learn.

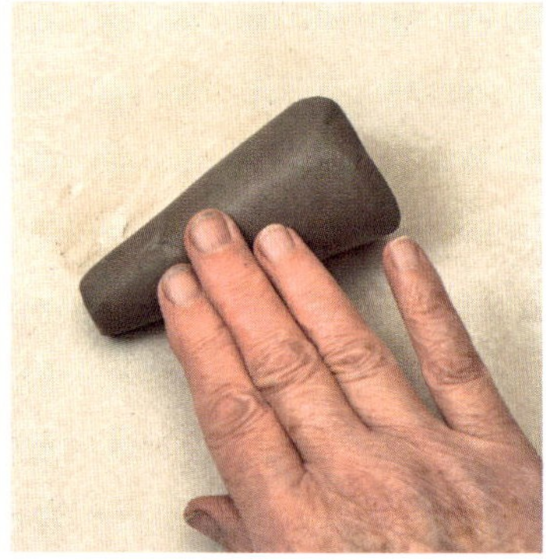

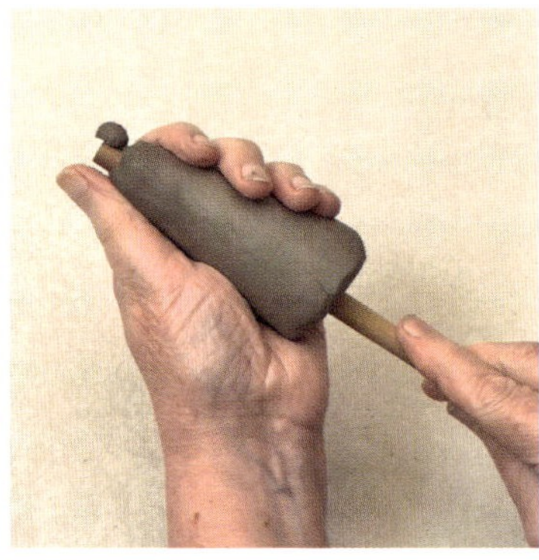

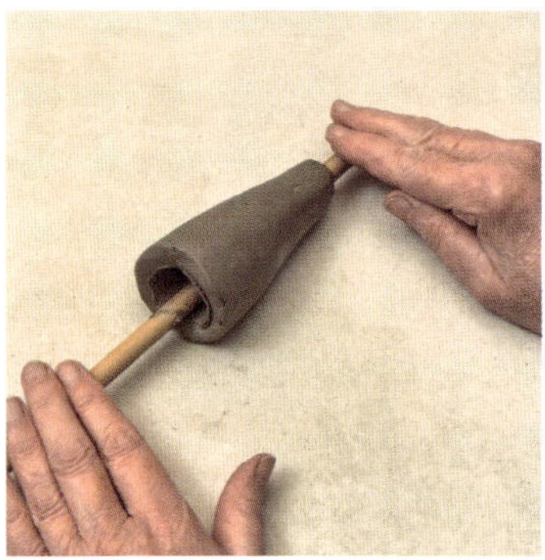

1 Form a small amount of clay into a conical shape, about 2¾in (7cm) long, narrow at one end, wide at the other.

2 Open out the center with a thin dowel rod.

3 Wiggle the dowel at the wide end until large enough to insert a finger or roll it on the dowel. Avoid enlarging the pouring end.

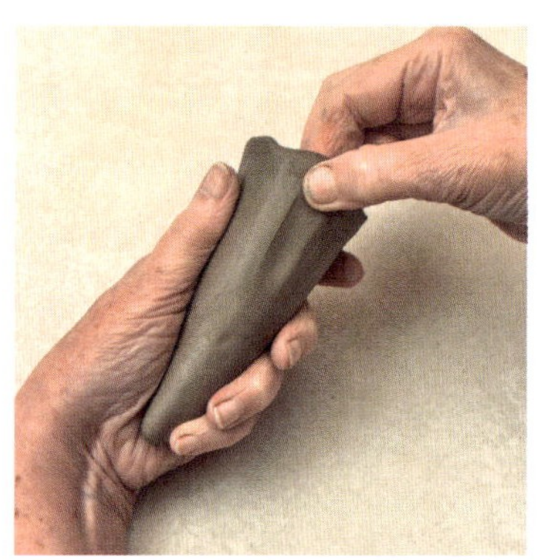

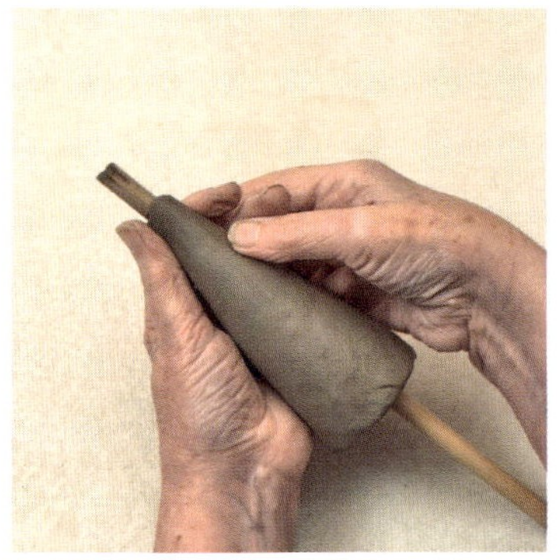

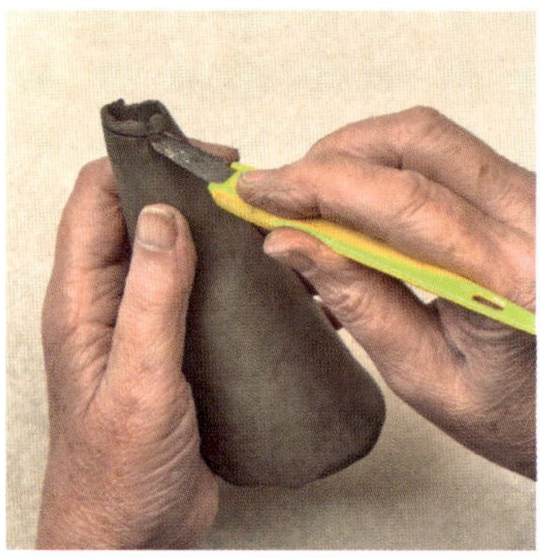

4 Pinch the shape from the wide end first, at the same time gently stroking the clay on the inside with your finger to extend it toward the opening and smooth the surface.

5 Now open up the narrow end to the required size by rotating the dowel inside. Aim to thin and extend the wall to the same thickness as the rest of the spout.

6 Carefully cut the pouring end of the spout to the required shape with a sharp knife.

7 To shape a spout (for a teapot), ease the clay into an outward curve from the inside and an inward curve from the outside by gently drawing a finger over the surface in the direction you want it to shape to. **Note**: The wide end of the form must be cut at the correct angle to fit the particular form it will be attached to.

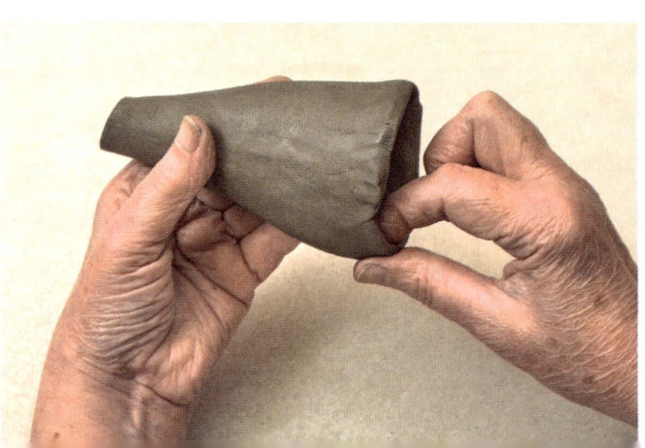

WIDE BOWLS OR PLATES

The technique for pinching wide, open forms is straightforward and only complicated by the clay's ability to hold the developing shape. To overcome this you can work in short stages, allowing the clay to firm up a little before moving on, or you can speed the process up periodically using a blow-dryer. **Note**: There is a fine line between clay that is too soft and too firm to pinch, so care must be taken when firming with a blow-dryer not to take it too far.

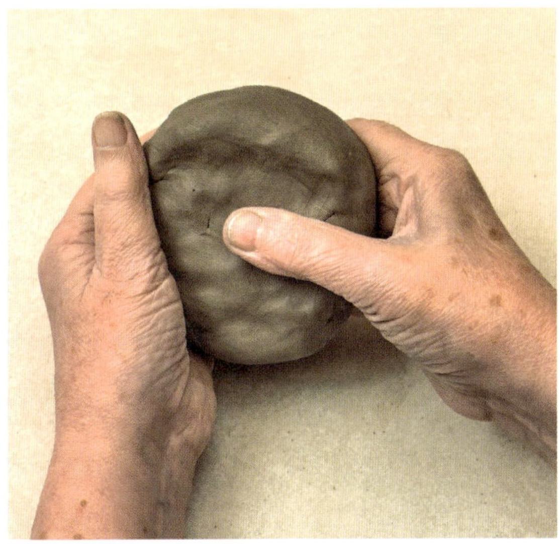

1 Flatten a ball of clay a little between the palms of your hands into a rough disc.

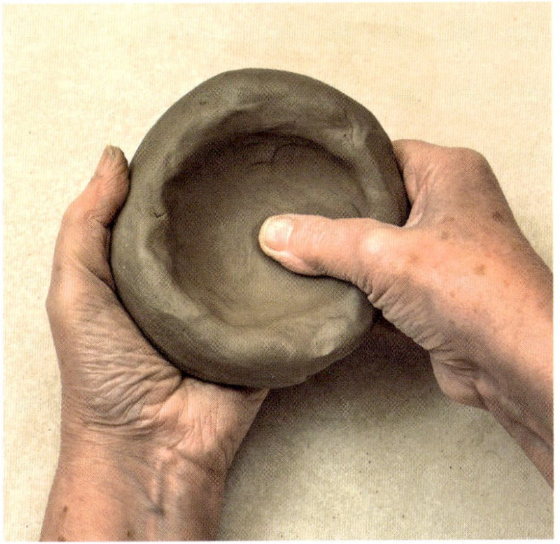

2 Pinch the shape out from the center, rotating the dish in small stages as you work. As with other forms, the rim should remain thick until the rest of the body has been shaped.

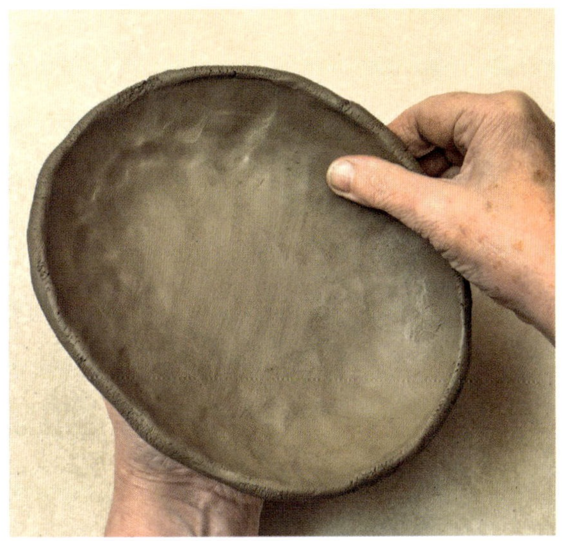

3 Keep a close eye on the profile to make sure it is what you are aiming for.

EXTENDING THE SIZE OF BOWLS AND PLATES

A really good way of extending the size of a form is with flattened coils of soft clay. These give great flexibility when developing a specific shape.

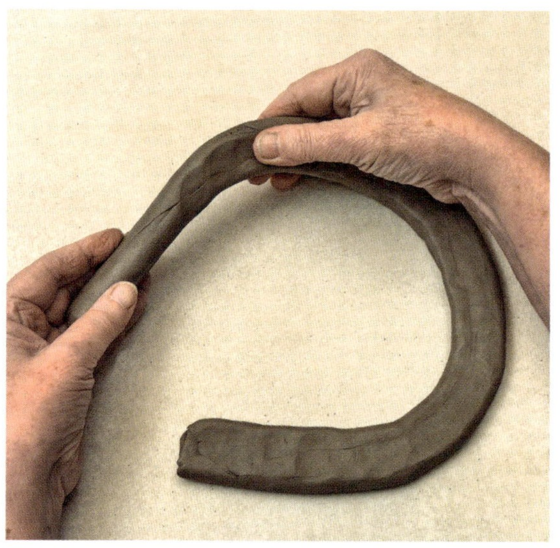

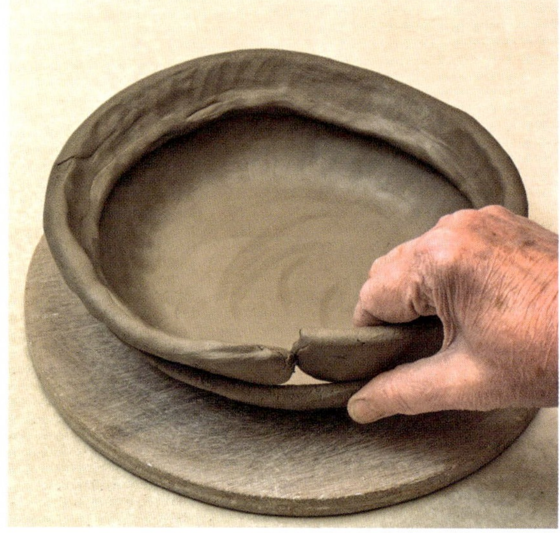

1 Roll a thick coil, long enough to fit around the rim of the base shape, then flatten it by pinching along its length, at the same time curving the coil into a semicircle.

2 Sit the coil just inside the rim of the base shape and secure it in place by drawing the clay upward from the base onto the coil. DO NOT join the ends of the coil until you reach the end because the length will extend as it is fixed onto the base.

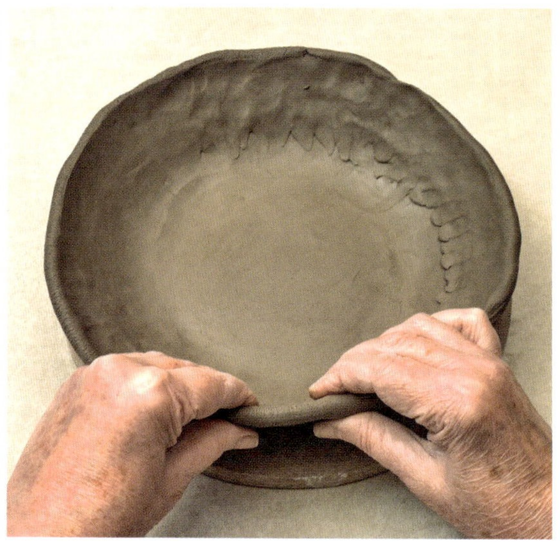

3 Work in the opposite way on the interior of the form, blending the clay from the coil down onto the base. Add more coils in the same way to extend the size even more. Neaten up with a rib after each new section has been joined.

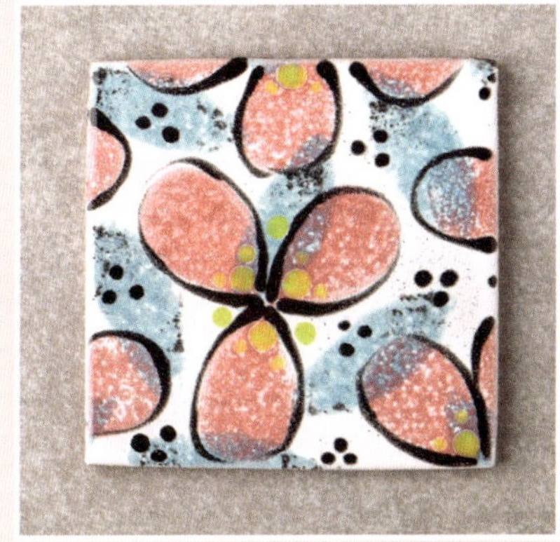
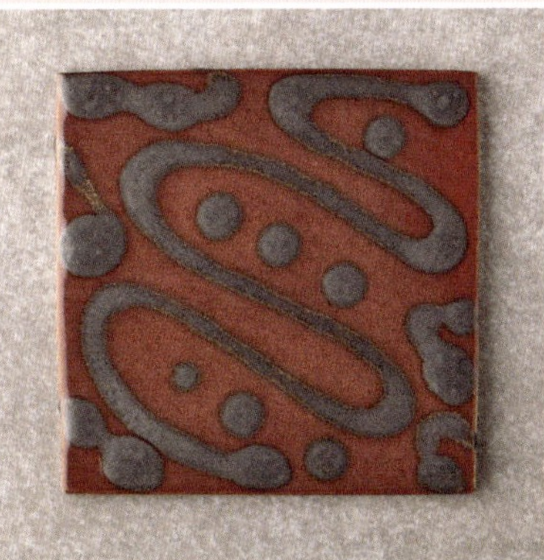
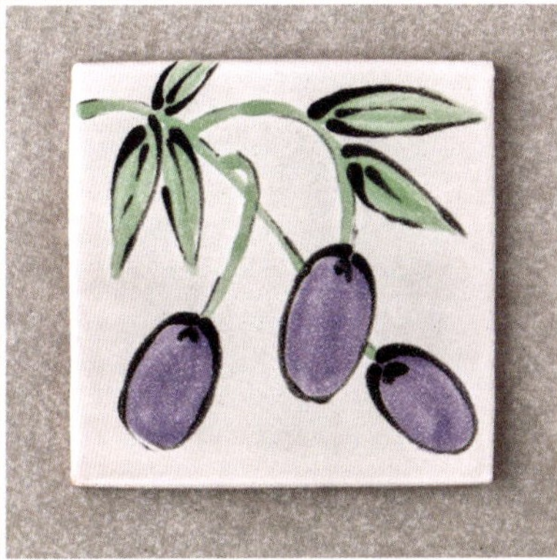

PROJECTS

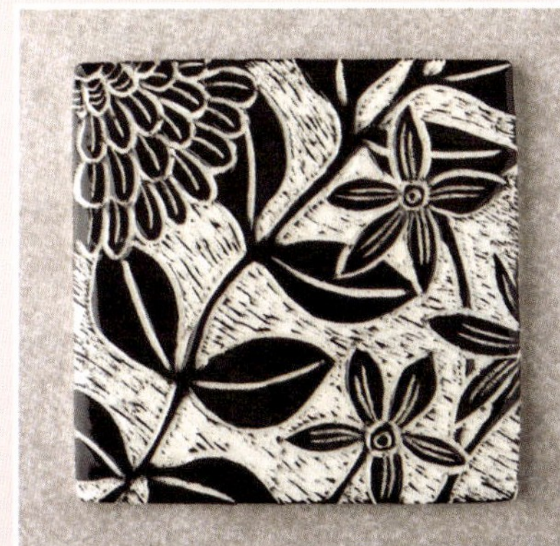
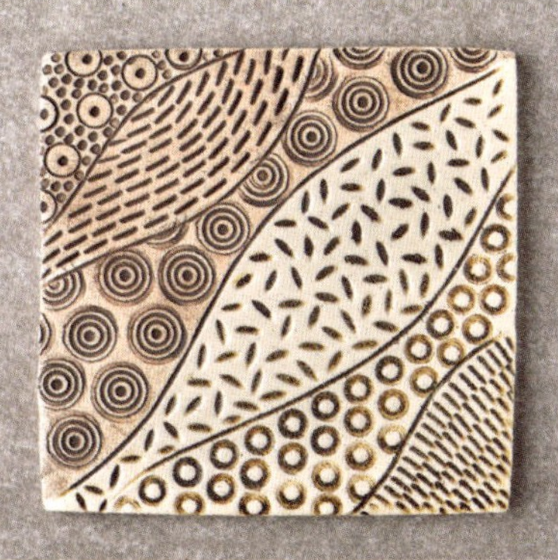
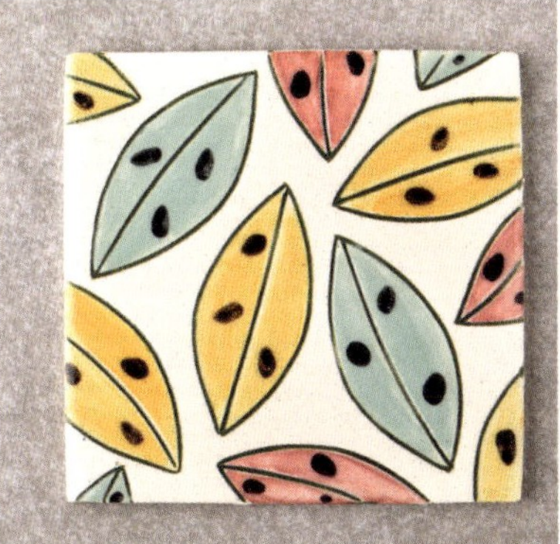
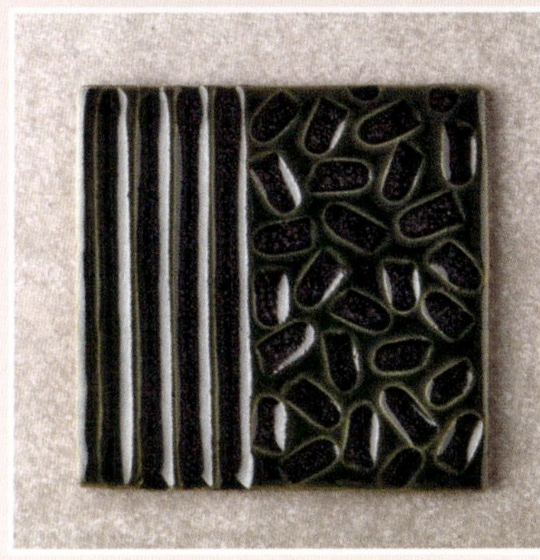
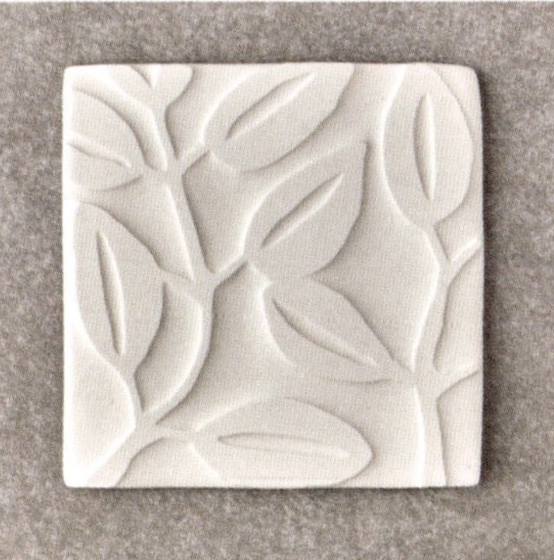
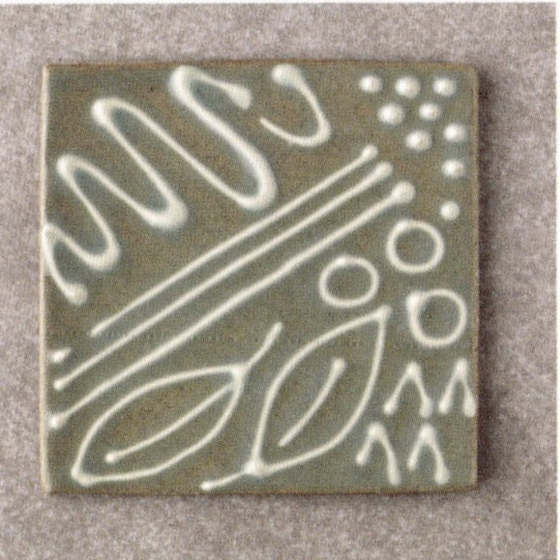

GENERAL GUIDELINES

1. Scale of difficulty is a relative thing, depending entirely on the maker's experience prior to working on the projects.
2. Weight conversion from imperial to metric is approximate in most cases to avoid having to weigh out fiddly amounts of clay. Generally, the metric weight will have been scaled up or down.
3. The given weights are for guidance only—in all cases they can be scaled up or down to make larger or smaller versions of the projects.
4. Clay type is for guidance only and each of the projects states the type used, but it is possible to use alternatives—different forms of a clay type or color can usually replace one another but items can also be made in lower or higher firing clays. In all cases, be aware that shrinkage rates can be different and firing requirements can change.
5. The tools list is not definitive and practiced makers will have their favorites to replace those recommended in this book.

Making specifics:

1. In ALL of the projects, sections are joined together by first scoring the relevant surfaces with a serrated kidney, then applying slip made from the same clay as the body used. Accept this as a given even if the text does not refer to it specifically; it is standard practice.
2. Not all the projects refer directly to refining the surface of a given item but this should also be accepted as standard practice—most surfaces need to be refined regularly using a rib or kidney to remove irregularities and excess weight, and to smooth the clay.
3. Be aware that the finished weight of each form will usually be reduced by scraping and refining the surface.

Drying and firing:

Finished projects must be allowed to dry out slowly and thoroughly in a warm place that is free of drafts prior to bisque firing: see page 174 for further guidance.

Decorating:

The decorating options are versatile enough to be interchangeable between forms. Just be aware of the difference between decorations applied to leather-hard clay as opposed to a bisque surface.

A note about molds:

In the *Nesting Plates* project on page 46, we refer to the use of molds and suggest three alternatives, but if you don't have either a suitable plaster, or bisque variety, then you can form the dishes in a sling mold made by loosely pinning a sheet of canvas to a wooden frame. If you can't make a wooden frame, try suspending the canvas sheet from the four legs of an upturned chair; it is an easy alternative and it doesn't even have to be canvas—a large, cotton dish towel will work as well as anything.

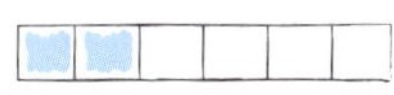

CEREAL BOWL

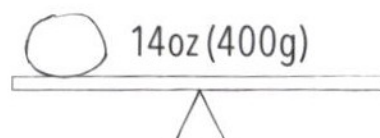

Diameter: 5in (12.5cm)
Height: 1¾in (4.5cm)

14oz (400g)

This is a straightforward, quick, and simple bowl to make in repeat, and is the ideal size for serving your breakfast muesli or a comforting dessert.

The added bonus of these bowls is that they stack neatly for easy storage—always a win when space is lacking.

YOU WILL NEED

TOOLS

- Small, rigid plastic or rubber kidney or rib
- Straight-sided metal palette
- Knife
- Surform or rasp blade
- Flexible metal kidney

CLAY

White stoneware
- 14oz (400g) per dish

DESIGN NOTE

For a deeper bowl, increase the weight of clay fractionally, then working to the same base width dimensions, pinch the wall to the height required.

DECORATION

The finished bowls have been simply decorated using a glaze-on-glaze technique. See pages 163–170 for this method and other decorating options.

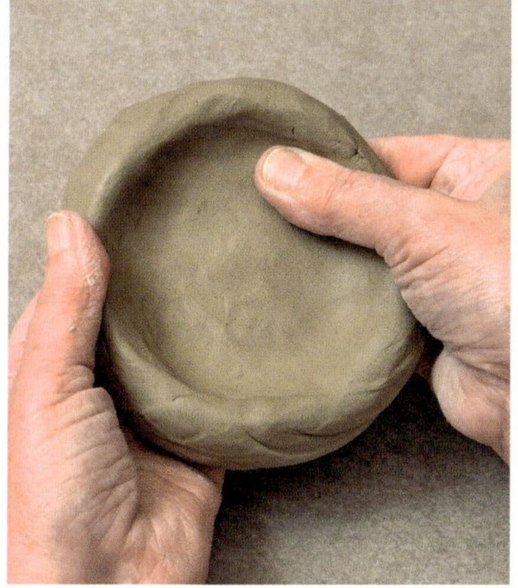

1 Form your clay into a ball. Open out the center of the clay, then pinch the shape to form a wide base, working as far as your fingers will allow you to reach.

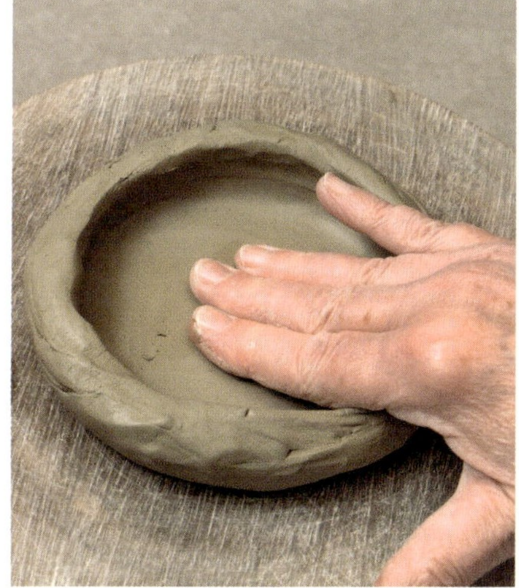

2 Place the rudimentary bowl on a wooden bat and continue to press and pinch the base outward until it is approximately 5in (13cm) wide, leaving a thick, donutlike wall. The base should be about ¼in (5mm) thick when finished.

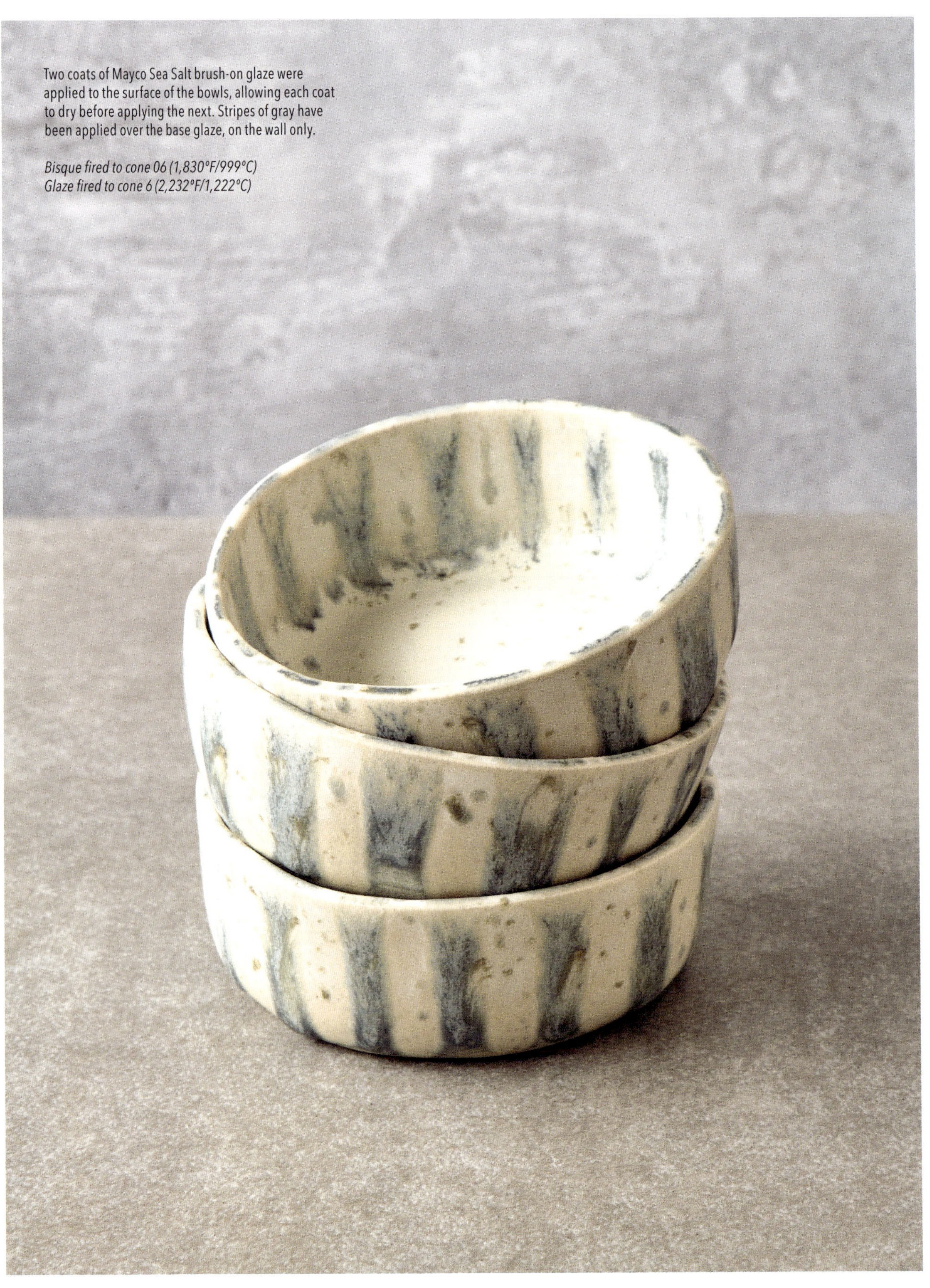

Two coats of Mayco Sea Salt brush-on glaze were applied to the surface of the bowls, allowing each coat to dry before applying the next. Stripes of gray have been applied over the base glaze, on the wall only.

Bisque fired to cone 06 (1,830°F/999°C)
Glaze fired to cone 6 (2,232°F/1,222°C)

3 Begin to pinch the wall vertically, working with both hands. DO NOT allow the shape to flare outward, as the aim is to create a straight-sided bowl. Work around the wall rhythmically, in small steps, to maintain control and ensure an even thickness.

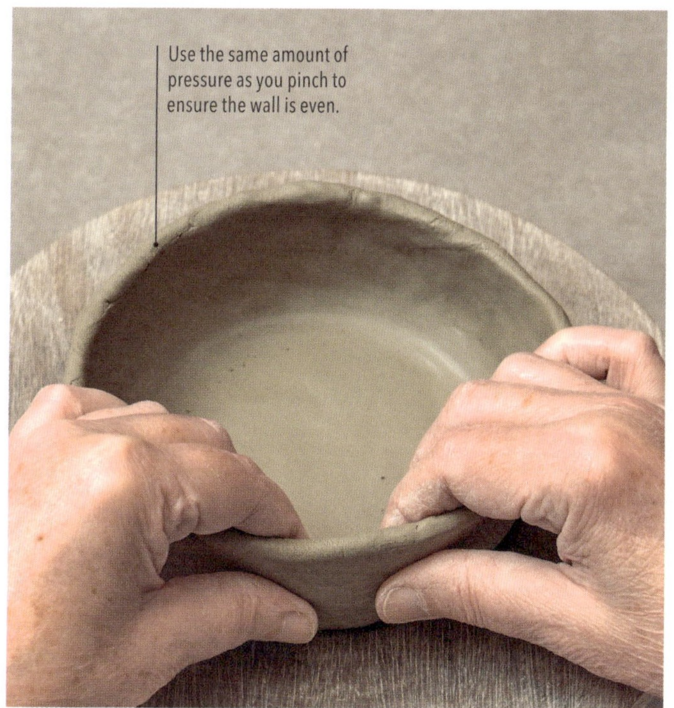
Use the same amount of pressure as you pinch to ensure the wall is even.

4 Sit the bat on a banding wheel, then, turning the wheel slowly as you work, smooth over the inner surface of the bowl with a small rib until all irregularities have been removed.

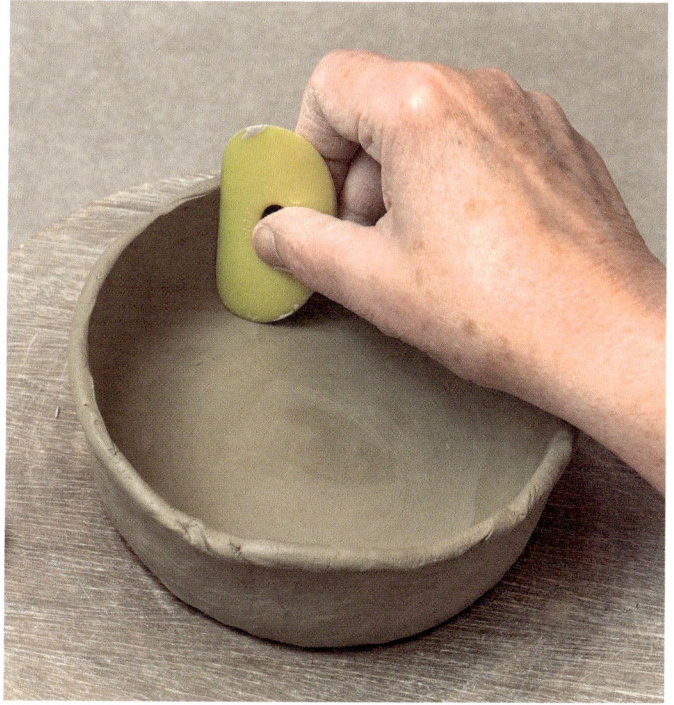

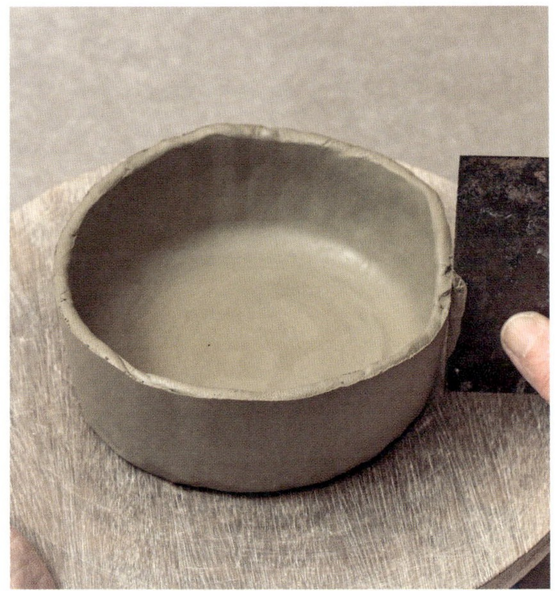

5 To even out and smooth the wall on the outside, work around the bowl with the metal palette sitting flat on the bat to maintain the straight side. Keeping the bat moving on the wheel as you work will help to ensure the shape remains round.

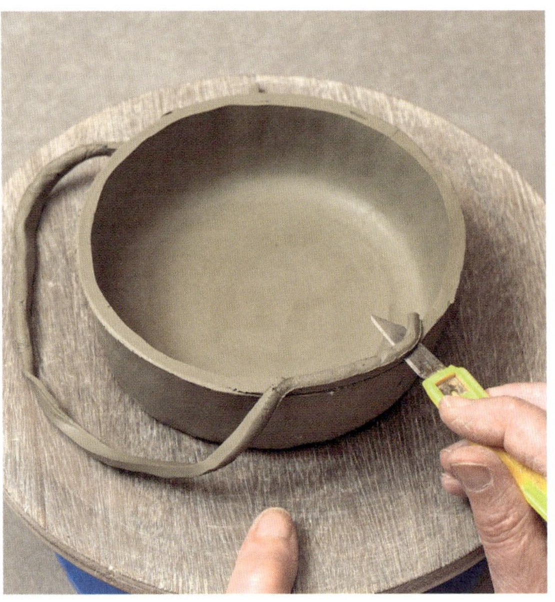

6 Holding a knife rigid in one hand as you move the wheel with the other, carefully level the rim of the bowl to 2in (5cm) high, or your preferred height.

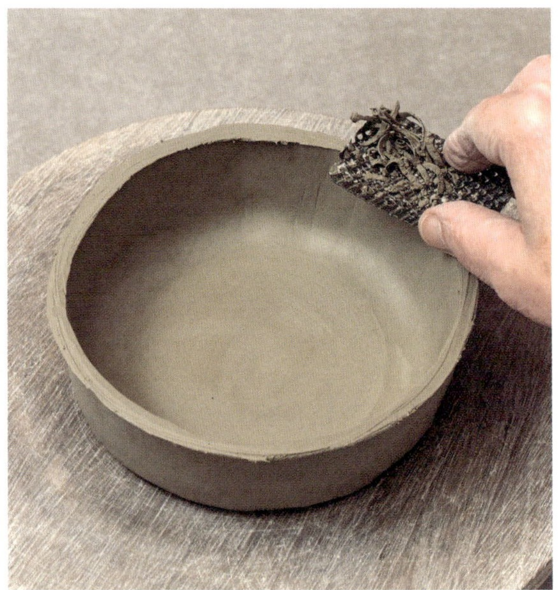

7 If you find the rim is not quite level after cutting off the excess, refine it further using a surform. Carefully neaten up with a rib when happy with the level but don't round the rim off; it should remain quite flat and square.

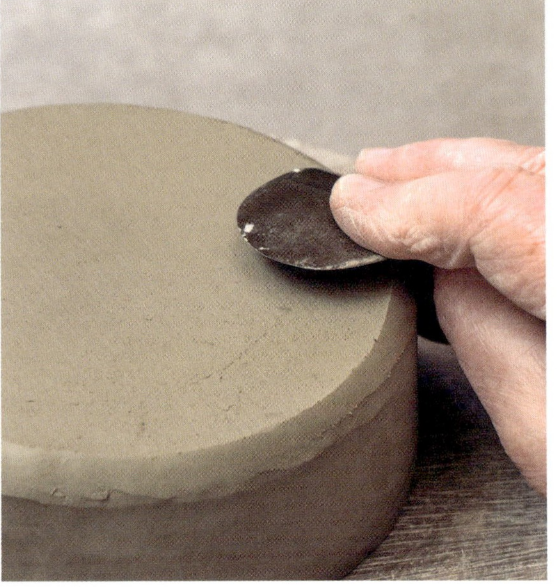

8 Turn the bowl over on the bat, then, turning the wheel as you work, round off the outer edge of the base using a flexible kidney held in a curved shape. Continue to work in this way until the base curves neatly around into the wall.

FRUIT BOWL

Width: 9½in (24cm)
Height: approx. 4in (10cm)
Length: approx. 11in (28cm)

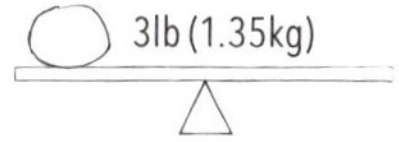

This project teaches you how to transform a relatively simple bowl shape into a spectacular vessel for displaying fruit, with a few easy cuts and some elaborate surface decoration.

The size of this bowl can easily be scaled up or down to make larger or smaller versions for other uses.

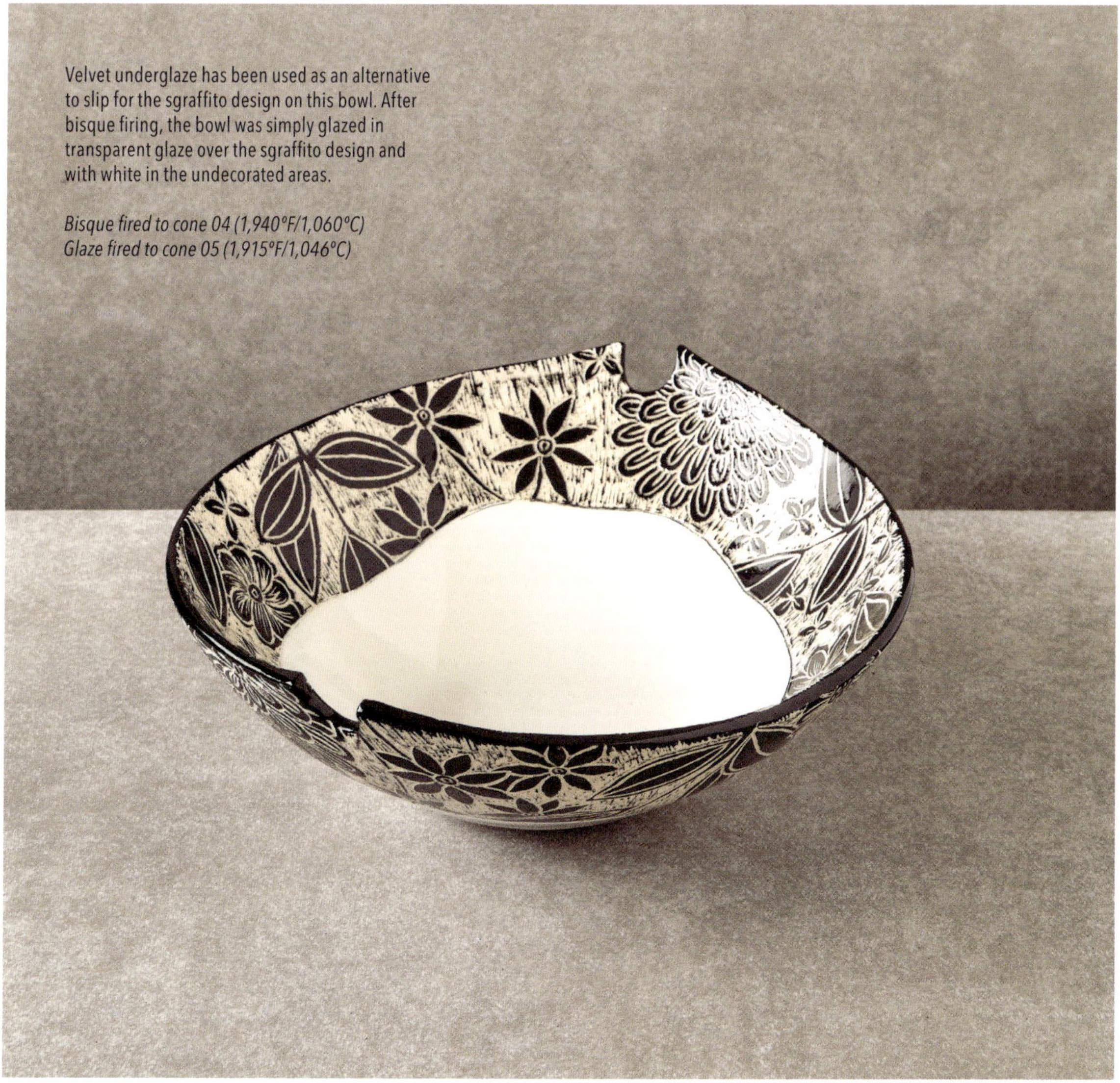

Velvet underglaze has been used as an alternative to slip for the sgraffito design on this bowl. After bisque firing, the bowl was simply glazed in transparent glaze over the sgraffito design and with white in the undecorated areas.

Bisque fired to cone 04 (1,940°F/1,060°C)
Glaze fired to cone 05 (1,915°F/1,046°C)

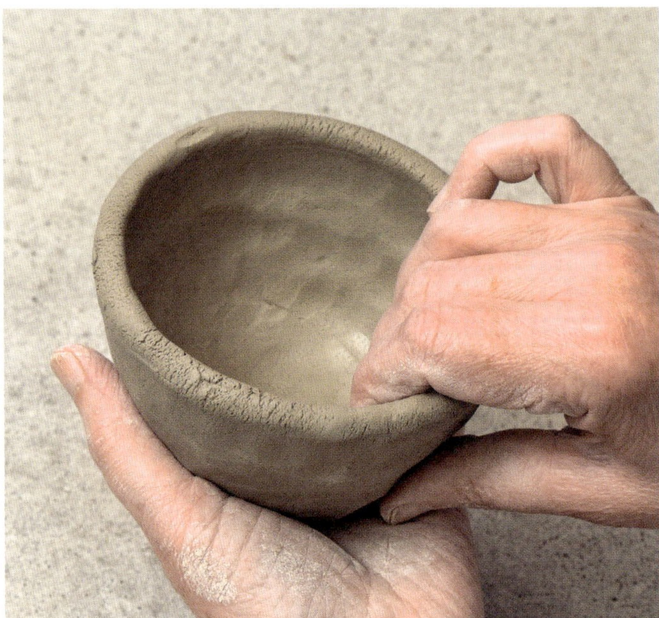

1 To begin, form your clay into a ball and pinch it to an open bowl shape, flaring from a narrow but sturdy base. Refine the inside surface of the bowl with a small stiff kidney, supporting the wall on the opposite side as you work.

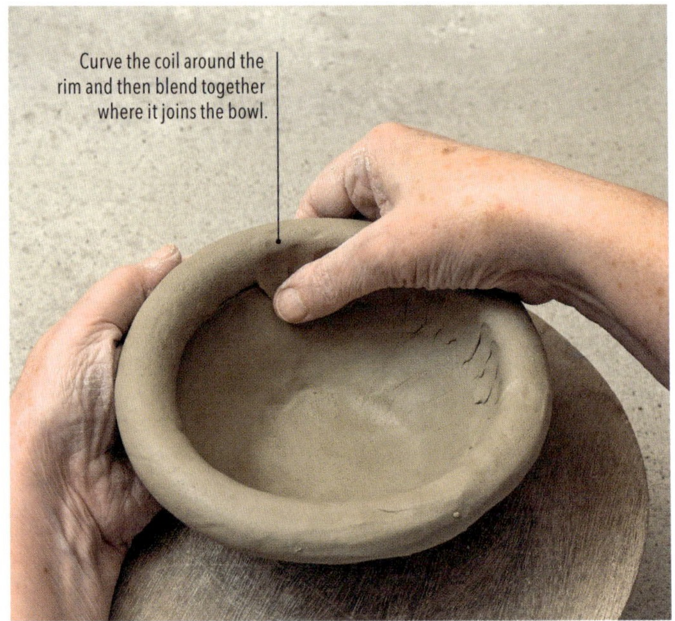

2 Allow the bowl to firm up a little, then form a rough, thick coil of clay, long enough to fit around the rim. Carefully blend the coil onto the base with a finger or thumb, inside and out.

YOU WILL NEED

TOOLS
- Small, rigid plastic or rubber kidney or rib
- Large metal kidney
- Pin
- Round-ended modeling tool
- Wooden modeling tool
- Knife

CLAY
Grogged white earthenware
- 14oz (400g) starting base weight, increasing incrementally with each additional coil. Total weight is dependent on the finished size of bowl, but approx. 3lb (1.35kg)

DESIGN NOTE
With this project, you must allow the clay to firm up at each level of the build, before attaching subsequent coils. The base has to be able to support additional weight and this is especially important if you are building a larger bowl than the one shown.

DECORATION
A floral sgraffito design in simple black and white is a super surface decoration that never fails to impress. See page 161 for this method and pages 156–172 for other options for decoration.

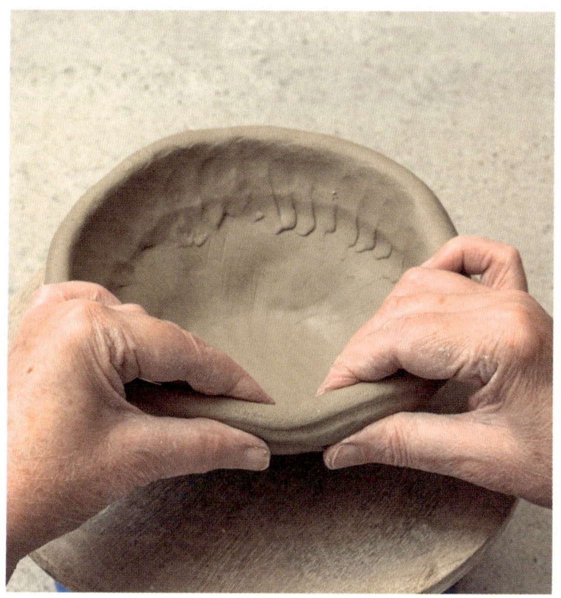

3 Once secure on the base, pinch the coil carefully, extending the outward flare until the added clay is the same thickness as the wall below.

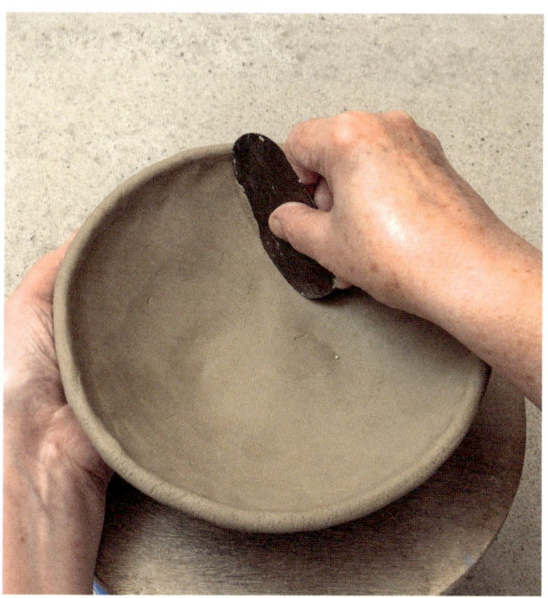

4 Supporting the wall from the underside with one hand, work over the inner surface with a metal kidney until all evidence of a join and pinch marks are removed. Allow the clay to firm up sufficiently to bear the weight of the next coil.

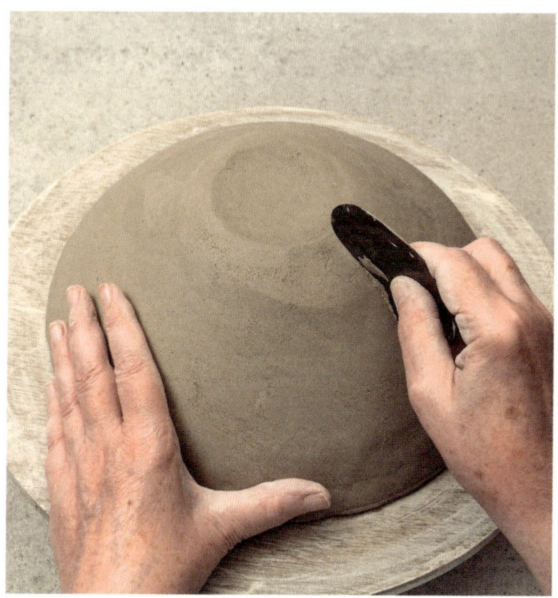

5 Continue to add coils in this way until the bowl is the height you require. Again, allow the clay to firm up, then turn the bowl over onto a bat and work over the surface with a kidney to neaten it up.

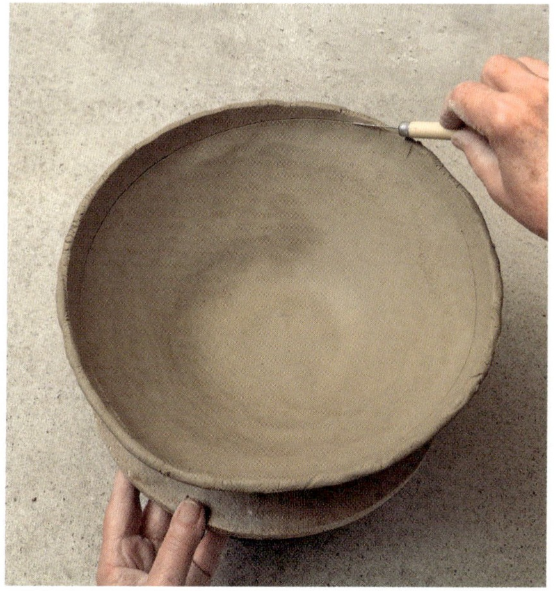

6 Turn the bowl upright again and divide the rim into two equal halves, marking the points with a pin. Score a line between the pin points on both sides of the bowl to make a leaflike shape.

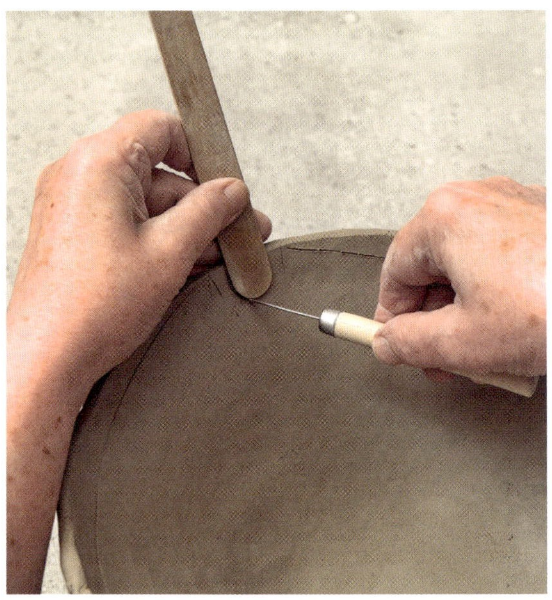

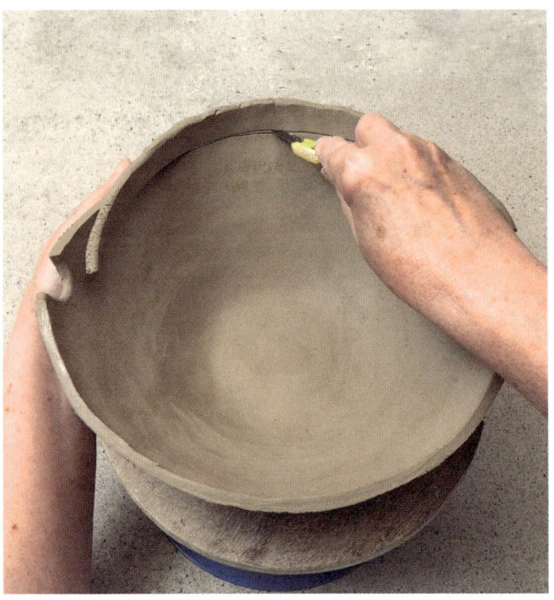

7 Using a round-ended tool as a template, score a semicircle on each side of the bowl at the point where the lines converge. Cut the semicircles out carefully, then neaten around the cut with a wooden modeling tool until gently rounded.

8 Use a knife to cut along the scored lines either side of the semicircles, then work over the cut edges with a rib to round them off and neaten up.

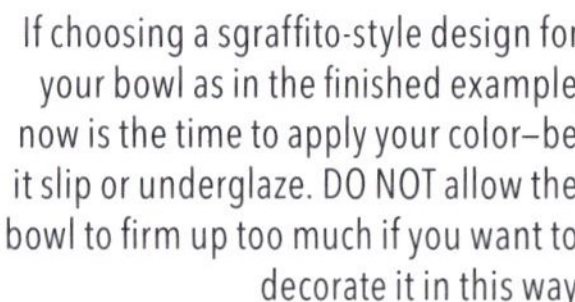

If choosing a sgraffito-style design for your bowl as in the finished example, now is the time to apply your color—be it slip or underglaze. DO NOT allow the bowl to firm up too much if you want to decorate it in this way.

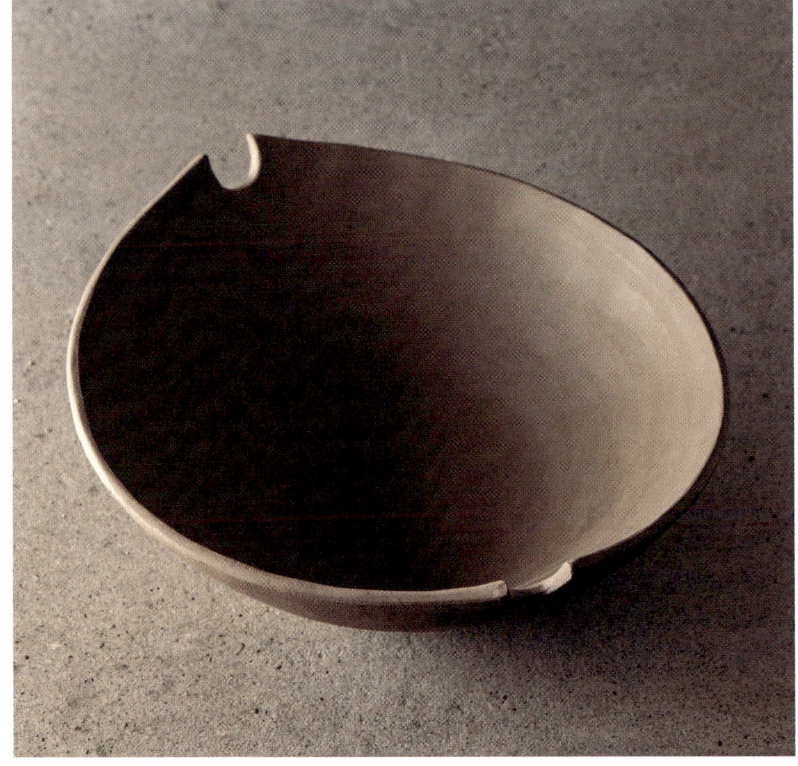

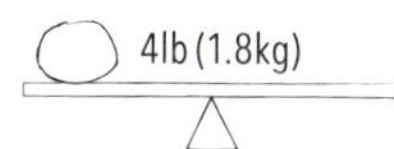

Diameter: 8½in (21.5cm) without handles; 11in (28cm) including handles
Height: 2in (5cm)

4lb (1.8kg)

BERRY BOWL WITH DRIP TRAY

Glazed in a stunning blue, this berry bowl looks fabulous stacked with luscious red fruit—it will wow both friends and family who will be sure to want one of their own.

YOU WILL NEED

TOOLS

- Metal palette
- Knife
- Kidney, metal or plastic
- Plaster hump mold or something similar, such as a large ball, to support the bowl
- Cookie cutters
- Pin
- Hole cutter or drill bit
- Thick foam block
- Small wooden bat, 5½in (14cm) diameter

CLAY

Buff stoneware

- 1½lb (675g) for bowl
- 14oz (400g) for foot
- 2oz (60g) for handles
- 1½lb (675g) for drip tray

DESIGN NOTE

To make a deeper bowl, simply pinch the clay to a more traditional rounded shape before adding the foot ring.

DECORATION

Berry fruits look stunning on blue backgrounds, so choose a simple glaze for this project—anything more elaborate would detract from the effect.

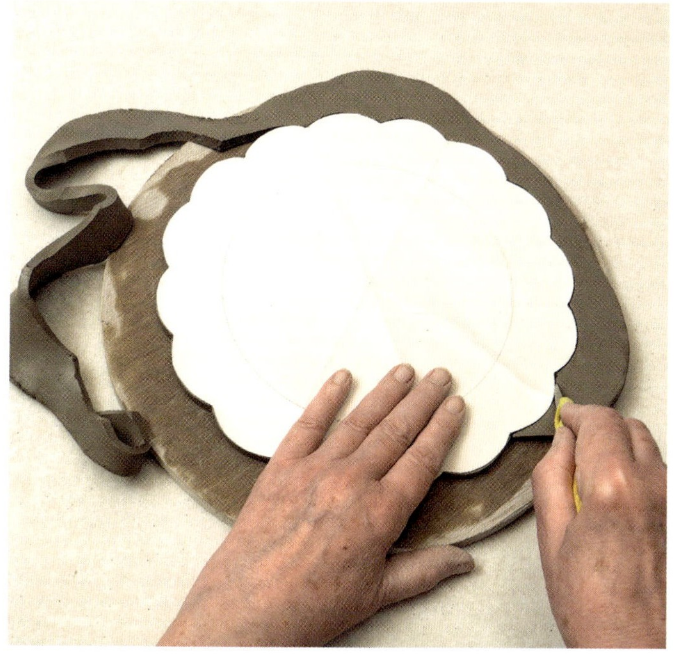

1 Draw and cut out a template, using the photograph above as a guide. Pinch and press a slab of clay for the bowl, large enough for the template to fit. Smooth over the slab with the metal palette to even the surface. Place the template on the slab and cut the shape out carefully following the scalloped edge.

Opposite: The berry bowl and tray are simply glazed with Amaco-Indigo Float brush-on glaze for dramatic effect.

Bisque fired to cone 06 (1,830°F/999°C)
Glaze fired to cone 6 (2,232°F/1,222°C)

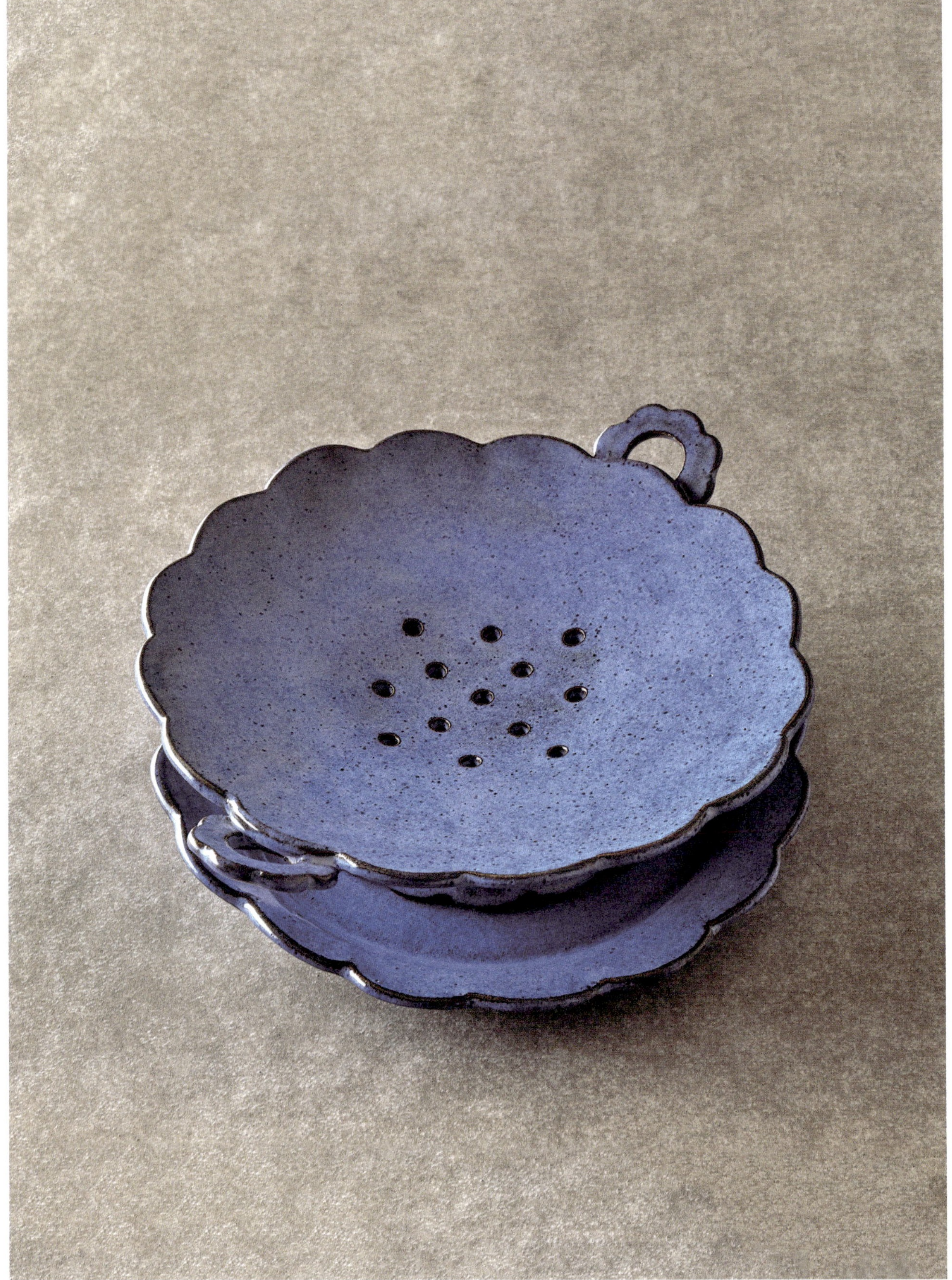

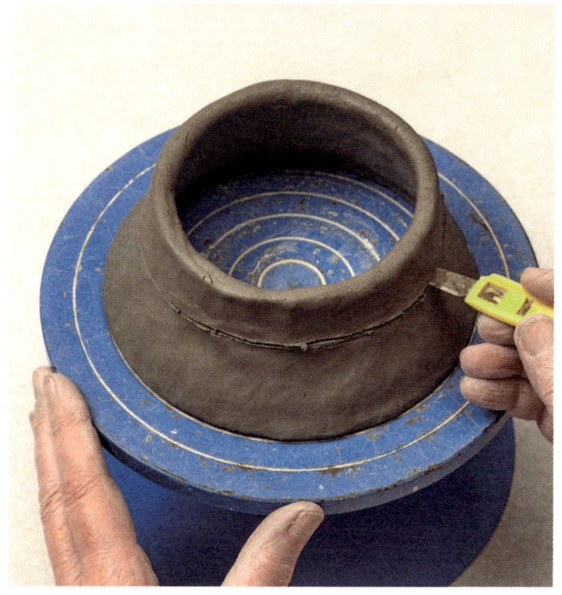

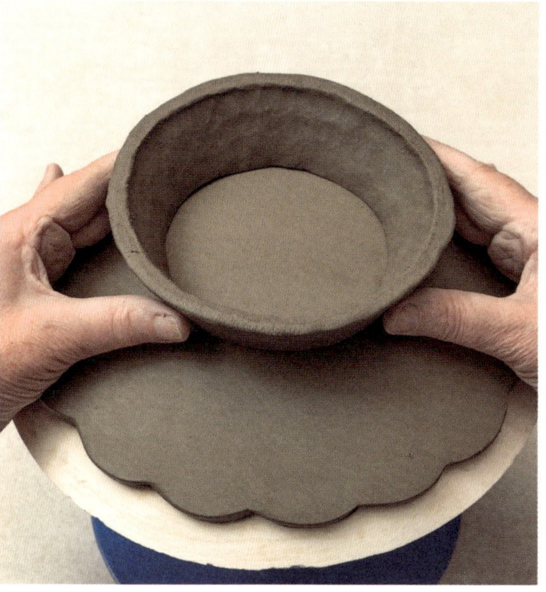

2 From the 14oz (400g) weight of clay, pinch an open ring into a conical shape, making it narrower at the top than the base. Cut the foot down to your chosen height, then neaten the surface of the ring using a kidney.

3 Drape the bowl slab over your support, then sit the foot on the surface to locate the central position—mark this with a pin. Fix the foot in place after scoring and slipping adjoining surfaces. Reinforce the join inside and out with coils of soft clay.

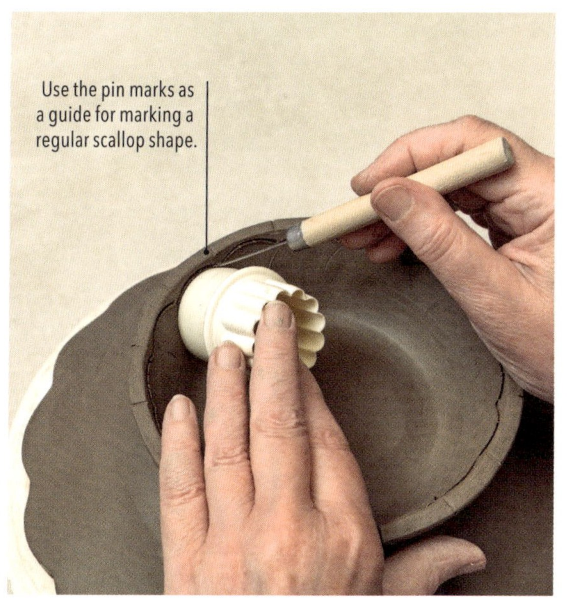

Use the pin marks as a guide for marking a regular scallop shape.

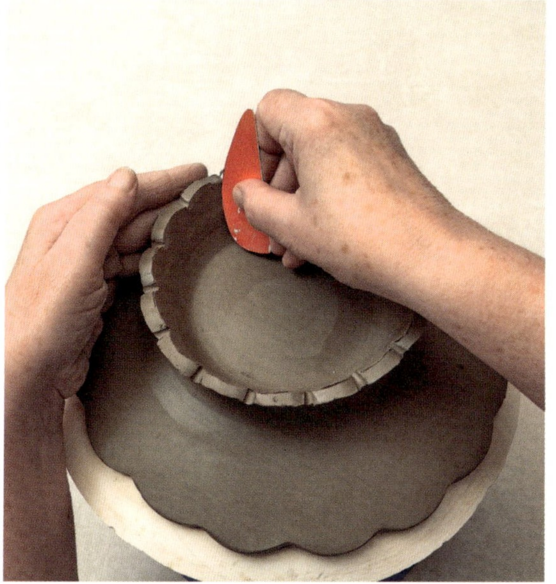

4 Divide the rim of the foot into equal sections with a pin mark. Place the cookie cutter between the marked lines and score around the curved edge to create a scallop shape.

5 Cut around the scored lines carefully, to form the scalloped rim. Neaten up around the cut edges with a kidney, then around the outside and underside of the foot generally until the clay is smooth.

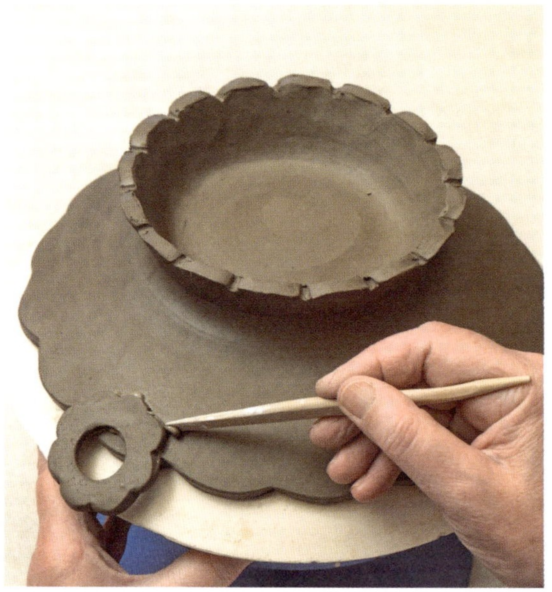

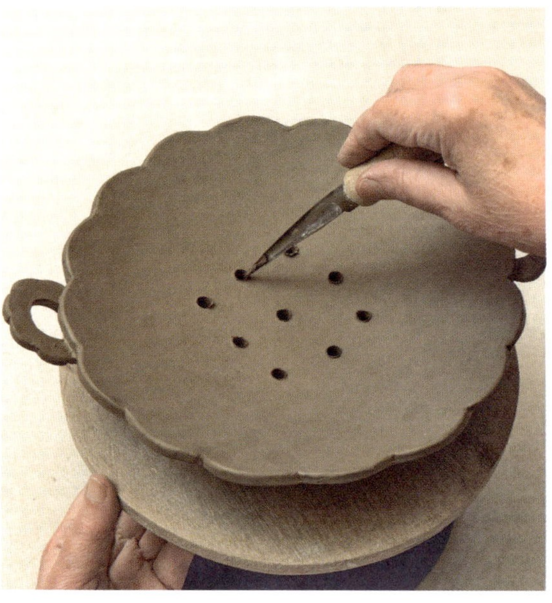

6 Pinch two small discs of equal size, then cut them to a perfect circle with the cookie cutter. Scallop around the edges of the discs and cut a smaller circle from the center. Fix the handles on opposite sides of the bowl after scoring and slipping adjoining surfaces.

7 Turn the bowl upright and cut as many holes as required on the center using a hole cutter or drill bit. Be careful where you locate the holes to avoid cutting into the foot beneath.

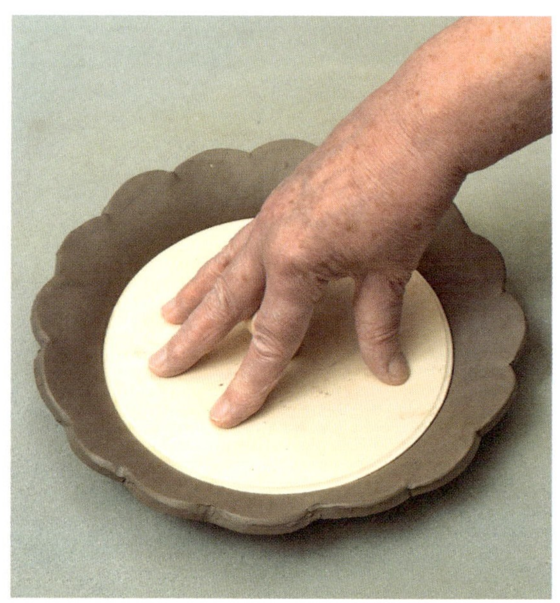

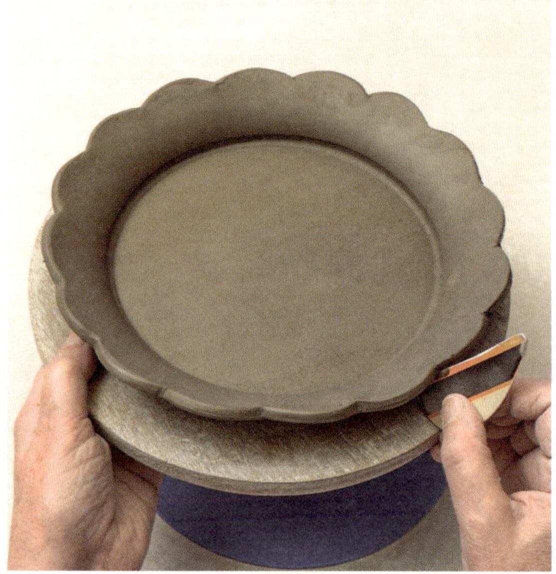

8 For the drip tray, pinch and cut out a second slab identical to the first, following step 1. Place the slab on the foam block and the wooden bat in the center of the shape. Press down firmly into the clay—the sides will rise up as you press to form a dish shape.

9 Use a kidney to neaten up the tray where required, ensuring both the inside and outside surfaces are smooth and the scallops defined.

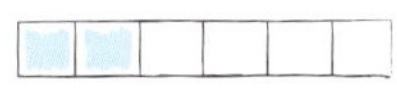

FOOTED DESSERT BOWL

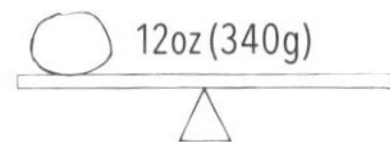

Diameter: 4½in (11cm)
Height: 3in (8cm)

12oz (340g)

These lovely little dessert bowls have been designed to use with the berry bowl on the previous pages. Glazed in a similar vibrant blue, your taste buds will be truly tantalized when dessert is served.

You can, of course, glaze the bowls in different shades of blue—so they still work as a set.

YOU WILL NEED

TOOLS
- Banding wheel (turntable)
- Metal kidney
- Surform or rasp blade
- Knife
- Round-ended wooden modeling tool
- Small rib or kidney

CLAY
Buff stoneware
- 8oz (225g) for bowl
- 4oz (115g) for foot

DESIGN NOTE
To match these bowls to the berry bowl exactly, scallop the rims and feet in the same way as demonstrated in steps 4 and 5 on page 30.

DECORATION
- If you want to use these bowls as a set with the berry bowl, simply decorate them in the same glaze.
- As an alternative, glaze each bowl in a different color to complement the berry bowl—jewel-like shades would look great.

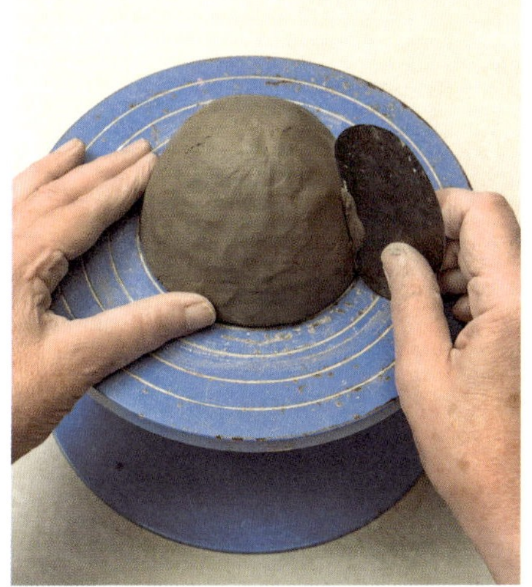

1 Working with an 8oz (225g) weight of clay, form it into a ball and pinch out an open bowl shape with a rounded base. Sit the bowl upside down on a banding wheel and work over the surface with a metal kidney to remove the pinch marks.

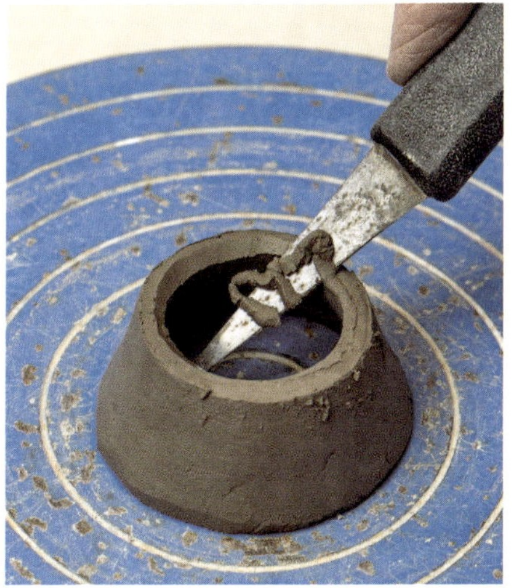

2 Pinch the remaining clay to an open, conical ring, which is narrower at the top than the bottom. Sit the ring on the wheel and level the narrow end using a surform. Now bevel the rim with a knife so the base of the bowl will sit on it comfortably.

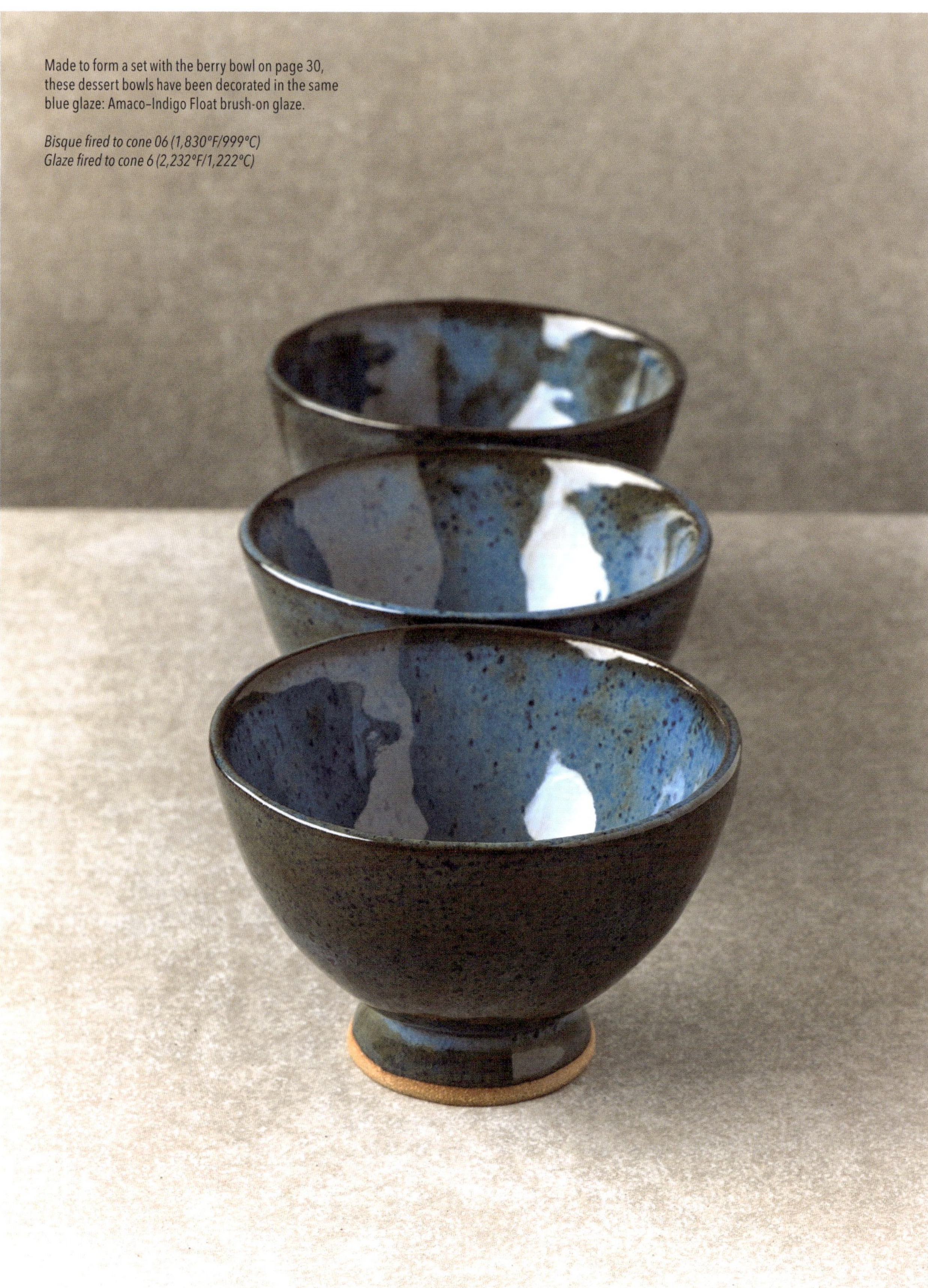

Made to form a set with the berry bowl on page 30, these dessert bowls have been decorated in the same blue glaze: Amaco–Indigo Float brush-on glaze.

Bisque fired to cone 06 (1,830°F/999°C)
Glaze fired to cone 6 (2,232°F/1,222°C)

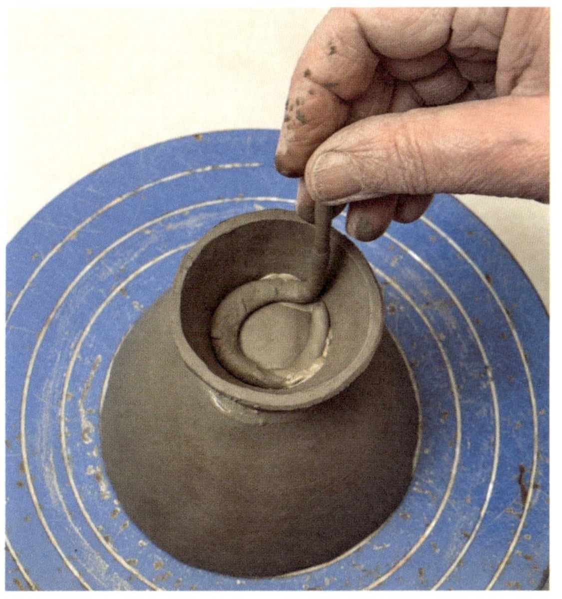

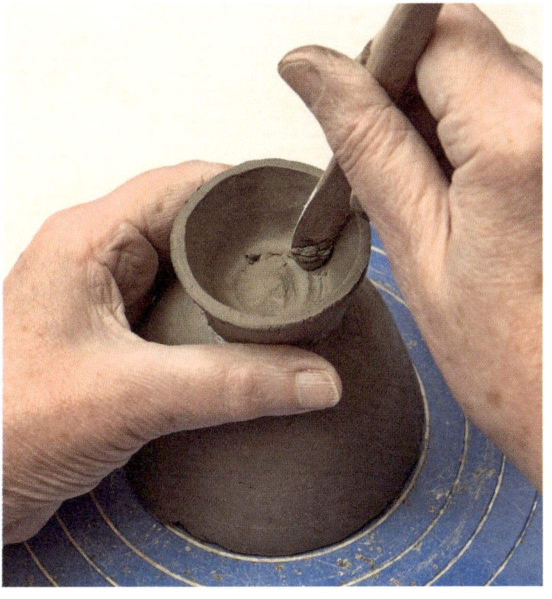

3 Mark and score the position for the foot on the underside of the bowl, then apply some slip to the adjoining surfaces and fix it in place. Reinforce the join on the inside of the foot with a coil of soft clay.

4 Blend the coil in thoroughly with a wooden tool, then use the same tool to neaten up. Take the time to finish the surface neatly using a small rib, if preferred.

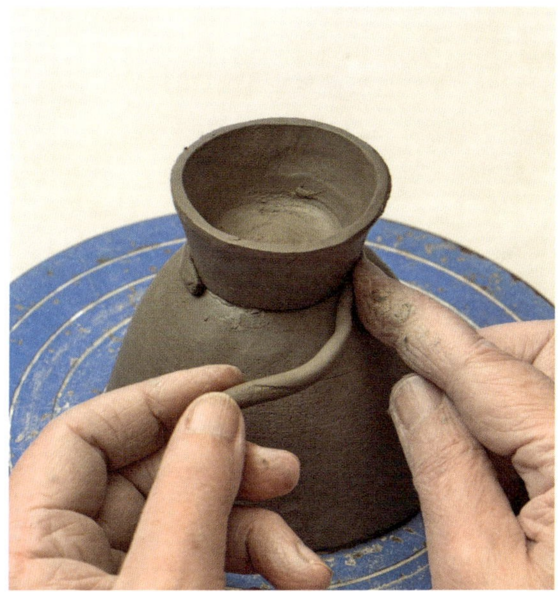

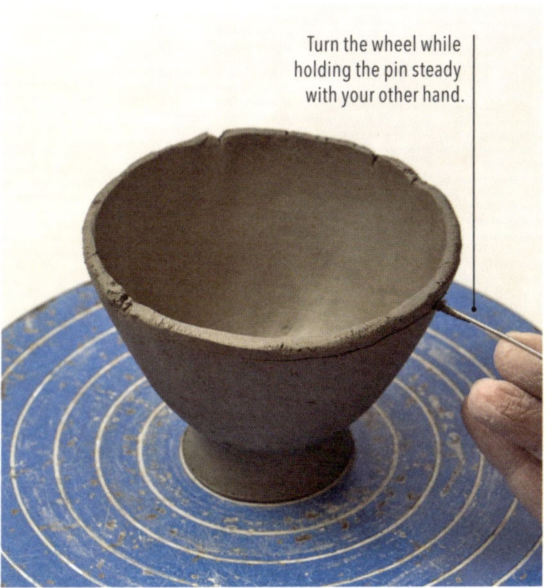

Turn the wheel while holding the pin steady with your other hand.

5 Repeat the process of reinforcing the join on the outside of the foot using another coil of soft clay. Neaten up using a rib once the coil has been seamlessly blended in.

6 Stand the bowl upright on the wheel, placing it as centrally as possible, then with a pin held rigid in your hand and turning the wheel slowly, score a level line for the rim.

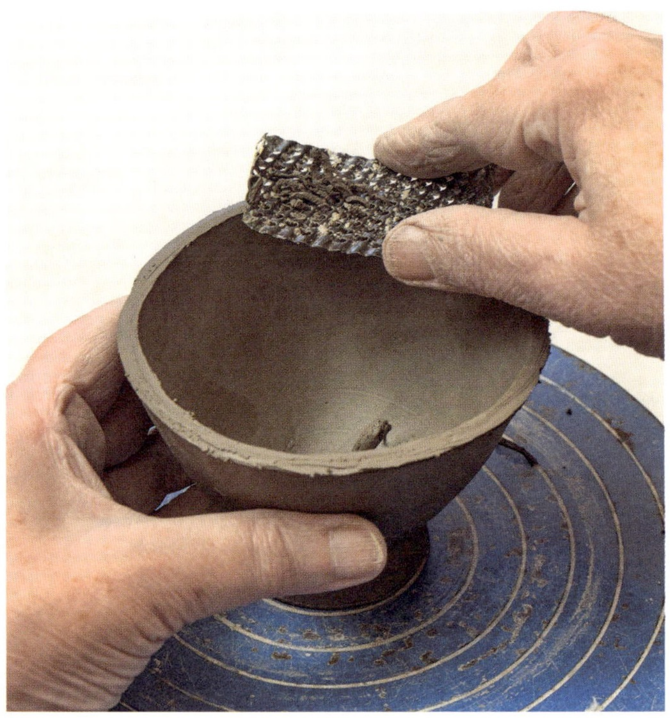

7 Surform the rim, working down to the scored line to level it. If there is a lot of clay to remove at the rim, cut along the score line first, then tidy up with the surform.

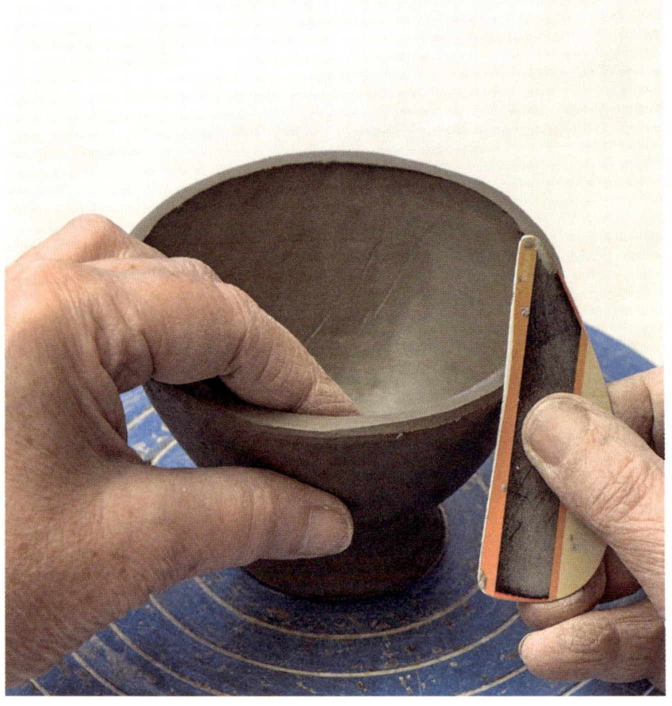

8 Neaten around the rim with a rib; aim for a pleasantly rounded finish which is smooth with an even thickness. Take the time to work on the rim; it is the first thing people will notice if it isn't smooth and regular.

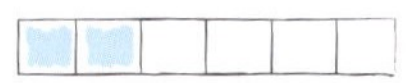

POURING BOWL

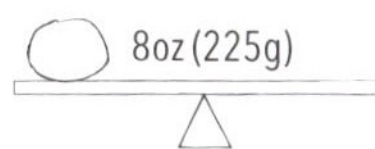

Width: 3in (7.5cm)
Height: approx. 3½in (9cm) at the highest point
Length: 6in (15cm)

8oz (225g)

These little pouring bowls are fabulous for sauces, dressings, or dips and look great on any table. Decorated in soft pastel shades for a really contemporary look, the bowls look particularly good in groups of three or more.

YOU WILL NEED

TOOLS
- Banding wheel (turntable)
- Wooden spatula
- Flexible metal kidney
- Small round object (cookie cutters are perfect)
- Small loop tool
- Brush for slip application

CLAY
Grogged white earthenware
- 8oz (225g) for each bowl
- Colored decorating slip

DESIGN NOTE
- This project is made from a white clay body but, alternatively, red terra-cotta can look really stunning with pale slip decoration.
- You could use a stoneware body but be aware the clay will shrink more in firing, resulting in a smaller bowl.

DECORATION
These practical little bowls look their best simply colored with slip on the inside and finished with a transparent glaze, but could be decorated more elaborately if preferred. See pages 156–172 for other options for decoration.

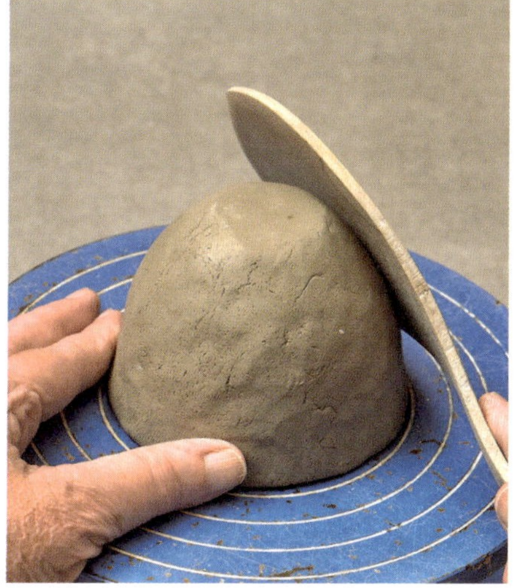

1 Pinch a basic bowl from the suggested quantity of clay. Place the bowl rim-down at the center of your banding wheel, then paddle the surface with the wooden spatula, to refine the shape.

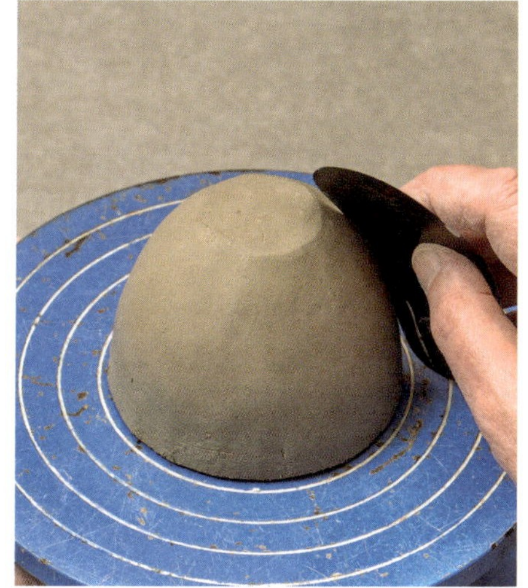

2 Maintaining the centered position on the wheel using the concentric lines as a guide, work over the surface of the bowl with a kidney to remove lumps and bumps and establish a definite, flat level for the base.

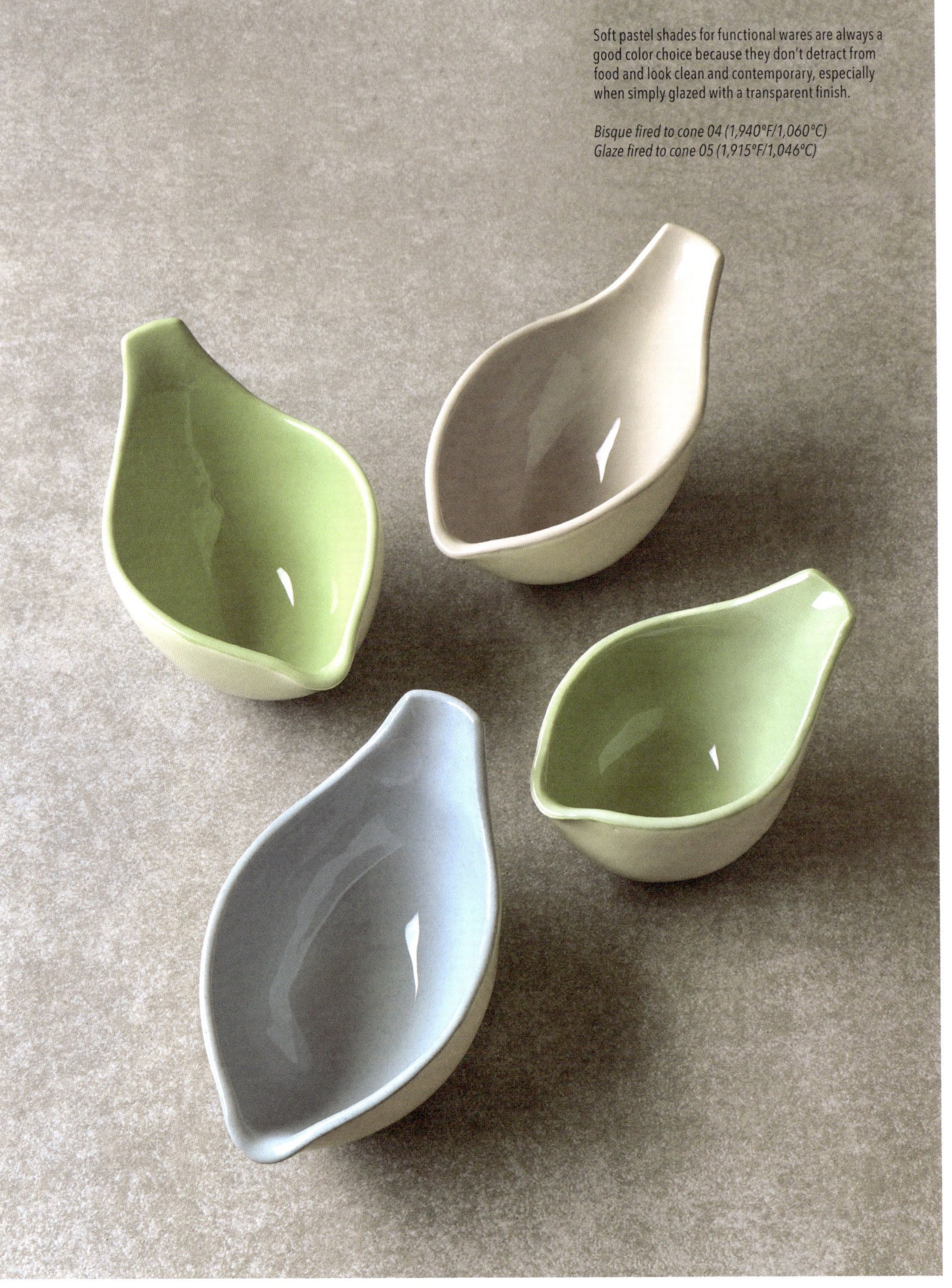

Soft pastel shades for functional wares are always a good color choice because they don't detract from food and look clean and contemporary, especially when simply glazed with a transparent finish.

Bisque fired to cone 04 (1,940°F/1,060°C)
Glaze fired to cone 05 (1,915°F/1,046°C)

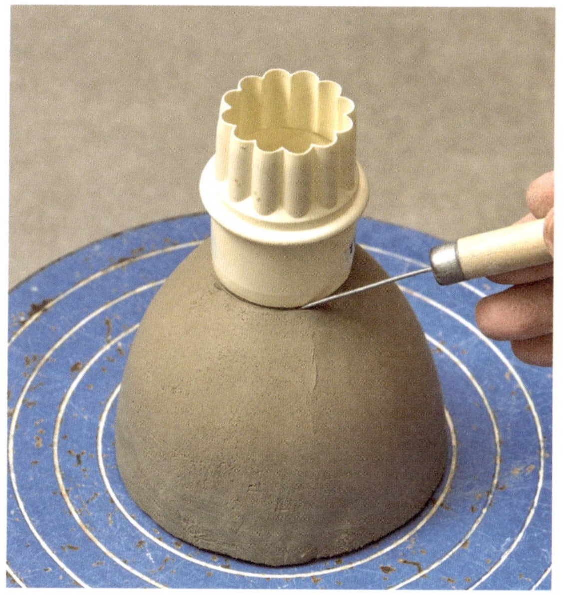

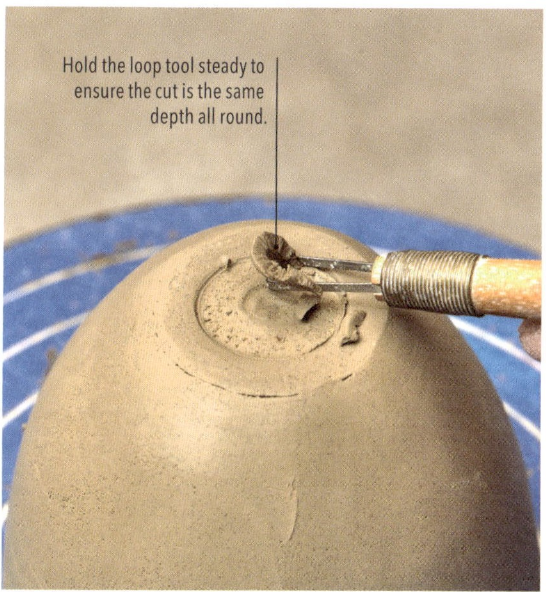

3 Position a small cookie cutter or similar round object centrally over the base. It will form the outer rim of a foot ring and therefore should be substantial enough in size for the bowl to sit safely and securely. Mark the position with a pin.

4 Turning the bowl on the banding wheel as you work, carefully trim away the clay from inside the marked circle to within ¼in (5mm) of the line, using the loop tool; this forms the foot. Leave the swirl created by the tool as a feature.

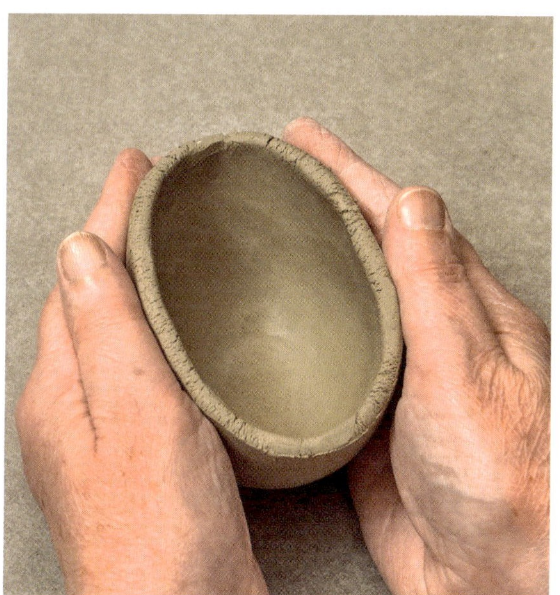

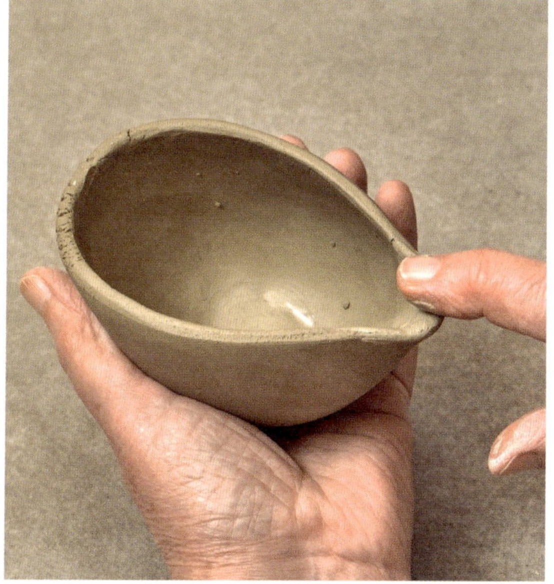

5 Sit the bowl upright on the work surface and gently squeeze the sides to change the shape from round to oval. Use a blow-dryer to firm the clay up a little until the shape holds in this position.

6 Gripping one end of the oval firmly, wet the forefinger of your other hand, then work it over the clay from side to side to form a pouring lip. You can make this narrow or wide depending on the intended use.

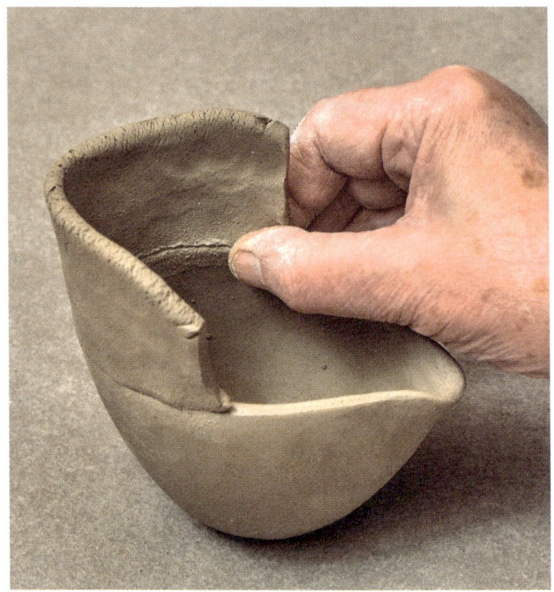

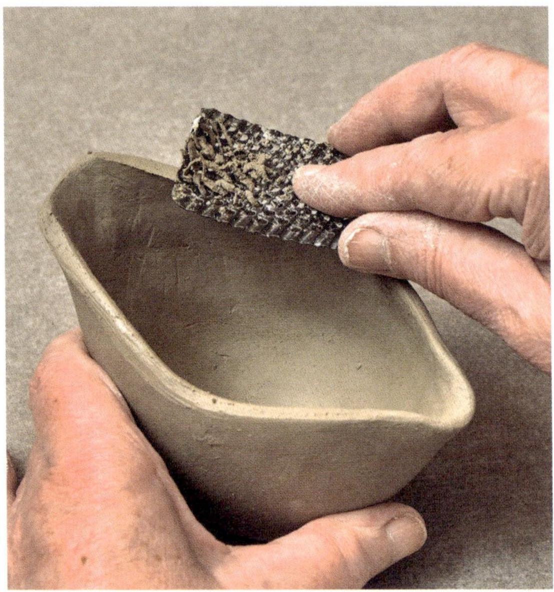

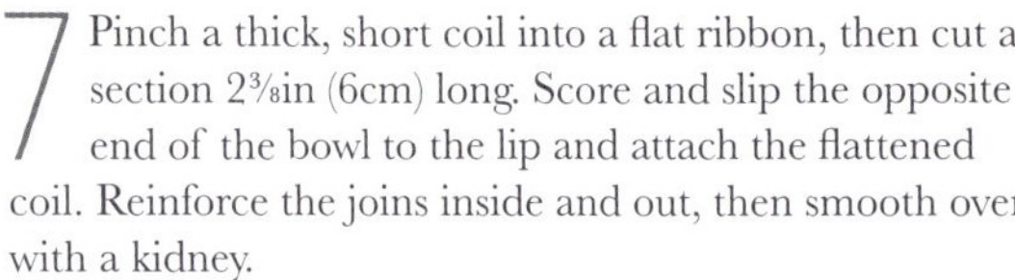

7 Pinch a thick, short coil into a flat ribbon, then cut a section 2⅜in (6cm) long. Score and slip the opposite end of the bowl to the lip and attach the flattened coil. Reinforce the joins inside and out, then smooth over with a kidney.

8 Shape the coil extension by shaving the clay with a surform to form a rudimentary handle or resting place for a spoon. From an aerial perspective the bowl should look leaf-shaped with the handle end cut level rather than forming a point.

9 Holding the bowl in the palm of one hand, brush the slip on the inside only. Apply three coats, allowing each coat to dry to the touch before applying the next. Extend the slip over the rim of the bowl but avoid the outer body.

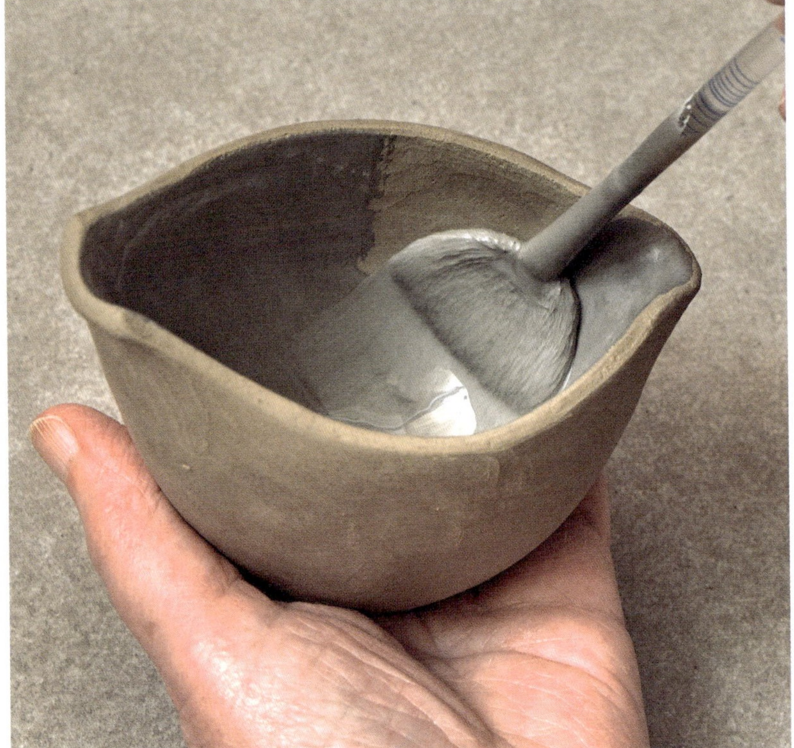

LIDDED SUGAR BOWL

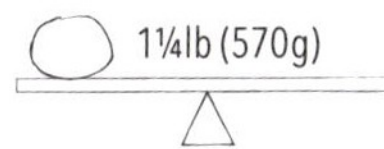

Diameter: 3in (7.5cm)
Height: 6¾in (17cm)

1¼lb (570g)

Sometimes it's nice to make something a little quirky, something unique, that breaks away from traditional shapes. This little sugar bowl, with its organic-shaped lid, certainly fits the bill in terms of quirkiness but it is totally fit for purpose, too, with a secure lid and spoon rest.

YOU WILL NEED

TOOLS
- Wooden spatula
- Flexible metal kidney
- Banding wheel (turntable)
- Knife
- Wooden modeling tool
- Slip trailer with fine nozzle

CLAY
Red earthenware
- 1lb (450g) for bowl, divided into 8oz (225g) for each half
- 4oz (115g) for locating ring
- White or colored decorating slip

DESIGN NOTE
- Red earthenware clay complements the organic form of the bowl and the white slip decoration contrasts beautifully on the surface.
- Use white clay with colored slip decoration as an alternative.

DECORATION
Slip trailing is an age-old method of surface decoration. See page 162 for this method and pages 156–172 for other options for decoration.

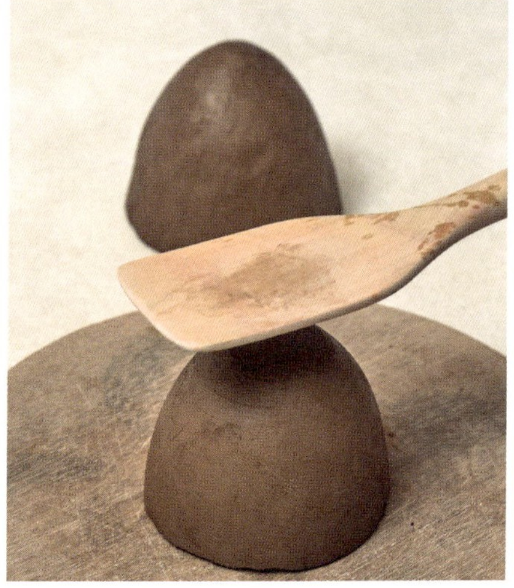

1 Divide the clay into two 8oz (225g) balls and pinch them to an identical basic bowl shape, narrower at the base and the same diameter at the rim. Flatten the base of one half with the spatula and refine the surface using a kidney.

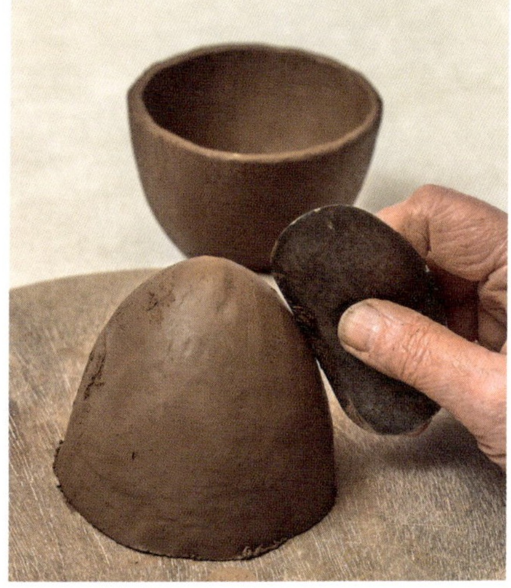

2 Maintaining the domed shape of the second pinched half (the lid), refine the surface with the kidney as you did the base, until all evidence of pinch marks have been scraped and smoothed away.

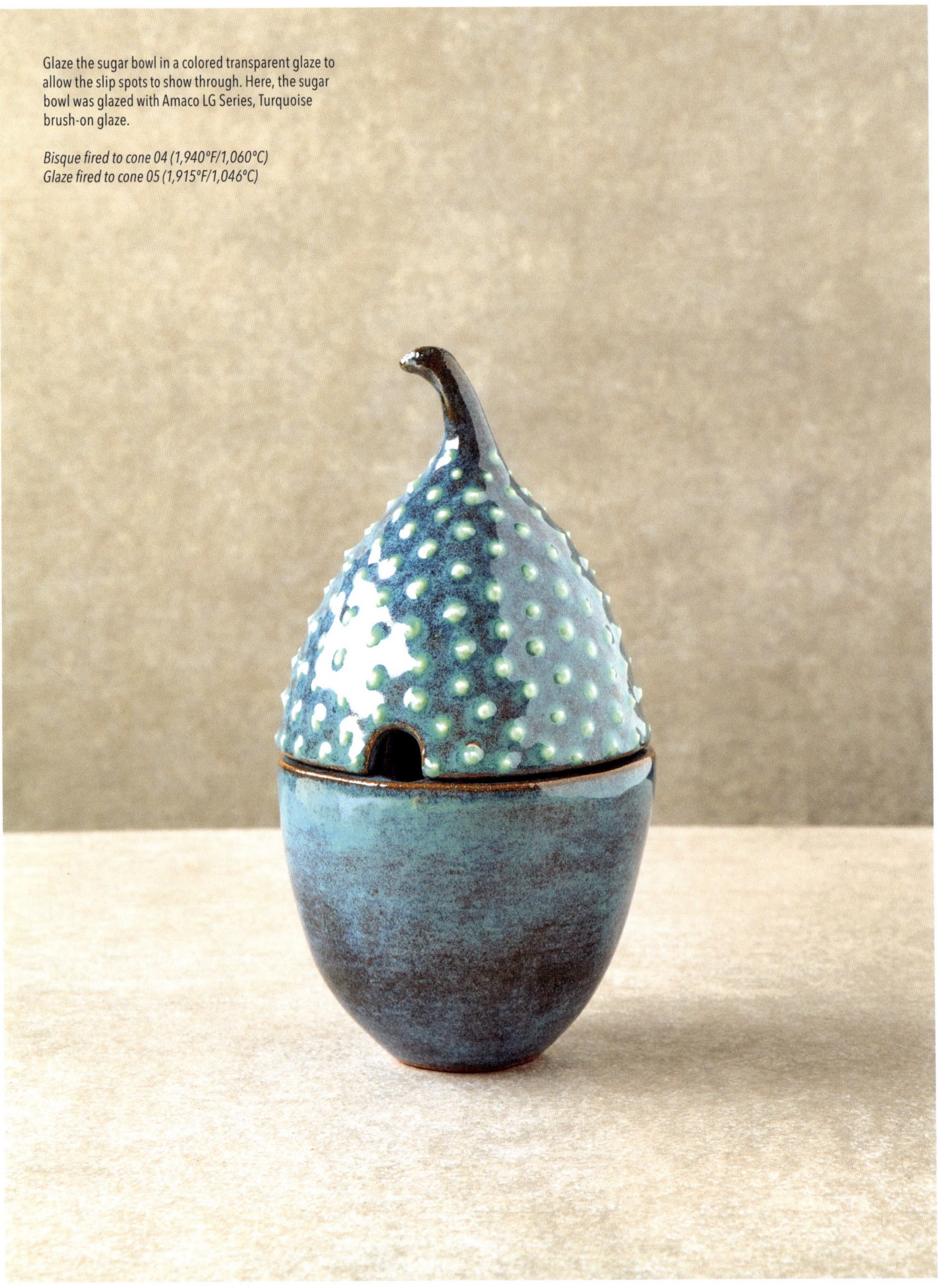

Glaze the sugar bowl in a colored transparent glaze to allow the slip spots to show through. Here, the sugar bowl was glazed with Amaco LG Series, Turquoise brush-on glaze.

Bisque fired to cone 04 (1,940°F/1,060°C)
Glaze fired to cone 05 (1,915°F/1,046°C)

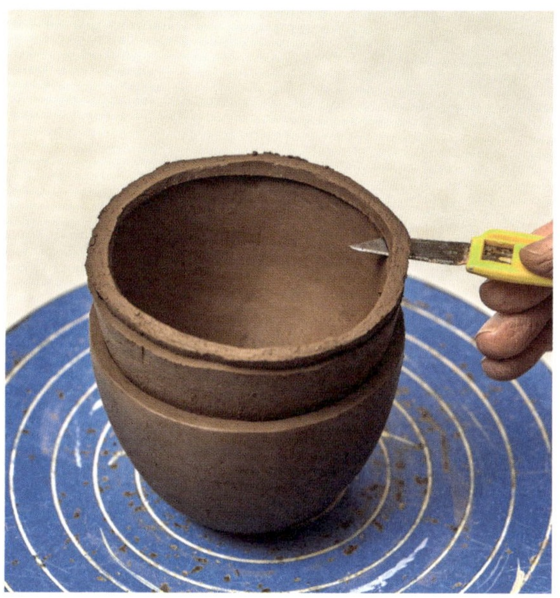

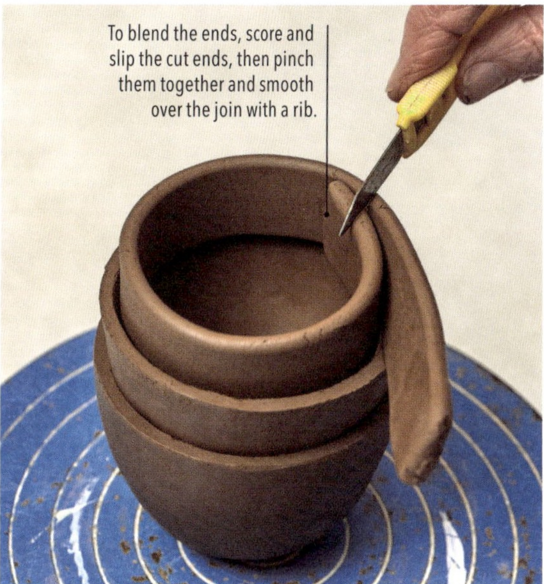

3 Invert the lid and place it inside the base, making sure it is aligned and level, then, holding a knife rigidly in your hand and turning the banding wheel slowly, cut the rim level. Neaten up the cut edge with a kidney when done.

4 From the remaining clay, pinch a short coil into a thin ribbon, long enough to form a locating ring inside the rim of the lid with some overlap. Place the ribbon inside the lid, then cut through the overlapped ends at an angle for a more secure join. Blend the ends to make a ring.

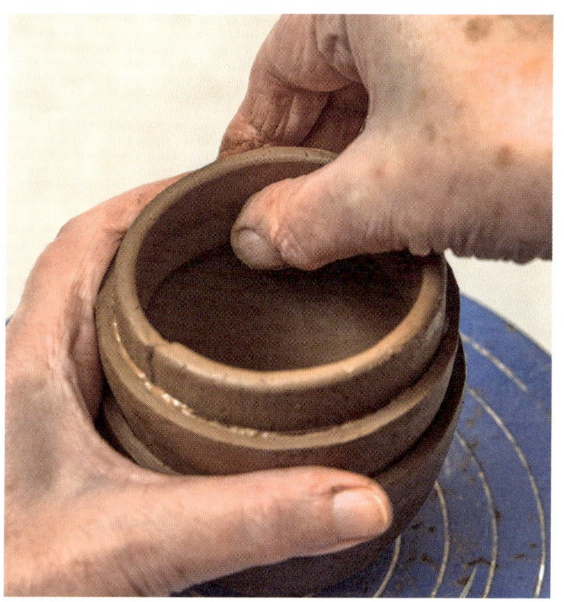

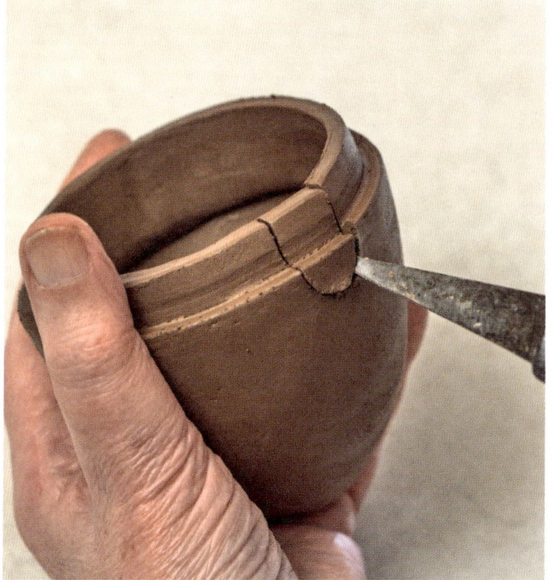

5 Remove the locating ring. Score and slip the place it will attach to and the corresponding area on the ring itself, then fix it back in place, pressing firmly with your thumb. Neaten around the ring with a modeling tool to remove excess slip.

6 Remove the lid from the base and check that it fits the base the right way up. Pare the walls back with a kidney if the two don't fit exactly. Now cut a U-shaped hole for a spoon rest through the lid and locating ring.

7 Pinch a small, stalklike handle for the top of the lid. Score and slip the area for the handle on the lid and adjoining end of the stalk, then fix it in place. Reinforce around the join with a coil of soft clay.

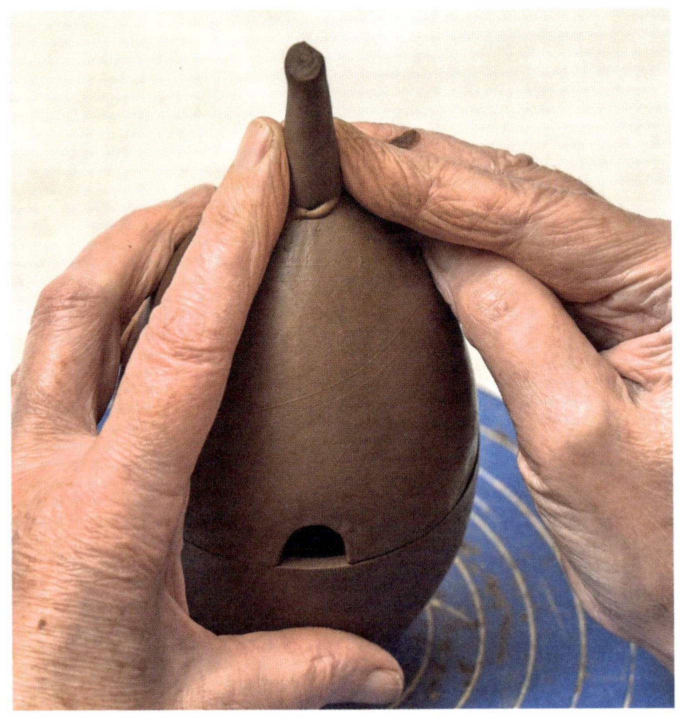

8 Allow the bowl to firm to leather-hard with the lid in place. Fill your slip trailing bottle with thickened slip and secure the nozzle in place. Add slip trail spots in a random pattern over the lid only.

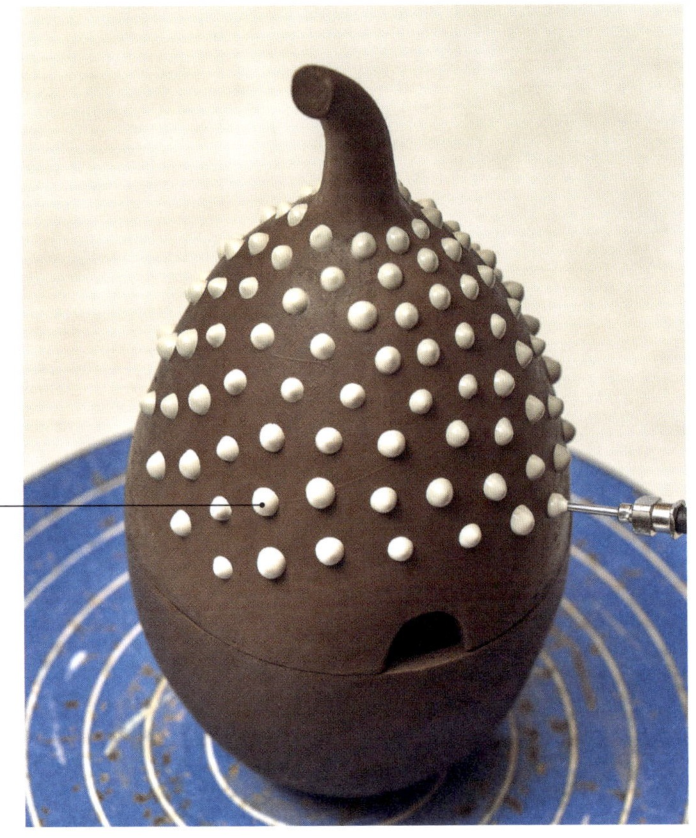

To avoid touching the slip, place the pot on a banding wheel and turn it to apply the pattern.

NESTING PLATES

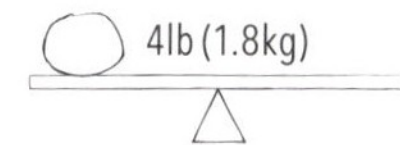

Largest size: 9½ x 7in (24 x 18cm)
Second size: 7 x 6in (18 x 15cm)
Third size: 5½ x 3½in (14 x 9cm)
Fourth size: 3 x 3in (8 x 8cm)
Smallest size: 2½ x 2in (6.5 x 5cm)

4lb (1.8kg)

There is a fine line between a plate and a dish, and this project falls somewhere between the two.

Make these plates in random shapes or in decreasing sizes of a standard circle or square—all styles look great when glazed in different colors.

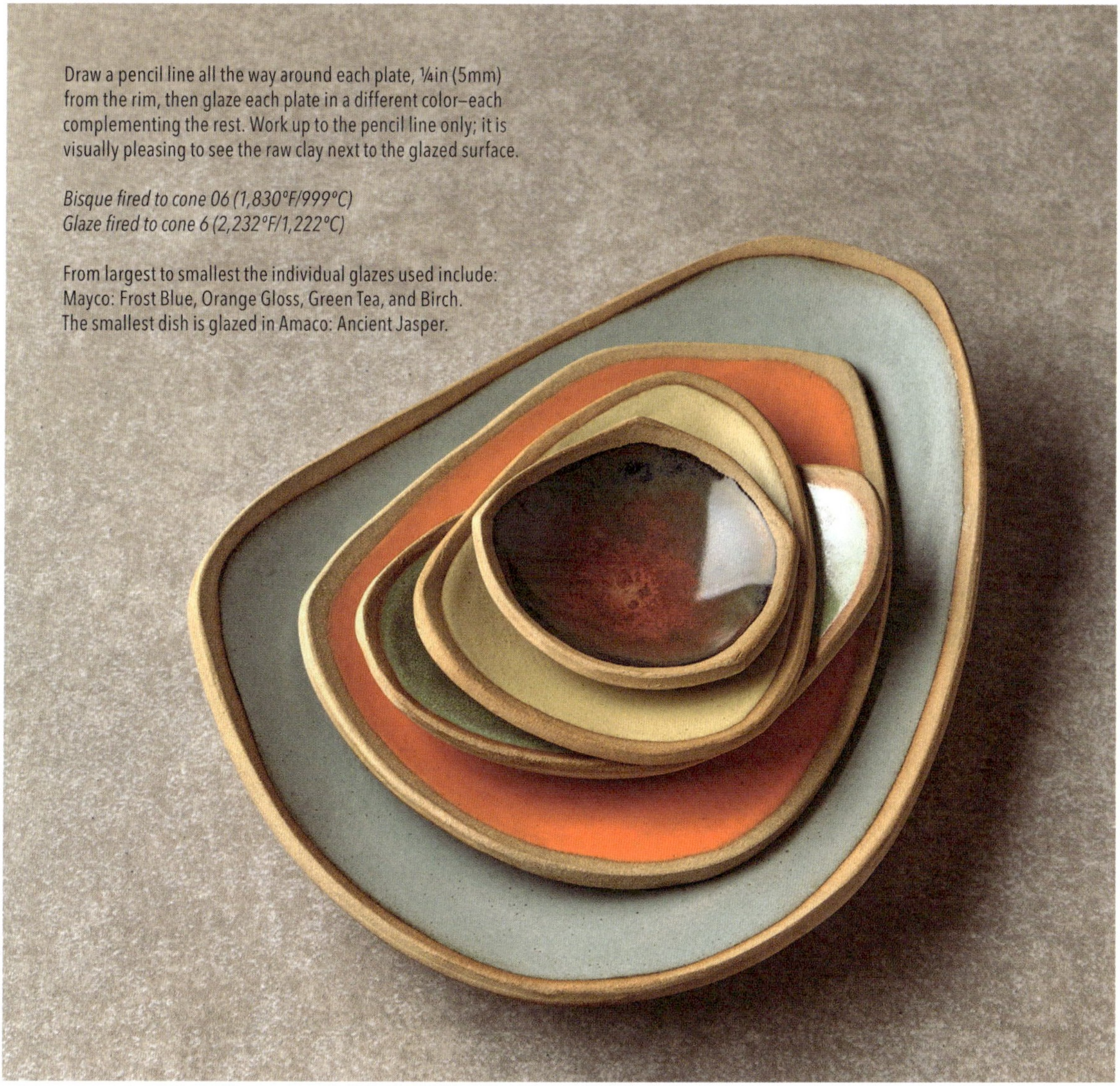

Draw a pencil line all the way around each plate, ¼in (5mm) from the rim, then glaze each plate in a different color–each complementing the rest. Work up to the pencil line only; it is visually pleasing to see the raw clay next to the glazed surface.

Bisque fired to cone 06 (1,830°F/999°C)
Glaze fired to cone 6 (2,232°F/1,222°C)

From largest to smallest the individual glazes used include: Mayco: Frost Blue, Orange Gloss, Green Tea, and Birch. The smallest dish is glazed in Amaco: Ancient Jasper.

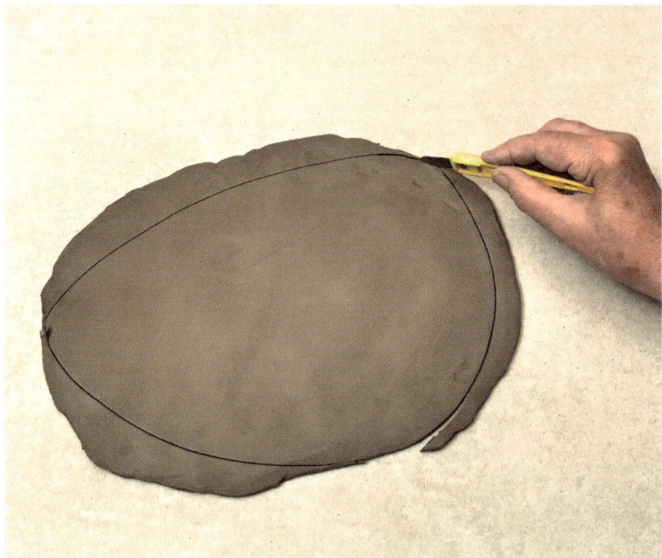

1 Beginning with the largest weight of clay, pinch out a flat slab until it is an even thickness of ¼in (5mm). Work over the surface of the slab with a metal palette to smooth the surface. Cut the slab to your chosen shape.

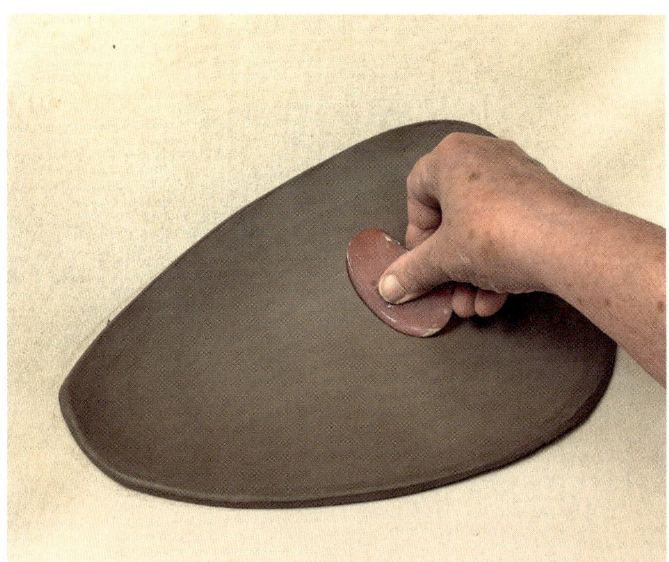

2 If using a sling mold, place the slab at the center and work over the surface with a soft kidney to develop a concave shape so that it can hold food. It can be gently rounded from the center or developed into a deeper container as required.

YOU WILL NEED

TOOLS

- Metal palette or rib
- Knife
- Soft rubber or plastic kidney
- Sling mold or plaster/bisque hump mold
- Curved kidney
- Pin
- Surform or rasp blade
- Curved rib (optional)

CLAY

Buff stoneware

- 1½lb (675g) for largest size
- 1lb (450g) for second size
- 12oz (340g) for third size
- 8oz (225g) for fourth size
- 4oz (115g) for smallest size

DESIGN NOTE

- There is little planning involved in the making of these plates; the shape is best dictated by the slab you pinch first.
- Thereafter, the shapes just have to vary as they decrease in size.

DECORATION

The attraction of these plates when stacked on top of one another is the contrasting color of the glazes. Only the upper surfaces are glazed but because they are fired to stoneware, the clay is vitrified, making it impermeable and safe for food.

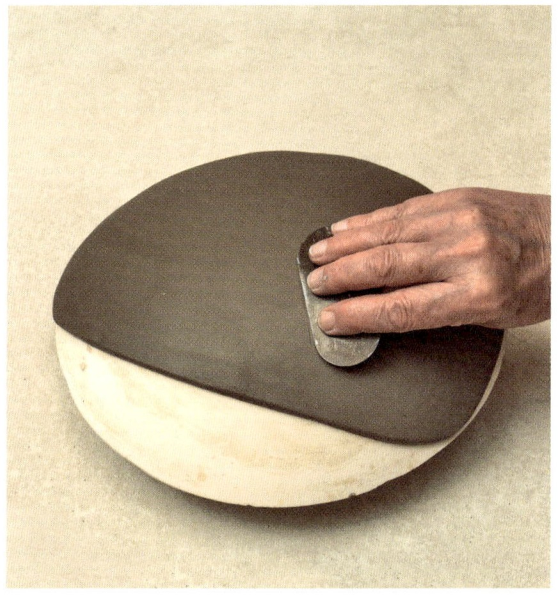

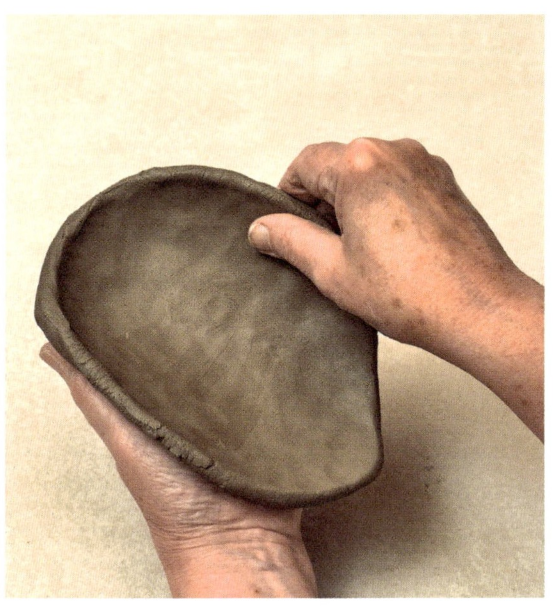

3 ALTERNATIVELY, drape the slab over a hump mold, then work over the surface with a kidney to ease the clay into shape. Whichever mold form used, allow the plates to firm to leather-hard in situ before handling them again.

4 The next plate can be made in the same way or formed directly from the basic weight. Pinch out the clay carefully, creating a gentle curve similar to the larger shape so that it will sit comfortably inside it when completed.

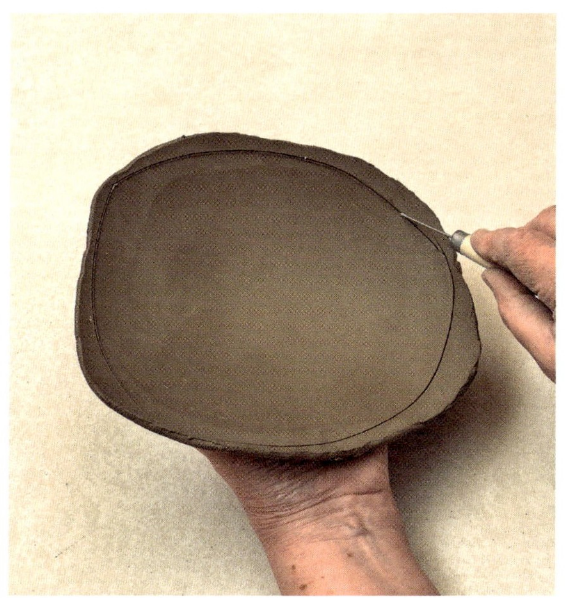

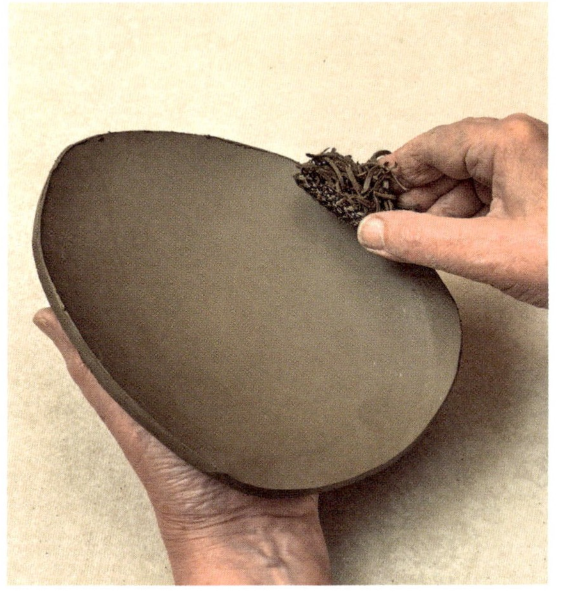

5 Once the slab is an even thickness and the rough shape required, work over the surface with a kidney to smooth the clay and refine the curved shape. Now score the outline shape of the plate with a pin, maximizing as much of the slab as possible.

6 Using a surform, shave away the excess clay around the scored line. If you're not happy with the shape when finished, simply shave a little more away until it pleases you more.

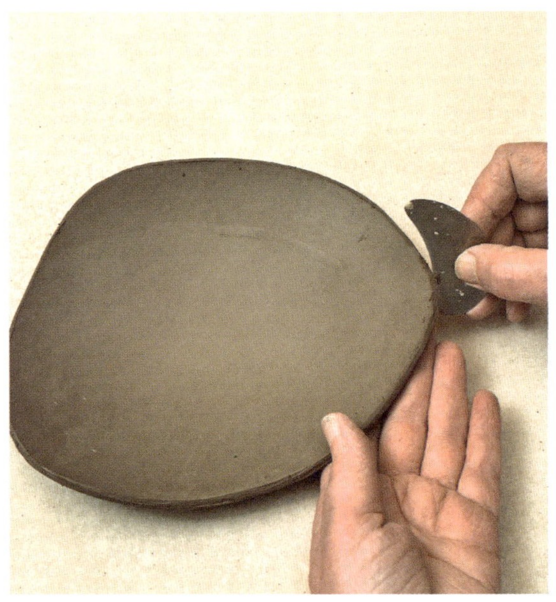

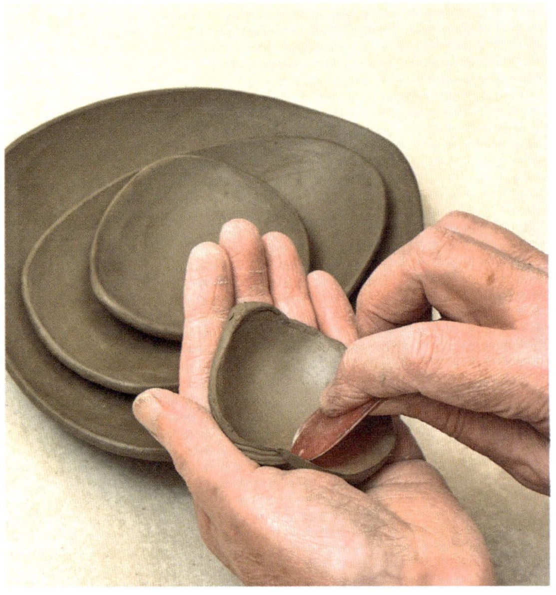

7 Use a curve-shaped rib or kidney to refine the surformed rim of the dish to a pleasing rounded shape. It is worth taking some time to get this right because rims are important—a bad one draws the eye immediately!

8 Reducing the weight of clay each time, continue to make the remaining plates in the same way. Consider the shape of each plate in relation to the one before as you make them, so that they create a pleasing arrangement when nesting inside one another.

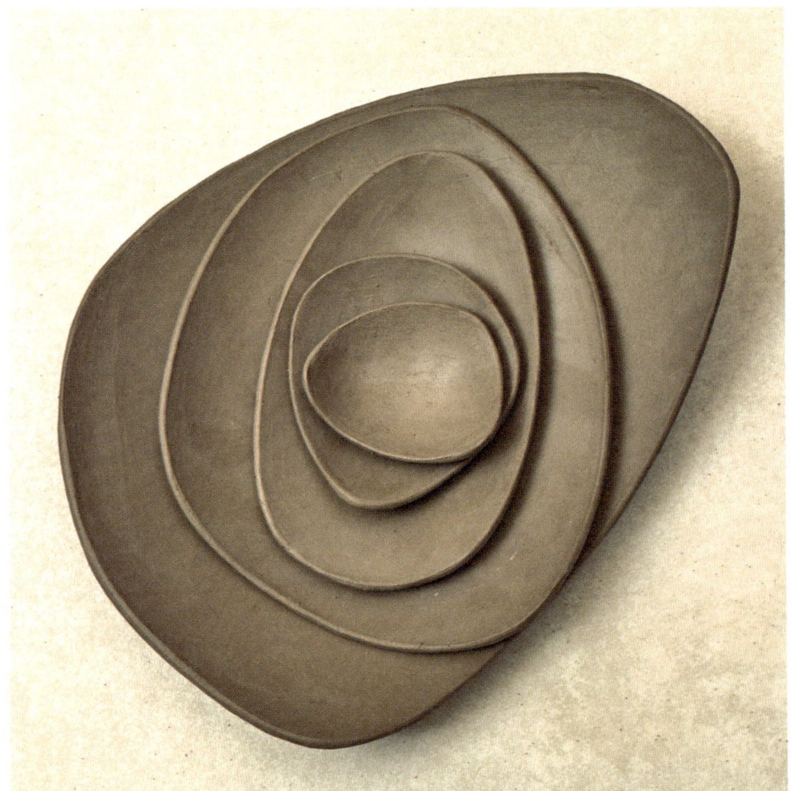

9 When all the plates have been completed, test how they look nesting inside one another. When you are satisfied with the arrangement, separate them out again to dry ready for bisque firing.

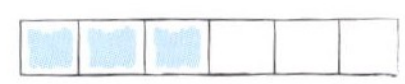

SECTIONAL DISH FOR DIPS

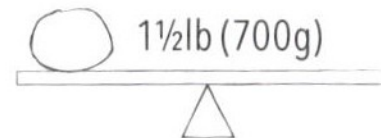

Width: 7in (18cm)
Height: 6in (15cm)

1½lb (700g)

This is a great little dish for center of table, to serve dips, sauces, or preserves. The generous handle makes it easy to carry and pass around and the design can readily be adapted in size for serving other dedicated food stuffs.

YOU WILL NEED

TOOLS
- Metal kidney or rib
- Wooden spatula
- Surform or rasp blade
- Wooden modeling tool

CLAY
White stoneware
- 6oz (170g) for each bowl
- 6oz (170g) for handle

DESIGN NOTE
The number of dishes can easily be increased from three to four if a square arrangement is preferred—the making principles are exactly the same.

DECORATION
The surface decoration on these dishes uses a glaze-on-glaze technique with wax resist. See page 168 for this method and pages 156–172 for other options for decoration.

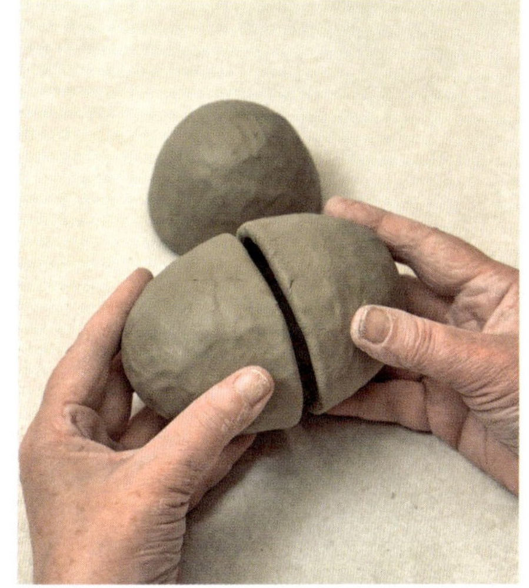

1 Divide the clay into four equal amounts of 6oz (170g) each, then pinch three of them into open bowl shapes, slightly wider at the rim than the base. When finished, all three bowls should be exactly the same size at the rim.

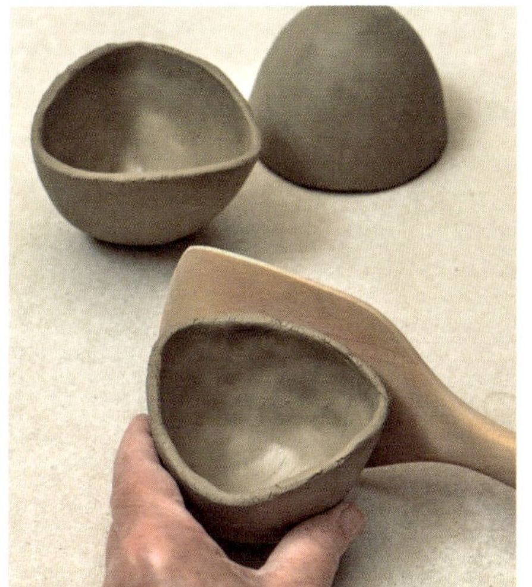

2 Work over the bowl shapes with a kidney to refine and smooth the surfaces inside and out. Now tap each bowl on the work surface lightly to establish a secure base, then triangulate their shape by gently flattening the sides with the wooden spatula.

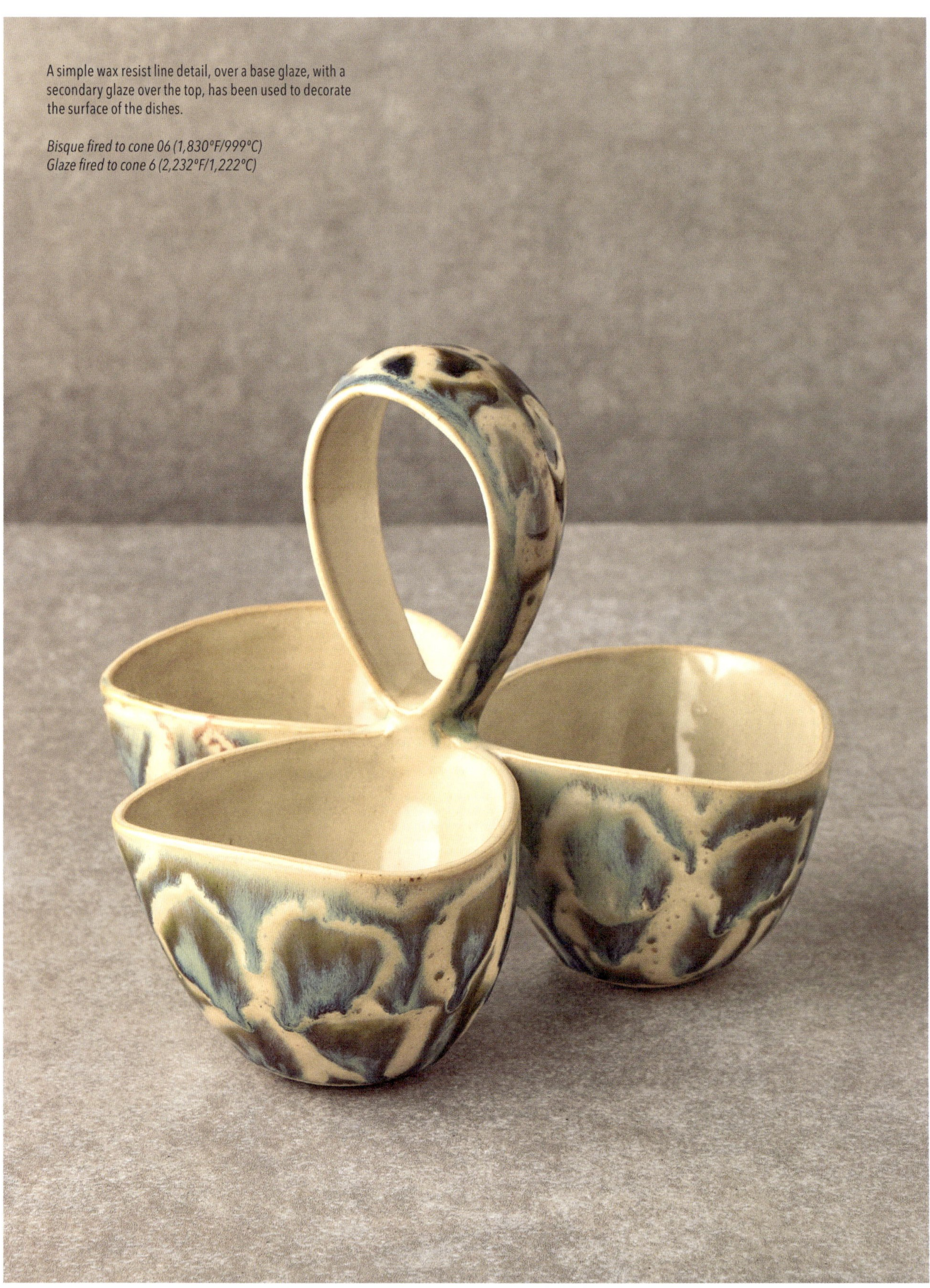

A simple wax resist line detail, over a base glaze, with a secondary glaze over the top, has been used to decorate the surface of the dishes.

Bisque fired to cone 06 (1,830°F/999°C)
Glaze fired to cone 6 (2,232°F/1,222°C)

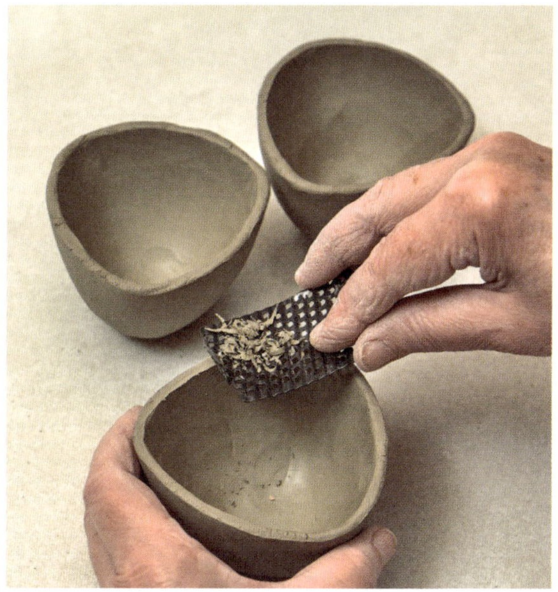

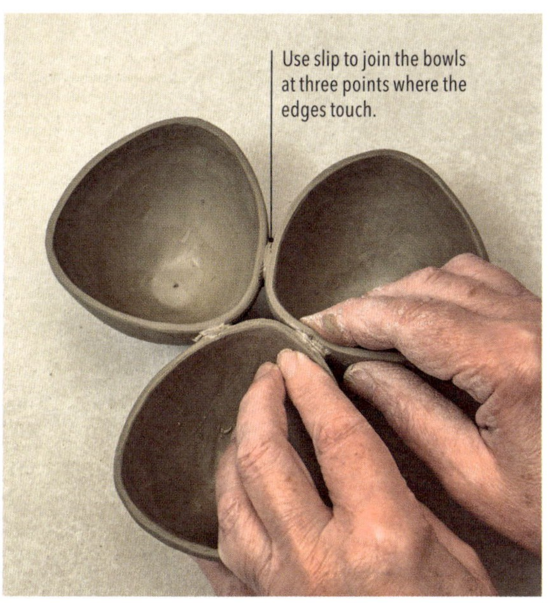

3 Sit the bowls together, then surform the rim of each to the same height. Once they are all reduced to an equal size, work over the rims with a kidney to neaten up and round them off. Pay attention to this detail—it is important to the visual effect.

4 Join the three dishes together at a triangulated end as shown, after first scoring and slipping the relevant joining areas. Pinch the dishes together securely, then neaten around the joins with a wooden tool to remove excess slip.

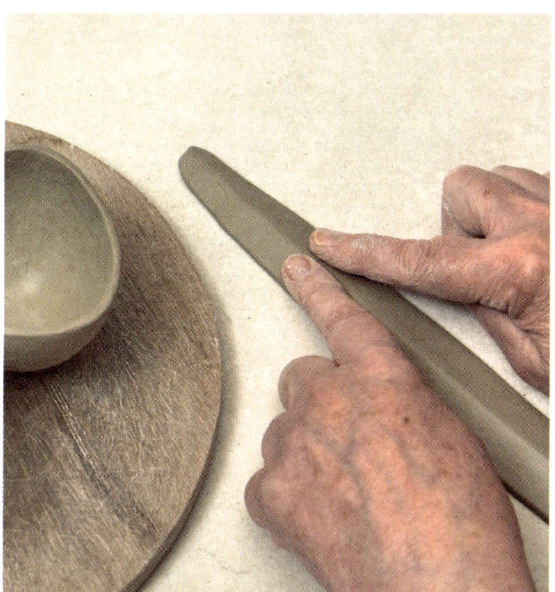

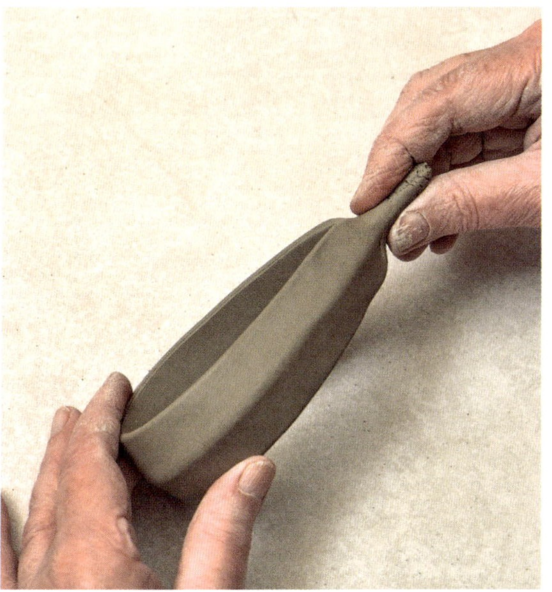

5 Form a coil for the handle from the remaining clay, approximately 6in (15cm) long—thinner at each end and fatter at the center. Place the coil on the work surface to flatten one side, then work along the length with your fingers to form a central ridge.

6 Curve the handle into a loop and pinch the ends together to form a coil, thin enough to fit through the space at the center of the dishes. Firm the handle up with a blow-dryer before attaching it so that it will hold its shape.

7 Apply a dab of slip to the end of the handle, then fit it through the space between the dishes. Holding the handle in place as you work, reinforce it with a coil of soft clay at the base and then neaten up on the underside when able.

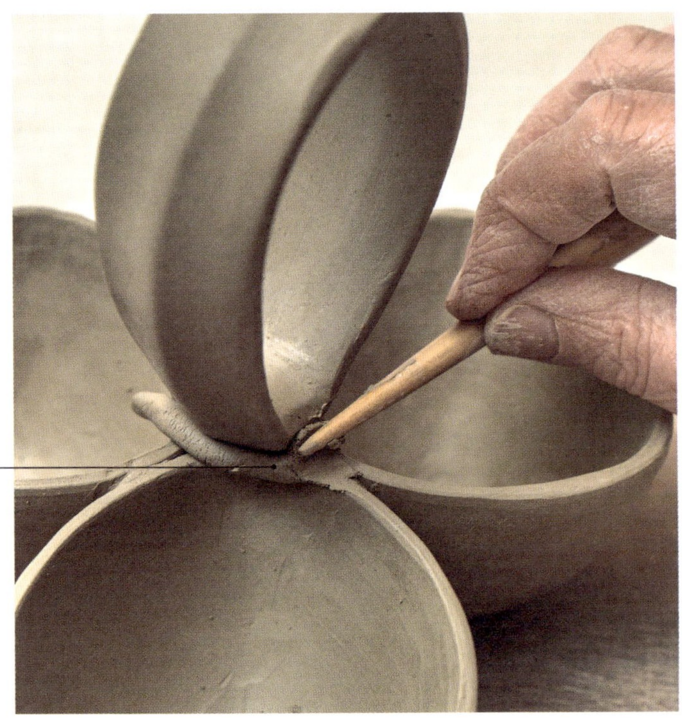

Blend the handle to the dishes around its base using soft clay worked in with a modeling tool.

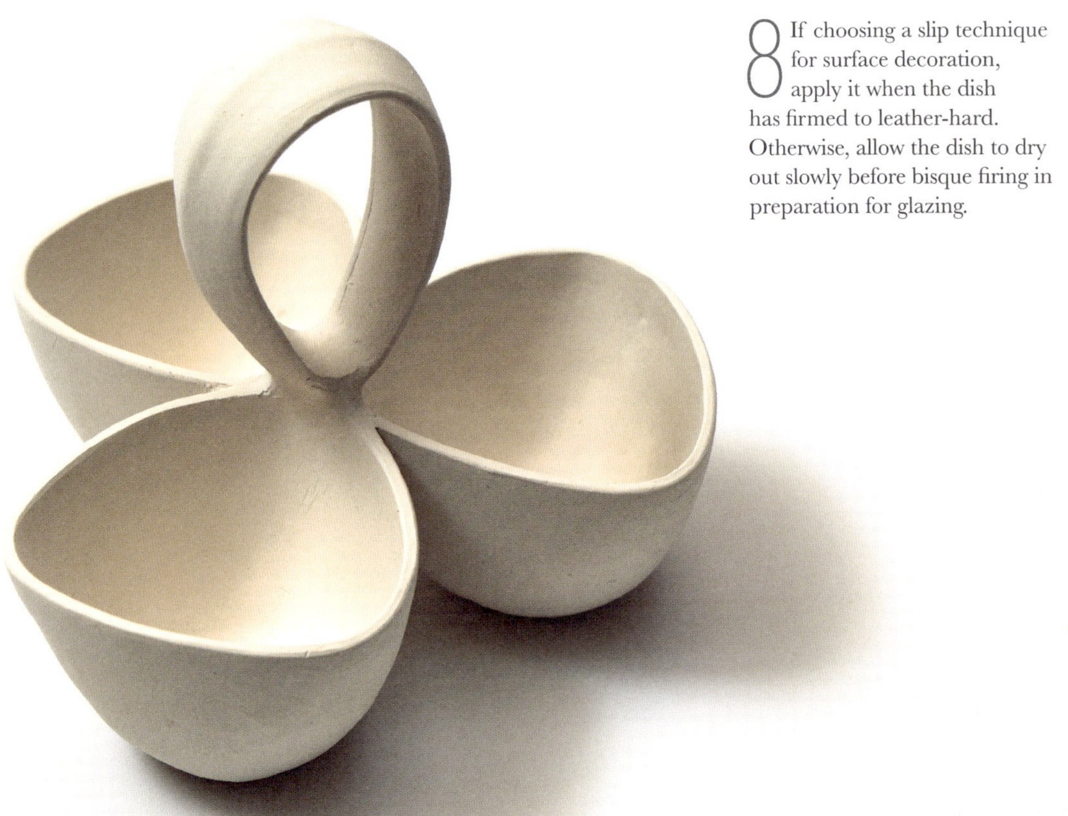

8 If choosing a slip technique for surface decoration, apply it when the dish has firmed to leather-hard. Otherwise, allow the dish to dry out slowly before bisque firing in preparation for glazing.

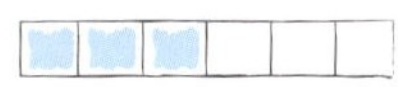

OLIVE DISH

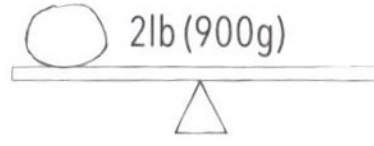

Width: 5in (13cm)
Height: 4in (10cm)
Length: 9in (23cm)

2lb (900g)

The divided sections of this dish are designed to serve different types of olives and it includes a bowl for toothpicks and another for stones. With its olive-tree, majolica-style decoration, there is no mistaking its function.

YOU WILL NEED

TOOLS
- Wooden bat
- Small kidney or store card rib, homemade to specific shape
- Pin
- Knife

CLAY
Red earthenware
- 1lb (450g) for main dish
- 3oz (85g) for each end dish
- 5oz (140g) each for the central divide and handle

DESIGN NOTE
Add more strips to divide the dish into smaller sections, or even add two more small dishes at the side for oil and vinegar.

DECORATION
A base white glaze with majolica-style decoration over the surface gives this dish a truly Mediterranean finish. See page 167 for a simple way to achieve this look.

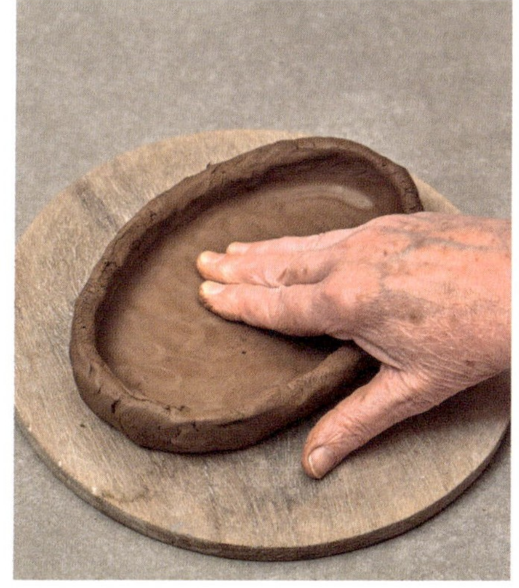

1 Using the clay for the main dish, pinch out an oval-shaped dish with a flat base as far as your fingers will reach, leaving a fat rim at the sides. Place the dish on a bat and pinch/press the base out further until ¼in (5mm) thick.

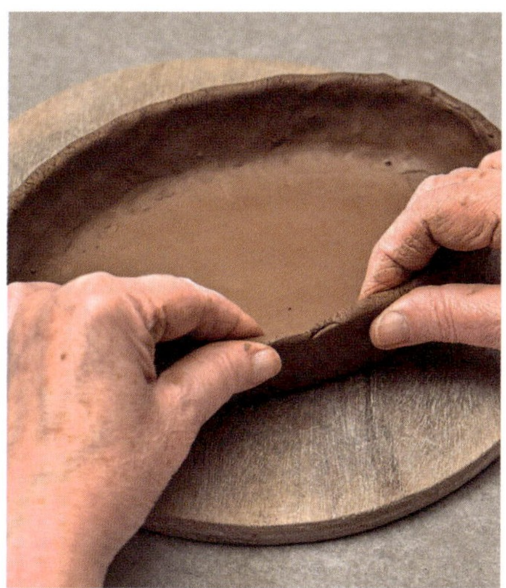

2 Pinch the thick rim vertically using both hands to keep control of the shape. Neaten the surface of the bowl inside and out with a rib, to remove all the pinch marks.

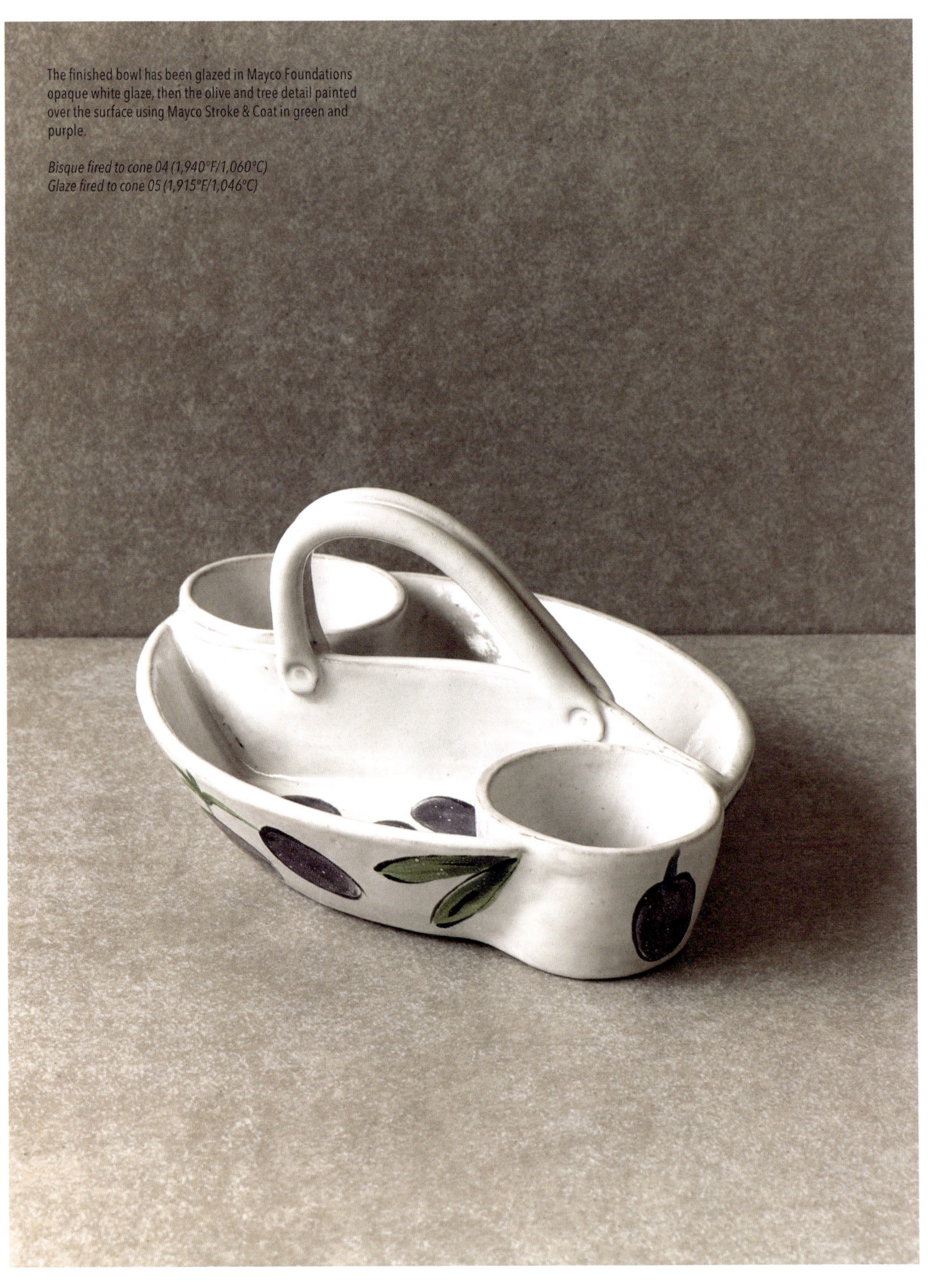
The finished bowl has been glazed in Mayco Foundations opaque white glaze, then the olive and tree detail painted over the surface using Mayco Stroke & Coat in green and purple.

Bisque fired to cone 04 (1,940°F/1,060°C)
Glaze fired to cone 05 (1,915°F/1,046°C)

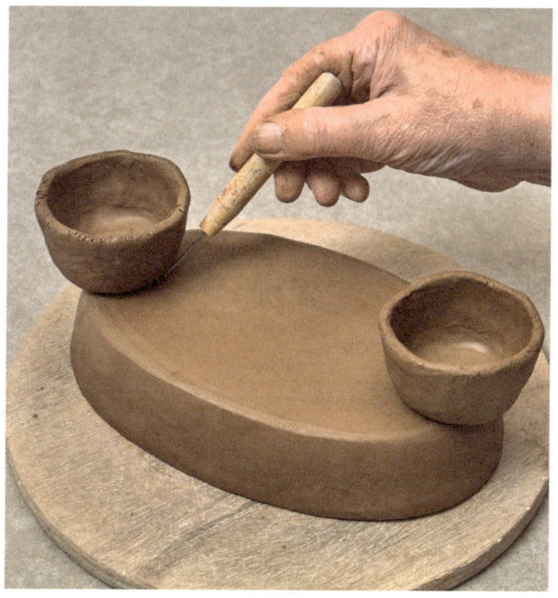

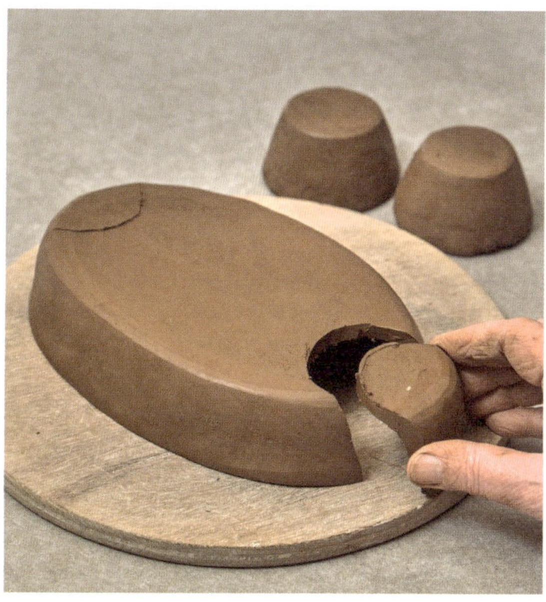

3 Using 3oz (85g) of clay for each, pinch two small, identically sized bowls with straight sides the same depth as the main dish. Turn the base dish over and sit the bowls at each end, overhanging the edge a little. Mark their positions with a pin.

4 Following the scored marks, carefully cut away the sections that the little bowls will fit into from each end of the main dish. Discard the cut-out sections.

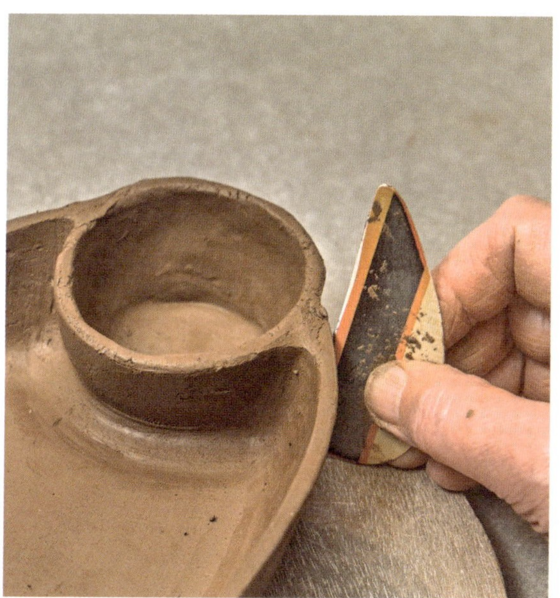

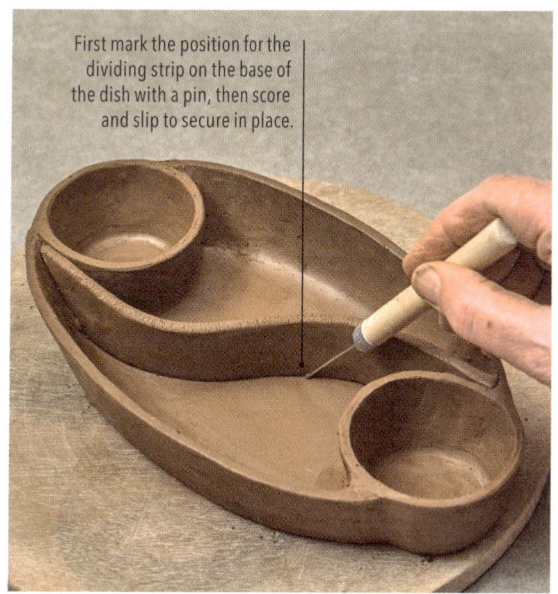

First mark the position for the dividing strip on the base of the dish with a pin, then score and slip to secure in place.

5 Score and slip the edge of the cut-away areas and the adjoining place on each dish, then fix them in place securely. Reinforce around the joins with coils of soft clay and blend them in thoroughly. Neaten up with a rib for a seamless surface.

6 From 5oz (140g) of clay, pinch a strip ¼in (5mm) narrower than the depth of the dish. Cut the strip to fit inside the dish in an S-shape. Fix the strip in place after marking, scoring, and slipping the position.

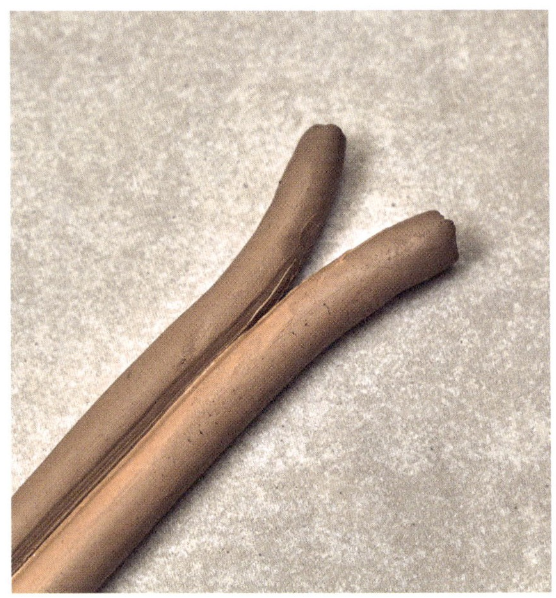

7 From the remaining clay, make two thin coils and join them along their length with slip to within 1in (2.5cm) of each end. Check the handle is long enough to fit the central divide of the dish.

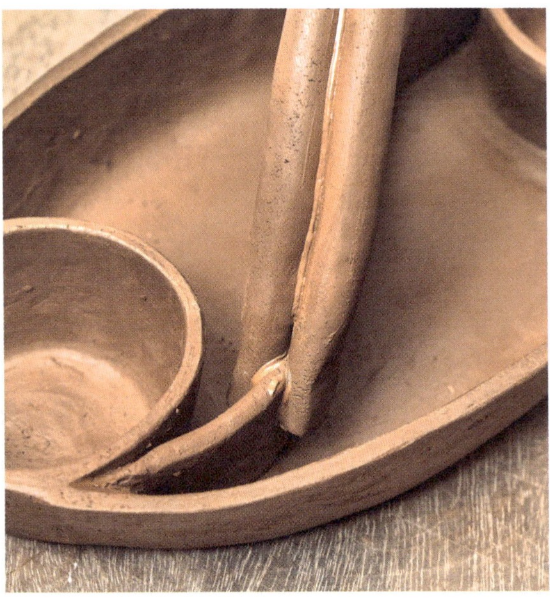

8 Firm the handle up a little with a blow-dryer until it will better hold its shape, then fix it in place, attaching the open ends over the dividing strip with a dab of slip. Pinch the handle ends together to secure them over the divide.

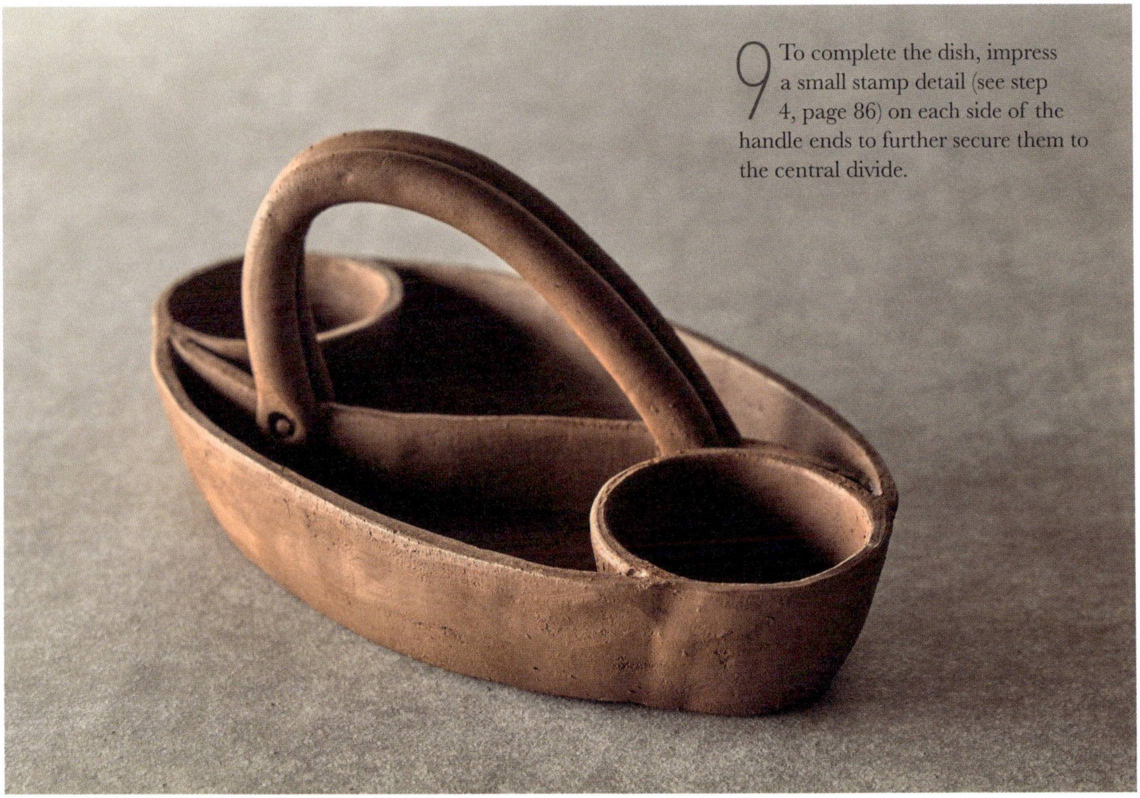

9 To complete the dish, impress a small stamp detail (see step 4, page 86) on each side of the handle ends to further secure them to the central divide.

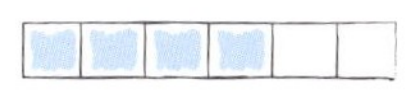

TEAPOT

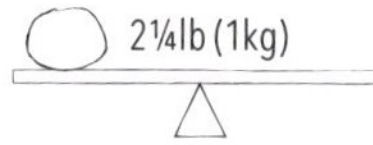

Width: 7½in (19cm) from tip of spout to handle
Height: 6in (15cm)

2¼lb (1kg)

Learning to make a good teapot is an aspiration for many people starting out in pottery. It is generally considered one of the most difficult items to make but it doesn't have to be if you follow the making process carefully.

YOU WILL NEED

TOOLS
- Banding wheel (turntable)
- Flexible metal kidney
- Pin
- Cookie cutters
- Knife
- Wooden modeling tools
- Hole maker or drill bit
- Foam support (thick foam disc with central hole)

CLAY
White stoneware
- 1½lb (675g) for the body and lid
- 8oz (225g) for the spout and handle
- 4oz (115g) for the feet

DESIGN NOTE
Change the teapot to a regular round shape by joining two equally sized pinched bowls together, then completing the rest of the build as shown.

DECORATION
The teapot is a blank canvas for decoration at the green stage or after bisque firing. Here a sgraffito and inlay technique was used with underglazes for color detail, then a transparent glaze (see pages 161–170).

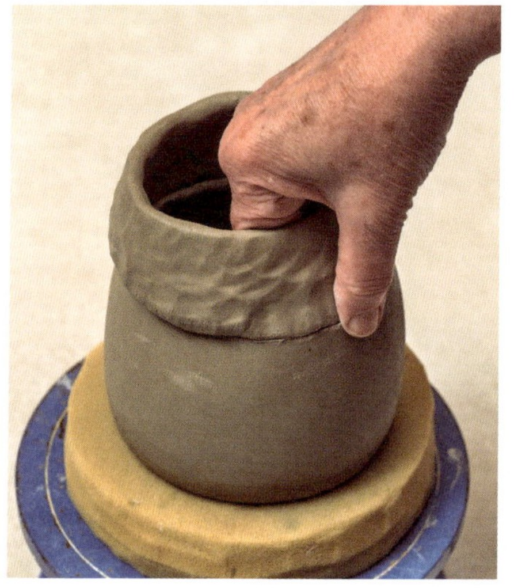

1 From 1lb (450g) of clay, pinch the base shape for the pot with a wide, flat bottom and slightly inward-tapering sides. Extend the height of the base with a pinched extension ring, maintaining the tapering shape. Reinforce the join, then neaten up using a kidney.

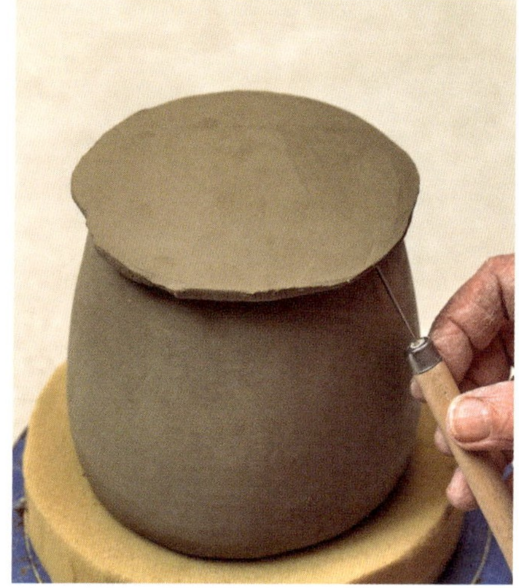

2 Pinch a slightly domed slab for the top section of the pot. Position the slab on the pot and score around the circumference on the underside. Cut the slab to size, then fix it back on the pot after scoring and slipping the joining areas. Neaten around the join.

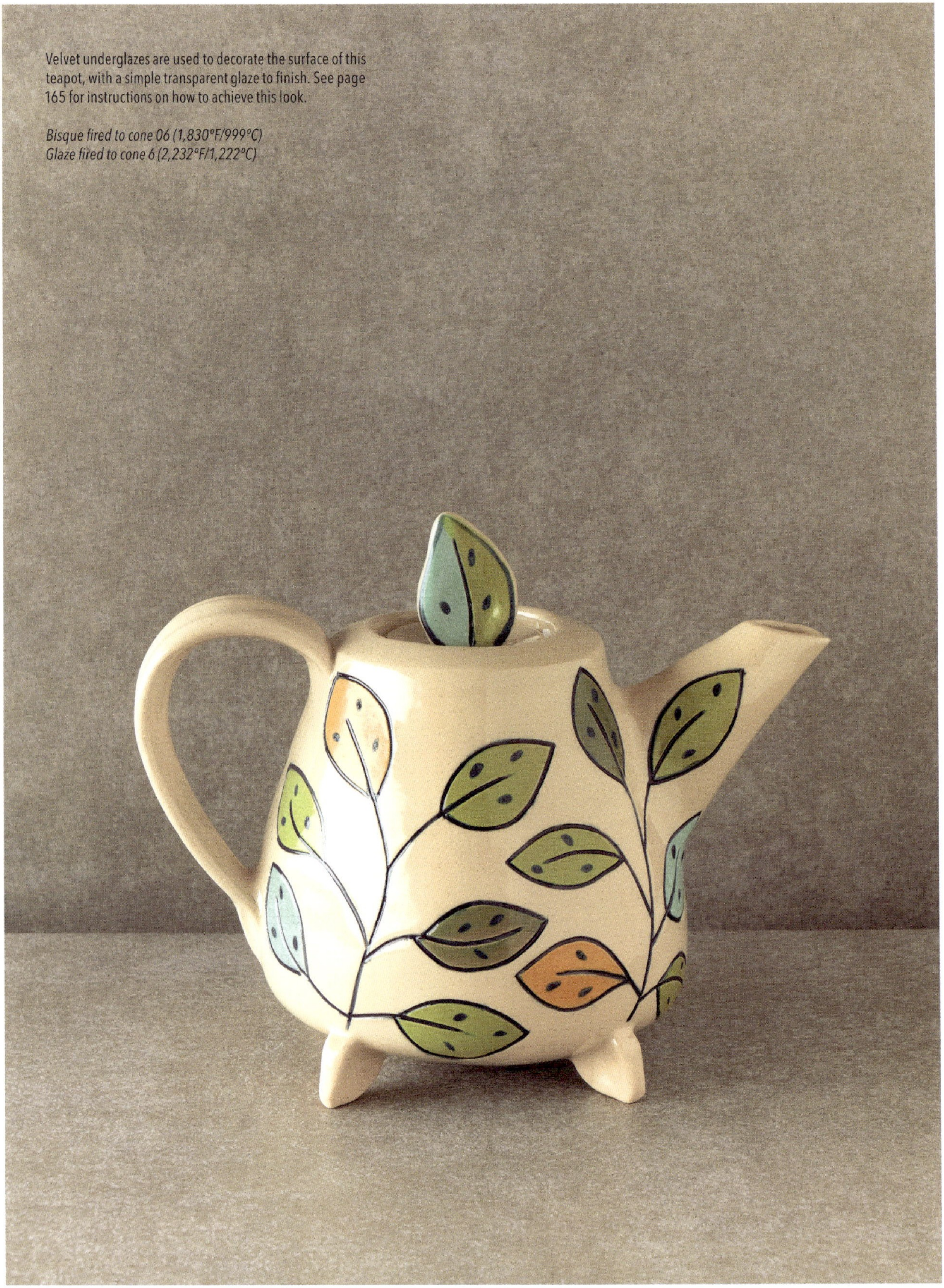

Velvet underglazes are used to decorate the surface of this teapot, with a simple transparent glaze to finish. See page 165 for instructions on how to achieve this look.

Bisque fired to cone 06 (1,830°F/999°C)
Glaze fired to cone 6 (2,232°F/1,222°C)

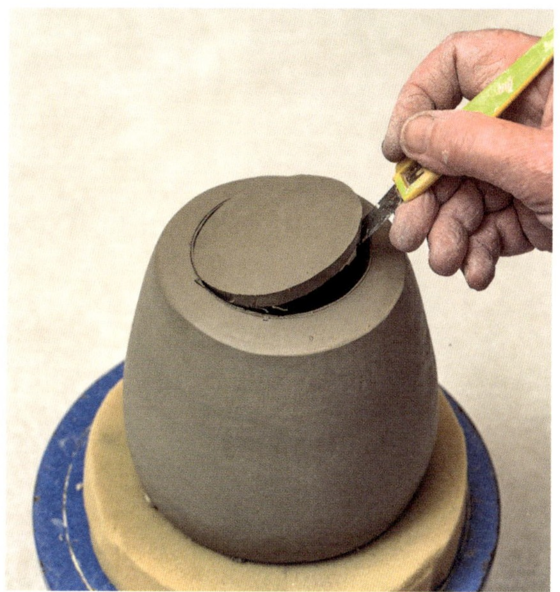

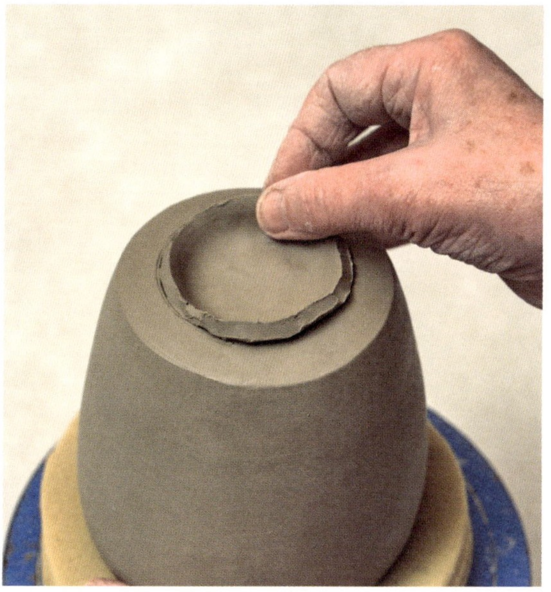

3 Using a cookie cutter to score around first, carefully cut out a circle from the top of the pot, allowing for a ½in (1cm) shoulder. Do this neatly—the cut-out section will be utilized in the next step.

4 Turn the cut-out circle over, then pinch around its edge to create a shallow wall. Score and slip the rim of the pot and the outer edge of the dishlike section, then fix it back in place on the pot. This forms the flange for the lid.

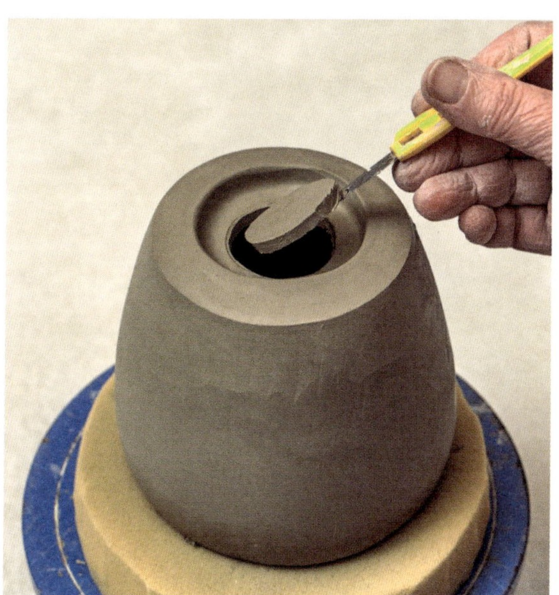

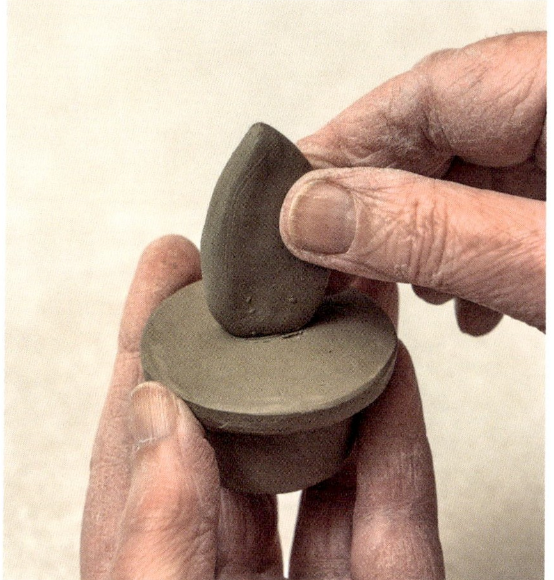

5 Use a smaller cookie cutter to mark a circle at the center of the newly formed flange, then cut the circle out carefully. Neaten around the opening with a wooden modeling tool, then use a rib for a seamless surface.

6 Pinch a small circle for the lid that will sit comfortably on the flange with a little wiggle room. Now pinch a locating ring to fit the pot opening and attach it to the underside of the lid. Finally, pinch and attach a leaf-shaped knob, then drill a small hole next to it for the release of steam.

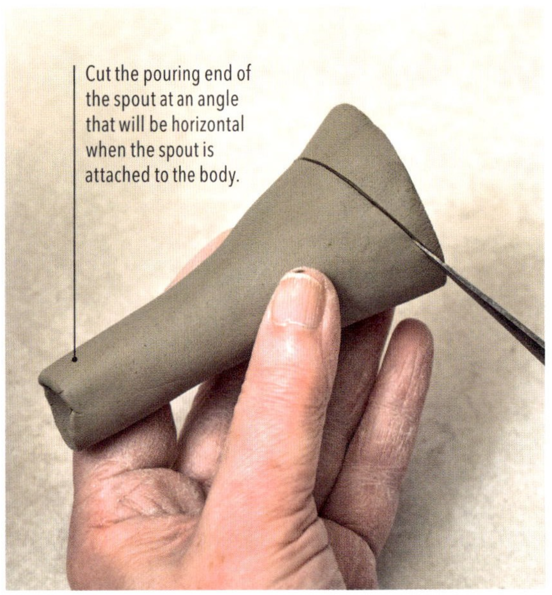

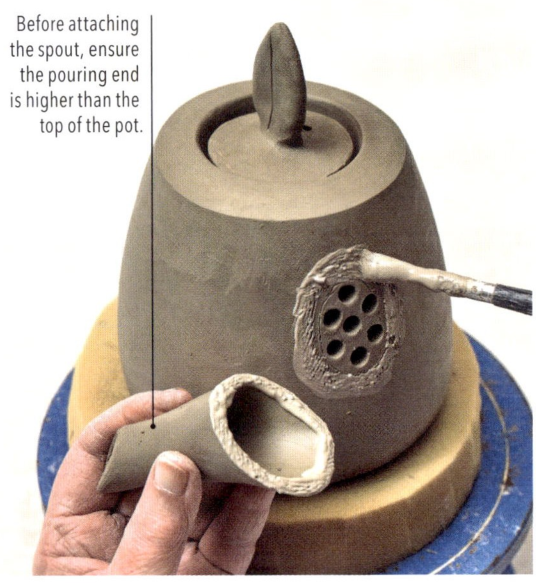

7 Pinch a conical tube for the spout, wide at one end, narrow at the other. Cut the wide end at an angle to fit onto the side of the pot and shape the tip. See page 16 for more detailed instructions on forming and shaping a teapot spout.

8 Score the position on the pot, then drill a series of holes inside the scored area. Score and slip the adjoining areas on the spout, then fix to the pot. Reinforce around the join with a coil of soft clay.

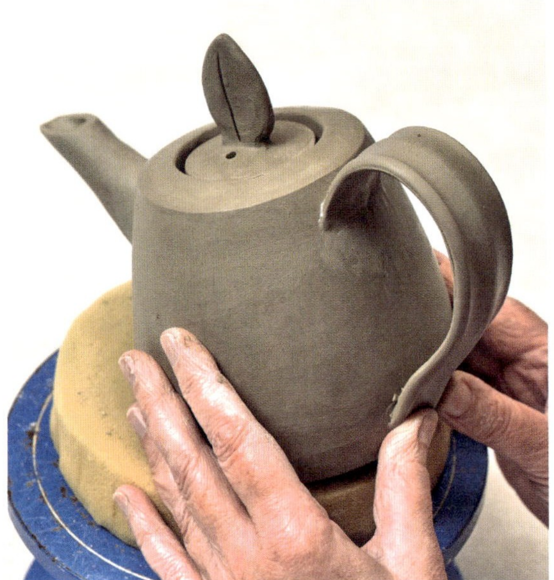

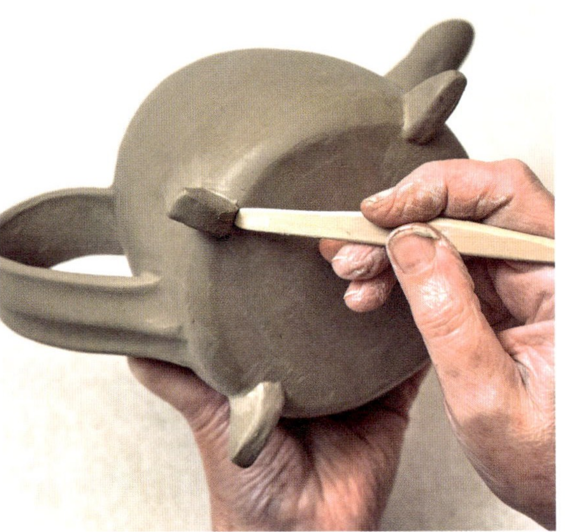

9 Form a short length of clay into a coil, then flatten it on the work surface. Run two fingers along the length of the strip to create a slight ridge at the center. Fix the handle onto the pot after scoring and slipping, then reinforce the joins.

10 Finally, pinch four feet to match the shape of the knob on the lid, then fix them to the underside of the pot, equally spaced apart. Neaten around the joins with a wooden modeling tool.

BREAKFAST CUP AND SAUCER

Cup height: 3–3¼in (7.5–8cm)
Cup diameter: 4½in (11.5cm)
Saucer diameter: 6in (15cm)

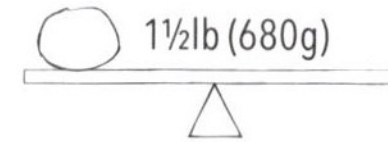

1½lb (680g)

With cheerful surface decoration and generous proportions, this cup and saucer is perfect for breakfast tea or coffee, and is sure to brighten the morning, no matter what the weather outside.

YOU WILL NEED

TOOLS
- Banding wheel (turntable)
- Flexible metal kidney
- 2in (5cm) cookie cutter
- Surform or rasp blade
- Pin
- Wooden modeling tool
- Knife
- Thick foam block
- 2in (5cm) rigid card disc

CLAY
White earthenware
- 10oz (285g) for cup
- 6oz (170g) for foot and handle
- 8oz (225g) for saucer

DESIGN NOTE
This cup also works well made from red earthenware clay, especially when decorating in majolica style. Vary the shape with handles of different proportions.

DECORATION
The cup is decorated in an adapted majolica technique using sponges to apply the secondary color and fine brushwork to define the design. See pages 66–67 for this method and pages 156–172 for other decorating options.

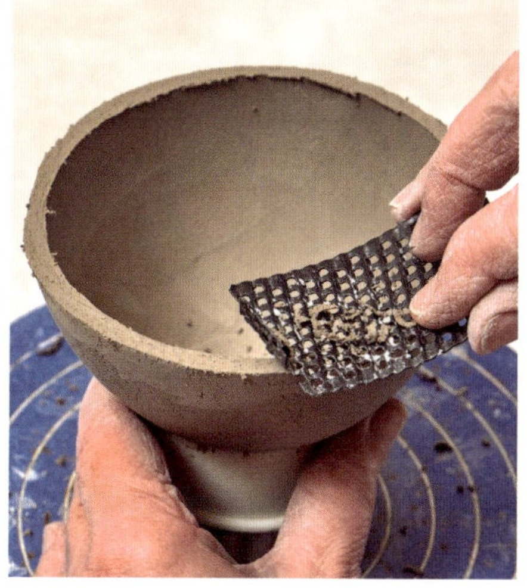

1 Using 10oz (285g) of clay, pinch an open cup shape with a gently rounded base. Refine the surface of the cup inside and out with a kidney. Sit the cup centrally on the cookie cutter, then surform the rim level. Refine the rim further with a kidney for a rounded finish.

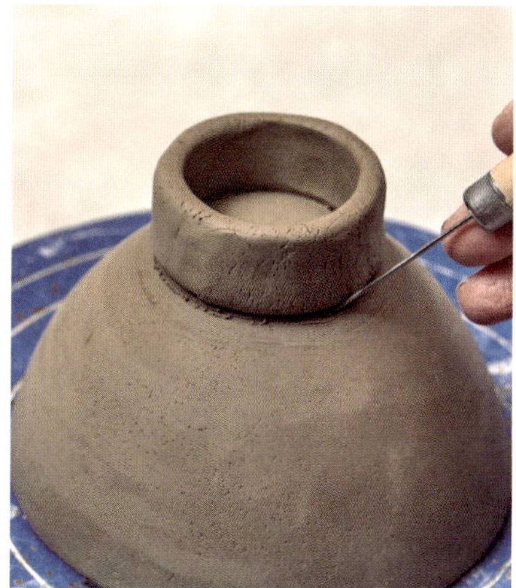

2 Pinch a small open ring for the foot with a diameter of 2in (5cm), from 4oz (115g) of clay. Position the ring centrally on the underside of the cup and mark the position with a pin. Fix the ring in place after scoring and slipping the adjoining surface areas.

The surface has been coated in a white, low-fire base glaze, then secondary colors applied, one over the other, with a sponge to create depth. A fine black outline defines the shapes, with a touch of bright color at the center to highlight.

Bisque fired to cone 04 (1,940°F/1,060°C)
Glaze fired to cone 05 (1,915°F/1,046°C)

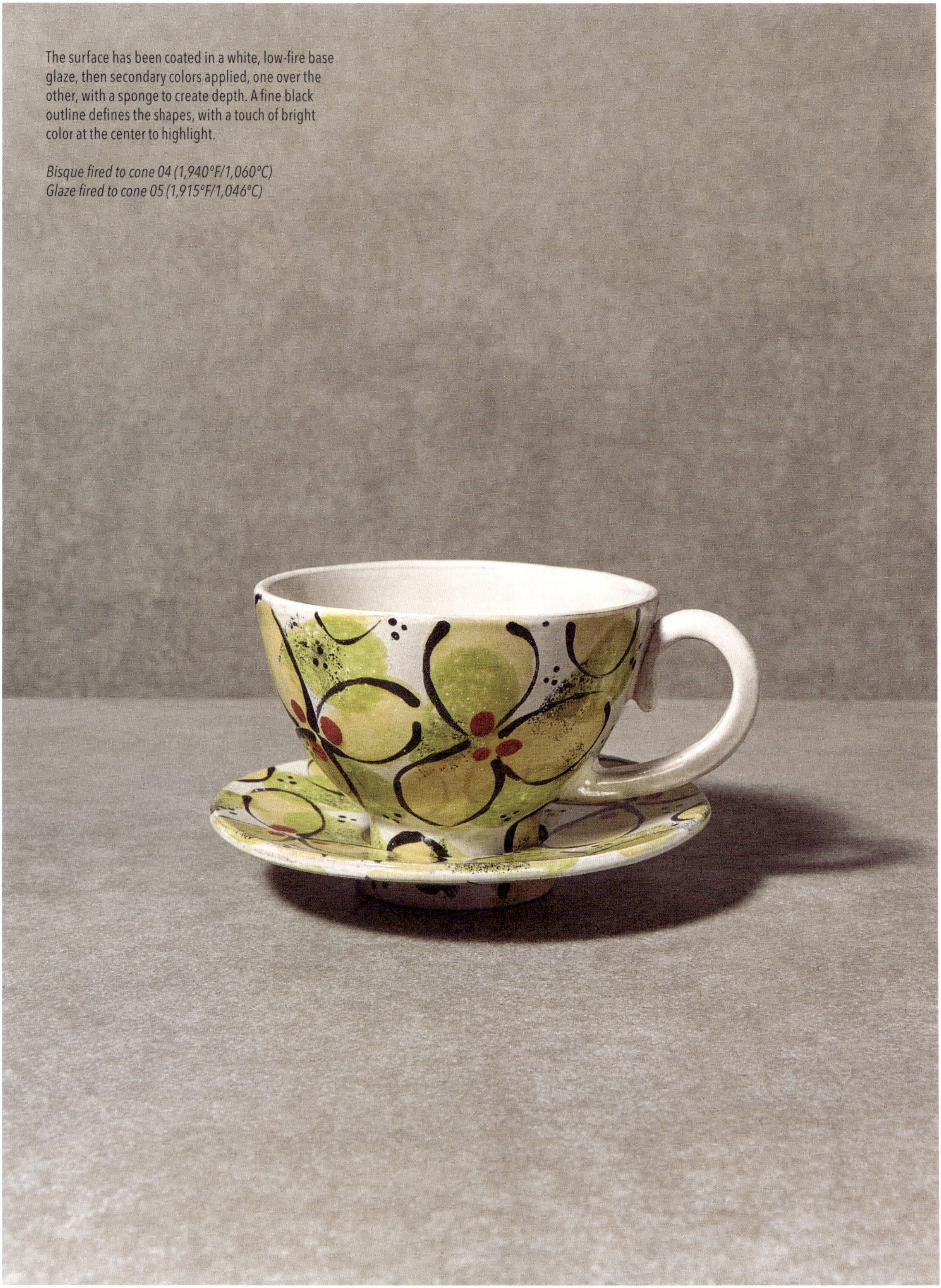

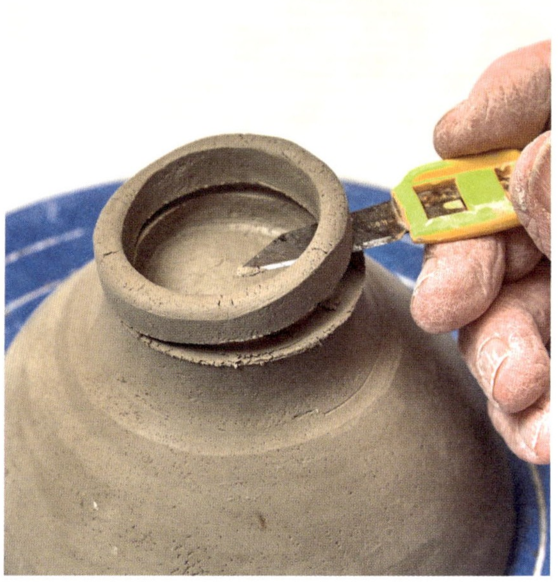

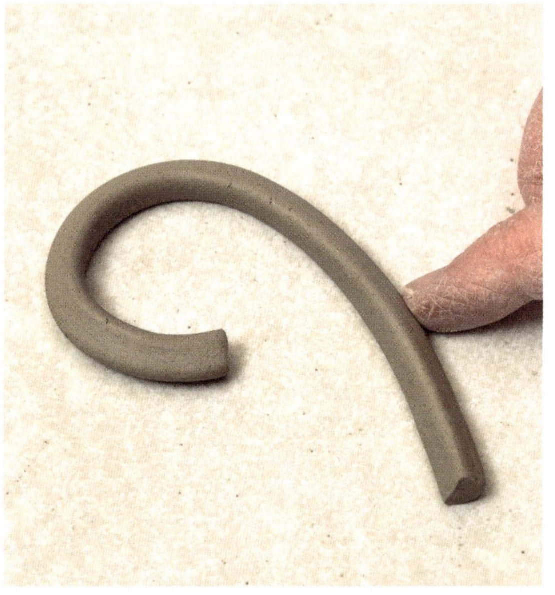

3 Reinforce the foot with coils of soft clay, inside and out. Blend the coils in until seamless. Sit the cup centrally on the banding wheel, then, turning the wheel slowly, cut the foot to the required depth using a knife held rigidly in your hand.

4 Form a short, thin coil for the handle, then softly triangulate the shape by placing it on the work surface and pinching evenly along its length. Bend the handle to the required shape and firm it up a little with a blow-dryer.

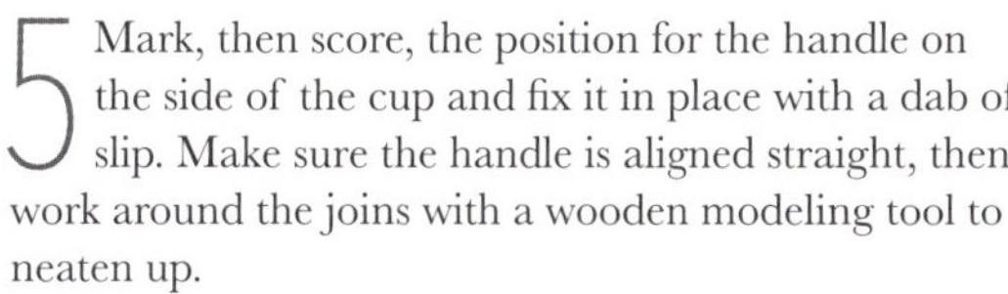

5 Mark, then score, the position for the handle on the side of the cup and fix it in place with a dab of slip. Make sure the handle is aligned straight, then work around the joins with a wooden modeling tool to neaten up.

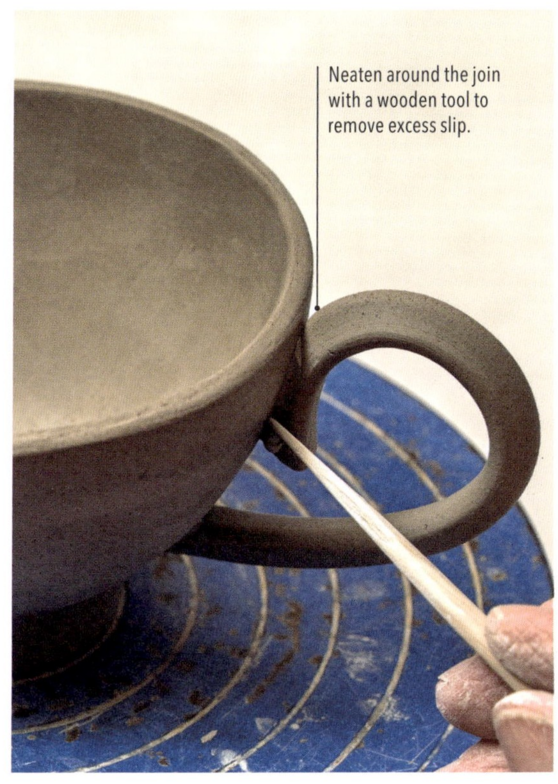

Neaten around the join with a wooden tool to remove excess slip.

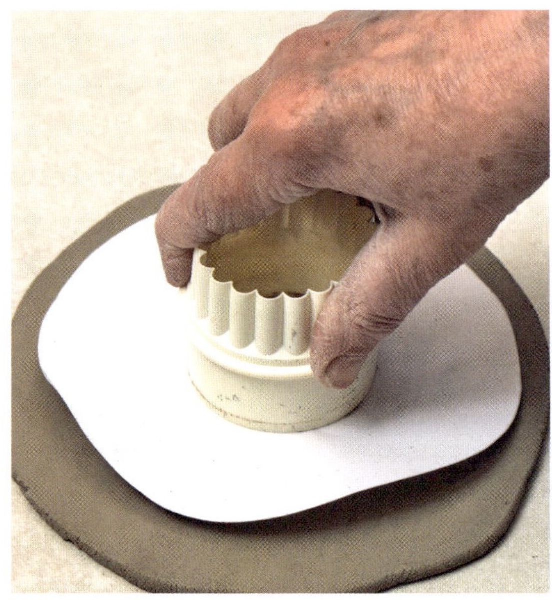

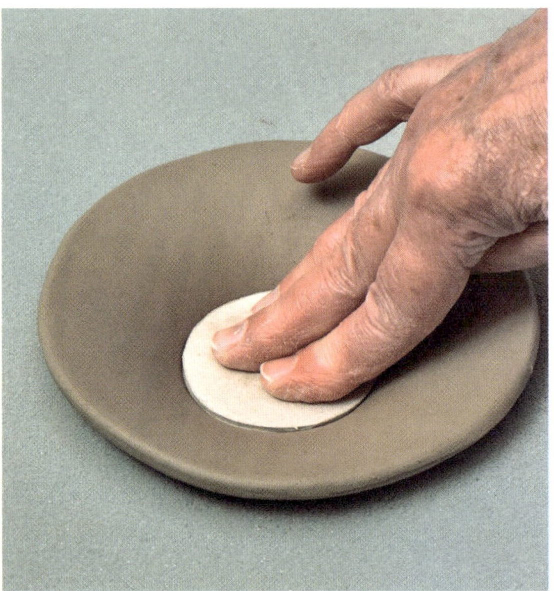

6 For the saucer, pinch a flat slab to an even thickness. Cut out a template for the saucer. Place the template on the slab and press down with the cookie cutter where the location ring for the cup is marked at the center, to lightly impress the position in the clay beneath.

7 Having first cut the saucer out and neatened the rim, place the slab on the foam block with the rigid card disc at the center where the location ring outline is impressed. Press the disc down firmly into the foam and the saucer sides will rise.

8 Neaten up the underside of the saucer where required. Test that the cup sits in the saucer comfortably, then allow them to dry out separately, ready for bisque firing.

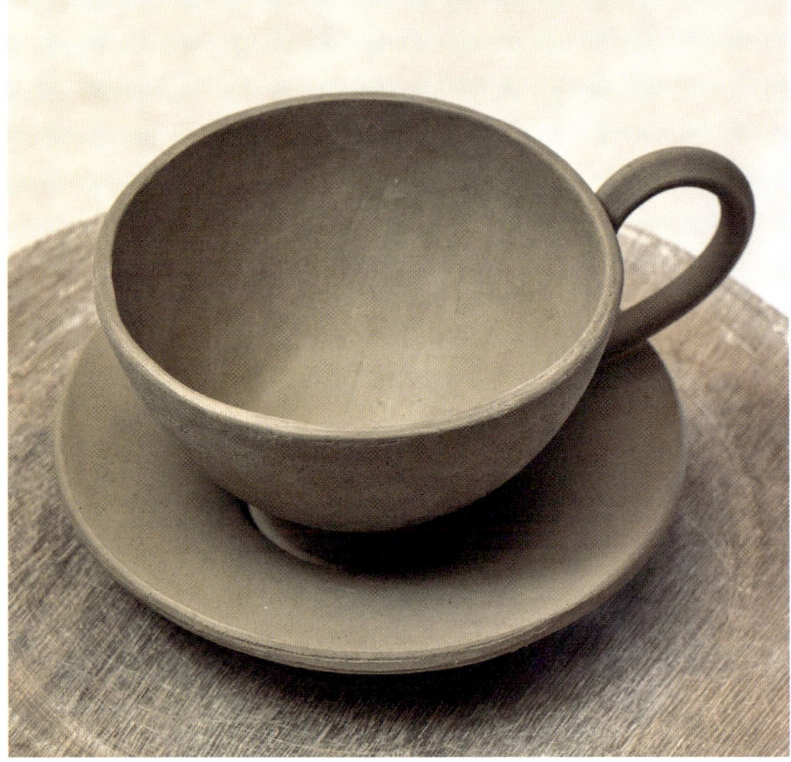

DECORATING USING GLAZE SPONGING

This is a decorating technique not unlike majolica, but the surface detail is sponged as opposed to painted and commercially prepared glazes replace the traditional tin glaze base and color decoration.

YOU WILL NEED

- Fan paintbrush for base glaze application
- Leaf-shaped sponge for surface design
- Fine liner brush
- Low-fire base glaze color
- A selection of glaze colors for sponge decoration (see Design Note, below)
- Black or other bold color glaze for outlining

DESIGN NOTE

- Mayco Foundations white opaque and Stroke & Coat colors—Sour Apple, Sunkissed, Ruby Red, and Tuxedo—are used to decorate this cup and saucer.
- These glazes have a wide firing range: cone 06 (1,828°F/998°C) to cone 10 (2,345°F/1,285°C).

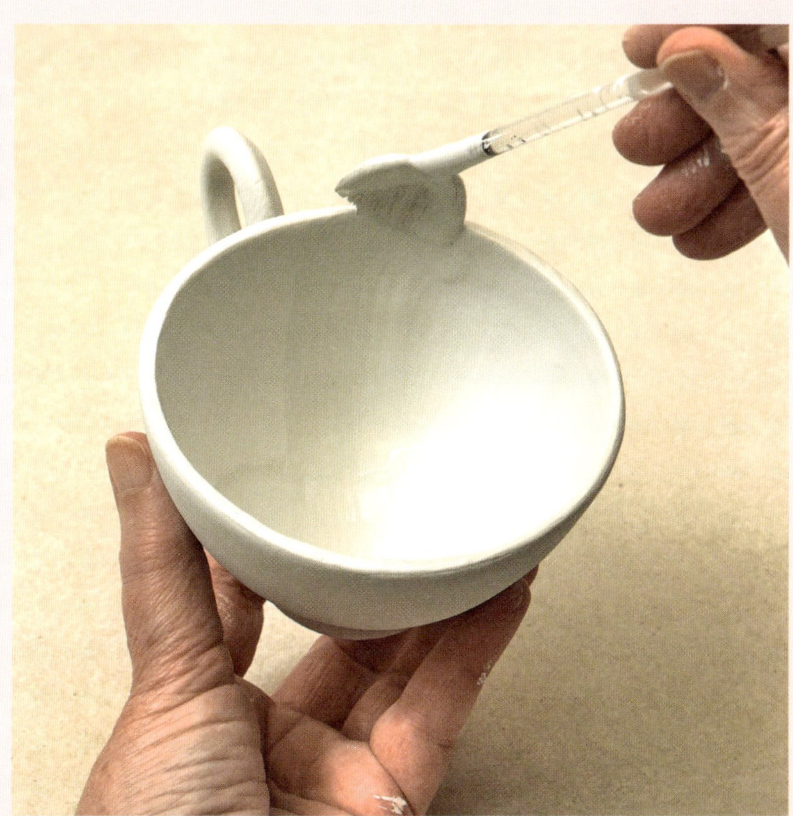

1 Load the fan brush with the base glaze and paint the entire surface of both the cup and saucer in an even covering. Allow the first coat to dry to the touch, then apply a second coat.

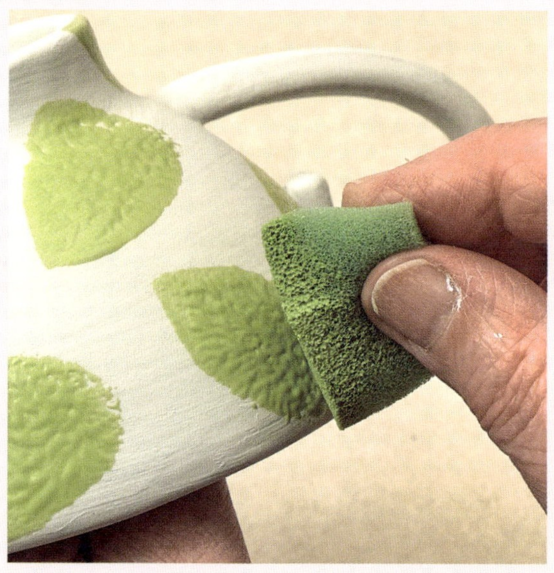

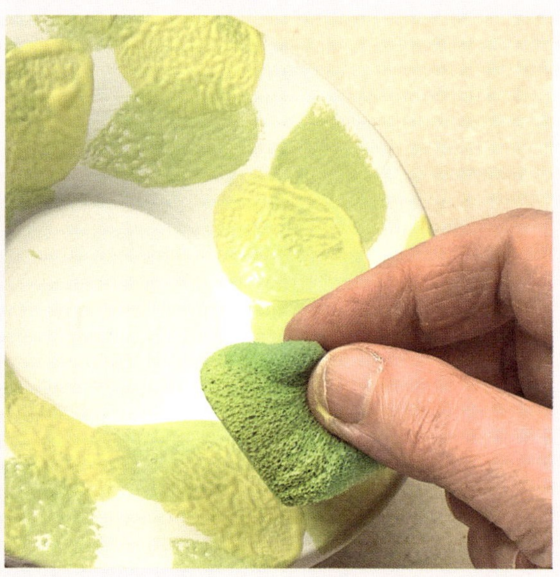

2 When the base coat is dry, using your first color of choice, load the leaf sponge and stamp the shape over the surface of the cup and saucer, positioning it at different angles each time for a balanced arrangement.

3 Wash the sponge clean, then, working with another color of glaze, sponge a three-petal flower over the top of the underlying shapes, on both the cup and saucer, as before. Sponge any light additional detail you want to add to highlight areas like the tips of the leaves.

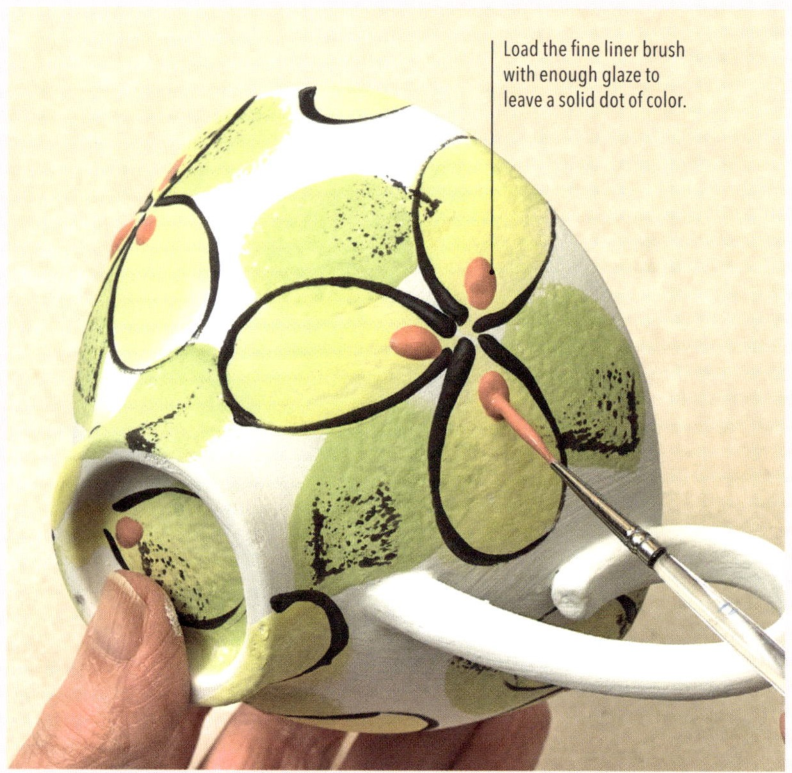

Load the fine liner brush with enough glaze to leave a solid dot of color.

4 Outline the flowers in a bold color using a fine liner brush, then finish the design with dots of a vivid color at the center of the flowers. You can also dot details between the flowers for additional decoration.

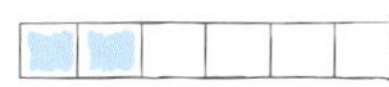

LARGE MUG

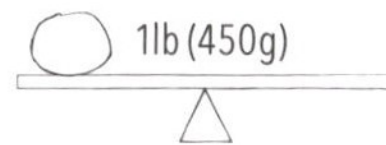

Height: 4in (10cm)
Diameter: 3½in (9cm)

1lb (450g)

If you like a generous mug for your tea or coffee, this is the one for you. With its stylish, mid-century, modern-shaped handle and 50s-inspired surface decoration, it will soon become a favorite.

Try making a few mugs in sets of different colorways using the same surface decoration for really great impact.

YOU WILL NEED

TOOLS
- Metal and plastic kidneys
- Loop tool
- Banding wheel (turntable)
- Wooden modeling tool

CLAY
White stoneware
- 1lb (450g) divided into small amounts for each part of the mug

DESIGN NOTE
The form of this mug can easily be adapted by changing the shape of the extension—give it a waist or flare it outward at the top instead of closing the shape in; the possibilities are many.

DECORATION
This mug is a blank canvas for decoration at either green stage or bisque, whether choosing a slip, glaze, underglaze, or combined techniques. See pages 156–172 for decorating options.

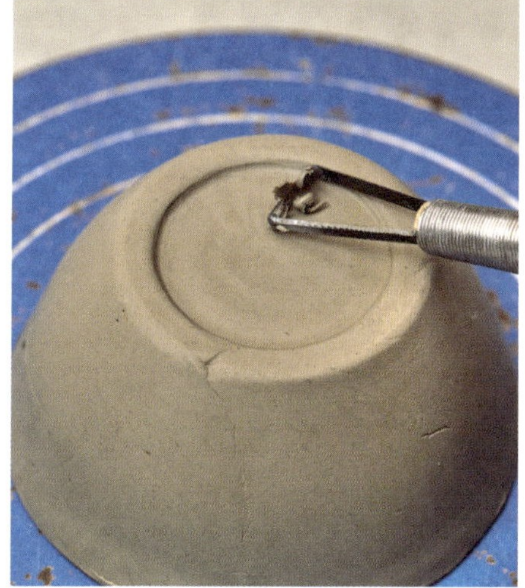

1 From 5oz (140g) of clay, pinch an open bowl that flares gently from a flat, sturdy base. Smooth the surface of the bowl inside and out with a kidney and level the rim. Center the bowl upside down on the banding wheel and score the position for a foot ring with a pin. Now trim the clay from the center of the circle using the loop tool.

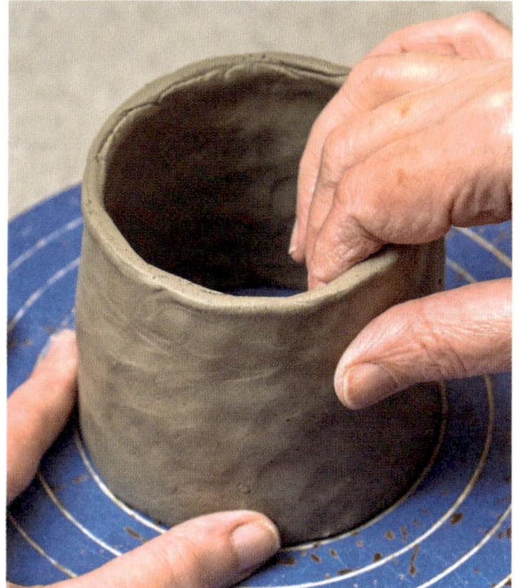

2 Pinch an open cylinder from 8oz (225g) of clay, using the concentric lines on the wheel to pinch it to the correct rim size to fit the base section.

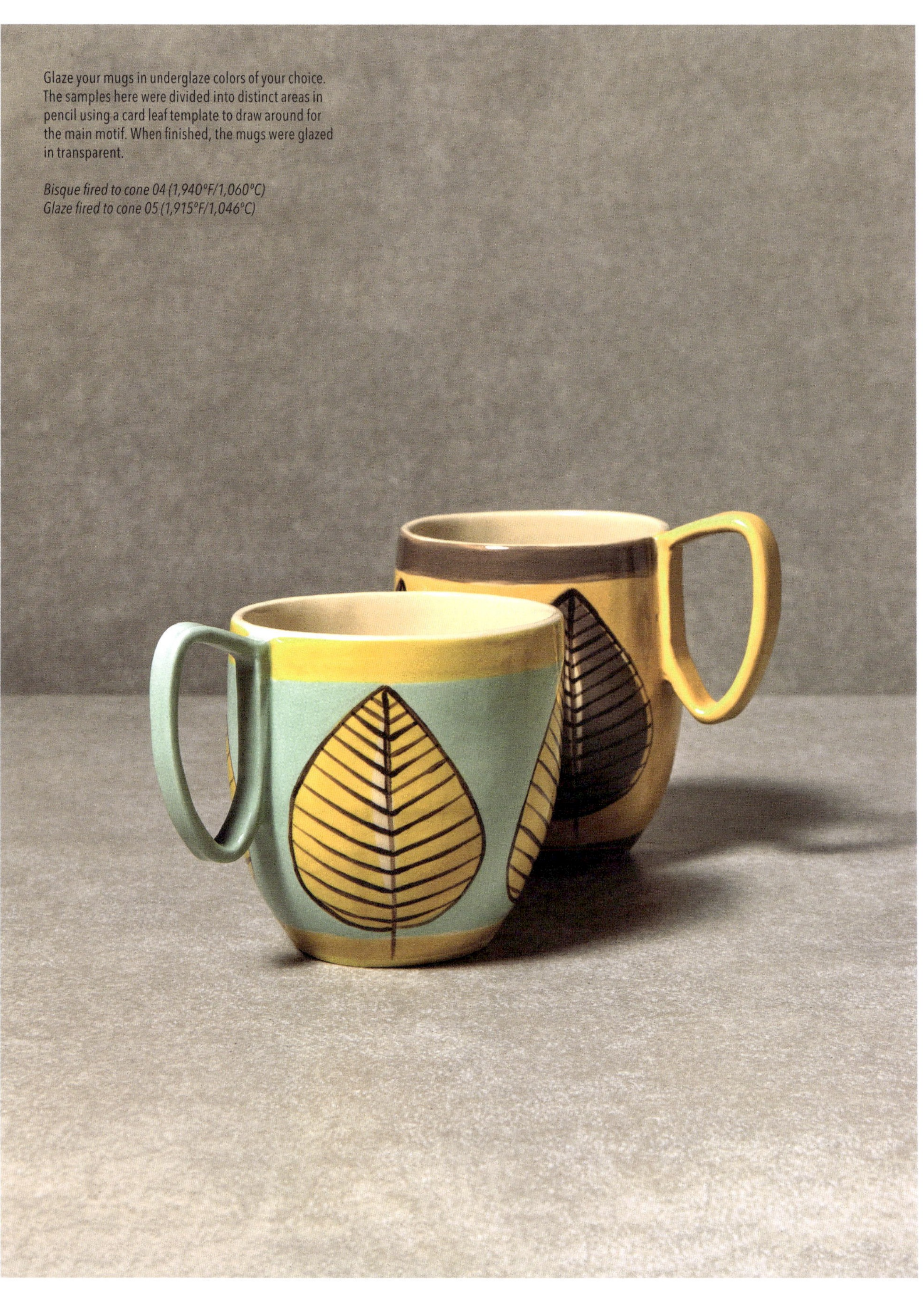

Glaze your mugs in underglaze colors of your choice. The samples here were divided into distinct areas in pencil using a card leaf template to draw around for the main motif. When finished, the mugs were glazed in transparent.

Bisque fired to cone 04 (1,940°F/1,060°C)
Glaze fired to cone 05 (1,915°F/1,046°C)

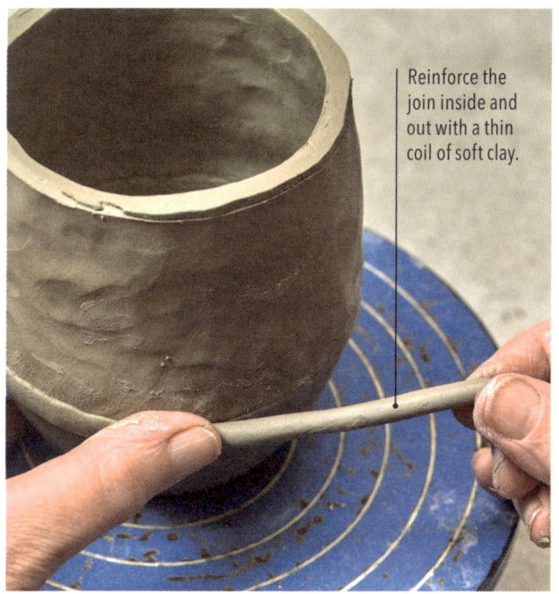

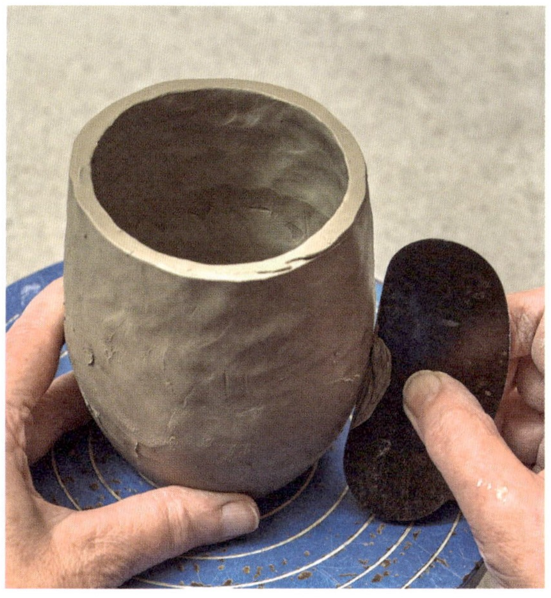

3 Ensure both rims are level, then score and slip the rim of the base and the adjoining rim on the extension. Pinch the two surfaces together carefully to secure them.

4 Work over the reinforced joins and the surface of the mug in its entirety with a kidney, to remove excess clay and pinch marks. NOTE: This is the stage at which the shape is determined and can be altered as preferred.

5 Work on the rim of the mug with a smaller kidney to reduce the thickness and create a good lip to drink from. Take the time to do this well as it is an important finishing touch.

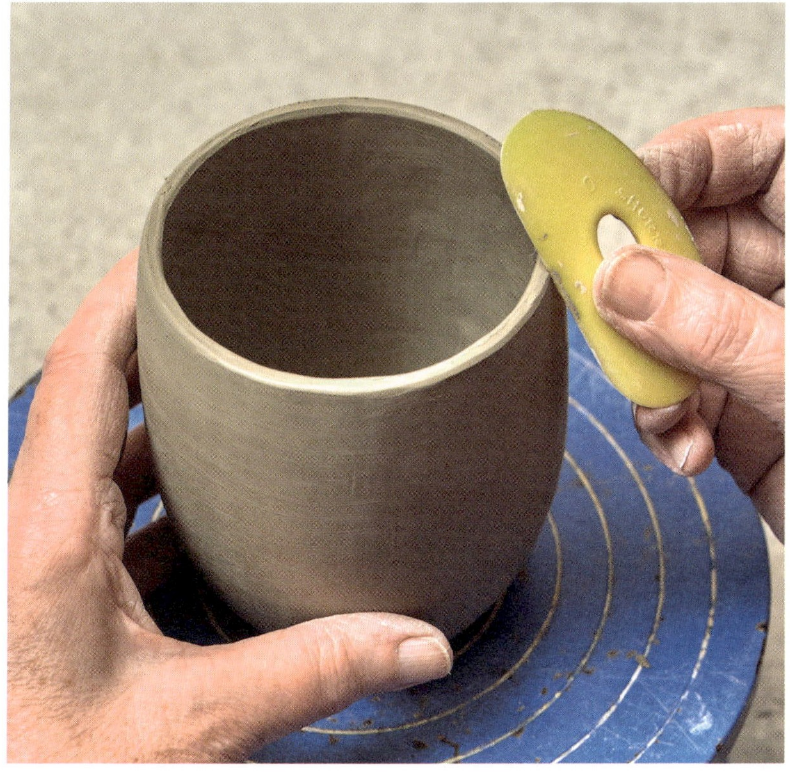

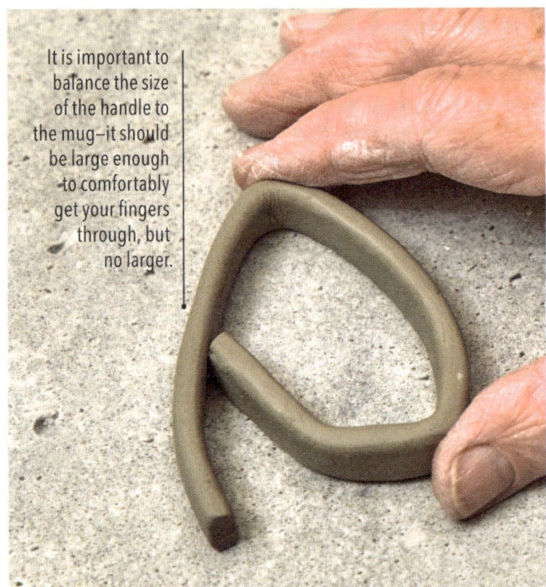

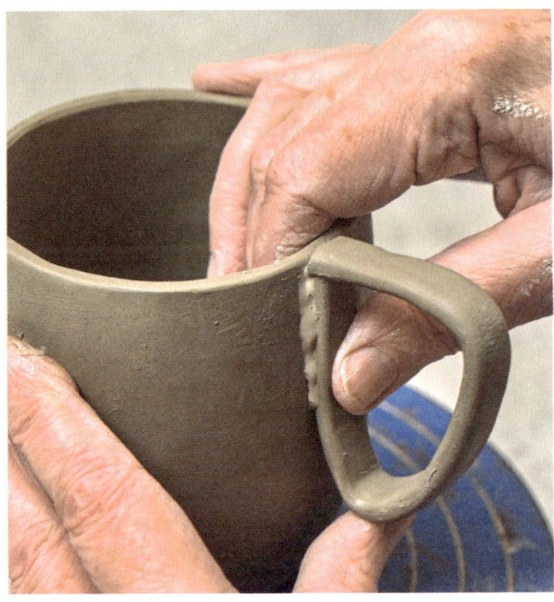

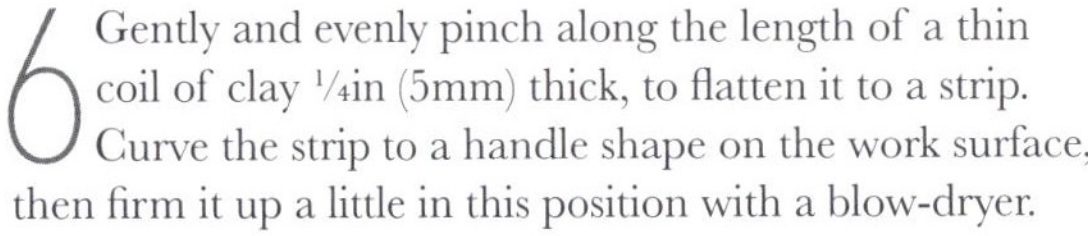

6 Gently and evenly pinch along the length of a thin coil of clay $\frac{1}{4}$in (5mm) thick, to flatten it to a strip. Curve the strip to a handle shape on the work surface, then firm it up a little in this position with a blow-dryer.

7 First, mark then score and slip the position for the handle on the side of the mug. Score and slip the corresponding surface on the handle, then fix it in place securely, making sure it is straight.

8 Neaten around the handle with a wooden tool to remove the excess slip. Decorate with slip or allow the mug to dry slowly ready for bisque firing and subsequent surface decoration.

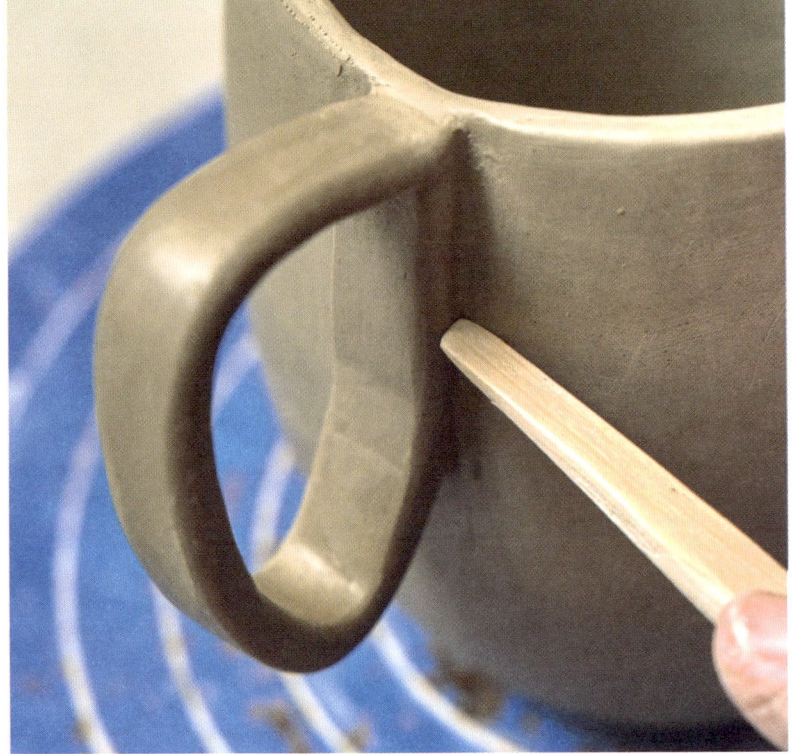

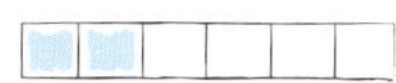

SMALL ESPRESSO CUP

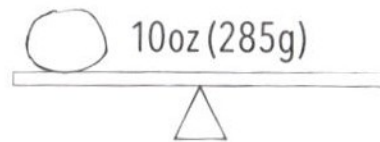

Height: 2½in (6.5cm)
Diameter: 2¾in (7cm)

10oz (285g)

This is the perfect little cup for serving a strong, espresso-style coffee. It is quick and easy to make, and the simple textured surface decoration is wonderfully highlighted by the celadon glaze.

To make a truly stunning set of these cups, glaze each one in shades of a single color.

YOU WILL NEED

TOOLS
- Small metal kidney or rib
- Banding wheel (turntable)
- Pin
- Wooden modeling tools
- Surform or rasp blade

CLAY
White stoneware
- 6oz (170g) for cup
- 4oz (115g) for foot and handle

DESIGN NOTE
Scale up the weight of clay to make this cup in a larger size or change its look with a more traditional handle shape.

DECORATION
These little cups look great decorated in different shades of transparent colored glaze like celadons, which beautifully pool in the textured marks to highlight detail.

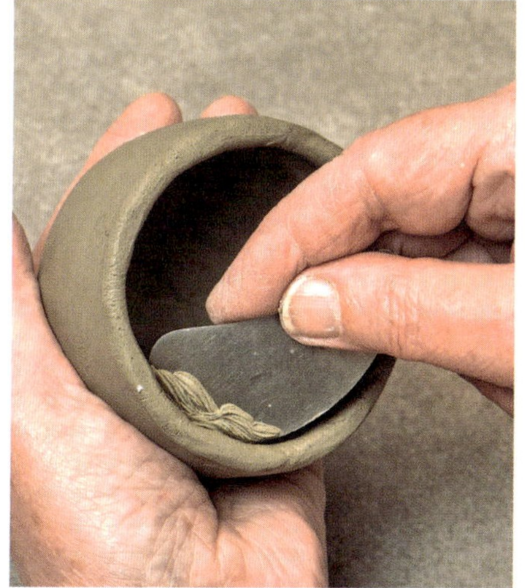

1 Beginning with 6oz (170g) of well-prepared clay, pinch a round-bottomed cup with straight sides. Using a small kidney, refine the surface of the cup inside and out, to even out the thickness of the wall.

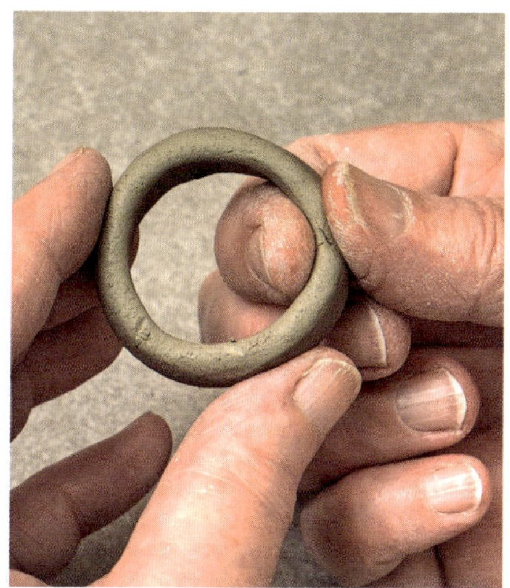

2 From 2oz (60g) of clay, pinch an open ring to a suitable diameter to form a sturdy foot for the cup. Place the ring centrally on the underside of the cup, then score the position with a pin.

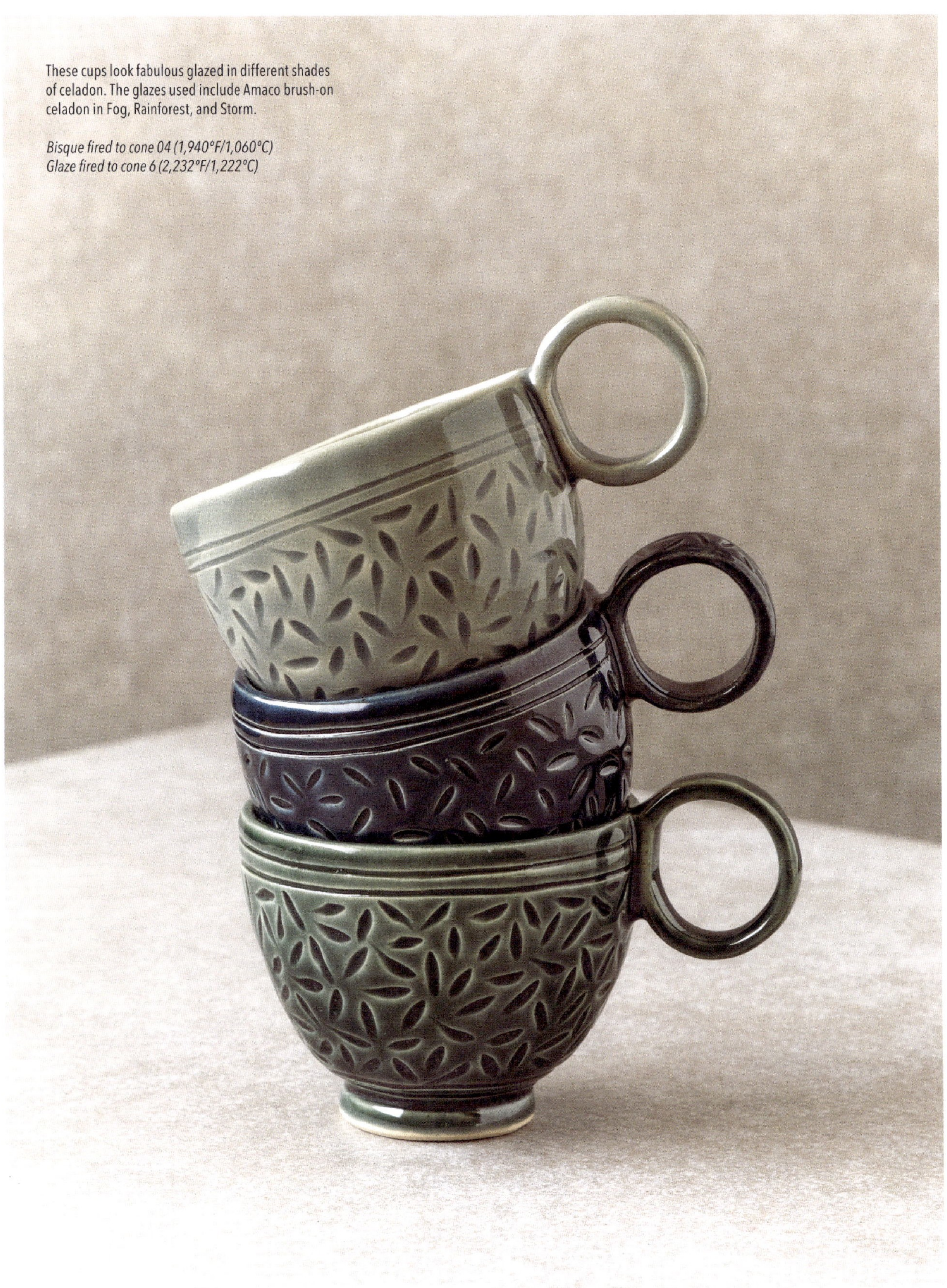

These cups look fabulous glazed in different shades of celadon. The glazes used include Amaco brush-on celadon in Fog, Rainforest, and Storm.

Bisque fired to cone 04 (1,940°F/1,060°C)
Glaze fired to cone 6 (2,232°F/1,222°C)

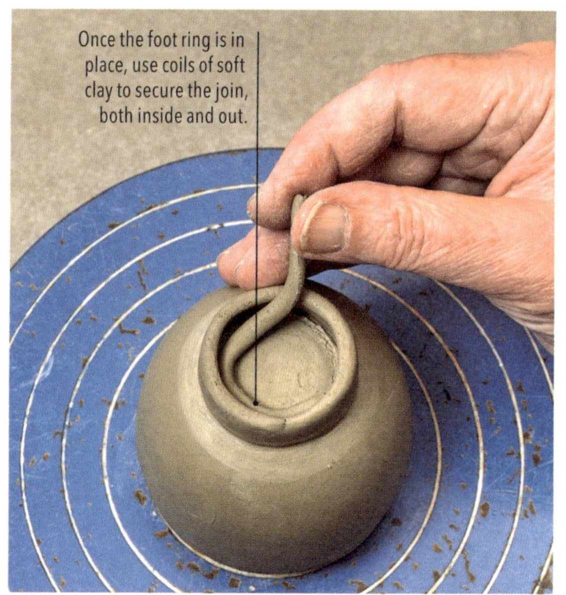

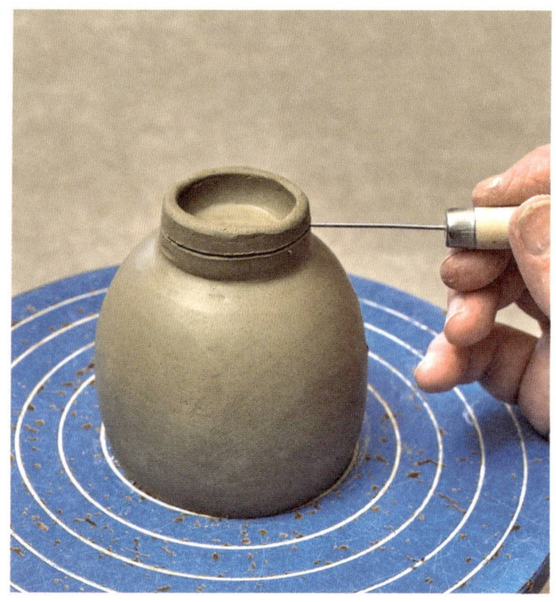

3 Score and slip the marked location for the foot on the cup and the adjoining rim of the foot itself, then fix them together. Reinforce the join, inside and out, with coils of soft clay and blend them in well using your fingers until seamless.

4 Place the cup upside down on the banding wheel, then, turning it slowly, score a level for the foot with a pin. NOTE: If you are happy with the depth of the foot you can omit this step.

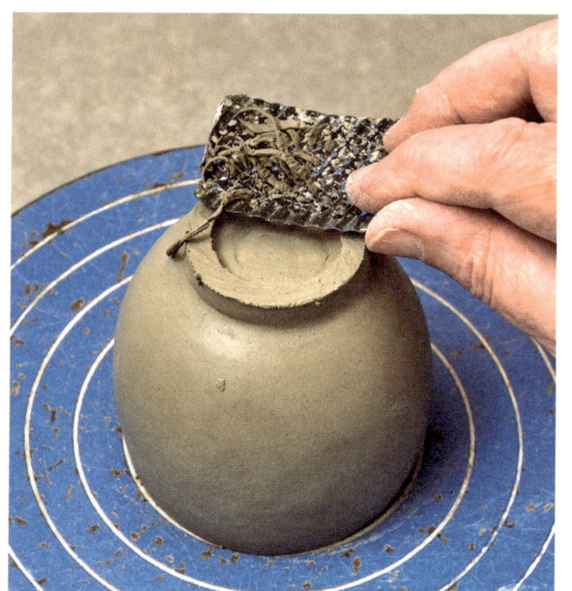

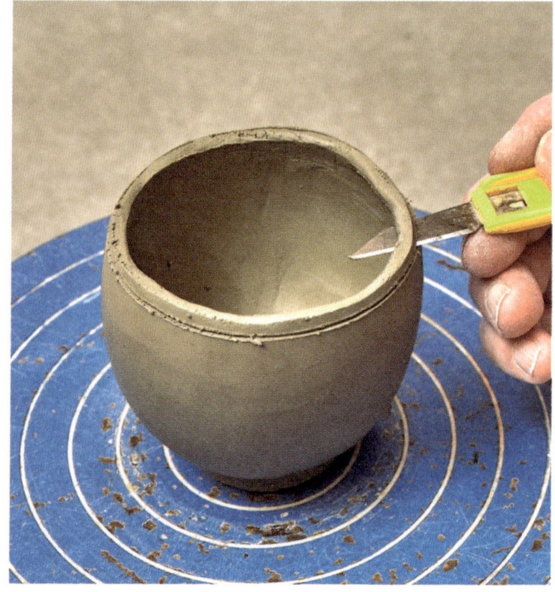

5 Reduce the level of the foot to the scored line using a surform or rasp blade. Work over the reduced foot rim with a kidney to refine the edge until neatly rounded and smooth.

6 Turn the cup upright and place it at the center of the wheel, then, turning the wheel slowly, score a level line with a pin. This time, cut the rim level with a knife held rigidly in your hand. Refine the rim with a kidney until evenly rounded and smooth.

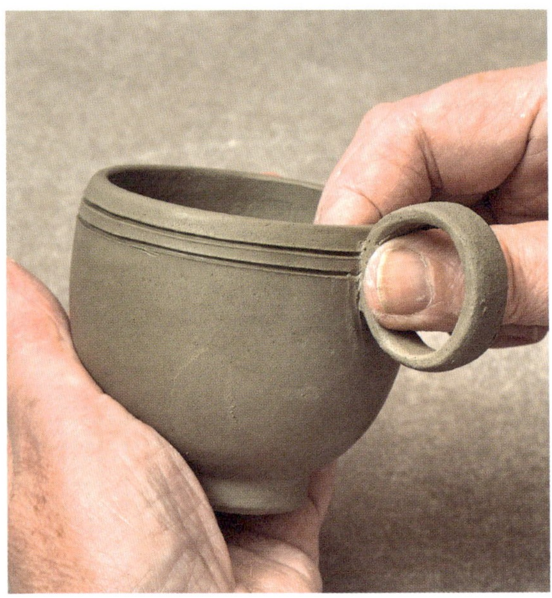

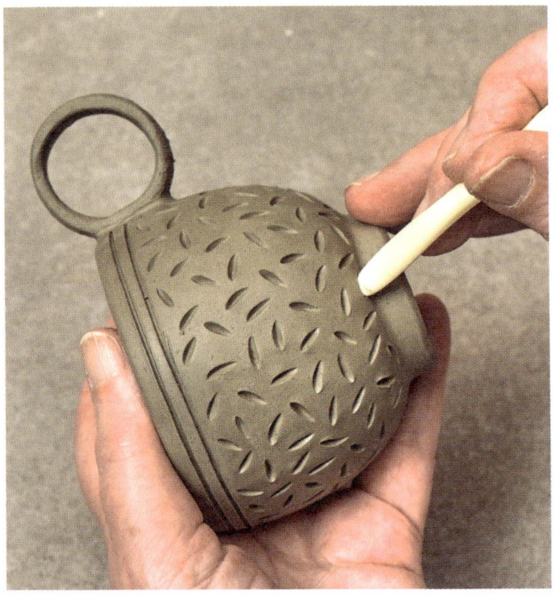

7 Score two decorative lines just below the rim of the cup, then pinch the remaining clay into a ring handle. Neaten the surface and edges of the handle, then attach it to the side of the cup after scoring and slipping all adjoining areas.

8 Working below the scored lines under the rim, texture the surface of the cup by impressing the end of a modeling tool into the clay at varying angles to replicate the seeding pattern used in embroidery.

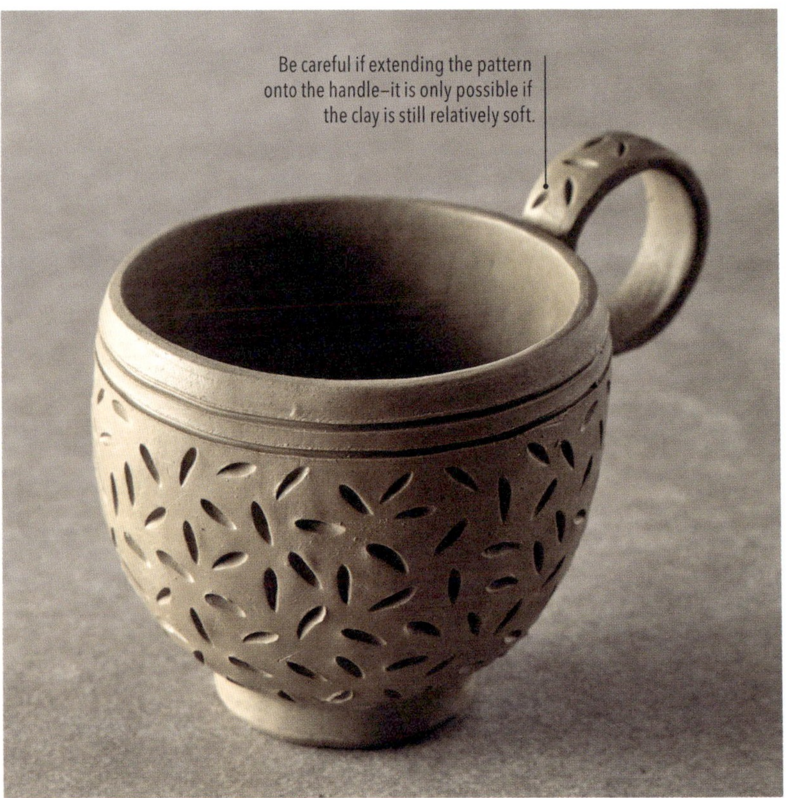

Be careful if extending the pattern onto the handle—it is only possible if the clay is still relatively soft.

9 The impressed seeding pattern texture can be extended to include the handle and inside of the foot ring, for added decorative detail.

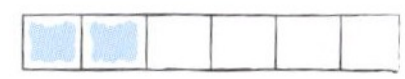

CREAMER

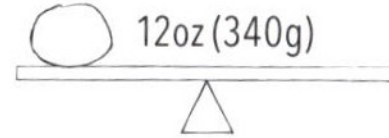

Width: 4in (10cm) from spout
Height: 4in (10cm)
Diameter: 1¾in (4.5cm)

12oz (340g)

The slender shape of this sweet little creamer makes it easy to use without the need for a handle. The pretty decoration can be adapted to suit any tableware or decor.

The shape can easily be scaled up to contain different fluids and a handle added for use with hot liquids.

YOU WILL NEED

TOOLS
- Metal rib or palette
- Soft rubber kidney or rib
- Pin
- Wooden modeling tool
- Knife
- Surform or rasp blade
- Pencil
- Fine tip brush

CLAY
White stoneware
- 8oz (225g) for body
- 4oz (115g) for base
- Decorating slip or underglaze in 4 colors

DESIGN NOTE
Scale the weight of clay up or down to adapt the size to a larger or smaller creamer. Be aware that the shape is not suitable made as a larger vessel to contain hot fluids.

DECORATION
The secret to the correct repeat pattern is to measure and draw out an accurate grid. Don't worry about pencil marks, as they will burn away in firing. For alternative decoration ideas, see pages 156–172.

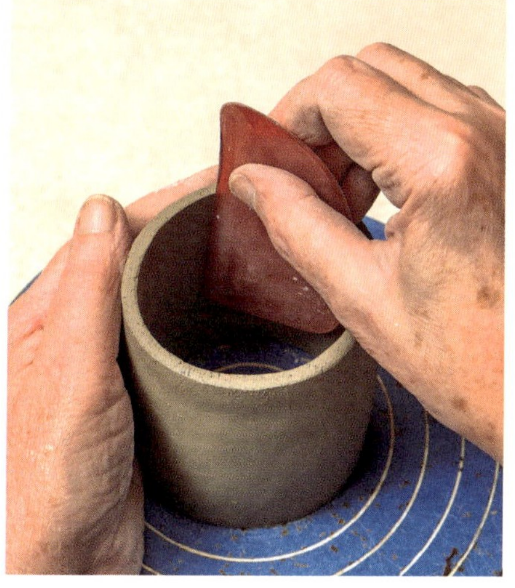

1 Pinch the body clay to an evenly thick, open, straight-sided cylinder. Work over the interior and exterior wall with a palette to refine the surface, then again with a soft rib to completely smooth it.

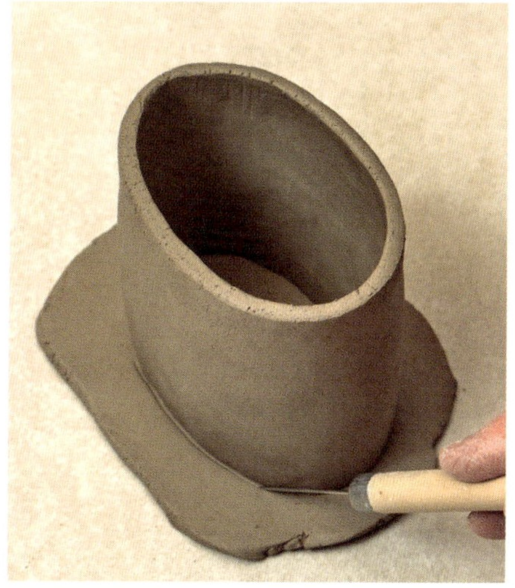

2 Gently squeeze the cylinder into an oval shape. Now pinch an oval-shaped slab from the remaining clay for the base, large enough to fit the body. Smooth over the slab with a palette, then place the body on the surface and mark the outline with a pin.

After bisque firing, simply glaze the creamer in transparent or a pale-colored transparent glaze to finish.

Bisque fired to cone 04 (1,940°F/1,060°C)
Glaze fired to cone 05 (1,915°F/1,046°C)

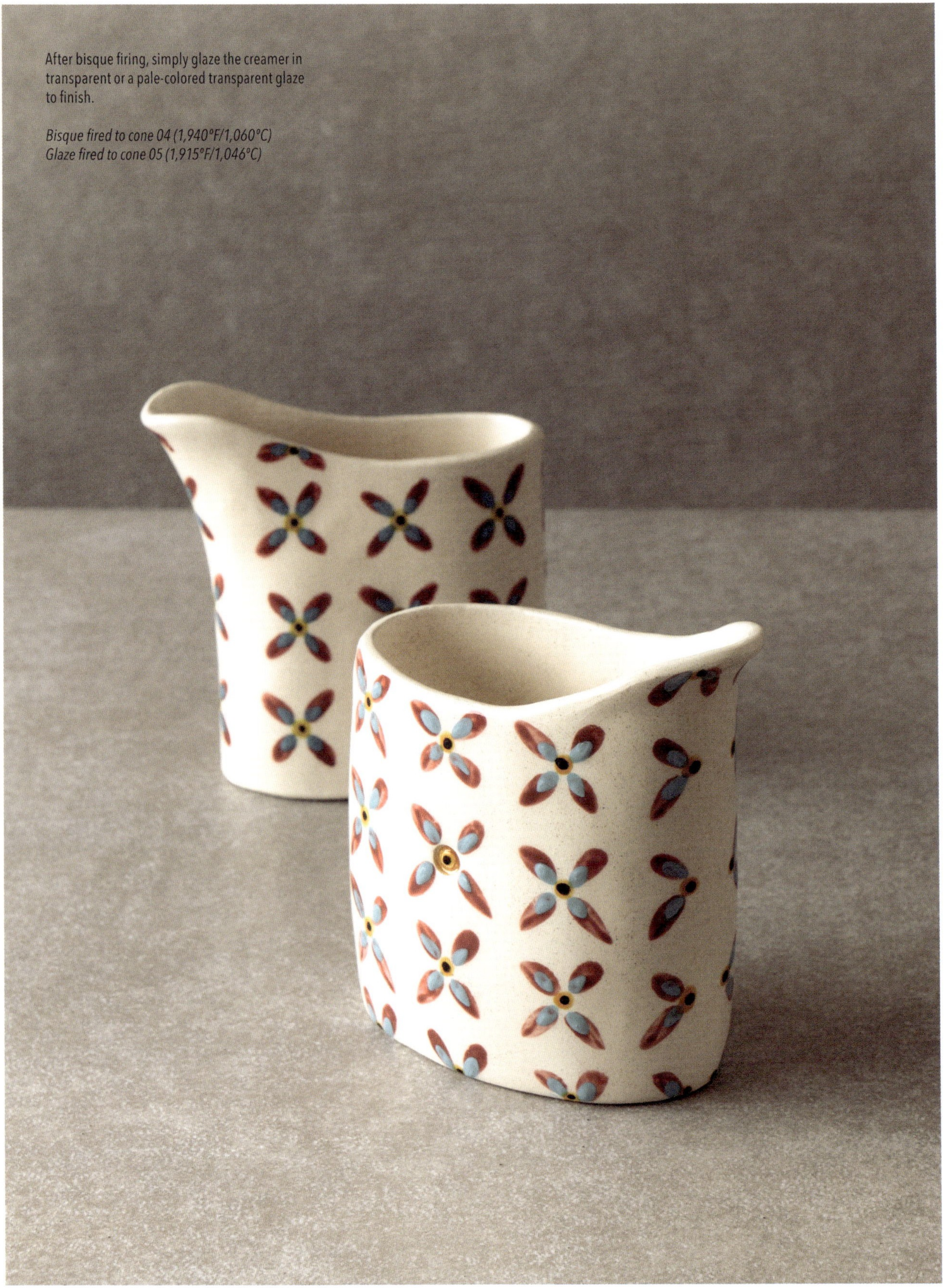

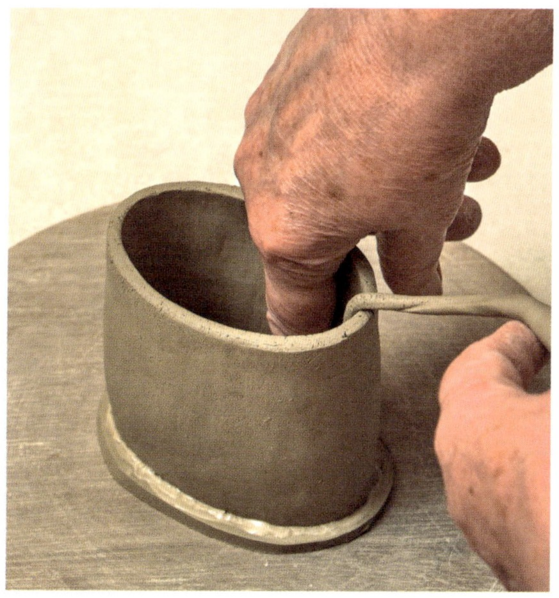

3 Cut the slab down to size. Score and slip all adjoining areas, then fix the body onto the base. Reinforce the internal join with a coil of soft clay and blend it in with a finger or suitable wooden tool.

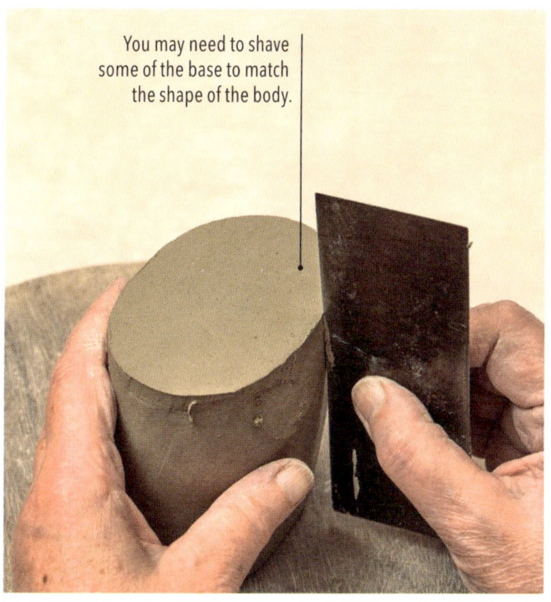

4 Turn the creamer upside down, then work over the join on the outside with a palette to remove any excess slip and refine the shape so that the base and body are identical.

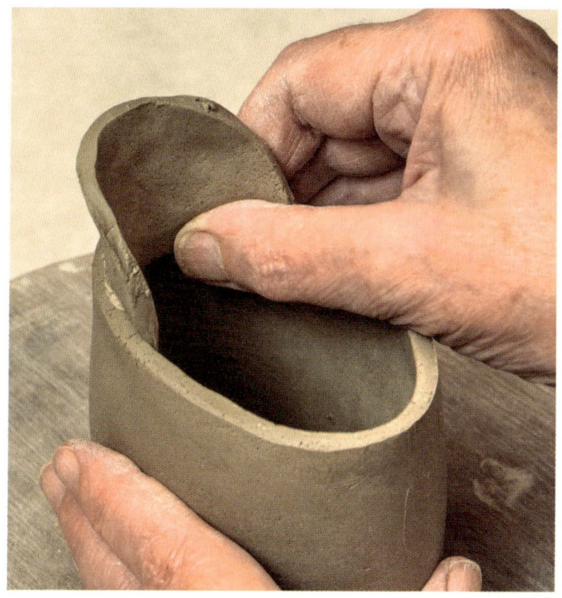

5 Pinch a small disc of clay and cut it into a semicircle, large enough to form the pouring lip. Fix it in place on the inside wall after scoring and slipping adjoining areas. Blend the lip onto the wall of the creamer, reinforcing if required.

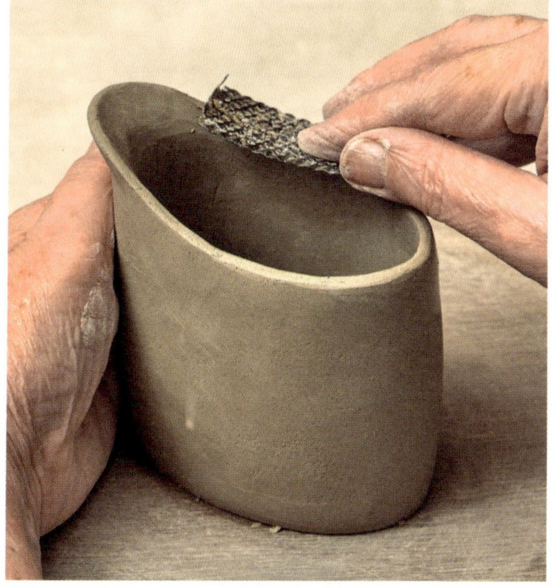

6 Surform the rim of the creamer until the line of the spout flows gently and seamlessly into the rim of the body. Neaten up the rim with a rib until it is an even thickness, nicely rounded, and smooth.

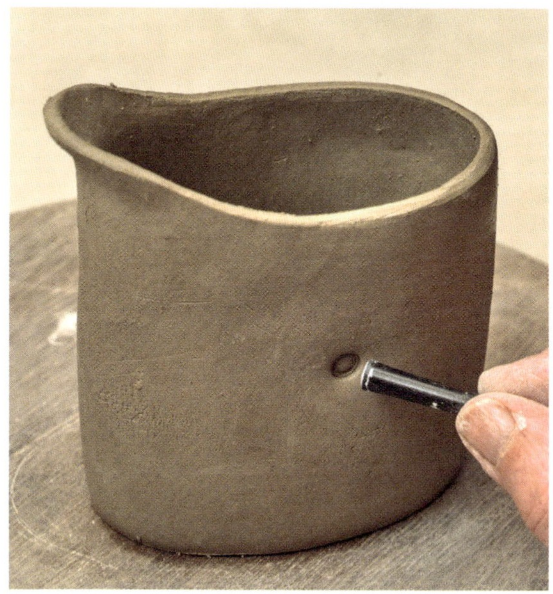

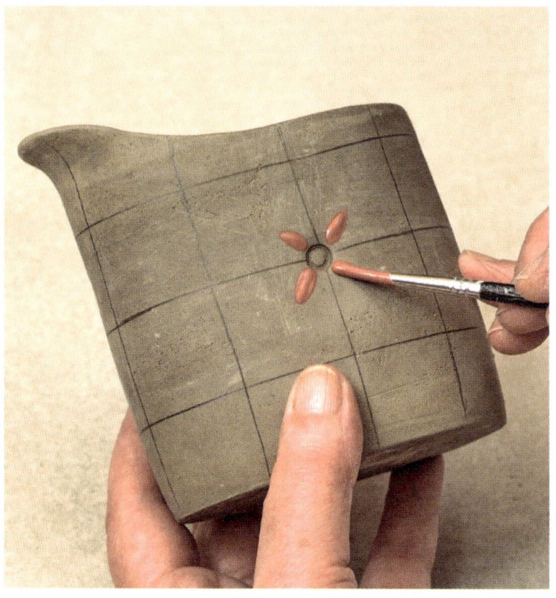

7 Calculate the spot where you would naturally lift the creamer and impress a small detail centered on each side where your finger and thumb grip. Anything can be used to impress a detail like this—the end of a pen for instance!

8 Measure and draw a square grid around the vessel using a soft pencil, starting from your impressed mark. Using the first color of slip or underglaze, paint four small petals radiating out as shown, beginning at the center impression.

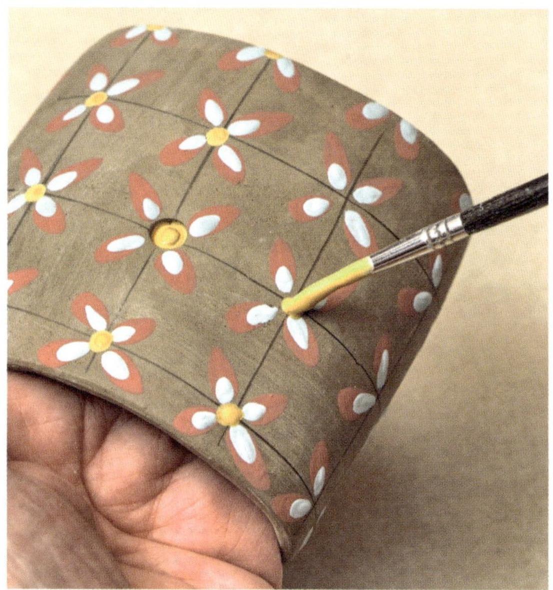

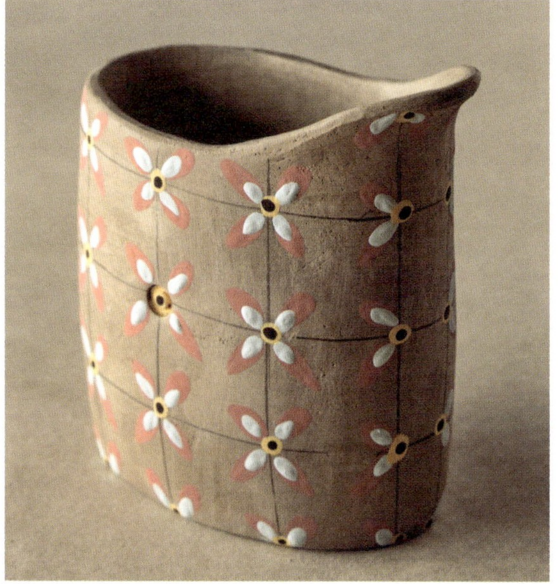

9 Continue to paint in the petals at the intersection of each point of the grid. When dry, work over the petals again with a smaller-sized petal in a contrasting color. Add a third color detail at the center of each flower.

10 Finish the decorating process with tiny dots of a strong color at the center of each flower as a highlight. NOTE: You can add more detail if preferred, more petals for example, or an added feature between the flowers; grid systems are great for this.

PITCHER

Width: 8in (20.5cm) from tip of lip to widest point of handle
Height: 6in (15cm)
Diameter: 4½in (11.5cm)

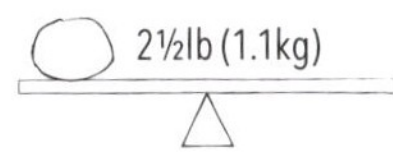
2½lb (1.1kg)

This contemporary, Scandi-style pitcher is a practical receptacle for any number of liquids. A simple design and bold color contrasts make it a stylish addition to the table at any time of day.

Scale the size up or down accordingly to make sets of pitchers for different uses.

YOU WILL NEED

TOOLS
- Banding wheel (turntable)
- Pin
- Loop tool
- Surform or rasp blade
- Knife
- Metal and flexible ribs
- Wooden batten or similar
- Wooden modeling tools

CLAY
Buff stoneware clay
- 1lb (450g) for base
- 1lb (450g) for extension
- 8oz (225g) for handle and lip

DESIGN NOTE
To make a larger pitcher, increase the weight of clay and pinch the base section to a wider diameter to balance the overall form and ensure it stands sturdily.

DECORATION
To get the Scandi look, opt for two matte glazes in strongly contrasting colors. The key to success is pared-back simplicity.

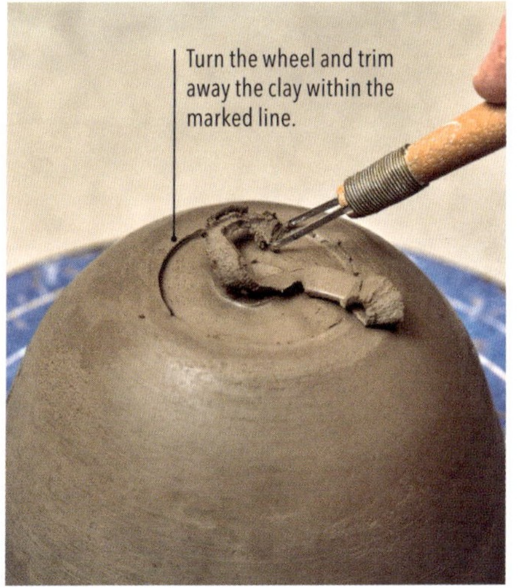

1 Pinch 1lb (450g) of clay to an open bowl shape, curving gently from a wide, sturdy base. Center the bowl on the banding wheel and score the position for a foot ring with a pin. Now trim the clay from the center of the circle using the loop tool.

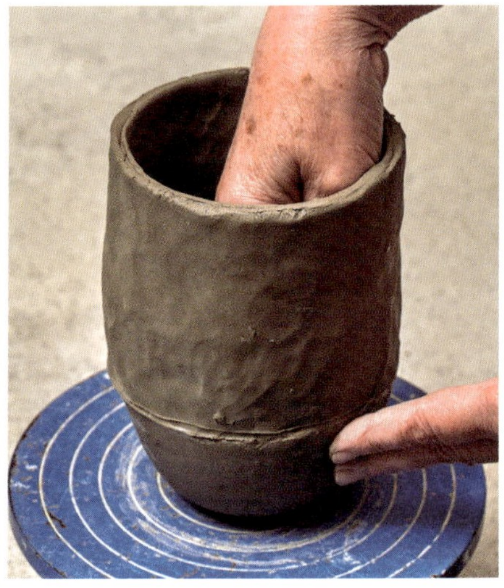

2 Pinch the second 1lb (450g) of clay to an open cylinder with the same diameter at the rim as that of the base. Fix the extension onto the base after scoring and slipping the adjoining rims. Reinforce, inside and out, with coils of soft clay.

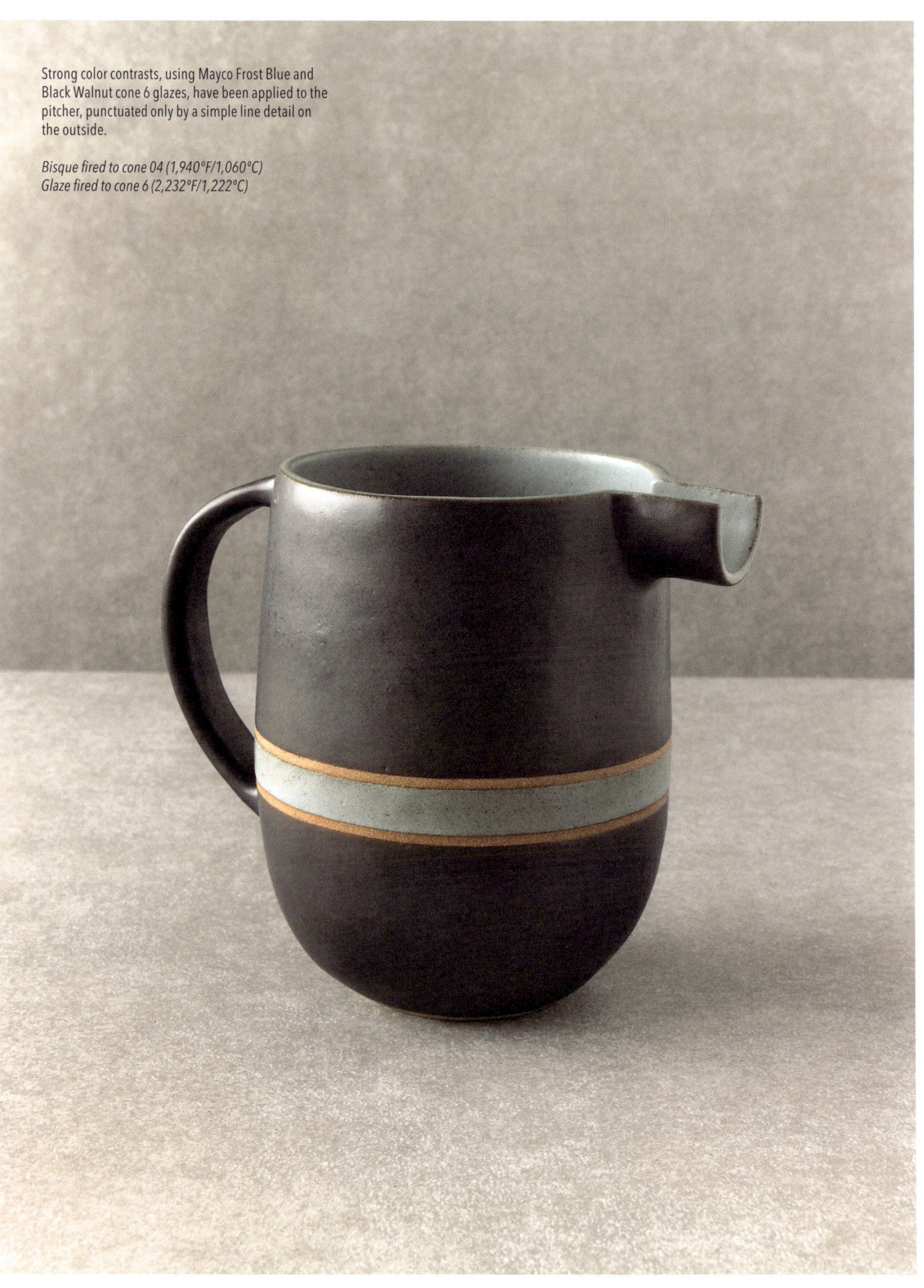

Strong color contrasts, using Mayco Frost Blue and Black Walnut cone 6 glazes, have been applied to the pitcher, punctuated only by a simple line detail on the outside.

Bisque fired to cone 04 (1,940°F/1,060°C)
Glaze fired to cone 6 (2,232°F/1,222°C)

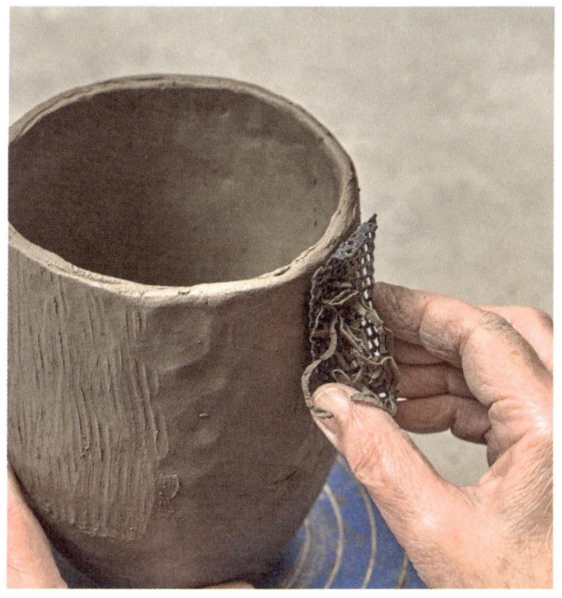

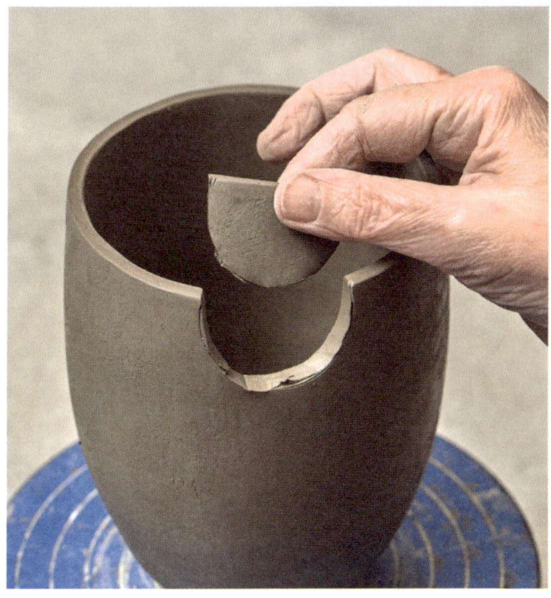

3 A quick way of reducing the thickness of the wall and refining the surface is to reduce the bulk with a surform. Work over the surface again with a rib when finished, to smooth it off.

4 Score a level line at the rim with a pin, then either cut or surform the clay back to the line. Neaten up with a small kidney or rib. Now cut a semicircle from the rim for the pouring lip.

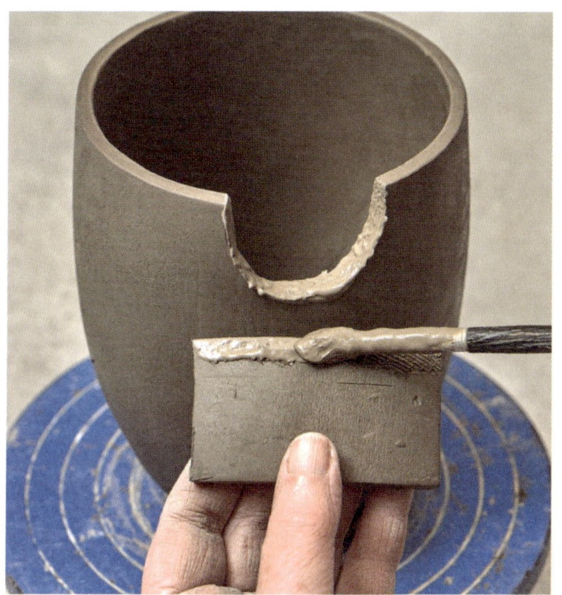

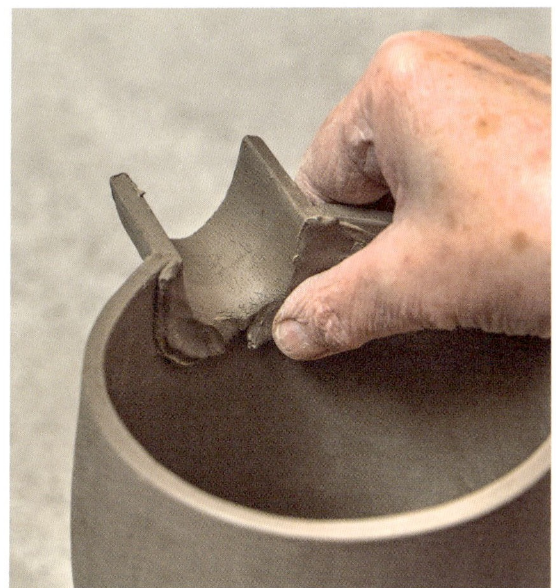

5 Pinch a small rectangular slab for the lip, long enough to fit the curve of the semicircle on the body. Score and slip the adjoining edges of the semicircle and lip.

6 Fit the lip slab in place and blend the clay onto the pitcher body on the inside. Reinforce around the join on the outside with a coil of soft clay, then blend it in until seamless.

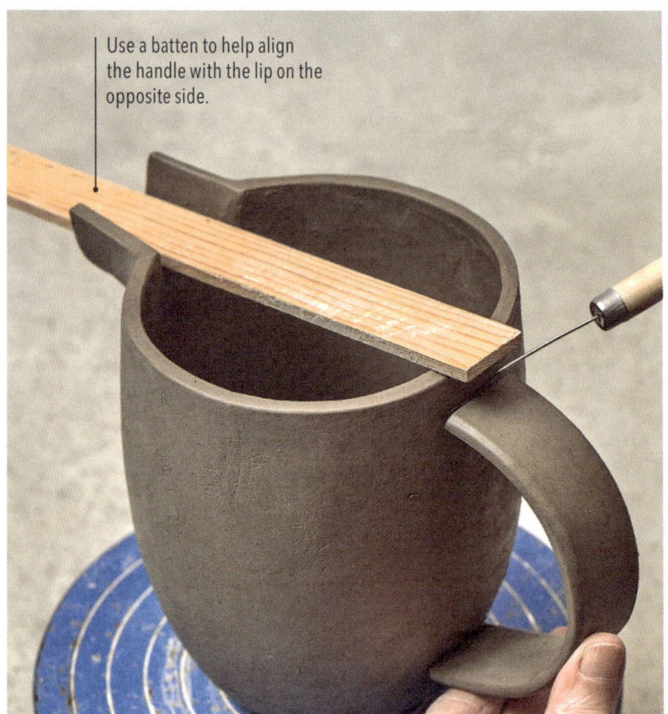

7 Pinch a simple strap handle no more than 1in (2.5cm) wide. Place a short length of batten, or similar, across the top of the pitcher, aligned with the lip to determine the position for the handle. Mark the position with a pin.

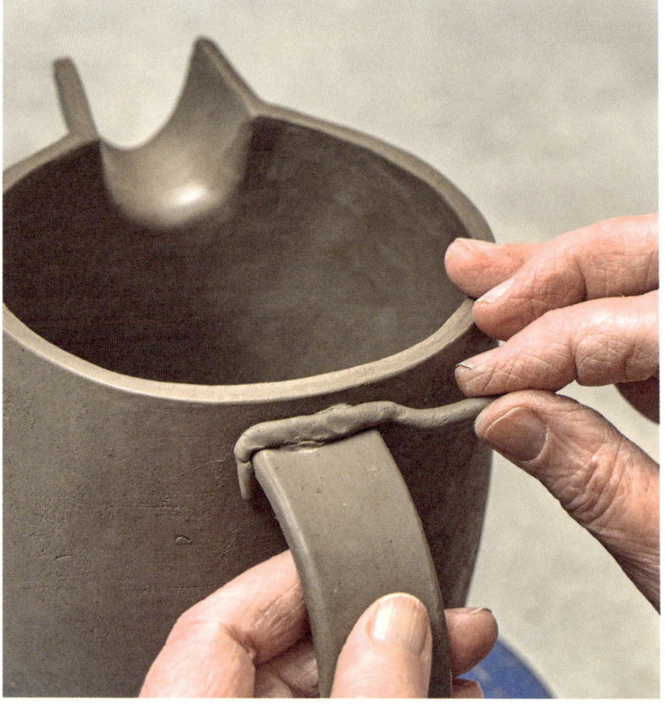

8 Fix the handle onto the pitcher after first scoring and slipping adjoining areas. Reinforce around the joins with coils of soft clay, then blend them in neatly with a wooden tool. Allow the pitcher to dry out slowly, ready for bisque firing.

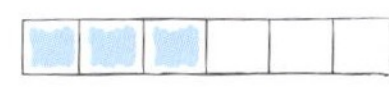

SALT AND PEPPER SHAKERS

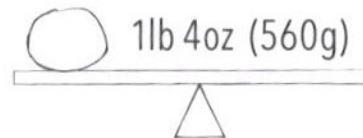

Height: 2¼in (6cm)

1lb 4oz (560g)

These sweet little salt and pepper shakers were inspired by a mid-century set and, although quite unusual, they are still perfectly practical and make a lovely centerpiece for the table.

The style of the birds here is generic, but they could easily be made to look like a specific species with more tailored features and coloring.

YOU WILL NEED

TOOLS

- Wooden modeling tool
- Pin
- Metal or plastic rib or kidney
- Suitable tool to impress an eye (an old pen top)
- Hole cutter
- Short length of ½in (12mm) dowel
- Rubber or cork stopper for the base

CLAY

White earthenware

- 10oz (280g) per shaker

DESIGN NOTE

Make these shakers as fruits, vegetables, or other animals as an alternative to birds. The principles for making and finishing are the same no matter what the shape.

DECORATION

Use underglaze colors with transparent glaze or low-fire brush-on glazes to decorate the surface of the birds for a realistic finish. See pages 156–172 for other options for surface decoration.

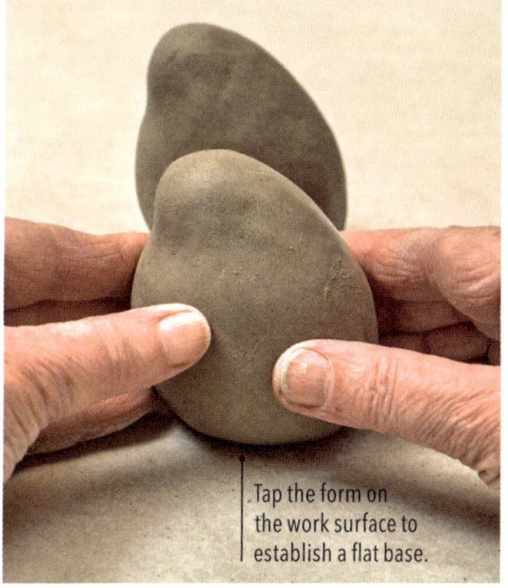

1 From 3oz (85g) of clay, pinch two equal, round-bottomed bowl sections, then fix them together and reinforce the join. Make a hole in the form at one end with a pin to allow for the release of air, then manipulate the shape to form the head. Fill the hole in when the shape is correct.

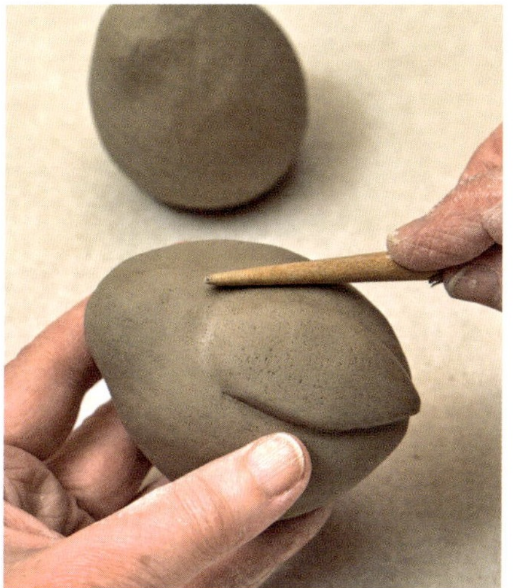

2 Pinch two thin, flat slabs to form the wings. Cut the wings to size, then attach one to each side of the body after scoring and slipping all adjoining areas. Blend each wing onto the body with a wooden tool.

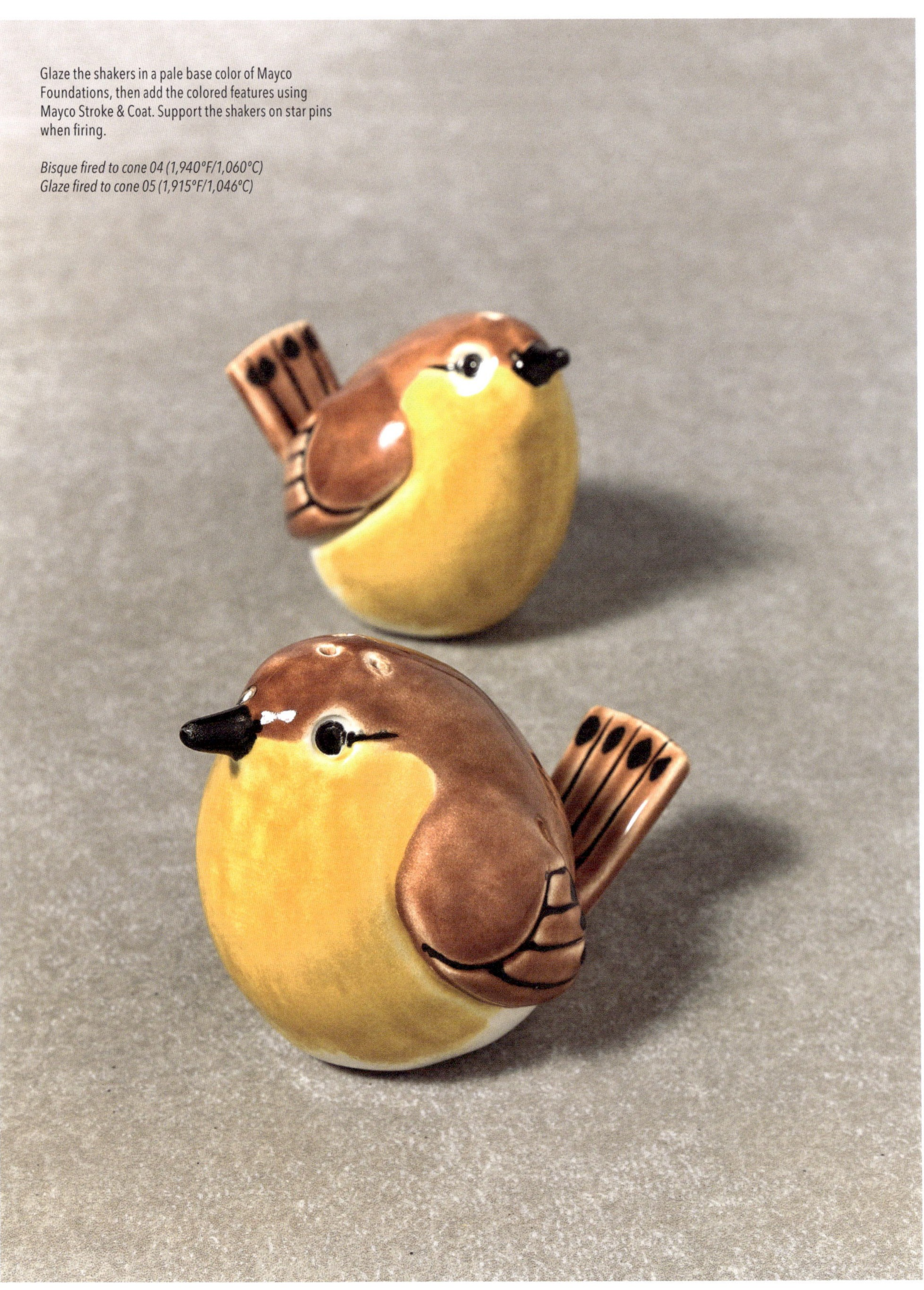

Glaze the shakers in a pale base color of Mayco Foundations, then add the colored features using Mayco Stroke & Coat. Support the shakers on star pins when firing.

Bisque fired to cone 04 (1,940°F/1,060°C)
Glaze fired to cone 05 (1,915°F/1,046°C)

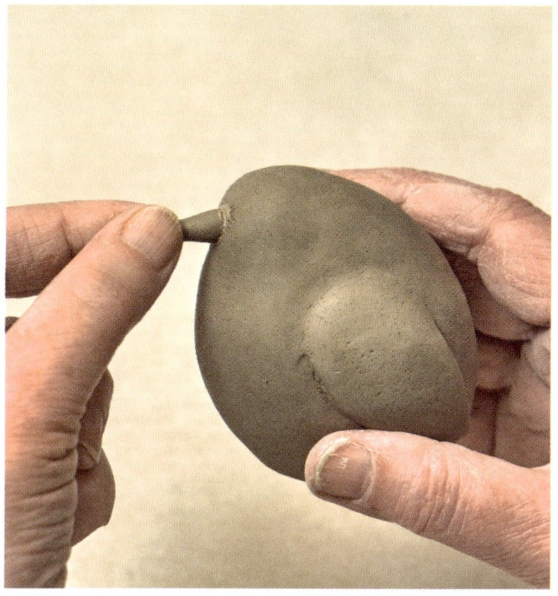

3 Form a tiny beak and attach it to the front of the head. Reinforce the join with the tiniest of soft coils, then blend it in carefully with a wooden tool.

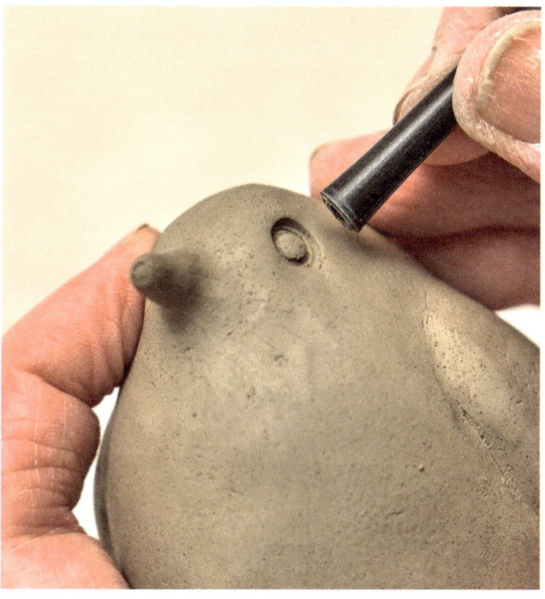

4 Impress the eyes, with a suitable tool—old pen tops are great for this; look for ones in different shapes. Then score the decorative feather detail of the wings using a pin.

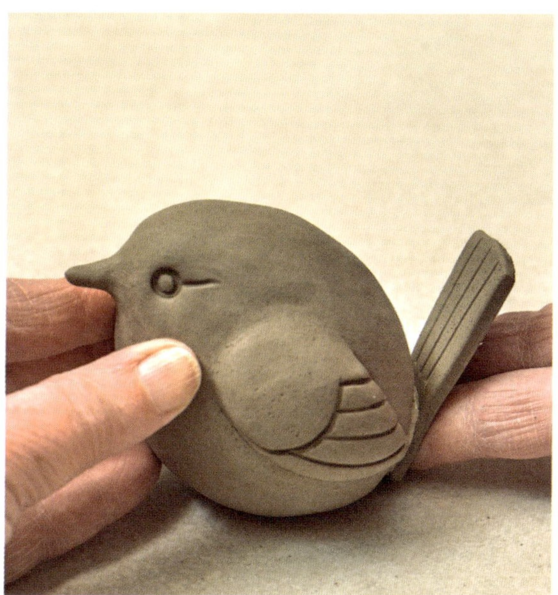

5 Pinch a final, small slab from the remaining clay, then cut it to form an upright tail feature. Score feather details, as for the wings in step 4. Attach the tail to the form after scoring and slipping the relevant areas. Blend the tail onto the body neatly with a kidney and reinforce, if required.

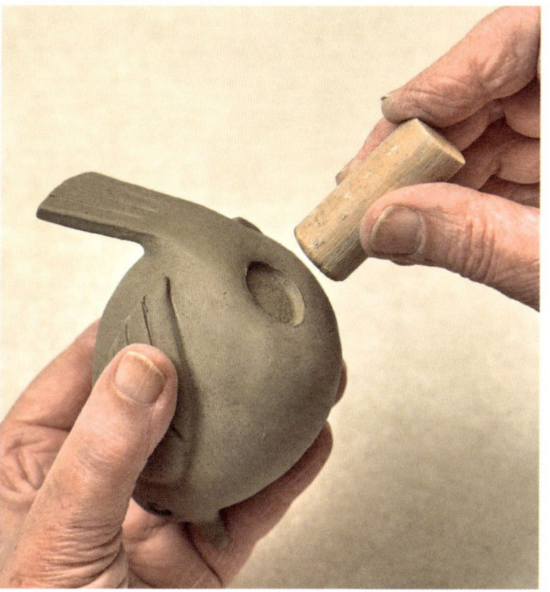

6 Place the stopper on the underside of the bird and lightly score the position with a pin. Gently impress the end of the dowel into the clay in the marked place on the underside, to form a recess for the stopper.

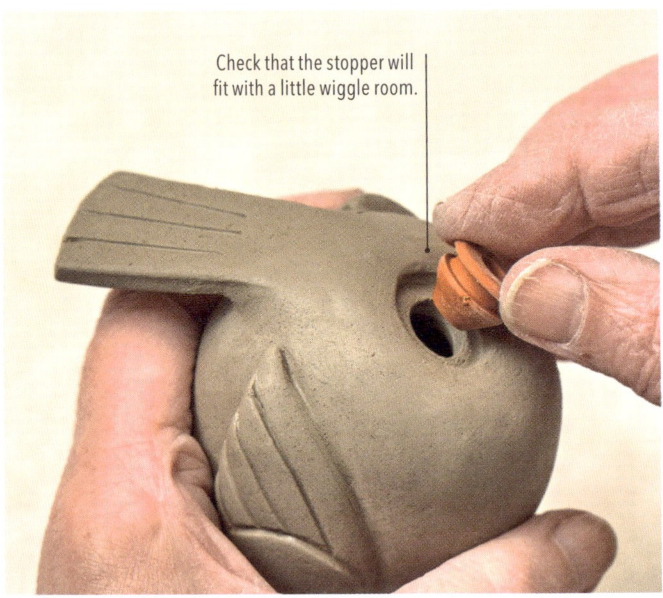

7 Cut a hole at the center of the recess, making it a little larger than the stopper, to allow for shrinkage in drying and firing.

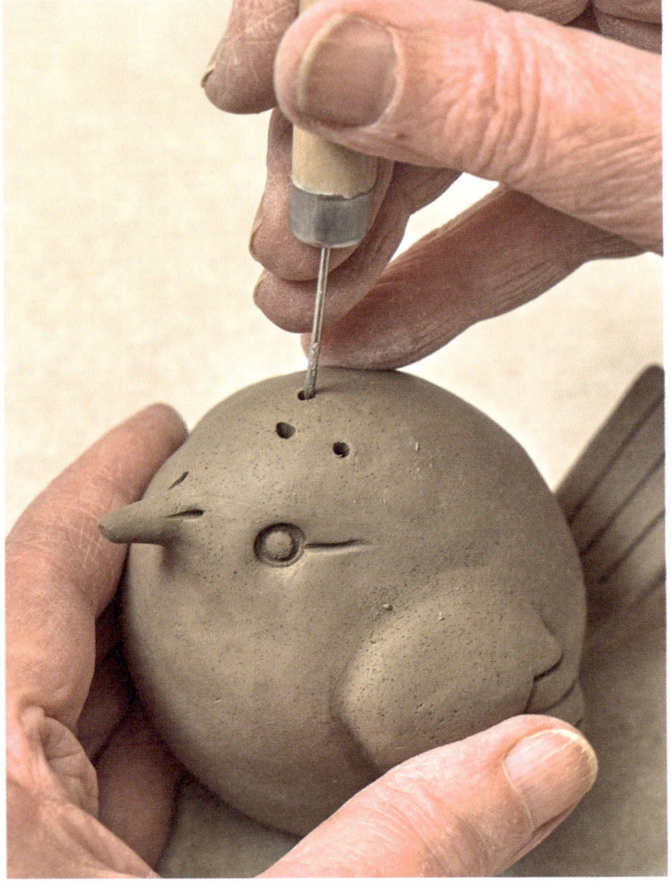

8 Using a pin, make holes in the top of the head: three for pepper; one for salt. Make the second shaker in exactly the same way.

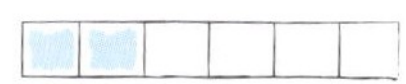

CONDIMENT BOTTLE

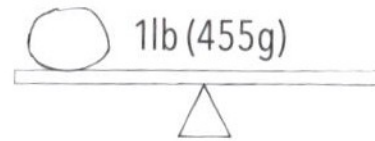

Width: 3¼in (8cm) at base
Height: 7in (18cm) to top of stopper

1lb (455g)

Bottles like these are useful for oil, vinegar, or salad dressings. Coordinate them with existing tableware by glazing in a similar or complementary colored glaze.

Make a larger version to use as a carafe for water or wine.

YOU WILL NEED

TOOLS
- Banding wheel (turntable)
- Metal or plastic kidney or rib
- Long throwing rib
- Wooden modeling tool

CLAY
White stoneware
- 14oz (400g) for body
- 2oz (55g) for stopper

DESIGN NOTE
- Make a straight-sided bottle by pinching the base wall straight and the top section as a straight-sided cylinder.
- Alternatively, make a rounded bottle from two pinched halves. In both cases the pouring lip extension must be pinched to fit the new shape.

DECORATION
Almost any decorating method can be applied to the surface of this bottle. A simple trailed glaze-on-glaze technique is used here, but see pages 156–172 for other options for surface decoration.

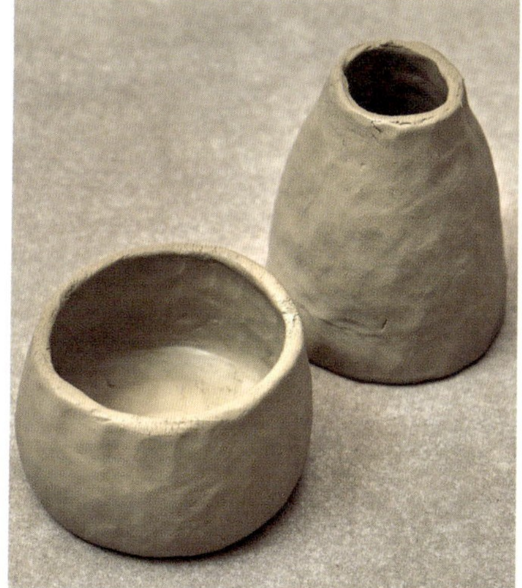

1 From 6oz (170g) of clay, pinch a bowl shape with a 3¼in (8cm) wide flat base and walls that narrow toward the rim. Pinch another 6oz (170g) of clay into an open-ended cone that will fit the base. Refine the inner surfaces with a kidney.

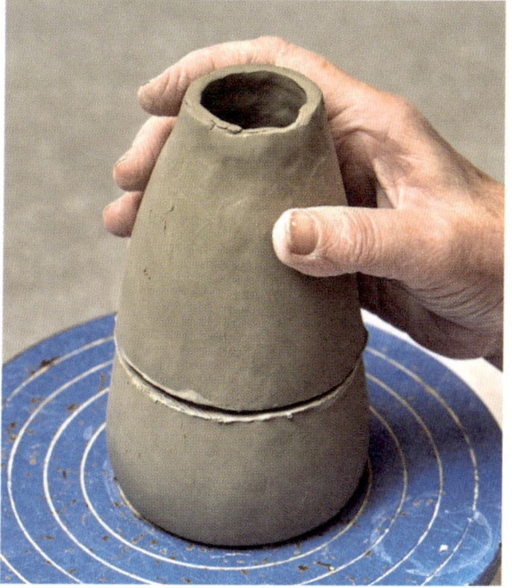

2 Level the rim of the base section with a knife or surform, then score and slip the surface and adjoining rim of the extension and fix the two together.

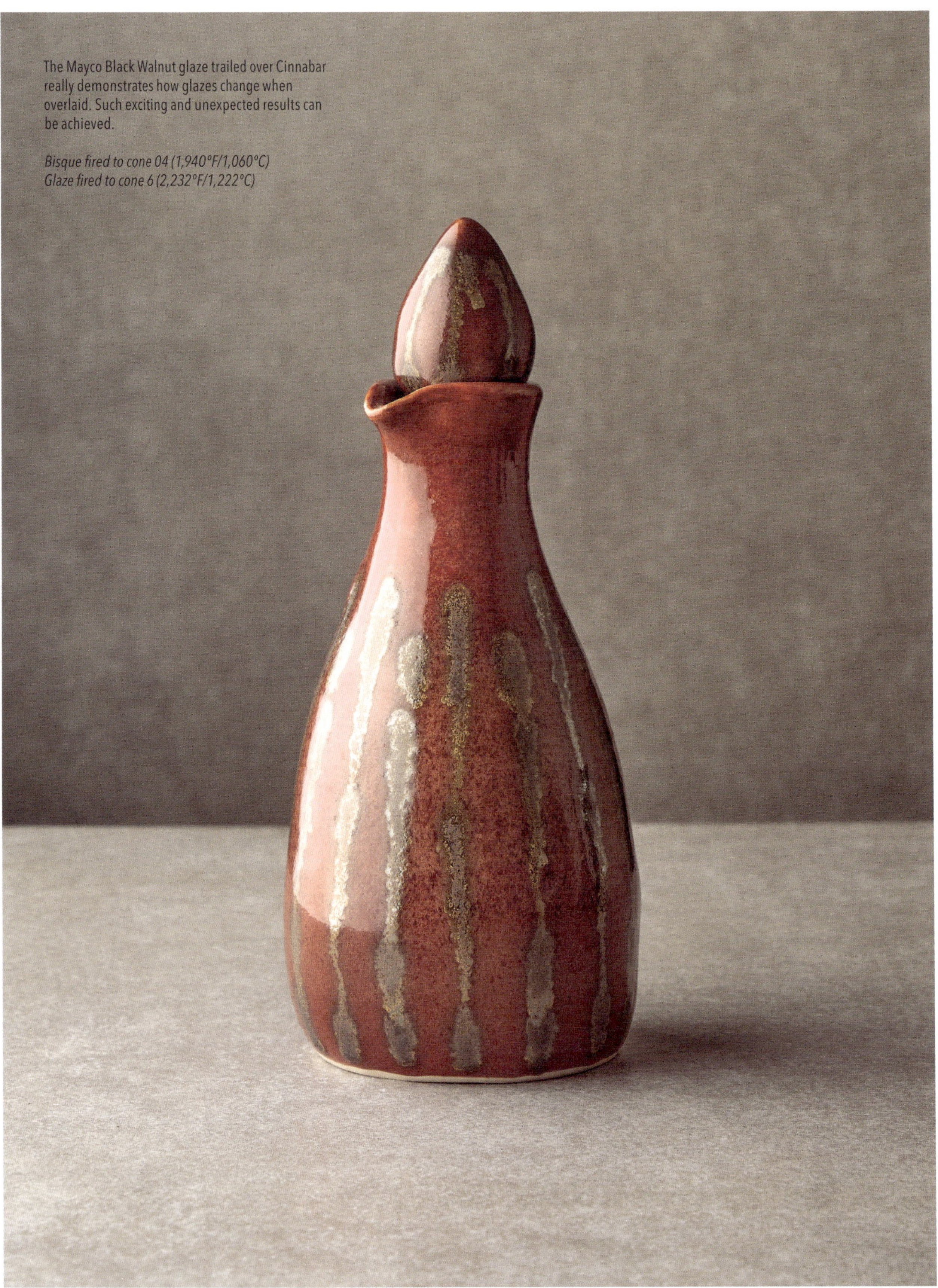

The Mayco Black Walnut glaze trailed over Cinnabar really demonstrates how glazes change when overlaid. Such exciting and unexpected results can be achieved.

Bisque fired to cone 04 (1,940°F/1,060°C)
Glaze fired to cone 6 (2,232°F/1,222°C)

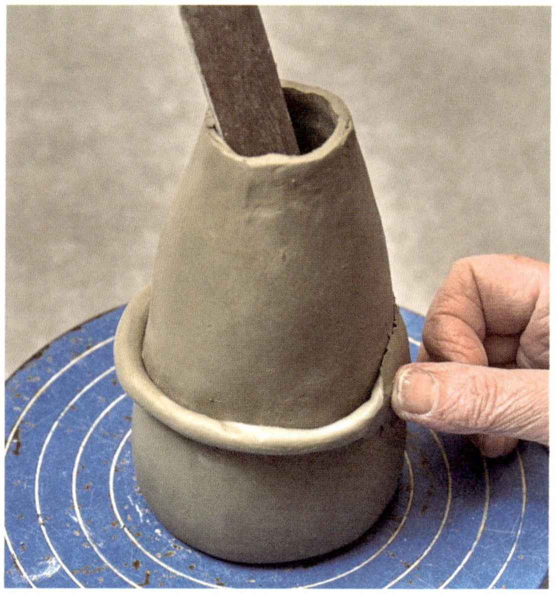

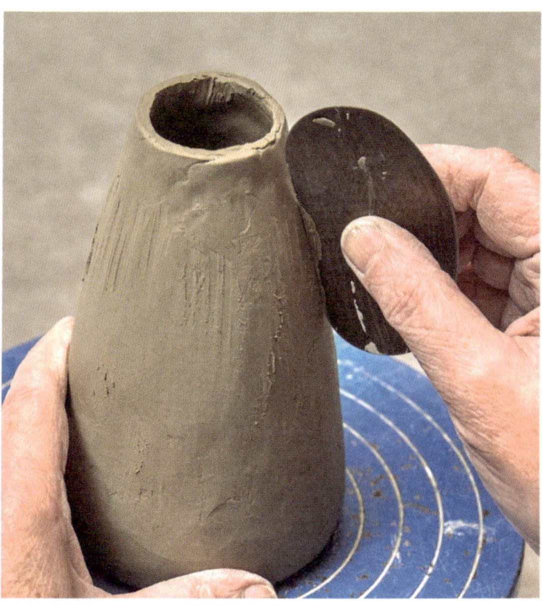

3 Reinforce the join on the outside with a coil of soft clay. Use a long throwing rib to support the wall on the inside as you blend the coil on the outside. Use the rib to correct any distortions in the shape from the inside when finished.

4 Work over the entire surface of the bottle with a kidney to refine and smooth away the pinch marks, removing clay as required for best effect.

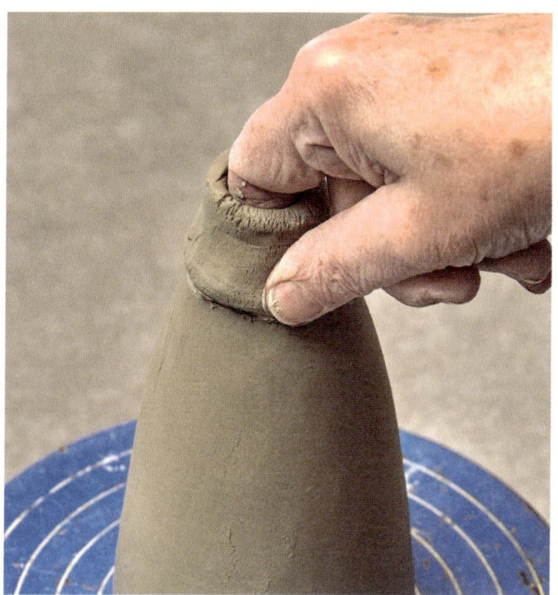

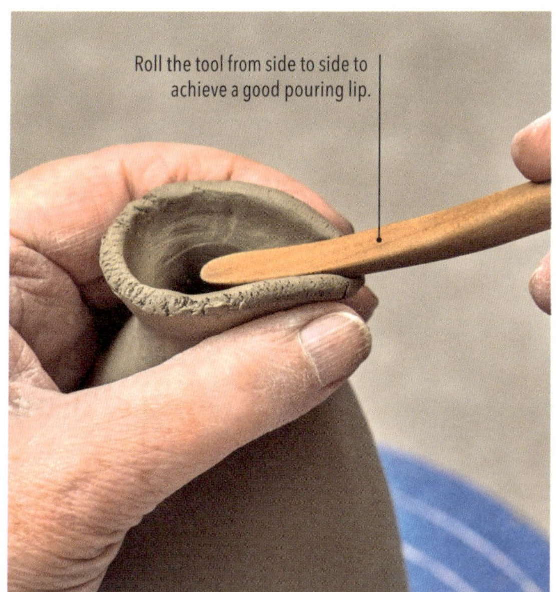

5 From 2oz (55g) of clay, pinch an open-ended, cone-shaped ring to form the pouring spout. Attach the ring to the body after scoring and slipping adjoining rims. Blend the ring onto the body, reinforcing if required.

6 Pinch one side of the rim between a finger and thumb to create an oval, then gently ease the clay into a pouring lip using a wooden modeling tool.

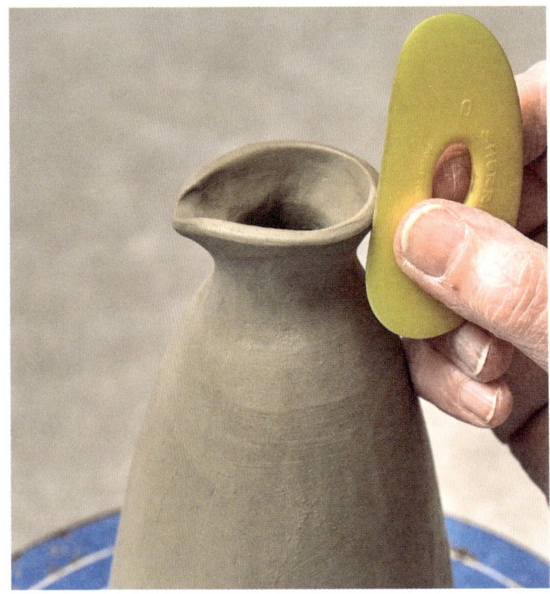

7 Work over the rim of the bottle with a flexible rib to level and smooth it to an even thickness. Take the time to do this well—the eye is always drawn to a bad rim even if the rest of the form is fantastic!

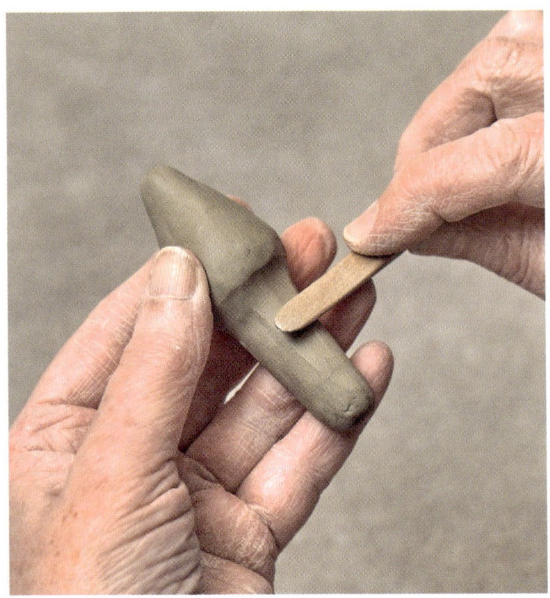

8 Form the remaining clay into a short, fat coil, then model one end into a minaret shape with a long stem below to fit into the neck of the bottle.

9 Dry and bisque fire the bottle with the stopper in place.

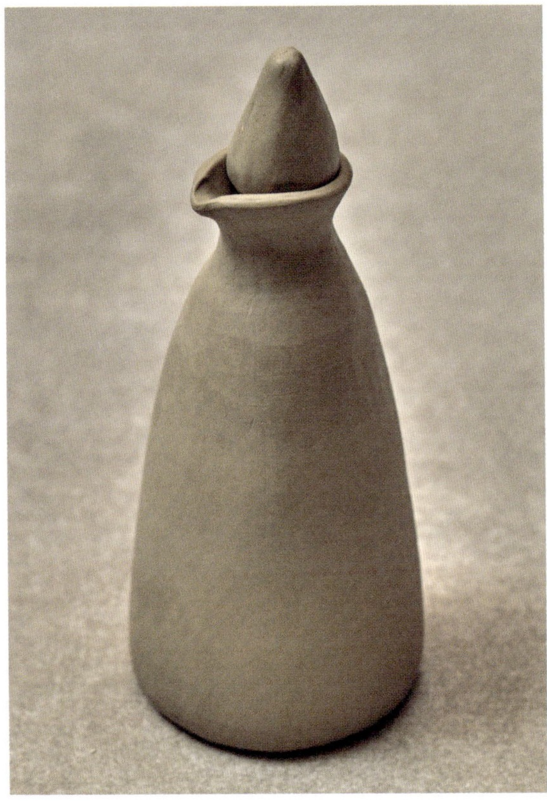

CHICKEN EGG CUP

Width: 4¾in (12cm) from tail to beak
Height: 3½in (9cm)

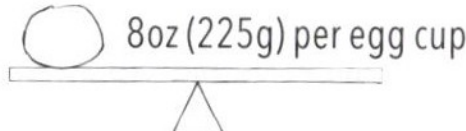
8oz (225g) per egg cup

An egg cup like this can cheer up any breakfast table and bring a smile to your face—even a reluctant child might be tempted to eat their egg if served in a chicken!

Make them colorful and fun with different surface decoration features.

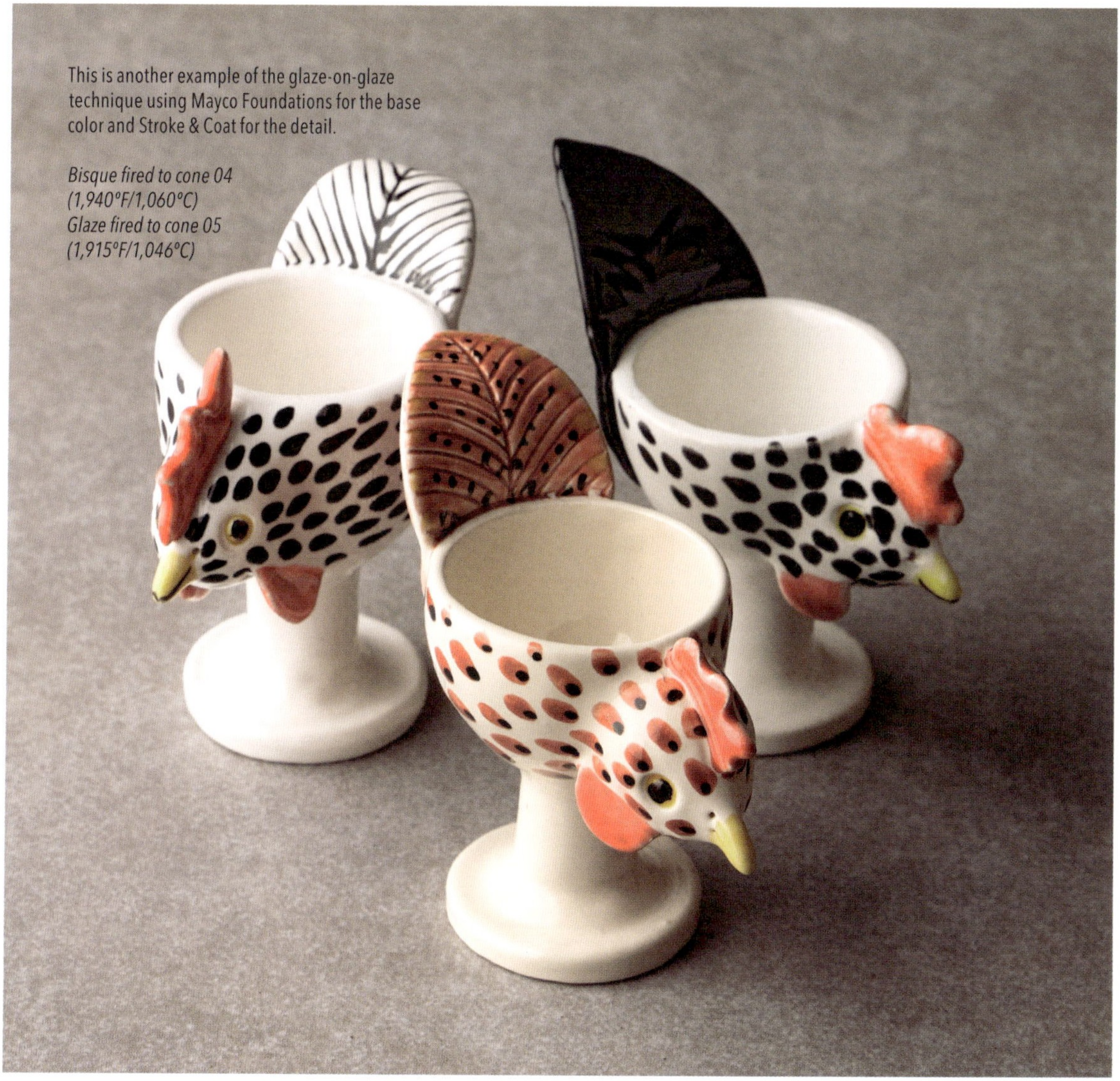

This is another example of the glaze-on-glaze technique using Mayco Foundations for the base color and Stroke & Coat for the detail.

Bisque fired to cone 04 (1,940°F/1,060°C)
Glaze fired to cone 05 (1,915°F/1,046°C)

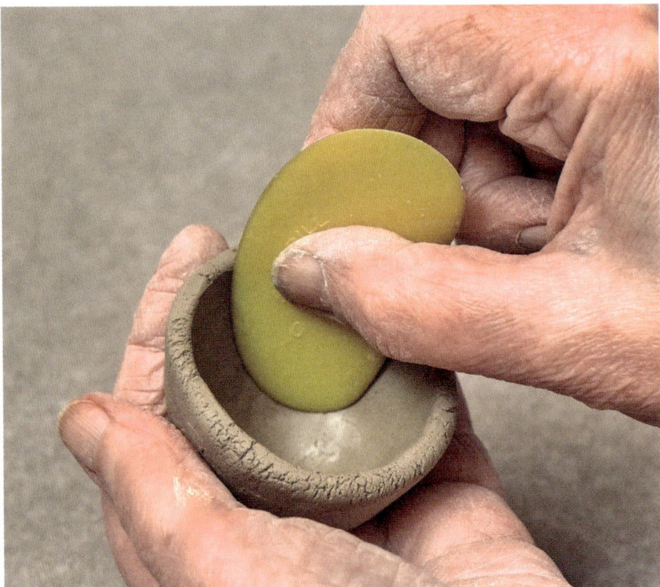

1 Form 2oz (55g) of clay into a ball and pinch the shape into a round-bottomed cup. Work over the interior surface of the cup with a rib to smooth and even out the thickness of the clay.

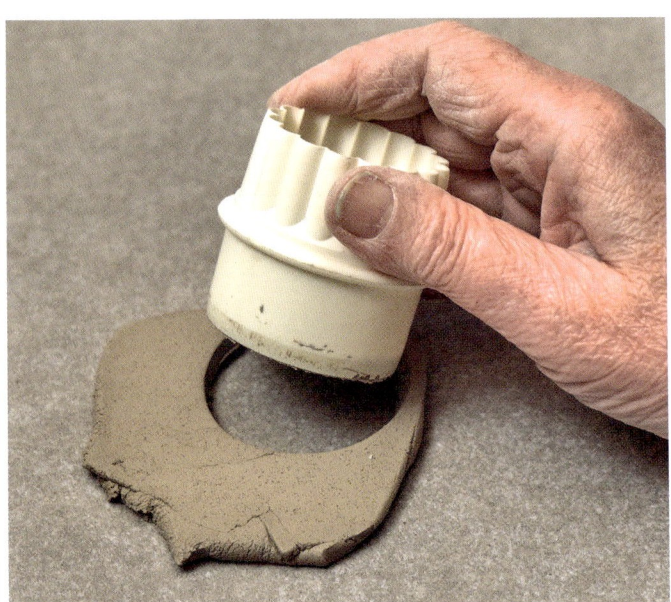

2 Pinch another 2oz (55g) of clay out into a flat disc about 1/4in (5mm) thick. Smooth over the surface of the disc with a rib to even out the thickness, then cut out a 1 1/2in (4cm) diameter circle using a cookie cutter.

YOU WILL NEED

TOOLS

- Small plastic kidney or rib
- 1 1/2in (4cm) cookie cutter
- Banding wheel (turntable)
- Wooden modeling tool
- Suitable tool to impress an eye (an old pen top)
- Pin

CLAY

White earthenware

- 8oz (225g) divided into small amounts for each part of the egg cup

DESIGN NOTE

Any bird or animal can be modeled to make an egg cup in this way; it is simply a matter of breaking the individual features of the creature down into relevant parts: head, tail, beak, etc. The principles for making are the same.

DECORATION

The egg cup can be decorated with slip or underglaze colors before bisque firing, then a transparent glaze applied after. Or, use low-fire glazes to achieve a similar effect after bisque firing. All are subtly different but equally good. See page 165 for this last method and pages 156–172 for other options for surface decoration.

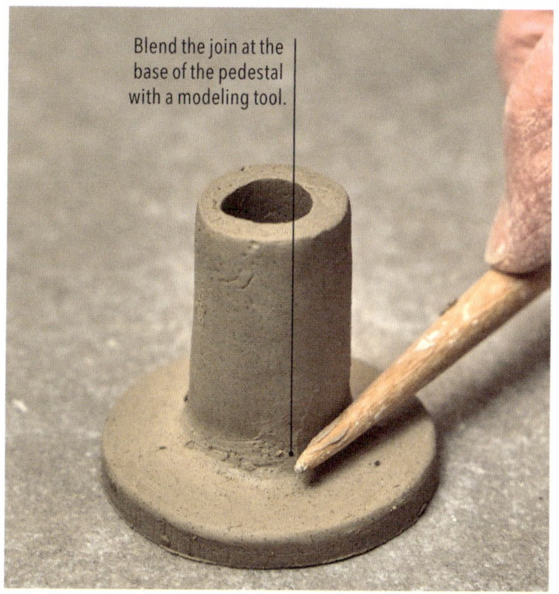

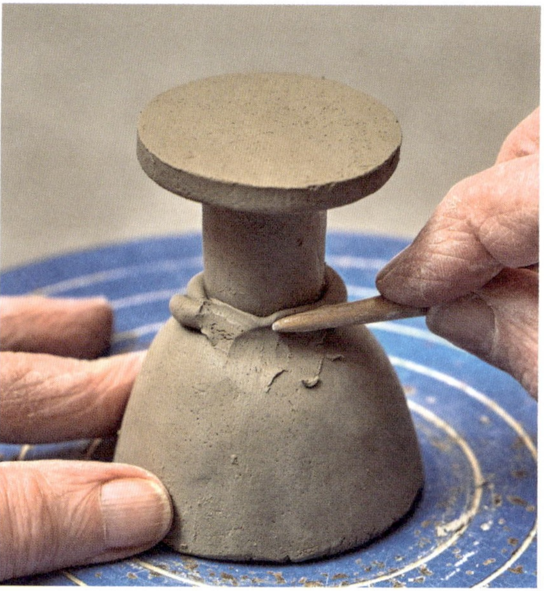

3 From another 2oz (55g) of clay, pinch a short, open-ended cylinder to a suitable height to form a pedestal for the cup, then fix it onto the base disc after scoring and slipping adjoining areas. Reinforce the join with a coil of soft clay.

4 Slip and score to fix the pedestal to the base of the cup and reinforce the join again with a coil of soft clay. Blend the coil onto the cup and pedestal equally for a neat finish.

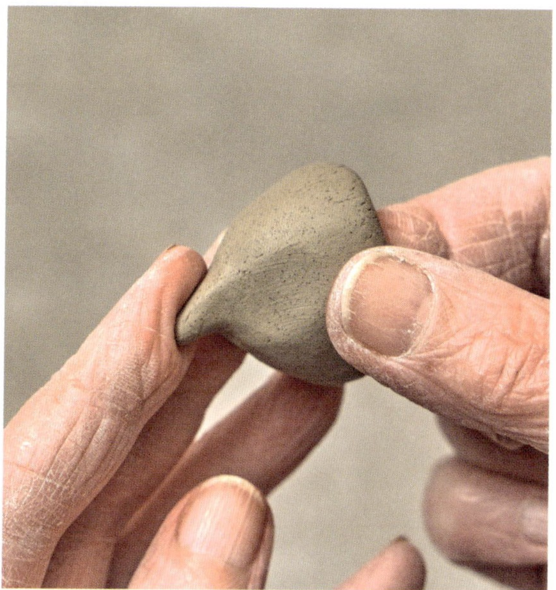

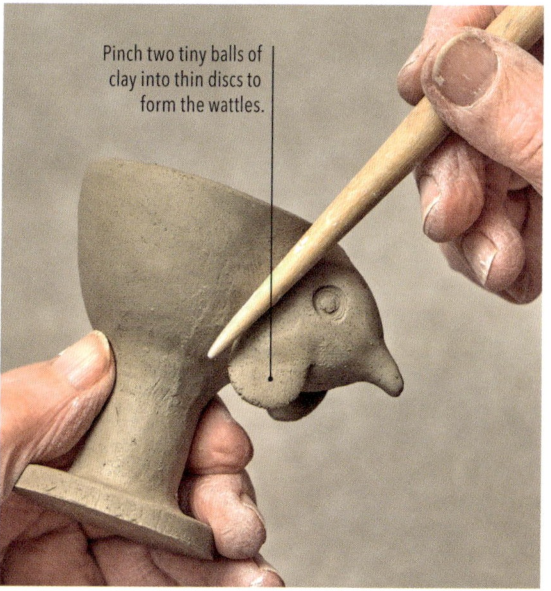

5 Pinch a tiny amount of clay into a bowl the size of the top of a finger, then manipulate the clay to shape a head with a beak. Attach the head to the side of the egg cup, with the top of the head level with the rim.

6 Pinch two small balls of clay into thin discs to form the wattles. Attach the wattles on each side of the head, below the beak, and blend them in seamlessly. Impress the eyes with a suitable tool and pierce the nostrils above the beak to allow for air release in firing.

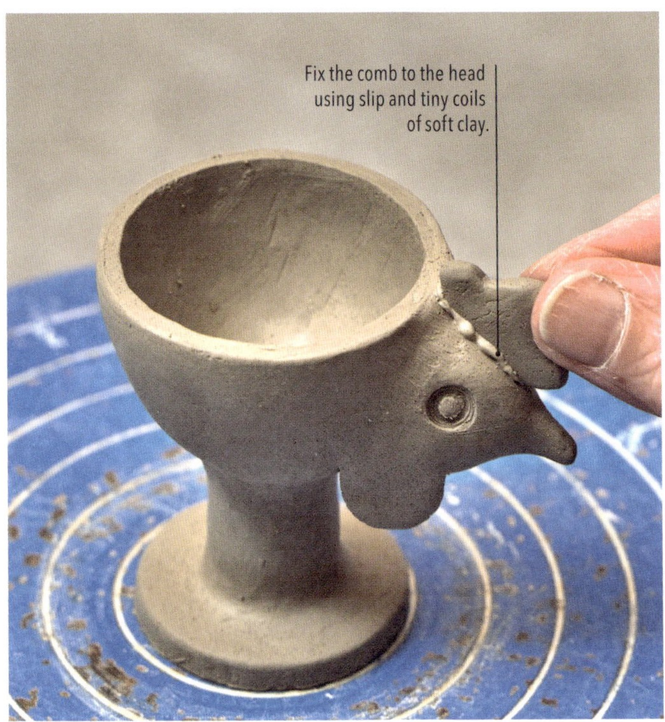

7 Now pinch a tiny amount of clay to form a frilly comb for the top of the head, and fix it in place with a dab of slip. Reinforce the join with tiny coils of soft clay and blend them in carefully.

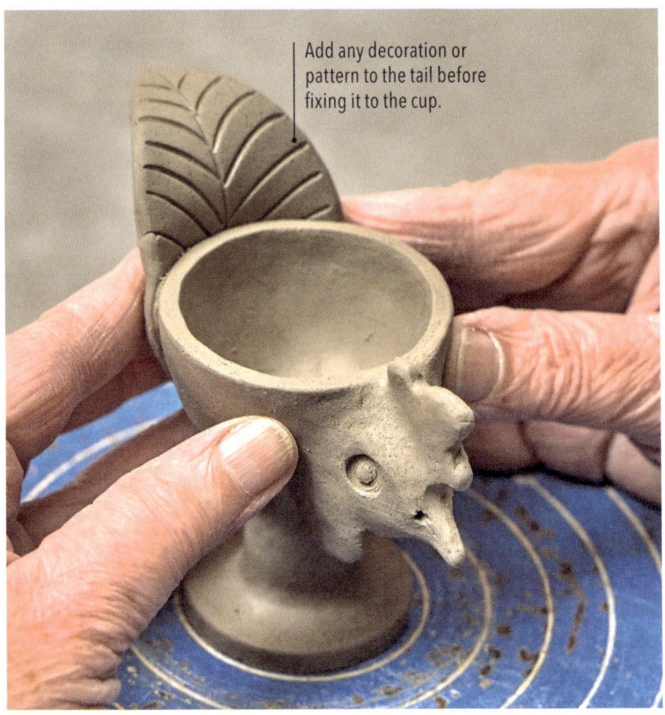

8 Pinch the remaining clay into a smooth slab and cut out a rudimentary leaf shape to form the tail feathers. Use a pin to score the feather details on the tail. Fix the tail onto the side of the cup opposite the head, after scoring and slipping the relevant areas.

GUINEA FOWL EGG CUP

Width: 4¾in (12cm) from tail to beak
Height: 3in (7.5cm)

8oz (225g) per egg cup

This fun but practical egg cup continues the bird theme to mix and match with the chicken version in the previous project. You could easily make a whole aviary of egg cups in this way if you wanted.

Try making garden birds like robins or blackbirds—or really exotic birds like ostrich or emu.

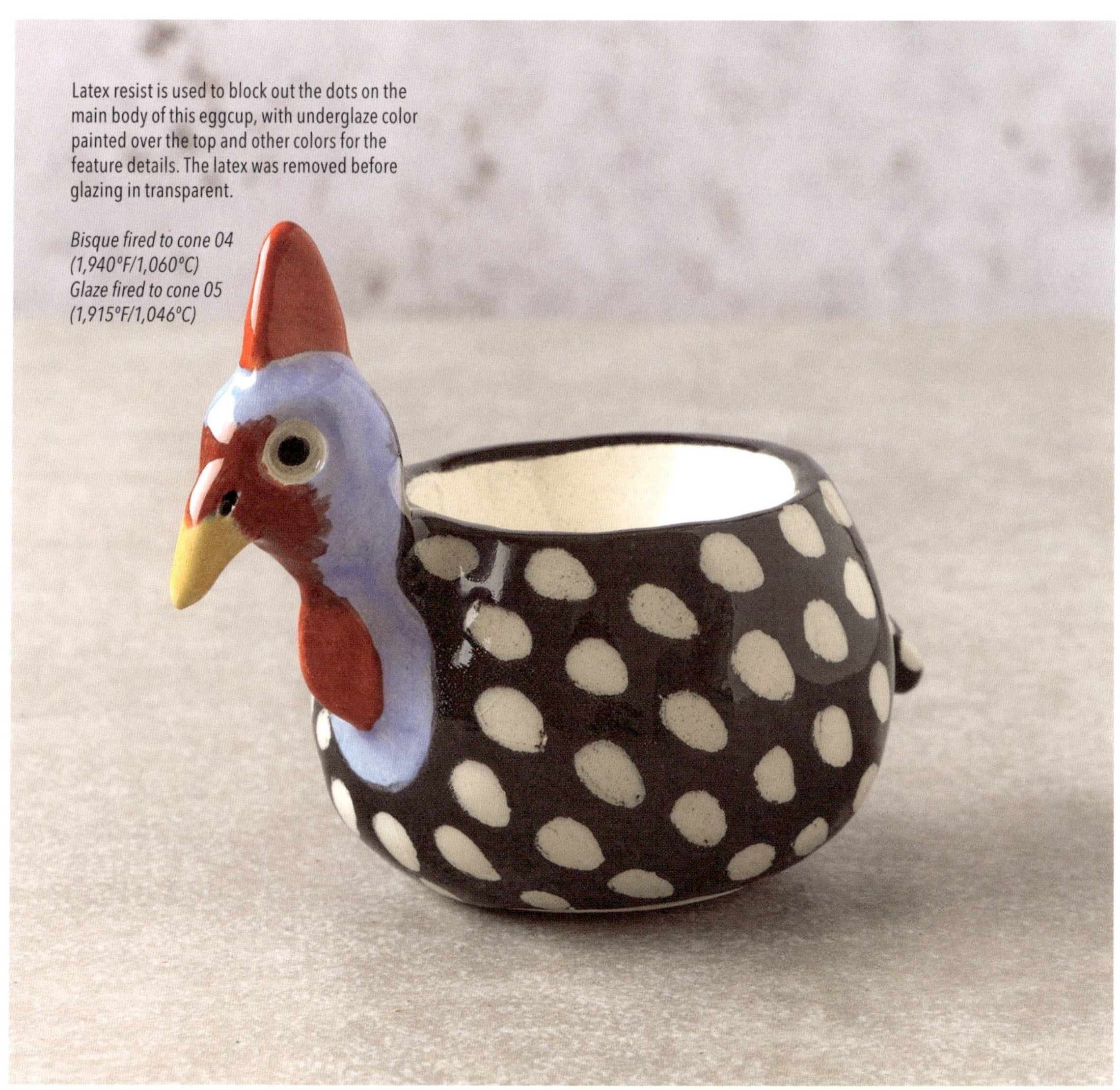

Latex resist is used to block out the dots on the main body of this eggcup, with underglaze color painted over the top and other colors for the feature details. The latex was removed before glazing in transparent.

Bisque fired to cone 04 (1,940°F/1,060°C)
Glaze fired to cone 05 (1,915°F/1,046°C)

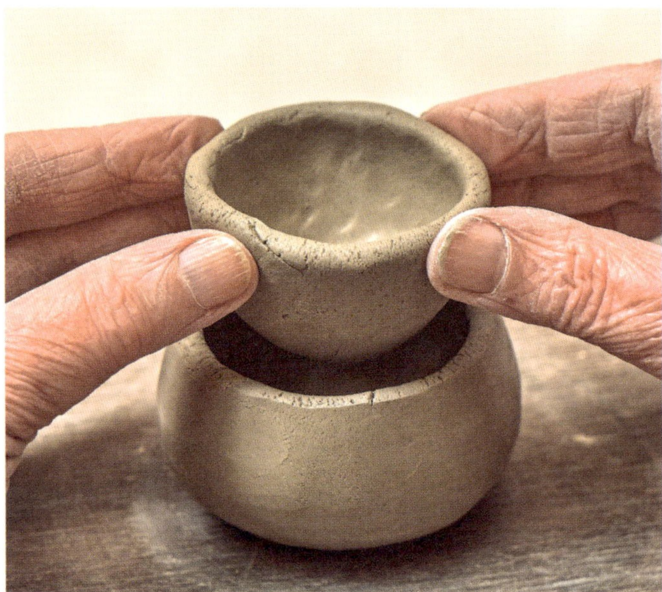

1 From 4oz (115g) of clay, pinch a spherical bowl with an opening at the rim wide enough to sit a large egg in. From 2oz (55g) of clay, pinch a second cup shape, just large enough to sit inside the spherical bowl.

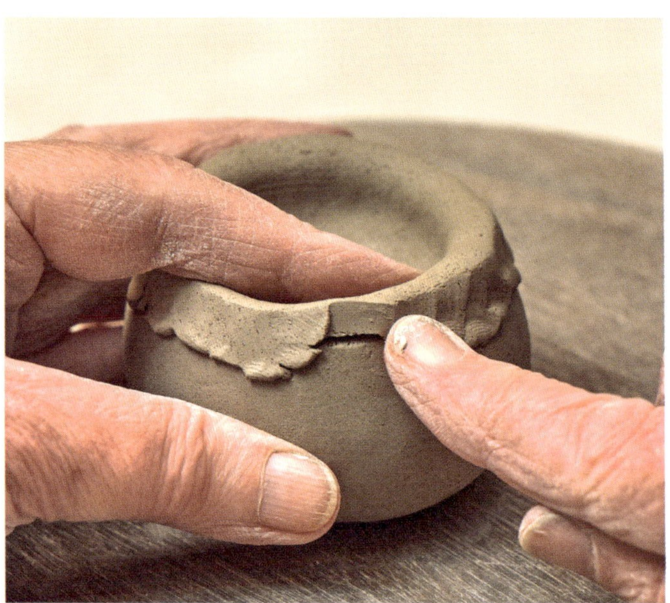

2 Score and slip the rim of the spherical bowl, then fix the cup inside and seal the two parts together by blending the clay from the inner cup over the rim and onto the main body. Neaten up with a rib once the sections are sealed.

YOU WILL NEED

TOOLS

- Wooden modeling tool
- Plastic or metal kidney or rib
- Pin
- Suitable tool to impress an eye (an old pen top)

CLAY

White earthenware

- 8oz (225g) divided into small amounts for each part of the egg cup

DESIGN NOTE

Why not make a selection of bird egg cups to create a set with the chicken on page 92? Garden birds, such as the blackbird or robin, would also work well because of their coloring; the principles for making are the same.

DECORATION

Much like the previous egg cup, this one can be decorated with slip or underglaze colors before bisque firing, then a transparent glaze applied after. Alternatively, low-fire glazes will achieve a similar effect after bisque firing. See page 165 for the method and pages 156–172 for other options for surface decoration.

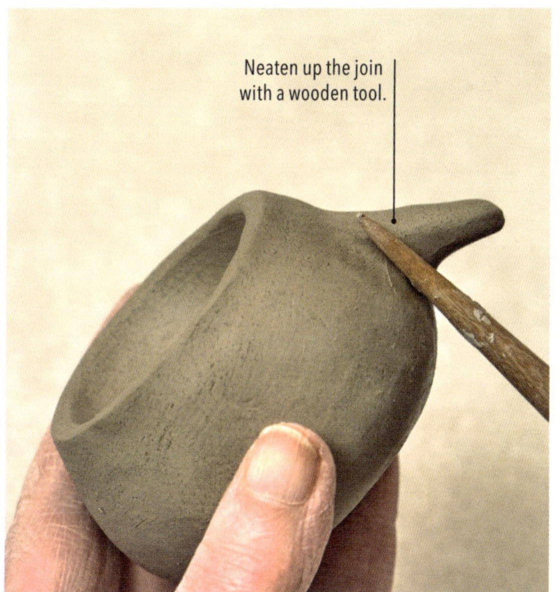

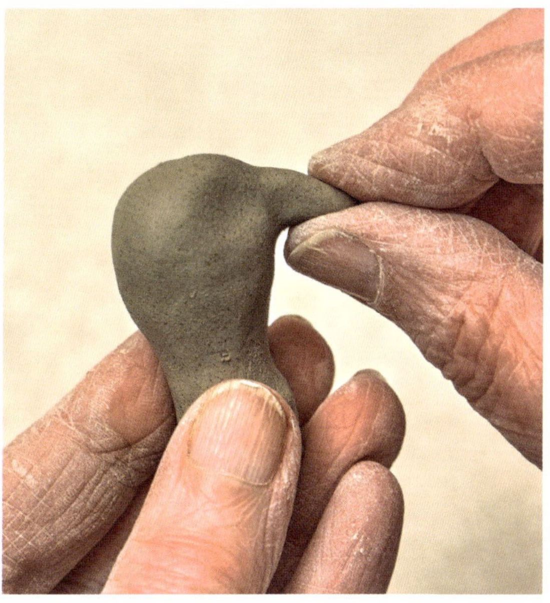

3 Pinch a small amount of clay into a cone shape to form the tail. Slip and score to fix the tail in place halfway down one side of the cup, positioned so that the tip sits just above the work surface in a downward direction.

4 Model a short length of clay into a slightly bulbous head with downward-curving beak, thin neck, and single wattle on the neck.

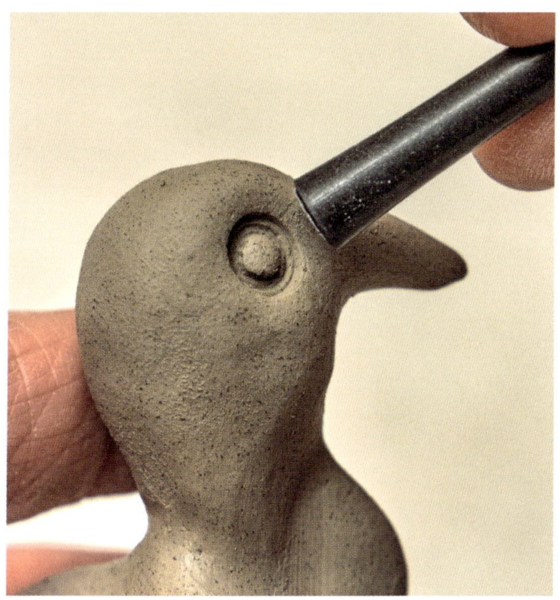

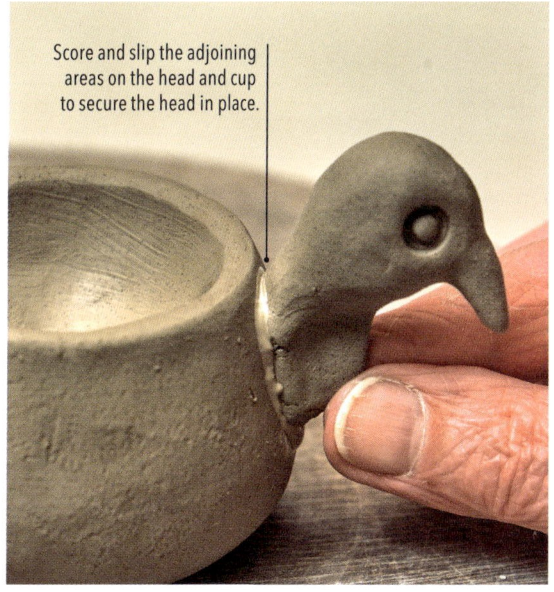

5 Carefully impress the eyes, either side of the head, using a suitable tool, such as the end of a pen top.

6 Fix the head onto the side of the egg cup opposite the tail, after scoring and slipping the relevant positions. Blend the join between the neck and the body neatly with a wooden tool.

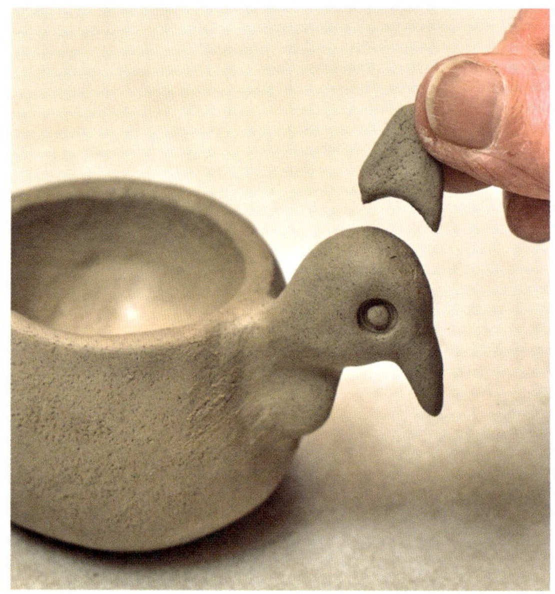

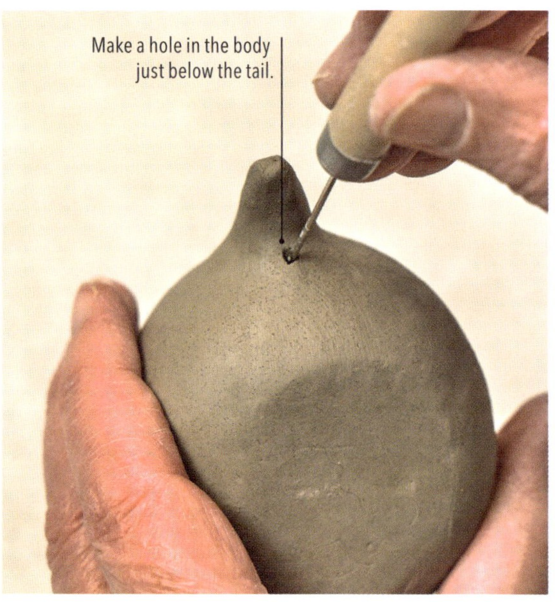

7 Now pinch a small amount of clay into a triangular shaped comb for the top of the head. Fix the comb in place with a dab of slip and reinforce the join with tiny coils of soft clay, blending in with a wooden tool.

8 Using a pin, make a hole in the body just below the tail to allow for the release of air in firing.

9 Add any final details, such as the nares, or nostrils, on the beak, or any feather patterns before the clay dries.

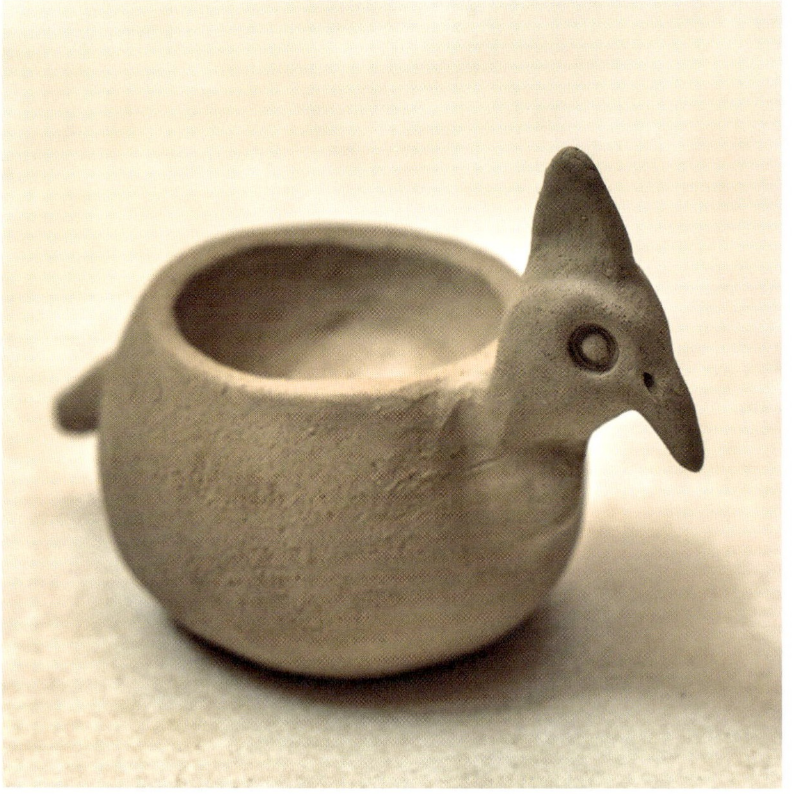

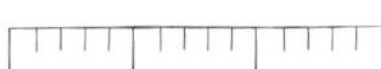

SPOON

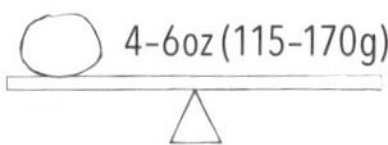

Length: from 4-5½in (10-14cm)

4-6oz (115-170g)

There are as many ways of making spoons as there are uses for them, so the method shown here demonstrates the process of making handy little scoops, which have a multitude of uses in the kitchen or at the table. The amount of clay required will depend on the preferred size of your spoon but the making process is the same.

YOU WILL NEED

TOOLS
- Surform or rasp blade
- Plastic or metal kidney or rib
- Suitable modeling tool to impress texture in clay
- Pin

CLAY
White stoneware
- 6½oz (180g) divided into three equal parts

DESIGN NOTE
The decorative detail of these spoons can be simply altered by impressing different marks in the handles. Similarly, the whole look of the spoons can be changed by using different colored clays and glazes.

DECORATION
The impressed marks in the spoon handles here are painted individually in different colors of glaze (see pages 104–105 for this method). Alternatively, you could use oxides or underglazes to highlight the detail in one color (see page 158 and pages 169–170, respectively).

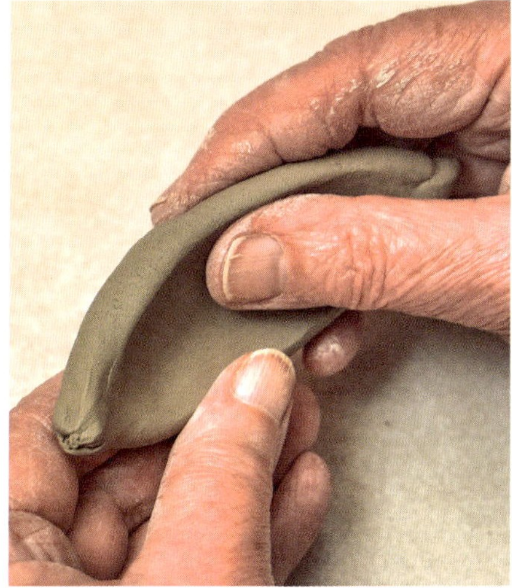

1 Form 2oz (60g) of clay into a rudimentary coil about 4in (10cm) long, then pinch it into a boat shape. Repeat to make a second, identical boat.

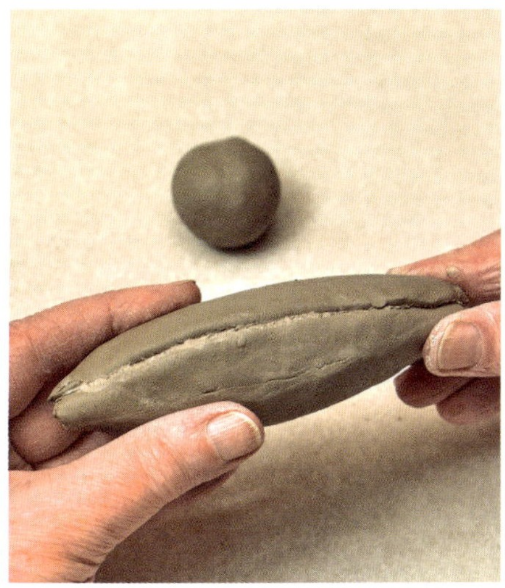

2 Score and slip the rims of the boats, then join them together to form a hollow pod shape. Work over the seams with a kidney or rib to neaten up.

Only the interior of the spoon is glazed to allow it to sit on the kiln shelf. The clay will vitrify at stoneware firing temperatures, making the spoon perfectly safe to use. The texture here is picked out in shades of celadon glaze on the handle to coordinate with the interior of the spoon.

Bisque fired to cone 04 (1,940°F/1,060°C)
Glaze fired to cone 6 (2,232°F/1,222°C)

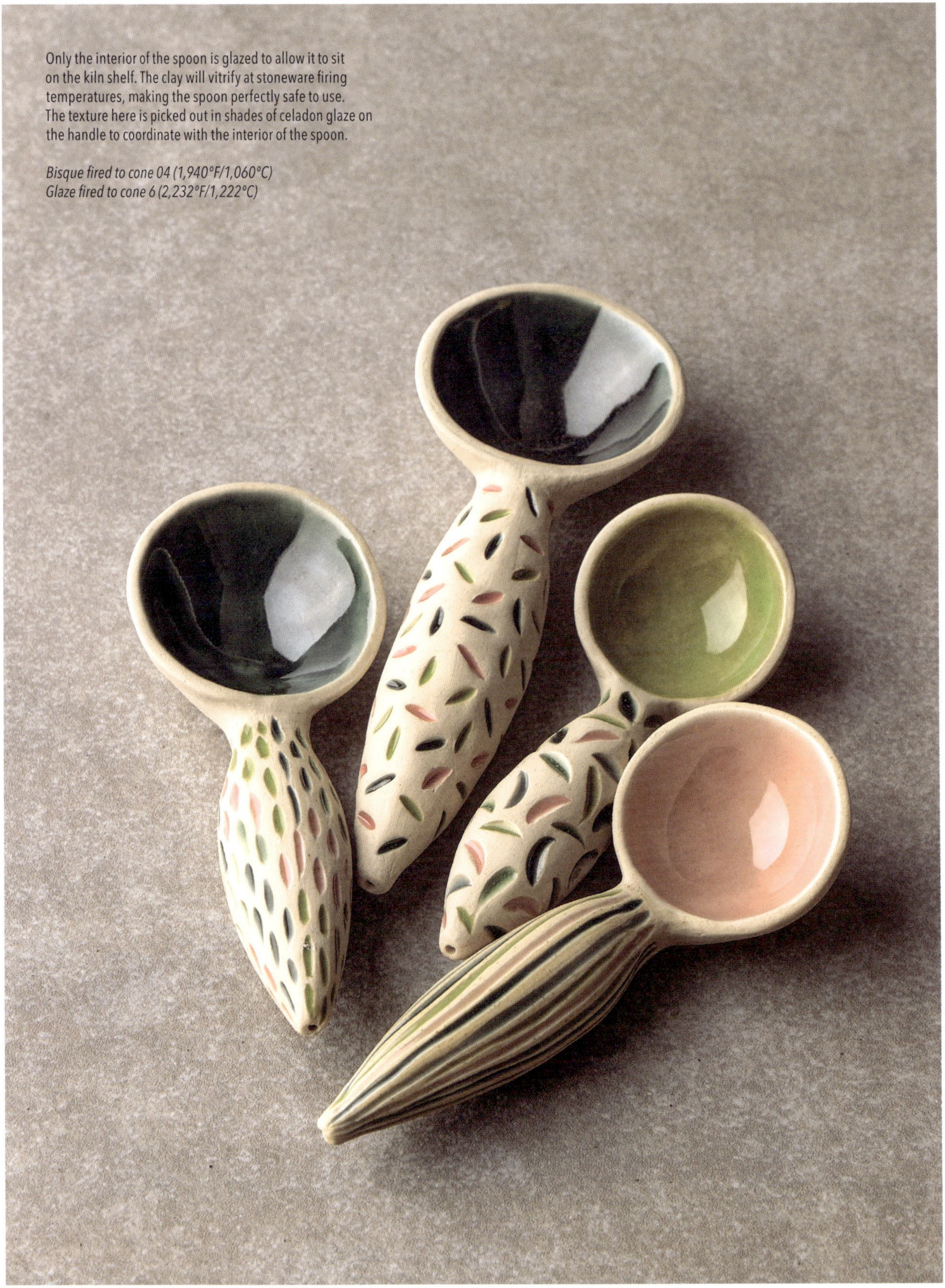

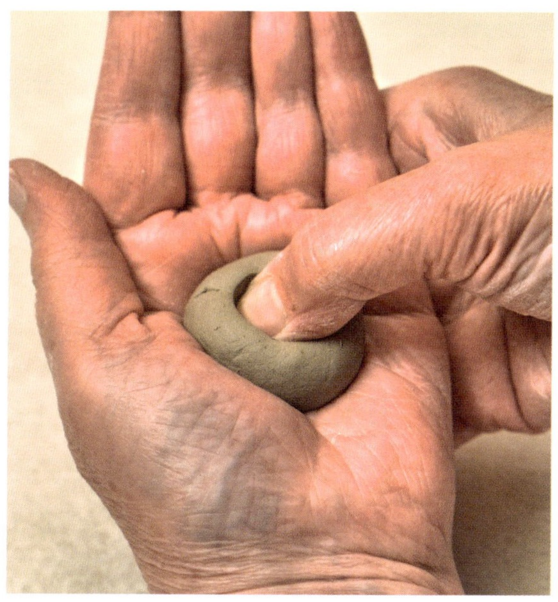

3 Pinch the remaining 2oz (60g) of clay into a perfectly round cup. This is a little tricky because it is a small amount of clay to work with, but pinch it out as finely as possible to maintain the shape.

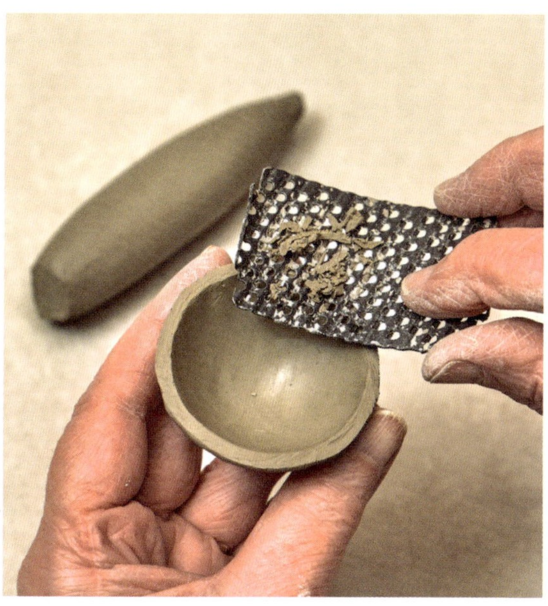

4 Surform the rim of the cup until level, then work over the area with a rib to neaten up.

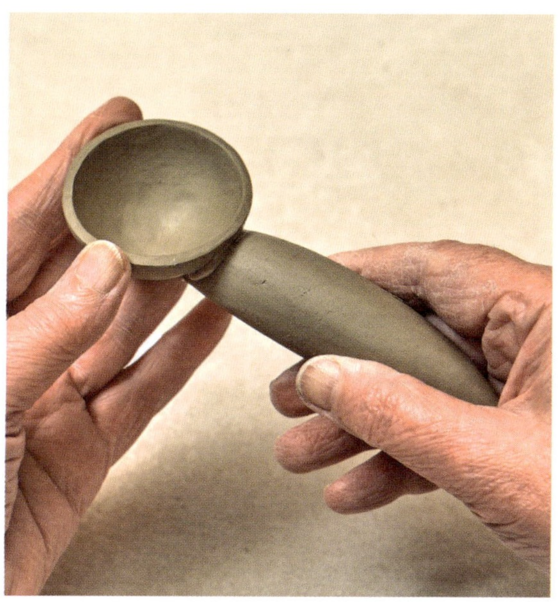

5 Cut one end of the handle at an angle that will allow the cup to sit against it comfortably, then score and slip the relevant areas and fix the two parts together.

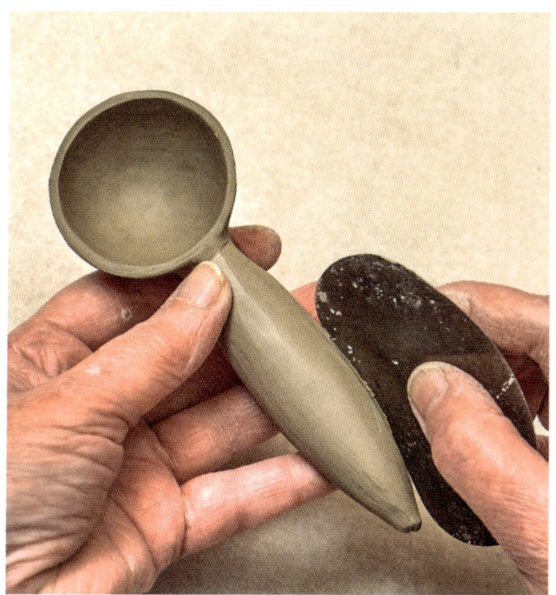

6 Reinforce the join of scoop to handle with a coil of soft clay, then blend it in until seamless. Finish up by working over the handle with a kidney to refine the surface and reduce the weight if it seems too heavy.

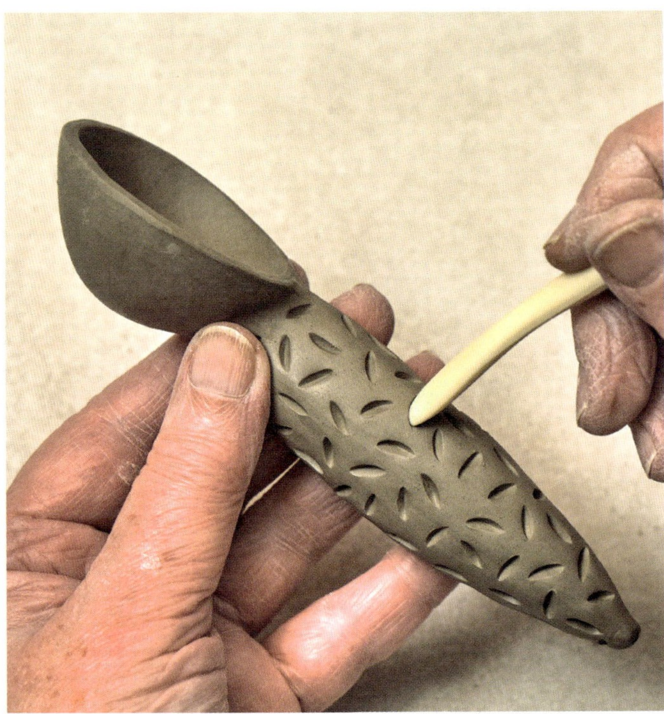

7 Using the end of a modeling tool, impress a textured pattern, similar to seeding used in embroidery, into the clay of the handle. Alternatively, score lines in the surface that are deep enough to hold glaze.

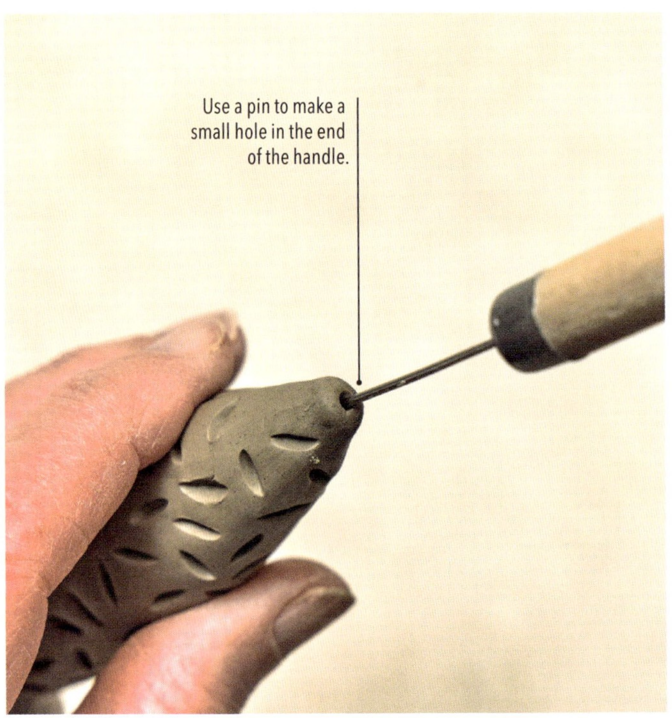

8 Make a small hole in the end of the handle to allow for the release of air in firing. This is an important detail to remember as, without the hole, the spoon could explode in the kiln.

DECORATING THE SPOON

This is a simple but effective way of decorating a textured surface where only the inside of the spoon and actual texture marks are glazed, thus allowing the spoon to be fired directly on the kiln shelf. The only requirement is patience and a steady hand.

YOU WILL NEED

- Bisque-fired spoon
- Glazes in your chosen colors
- Paintbrush
- Fine liner brush
- Dust mask
- Sanding block

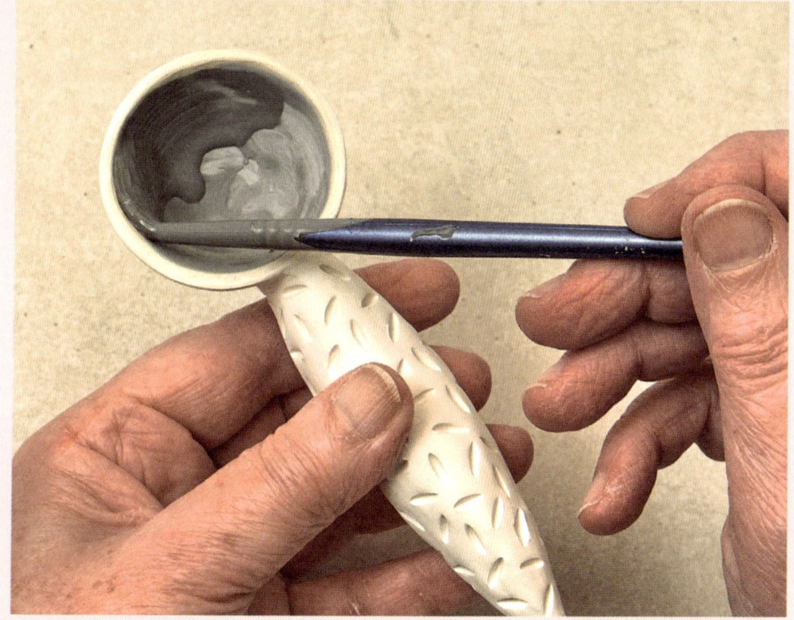

1 Paint your chosen color glaze in the well of the spoon only, working just up to the rim. Apply the glaze in two or three coats, allowing each to dry before applying the next.

2 Using the same glaze and a fine liner brush, paint in selected areas of the textured marks, making them as equally spaced apart as possible.

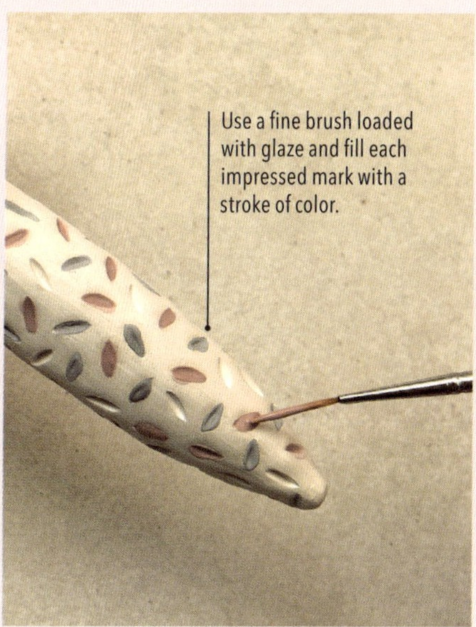

Use a fine brush loaded with glaze and fill each impressed mark with a stroke of color.

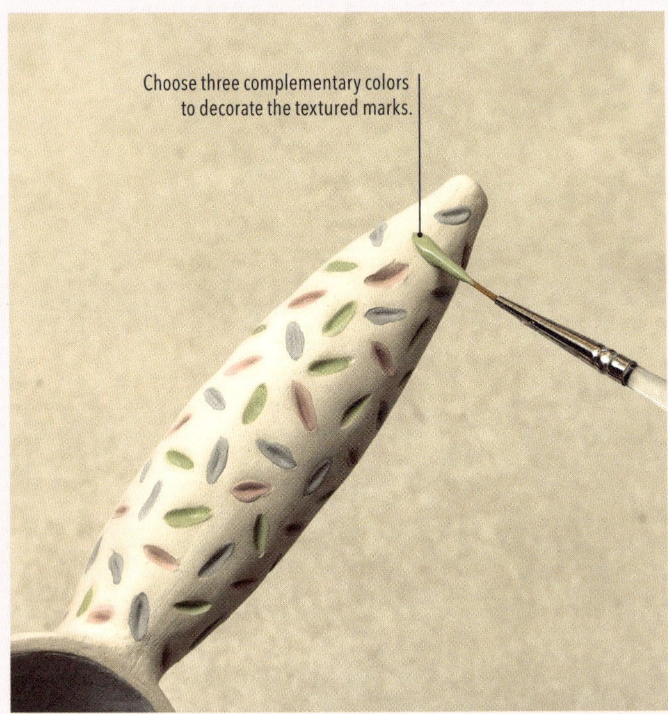

3 Fill in the rest of the texture with additional colored glazes that complement each other, again spacing them equally apart until all are filled. Allow the glaze to dry.

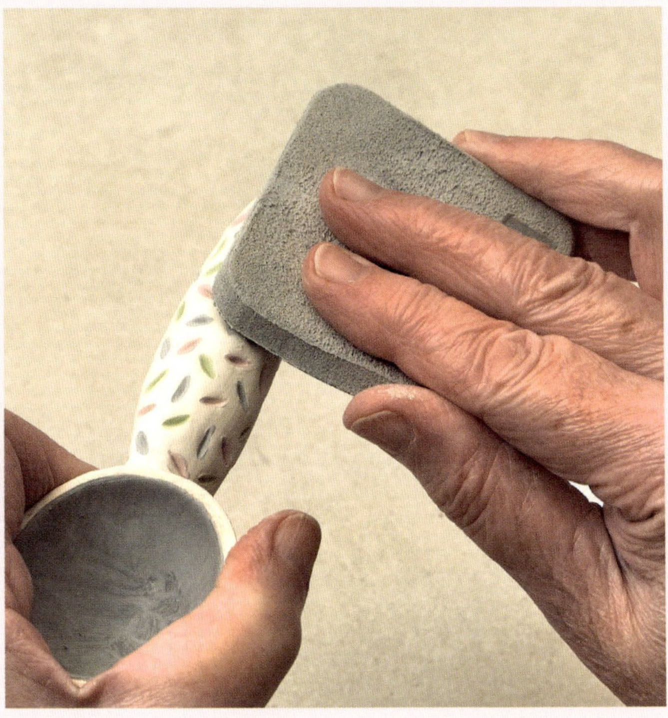

4 Wearing a dust mask, sand over the handle to level the glaze so that it remains only in the impressed marks. Brush away and dispose of the dust very carefully.

UTENSIL HANDLES

Width: 1½in (4cm)
Length: 4in (10cm)

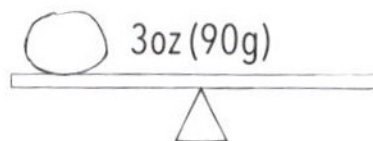

This is a great way of personalizing kitchen utensils like spoons, sieves, cake slices, and so on. Look out for utensils that can be easily separated from their original handles and set them into their new ones using epoxy resin. Or alternatively, look online for new utensil parts, as they are widely available.

YOU WILL NEED

TOOLS
- Knife
- 4–6in (10–15cm) length of ¼in (5mm) dowel
- Wooden spatula
- Metal or plastic kidney or rib
- Hole cutter

CLAY
Red earthenware
- 3oz (90g) per handle plus a small amount for the hilt Note: This weight can be adjusted to make smaller or larger handles.

DESIGN NOTE
Scale your drawn template up or down to make larger or smaller handles. You can buy utensil parts online or simply cut old ones with a saw to repurpose them.

DECORATION
These handles also look good when textured and then decorated in a glaze that pools in the texture marks. See pages 110–111 for an attractive decorating method and pages 156–172 for further ideas.

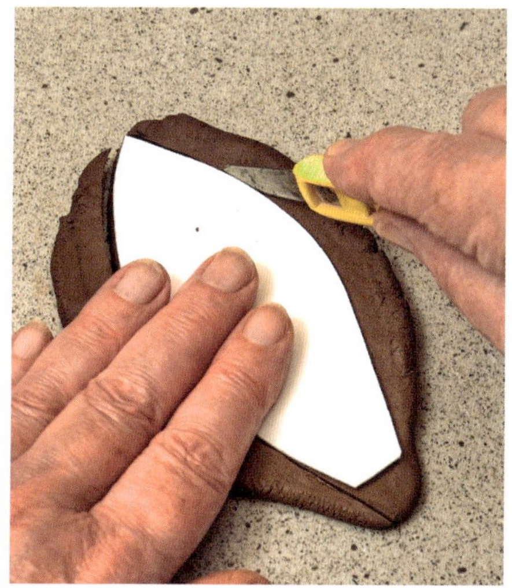

1 Cut out a template with your chosen shape. I have made mine in the shape of a leaf. Pinch 1½oz (45g) of clay to a roughly leaf-shaped slab, ¼in (5mm) thick. Place the template on the slab and cut out the shape. Repeat to produce a second leaf shape.

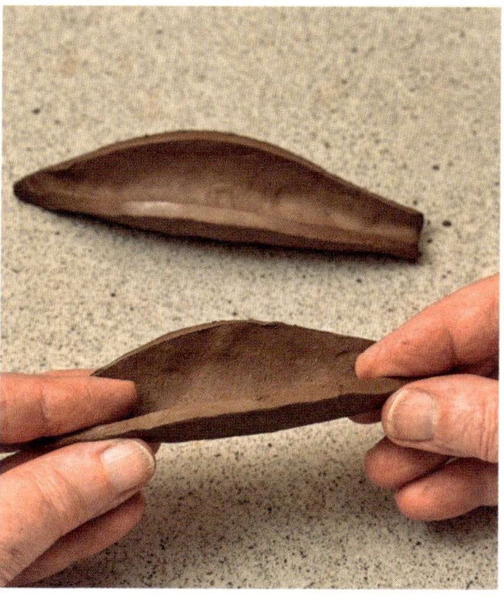

2 Curl the shapes into a boat form between your fingers and thumbs, then score and slip the edges ready to join.

The handle was fired on a star prop to elevate it from the kiln shelf. After firing, the utensil was cut to size using a hacksaw, then fixed into the handle with epoxy resin. This is a great way of repurposing old utensils rather than throwing them away.

Bisque fired to cone 04 (1,940°F/1,060°C)
Glaze fired to cone 05 (1,915°F/1,046°C)

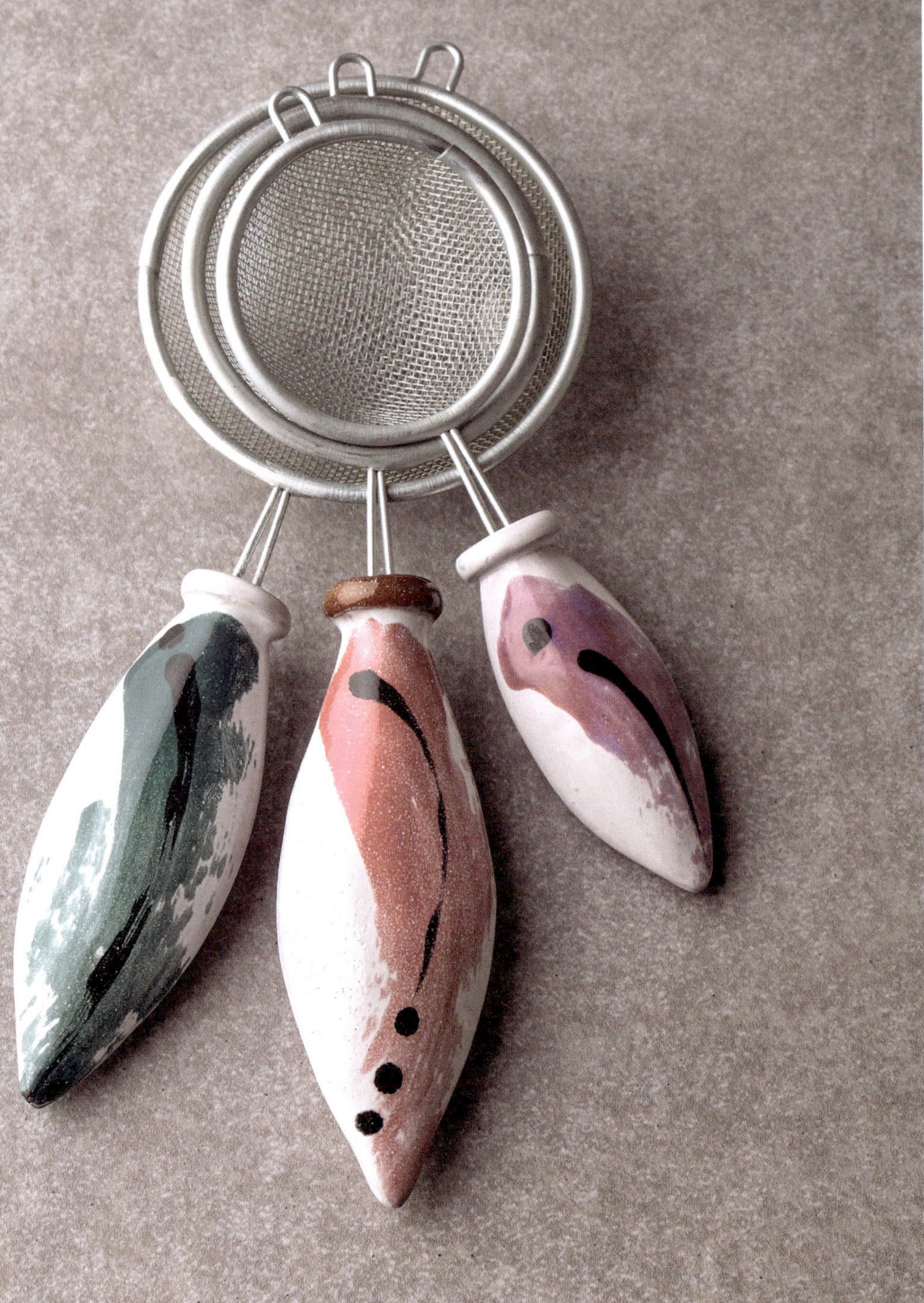

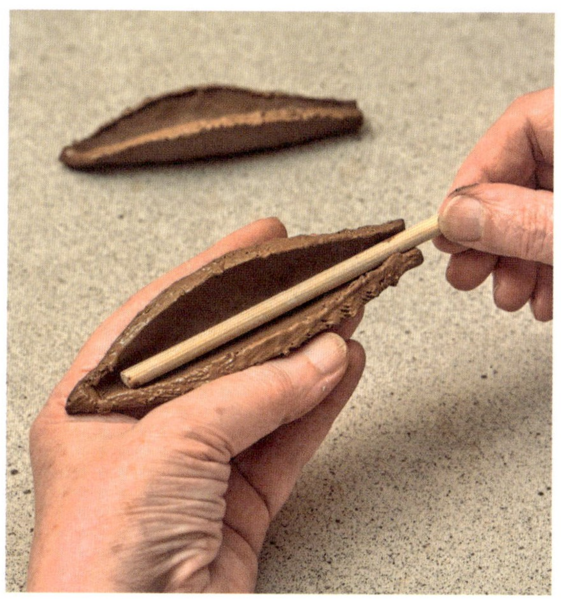

3 Lay the dowel along the length of one section, then join the two halves together with the dowel in situ. Pinch the edges together firmly to seal them.

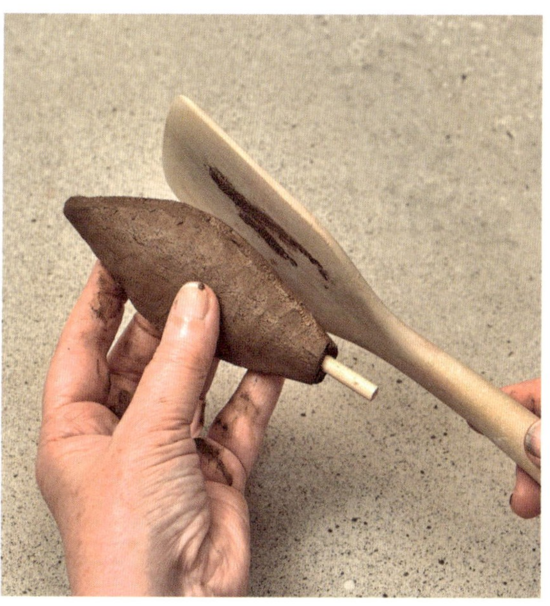

4 Paddle over the edges of the handle with the wooden spatula to ensure a good seal. This will also help to refine the shape.

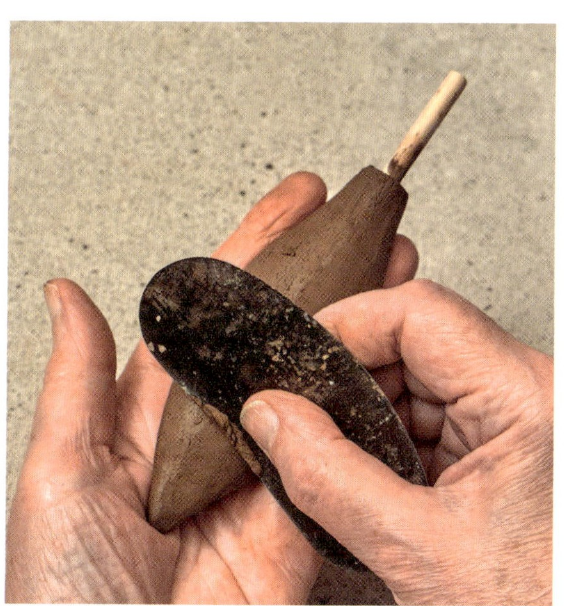

5 Neaten the surface of the handle with a kidney, removing clay in the process as required for a smooth and even finish.

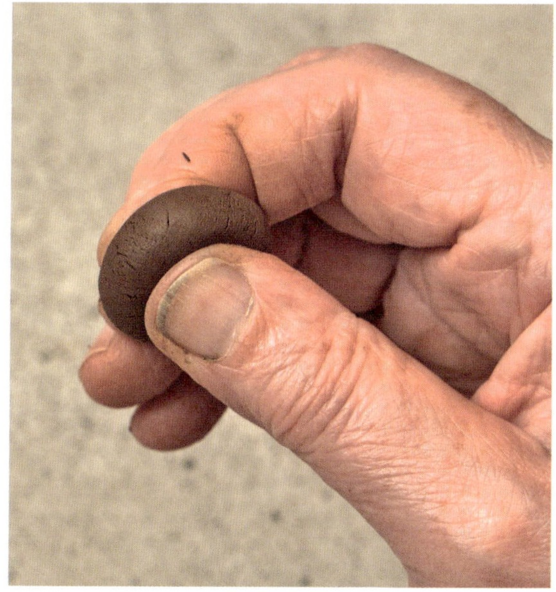

6 Roll a small amount of clay into a ball in the palm of your hand, then pinch it into a flattened disc about ¼in (5mm) thick.

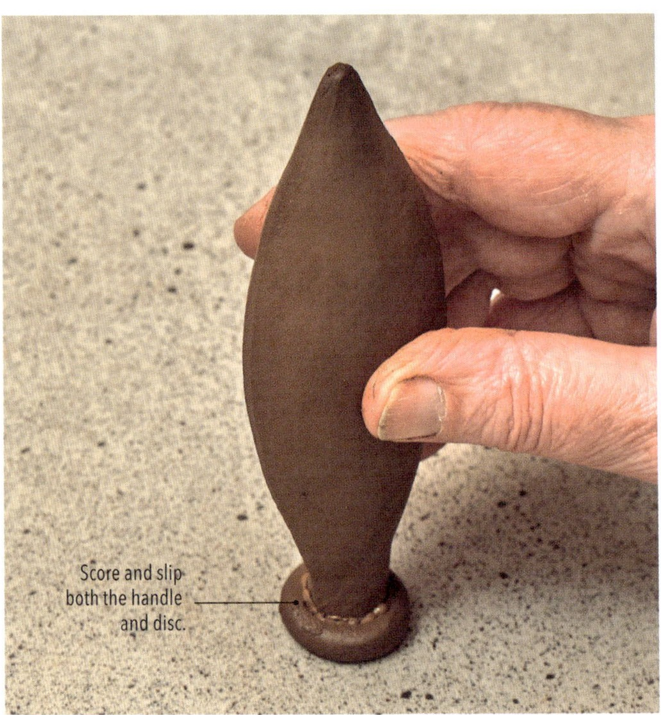

7 Remove the dowel from the handle and fix the disc onto the open end after first scoring and slipping adjoining surfaces. Reinforce around the join with a coil of soft clay, blending it in neatly.

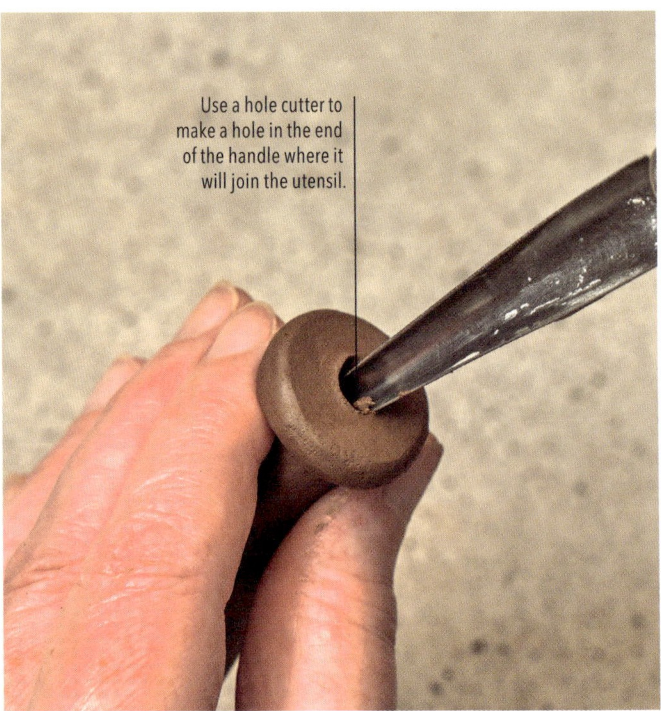

8 Make a hole through the hilt, into the cavity of the handle. It must be large enough to fit the diameter of the chosen utensil with a little wiggle room to allow for shrinkage in firing.

PAINTING WITH GLAZE

This is a simple but highly effective way of using glaze in a painterly way. Practice the technique on paper first until confident to work on the handle.

YOU WILL NEED

- Low-fire, brush-on glazes in white or a pale shade, plus 2 strongly contrasting colors
- Fan paintbrush
- Length of dowel
- Fine liner brush

FIRING DETAILS

- Bisque fired to cone 04 (1,940°F/1,060°C)
- Glaze fired to cone 05 (1,915°F/1,046°C)

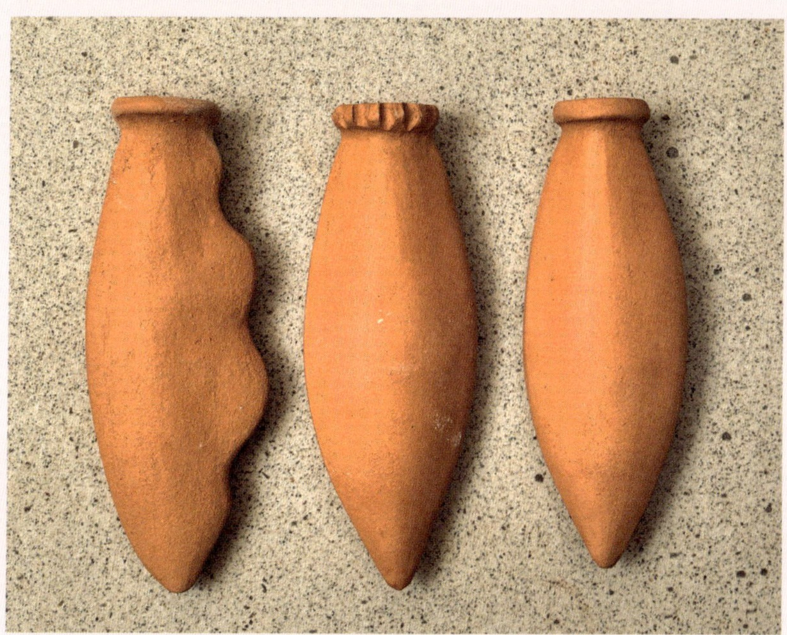

1 You can adapt the handle shape in many ways. Here, the base shape (right) has been altered with simple variations to add a shaped hand grip (left) and a ridged rim (center).

2 Cover the whole bisque-fired handle in two coats of the brush-on base glaze, allowing the first coat to dry before applying the second. Suspend the handle on a length of dowel as you work.

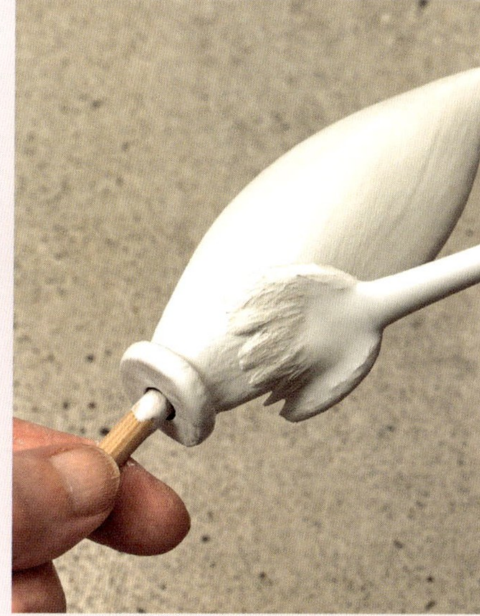

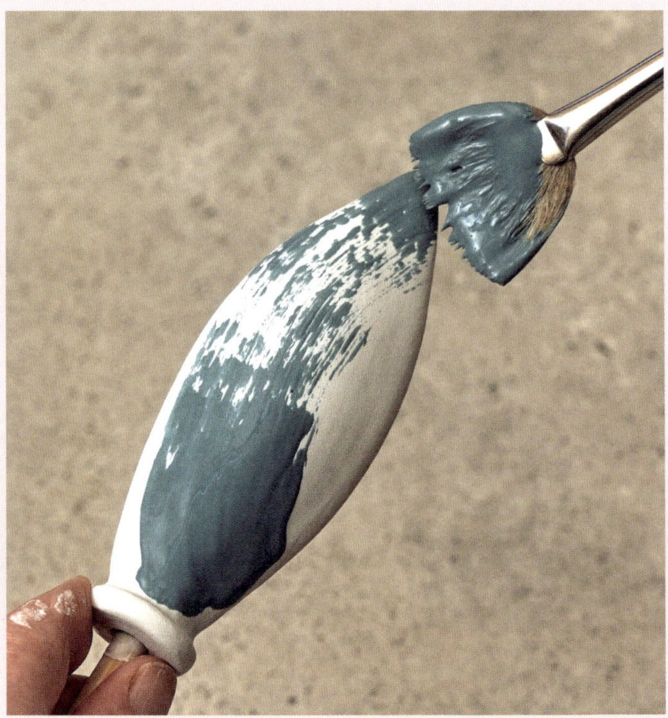

3 Load your fan brush with the first contrasting glaze, then, beginning just below the hilt, sweep the brush down the length of the handle in an arc. Don't worry that the color thins toward the end of the sweep—this is the desired effect.

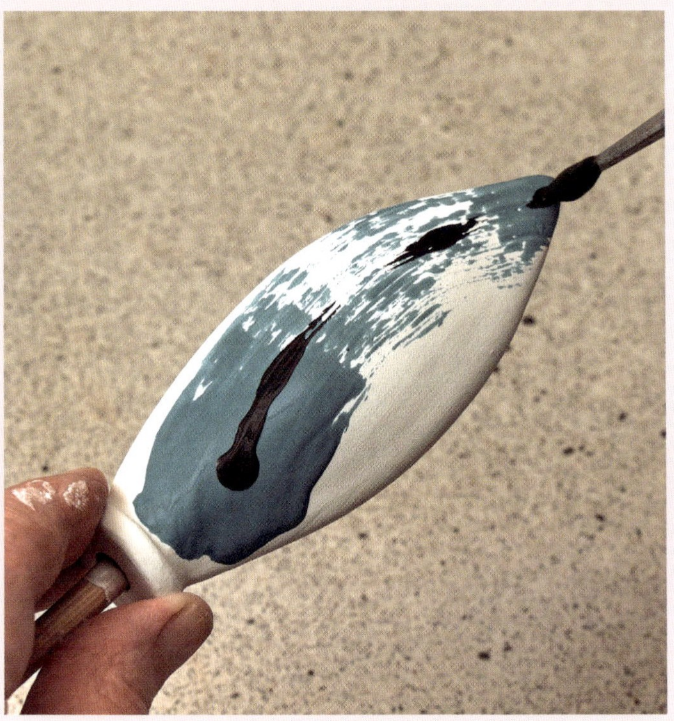

4 Complete the decoration with some line detail in a bold alternative color glaze applied with a thinner brush. Fire to the required temperature.

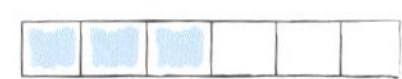

CYLINDER VASE

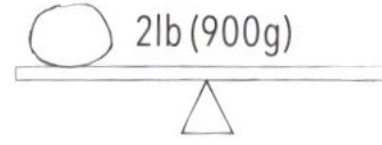

Width: 5½in (14cm)
Height: 8in (20cm)
Depth: 2¼in (6cm)

2lb (900g)

This vase demonstrates how a basic form can be adapted to create a stylish and individual vessel with simple, small adjustments and additional decorative elements.

If you prefer, you can make the vase square or triangular, or the ends of the oval can be squared to make a rectangle. There are many possible variations.

YOU WILL NEED

TOOLS
- Pin
- Metal palette
- Surform or rasp blade
- Wooden modeling tool
- Knife

CLAY
White stoneware
- 1½lb (680g) for main body
- ½lb (220g) for base and wings

DESIGN NOTE
The shape of the basic cylinder can be adapted to several other shapes if preferred. Try triangulating or squaring the shape. The oval can also be formed into a rectangle by squaring the ends.

DECORATION
Almost any surface decoration technique can be applied to this form—it is a blank canvas. For the decoration shown here, see pages 116–117. See pages 156–172 for other ideas.

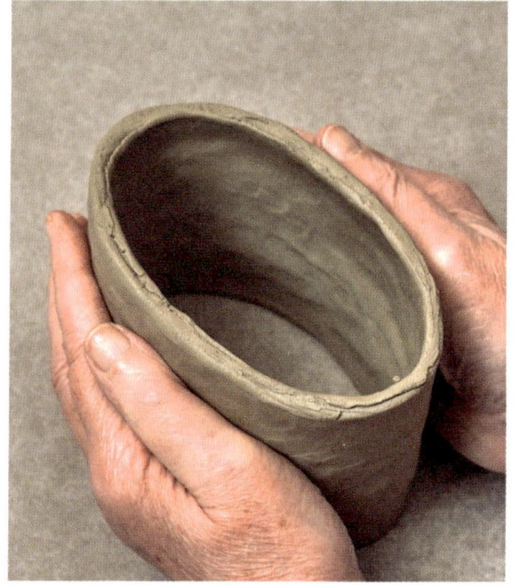

1 Pinch 1lb (450g) of clay to an open cylinder, approximately 4¾in (12cm) in diameter with an evenly thick wall all round. When ready, squeeze the cylinder into an oval between both hands.

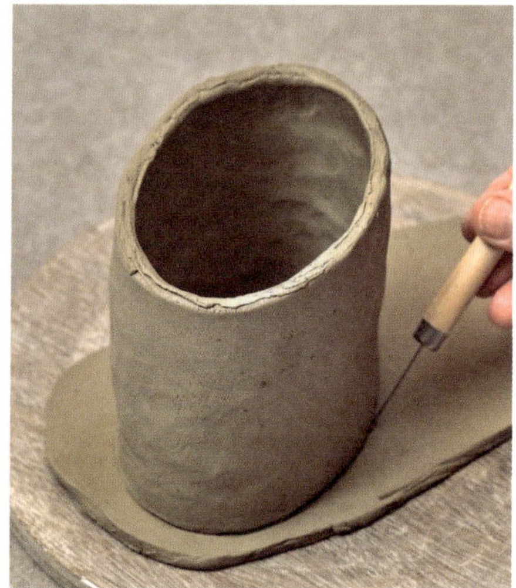

2 From approximately 6oz (170g) of clay, pinch a flat slab, large enough to fit the oval body. Place the body on the slab and score the position with a pin. Remove the body and cut out the base.

The surface of this vessel incorporates underglaze pencil decoration with matte-colored glaze and shiny transparent glaze. The different areas are separated by tape resist for the purposes of application.

Bisque fired to cone 04 (1,940°F/1,060°C)
Glaze fired to cone 6 (2,232°F/1,222°C)

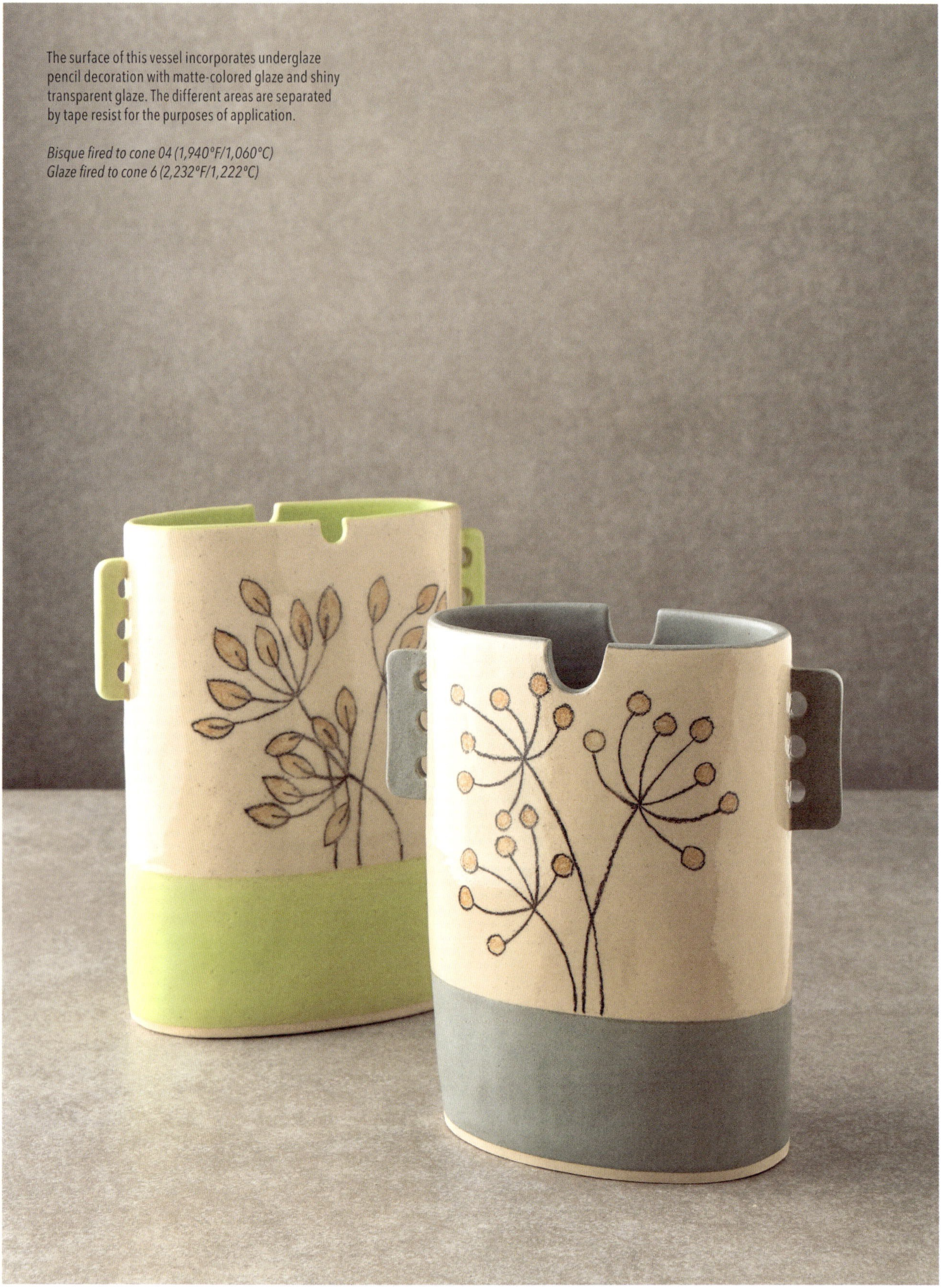

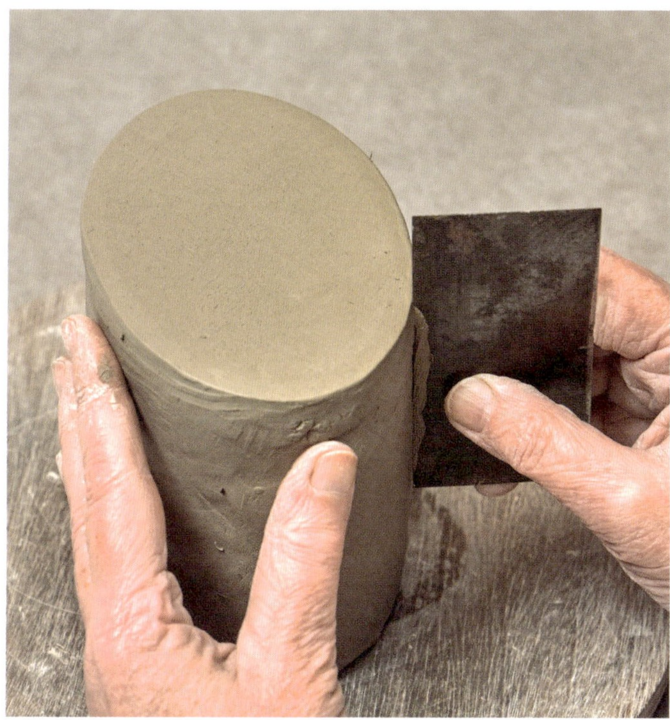

3 Score and slip around the edge of the base slab and corresponding rim of the base, then fix them together. Reinforce the join on the inside with a coil of soft clay. Turn the vase over and neaten the outer join with a metal palette.

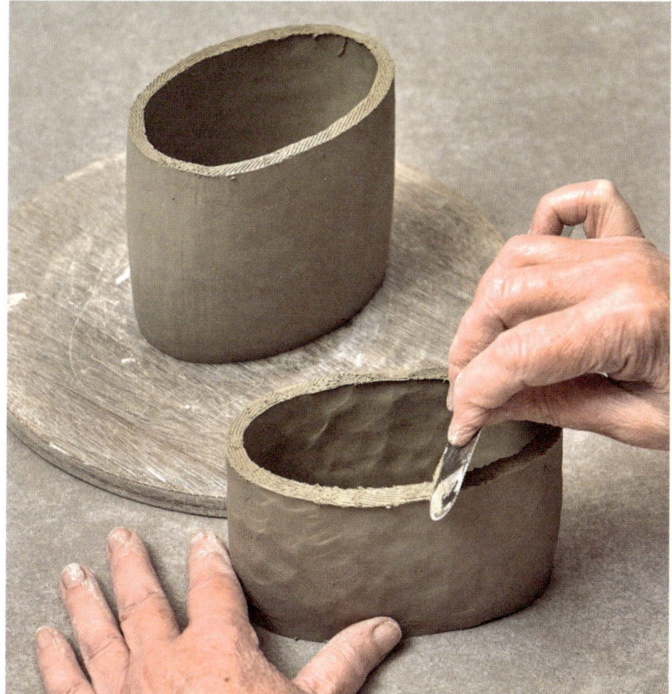

4 Level the top of the vase with the surform, then pinch a second, shorter open cylinder to the same dimensions, from ½lb (220g) of clay. Score the rim of the base and adjoining rim of the extension.

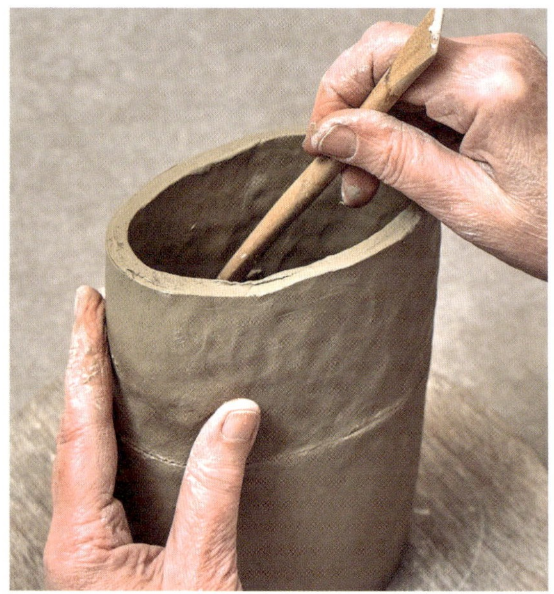

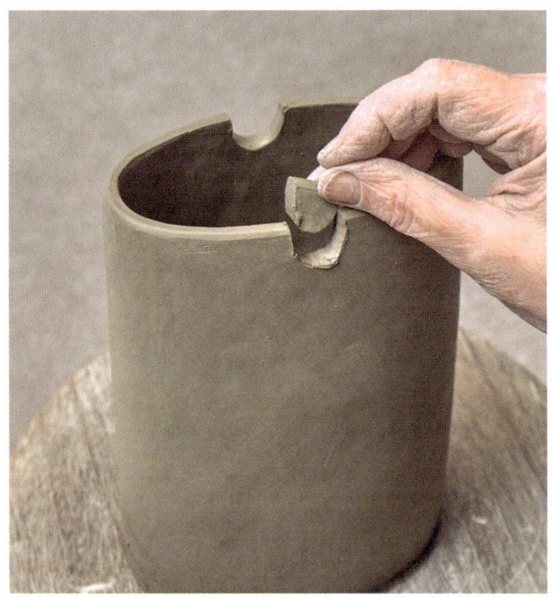

5 Slip the scored rims, then join the two sections together. Reinforce the join on the inside with a coil of soft clay, blending it in well with a wooden tool, then repeat on the exterior. Work over the entire surface with a palette to neaten up.

6 Cut a small semicircle from the center of the rim, on opposite sides of the vase. Neaten around the cut-out areas and the rest of the rim with a wooden tool or rib, until level and gently rounded.

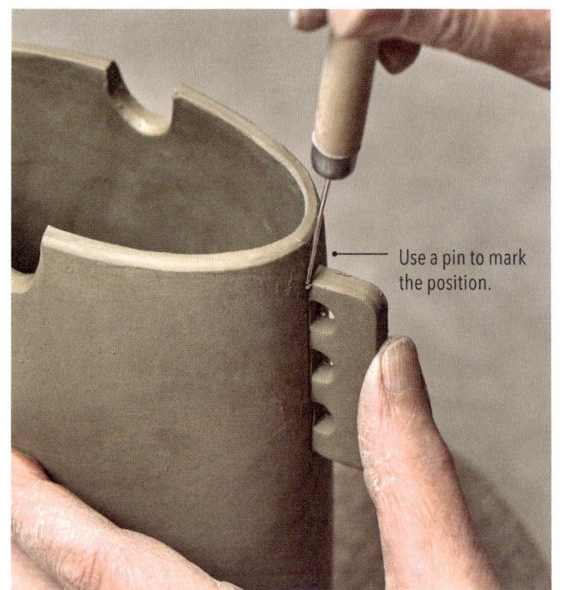

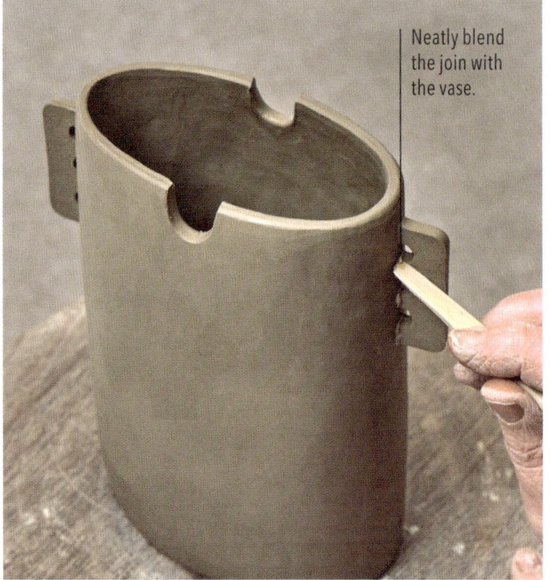

7 Pinch the remaining clay into a flat slab, then cut out two small, matching wings to fit the side of the vase—the wings can be any shape you like. Mark the position for the wings on opposite sides of the vase just below the rim, using a pin.

8 Fix the wings in place after scoring and slipping the marked positions and adjoining edges of the wings themselves. Neaten around the joins with a wooden tool to finish.

DECORATING USING UNDERGLAZE PENCILS

The surface decoration for this cylinder combines underglaze pencil drawing with glaze. Care will need to be taken with the pencils because they can easily smudge, but they offer wonderful potential for those who enjoy drawing and have sought a medium that will allow them to transpose their imagery to clay.

YOU WILL NEED

- Thin adhesive paper tape
- Colored glaze
- Transparent glaze
- Tracing paper
- Soft pencil
- Mop brush for glaze application
- Underglaze pencils in colors of choice

BEFORE YOU BEGIN

- Measure the space available on each side of the pot for your pencil design and cut a piece of tracing paper to the appropriate size.
- Draw your design onto the paper in soft pencil to allow the image to be transferred to the pot.

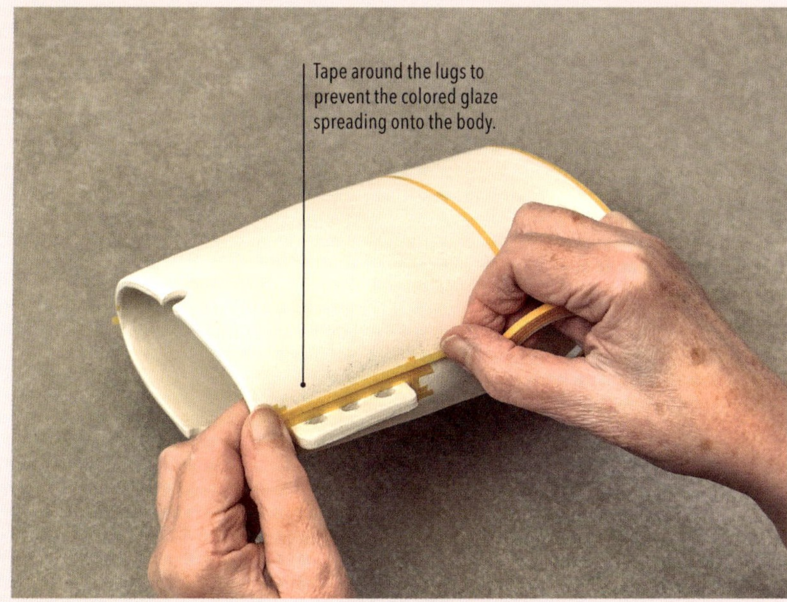

Tape around the lugs to prevent the colored glaze spreading onto the body.

1 Fix a length of tape along the lower edge of the pot as a line to glaze up to, then add another line a third of the way up from the base. Measure the distance first to ensure a level line. Add tape around the side lugs.

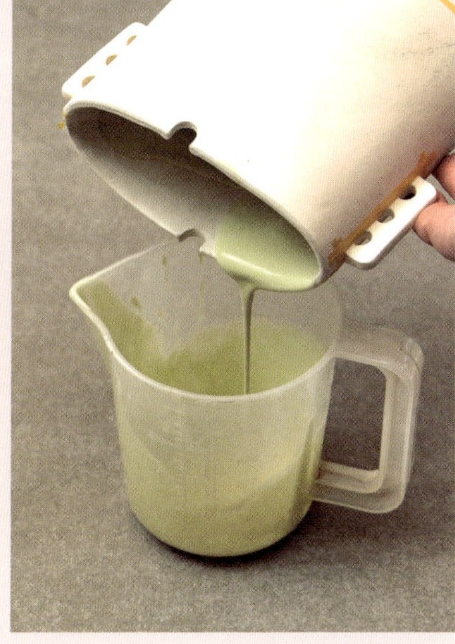

2 Prepare your chosen glaze and pour enough into the interior of the pot to allow the surface to be covered in one application. For even coverage, rotate the pot as you pour the glaze out, trying to avoid it spilling onto the exterior wall. Wipe the glaze away with a sponge if it does go over the rim.

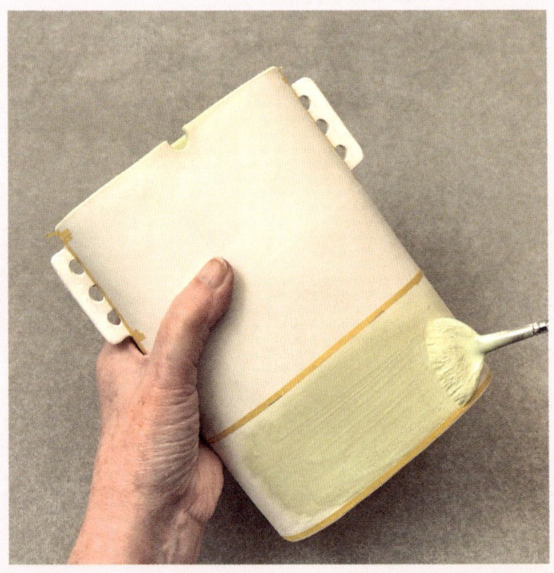

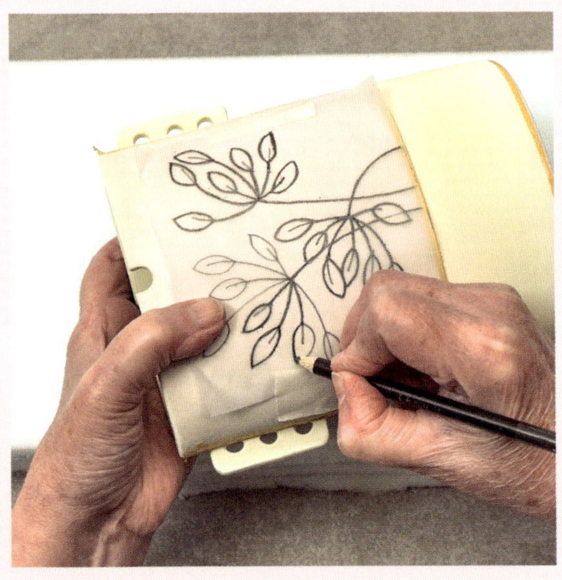

3 Paint in the lugs carefully in the same color glaze, making sure you do not go over the tape lines. Paint in the sectioned-off area at the lower end of the pot to complete the decoration with this glaze.

4 Fix your tracing paper, pencil side down, on the first side of the pot and secure it with paper tape at the sides to hold it in position. Transfer the design by firmly working over the lines with a pencil again. Repeat on the opposite side of the pot.

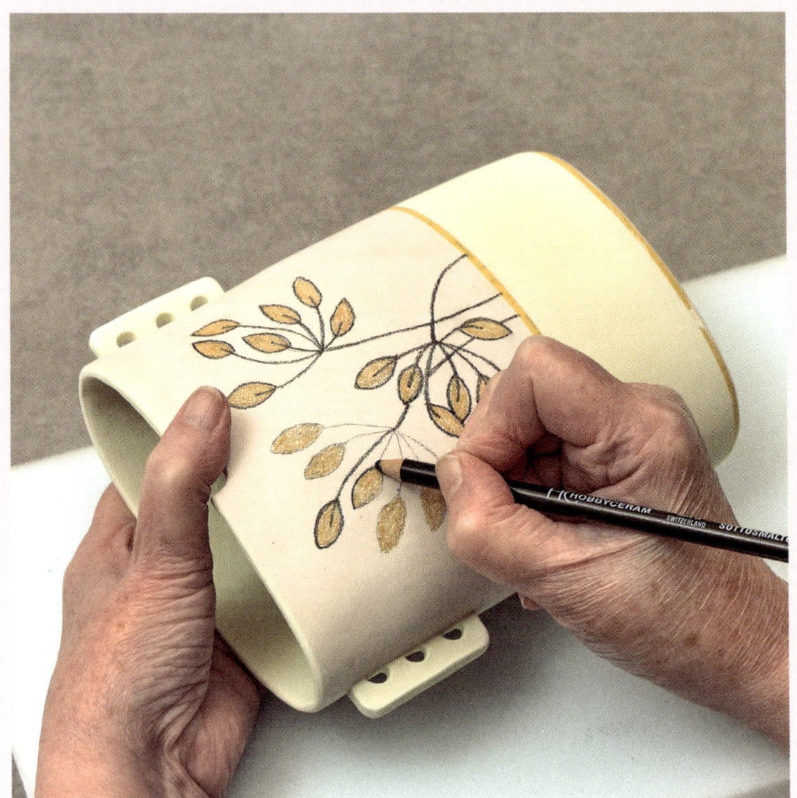

5 Fill in the feature detail of your design with underglaze pencil shades of choice, then outline the design in black or another bold shade. Apply transparent glaze over the pencil-decorated section of the pot when ready.

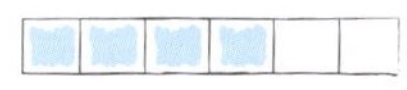

SECTIONAL VASE

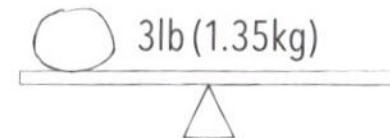

Height: 8in (20cm)
Diameter: 4½in (11cm)

3lb (1.35kg)

This project utilizes three basic techniques to create a composite form that demonstrates the versatility of the pinching method.

It is possible to build forms of great complexity using this approach, because sections can be attached to the sides to extend the form outward, in addition to upward.

YOU WILL NEED

TOOLS
- Wooden bat
- Pin
- Wooden spatula
- Foam block
- Small loop tool
- Banding wheel (turntable)
- Knife
- Surform or rasp blade
- Metal or plastic kidney or rib

CLAY
Buff stoneware
- 1lb (450g) for each composite part of the vase

DESIGN NOTE
Any shape can be attached to another providing the joining openings are the same size: flared extensions to straight sections; round forms to other round forms, and so on.

DECORATION
Almost any decoration method can be applied to the surface of this vase; see pages 156–172 for other decorating options.

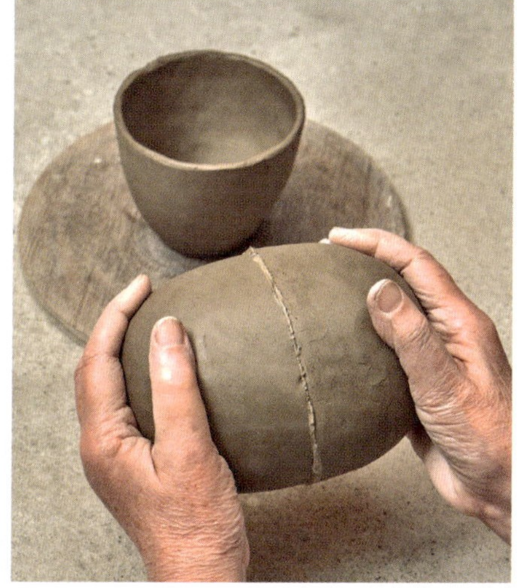

1 Make a joined pinch form from two 1lb (450g) weights of clay. Pinch a third open-ended conical bowl shape from the remaining 1lb (450g) of clay.

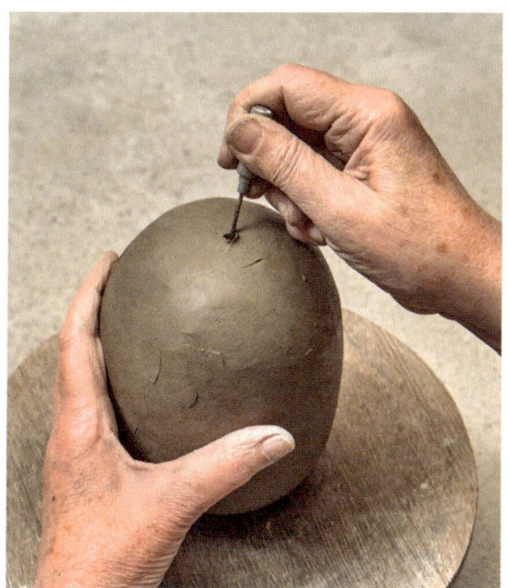

2 Sit the joined form on a wooden bat to establish a flat base, then pierce the clay with a pin to allow the shape to be manipulated.

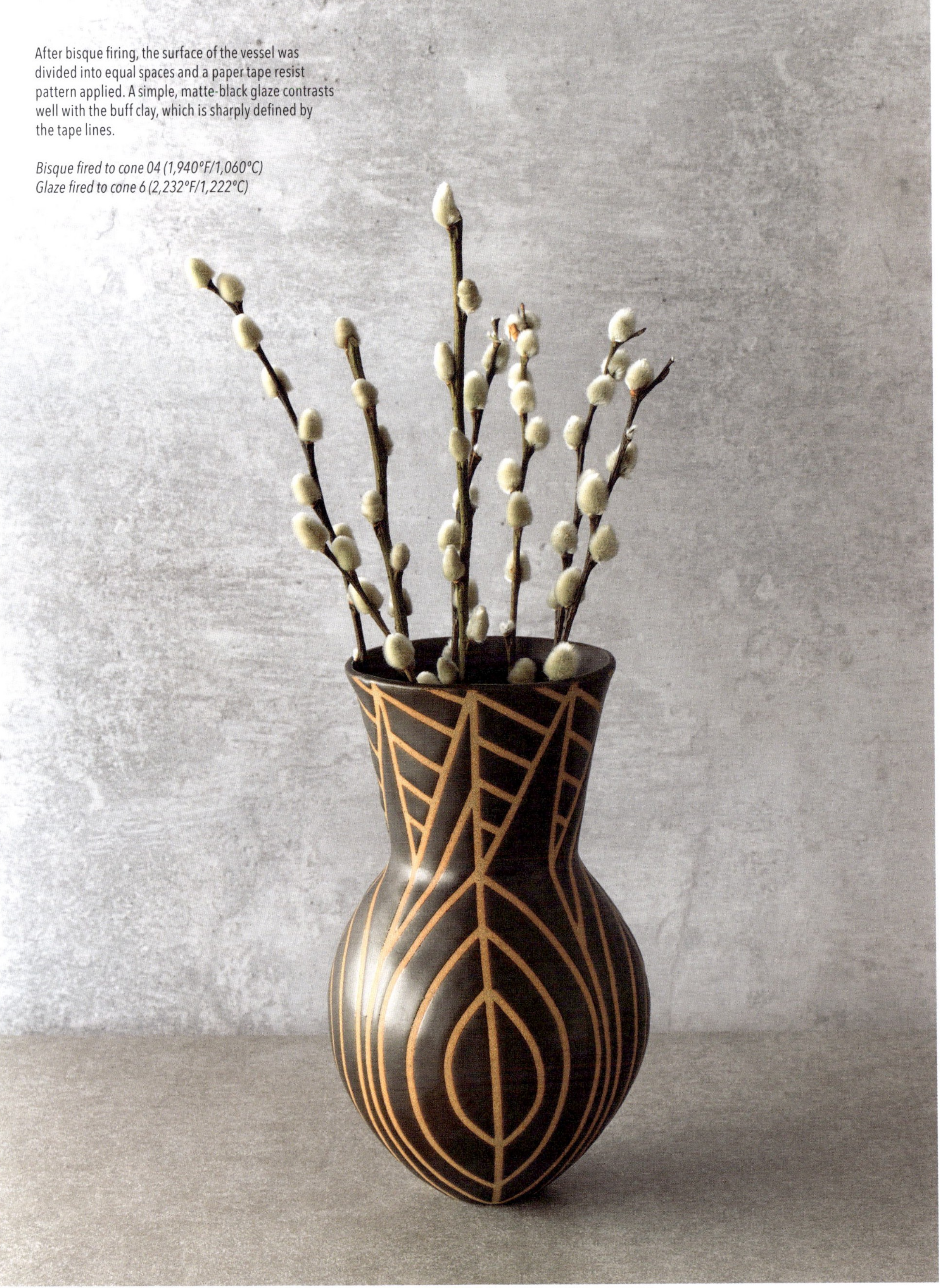

After bisque firing, the surface of the vessel was divided into equal spaces and a paper tape resist pattern applied. A simple, matte-black glaze contrasts well with the buff clay, which is sharply defined by the tape lines.

Bisque fired to cone 04 (1,940°F/1,060°C)
Glaze fired to cone 6 (2,232°F/1,222°C)

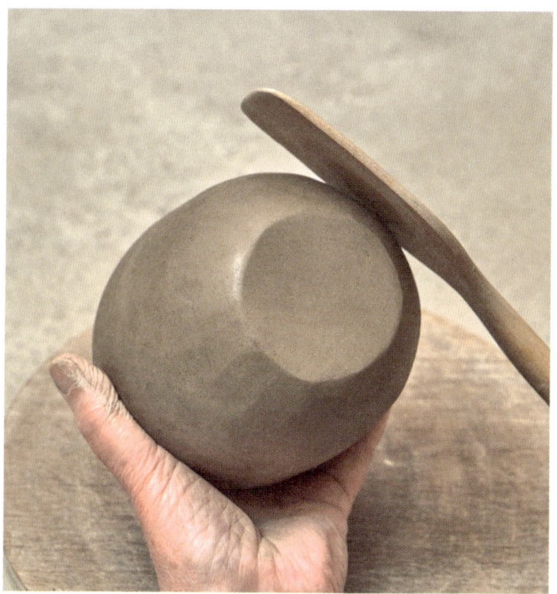

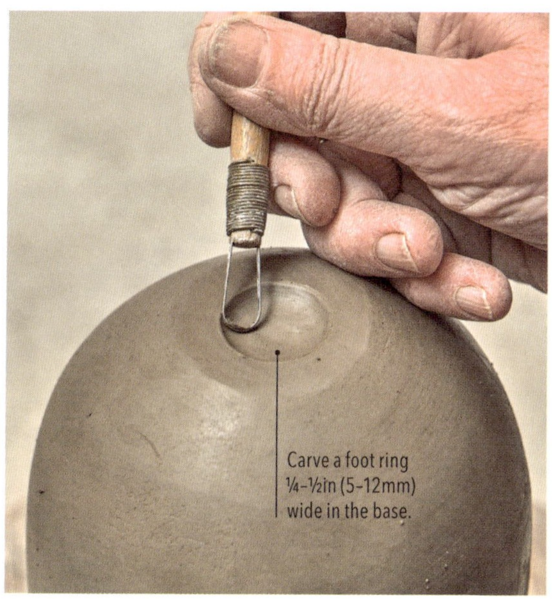

3 Turn the form over and paddle around the flat base to develop the body to a pleasing shape and the base to a balanced size. Plug the hole back up when finished to prevent the shape distorting further as you work on it.

4 Support the shape on a foam block with a hole cut out of the middle. Still working on the base, create a foot ring by carving out a hollow at the center using a small loop tool. The ring should measure ¼–½in (5–12mm) wide.

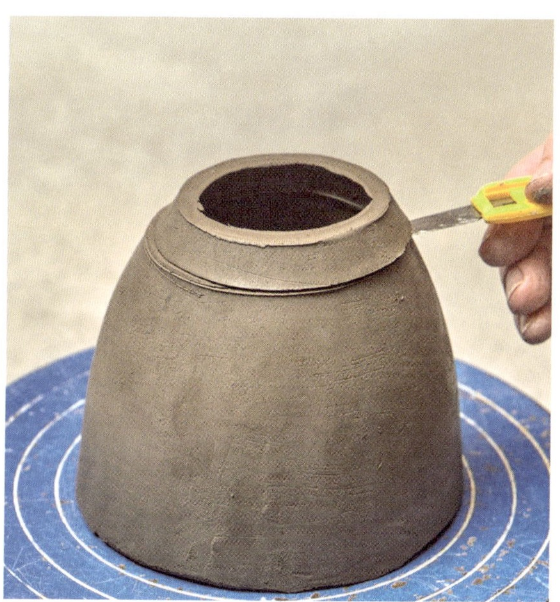

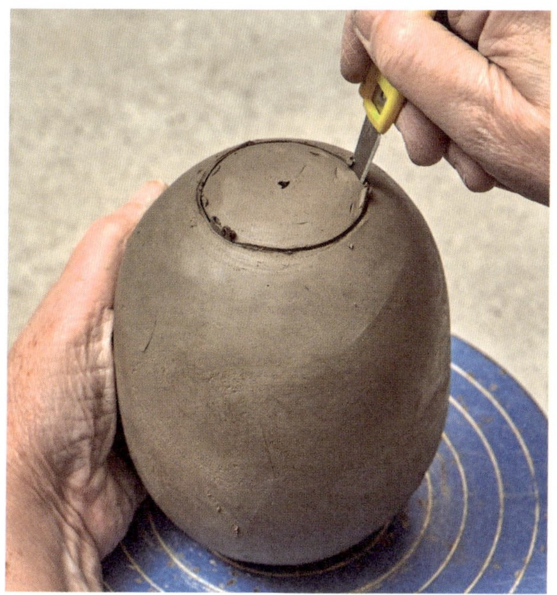

5 Center the extension section upside down on a banding wheel. Holding a knife rigid in one hand as you move the wheel with the other, carefully cut the section down to a size that balances in proportion with the base section.

6 Sit the extension on top of the base and mark the position with a pin. Carefully cut out the opening for the extension. Neaten the interior of the base with a wooden tool as far as is possible before adding the extension.

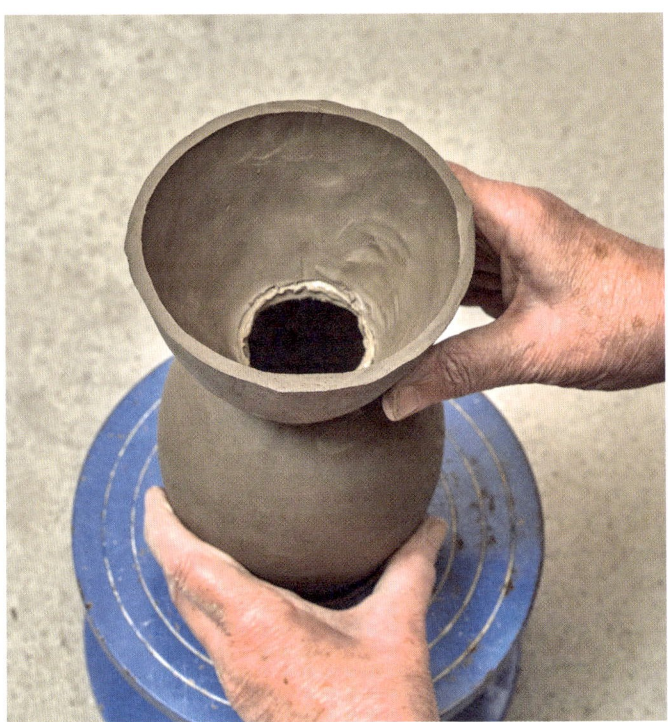

7 Score and slip the rim of the base and corresponding rim of the extension, then join the parts together. Reinforce the join on the outside with a coil of soft clay and neaten around the join on the interior with a wooden tool.

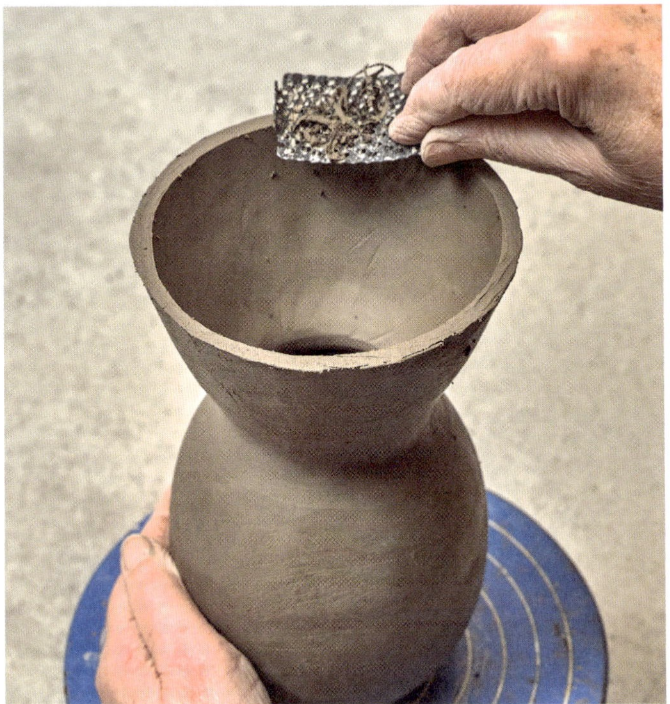

8 Surform the rim of the vase to establish a level, then work over it with a rib to neaten up and gently round off the edges.

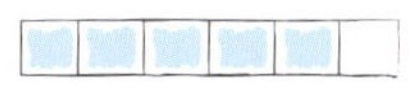

FLOWER VASE

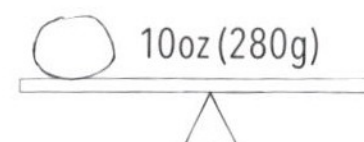

Width: 3in (8cm)
Height: 3in (8cm)

10oz (280g)

The challenge of this project lies in making the petals and then the construction of the flowers themselves. A delicate touch is required to execute the process well, but the key to success lies in practice and choosing the right clay.

YOU WILL NEED

TOOLS
- Metal or plastic kidney or rib
- Wooden bat
- Small cookie cutter measuring 1in (2.5cm)
- Pin
- Surform or rasp blade
- Pointed, wooden modeling tool

CLAY
White stoneware
- 8oz (220g) for vase
- 2oz (60g) for petals

DESIGN NOTE
The vase can be altered significantly by arranging the flowers in different ways on the surface—a shower down one side, for example, or covering the entire form.

DECORATION
Choose glazes like celadons that pick up the delicate quality of the form; work in two or more colors if possible but a single pale shade looks just as lovely. See pages 156–172 for other decorating options.

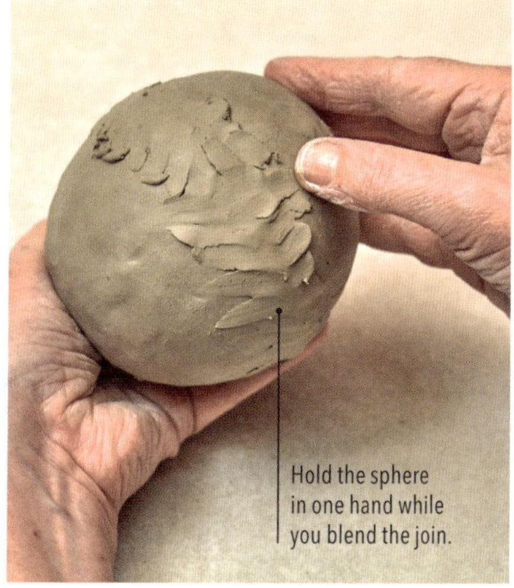

Hold the sphere in one hand while you blend the join.

1 From two 4oz (110g) balls of clay, pinch two identical open bowl shapes, then join them together to form a sphere. Reinforce the join with a coil of soft clay and blend it in with your fingers first.

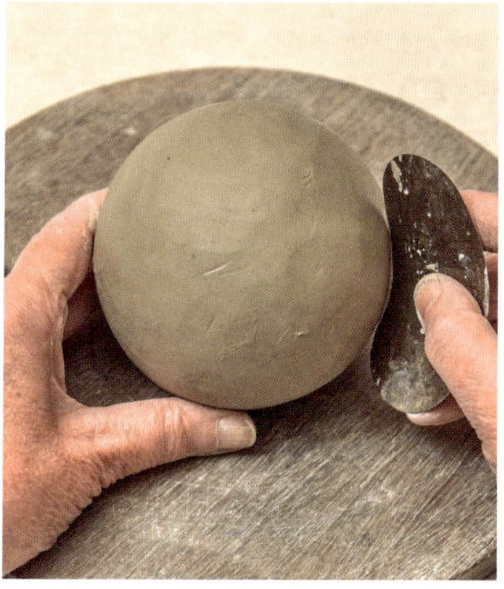

2 Work over the sphere with a kidney, removing excess clay as required to create a perfectly smooth surface.

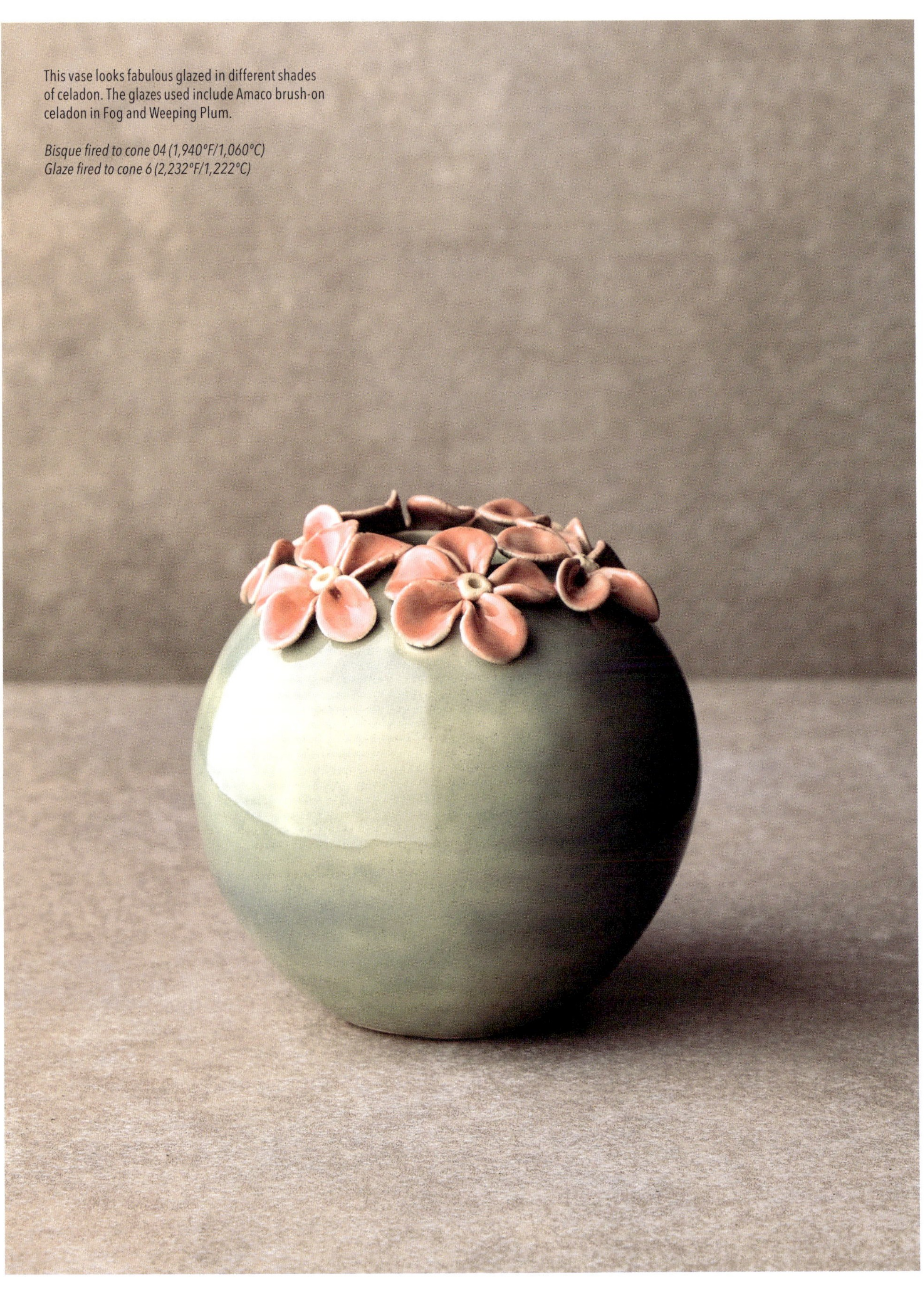

This vase looks fabulous glazed in different shades of celadon. The glazes used include Amaco brush-on celadon in Fog and Weeping Plum.

Bisque fired to cone 04 (1,940°F/1,060°C)
Glaze fired to cone 6 (2,232°F/1,222°C)

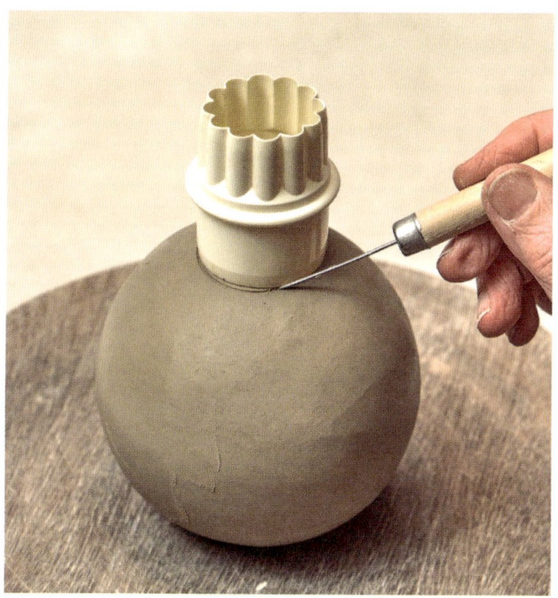

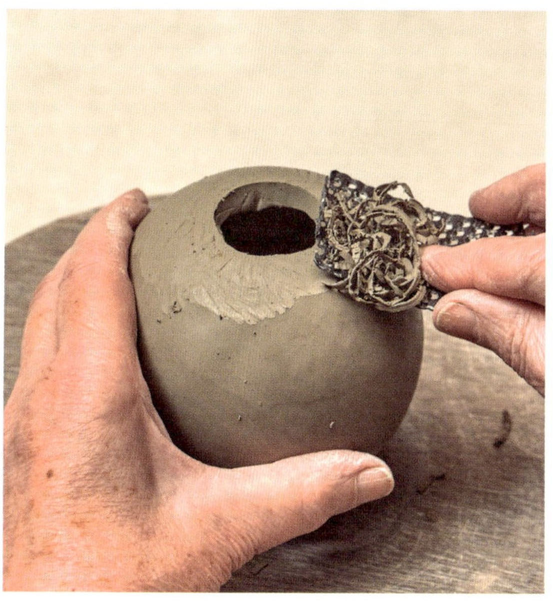

3 Sit the sphere on the bat and tap it down gently a couple of times to establish a small flat base. Place the cookie cutter centrally on top of the sphere and score around the circumference.

4 Cut the opening out carefully. If you feel the thickness of the clay wall is too bulky, reduce it by shaving the surface with a surform. Smooth over the surface again with a kidney when you are happy with the result.

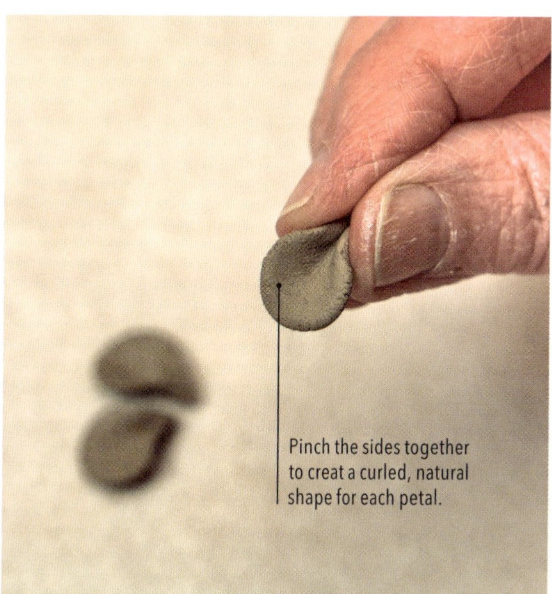

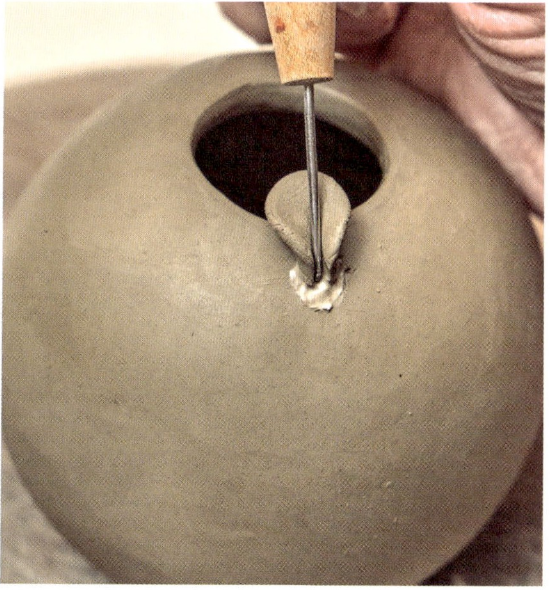

5 Form a series of five equally tiny amounts of clay into balls, then squeeze them between finger and thumb to make delicate petals. Pinch one end of the flattened shape together to create a realistic petal.

6 Fix the first petal onto the sphere with a dab of slip, using a pin to ease it into position and help it adhere to the surface. The petal should slightly overhang the rim for best effect.

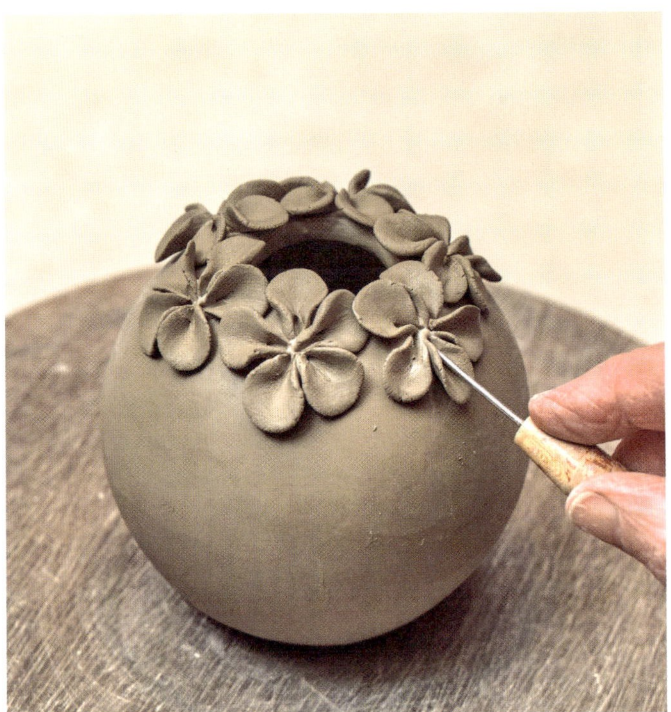

7 Continue to put the flowers together in groups of five petals, using the pin to secure each one in place. Measure the span of the first flower and divide the rim into sections to accommodate as many flowers as will fit the space neatly.

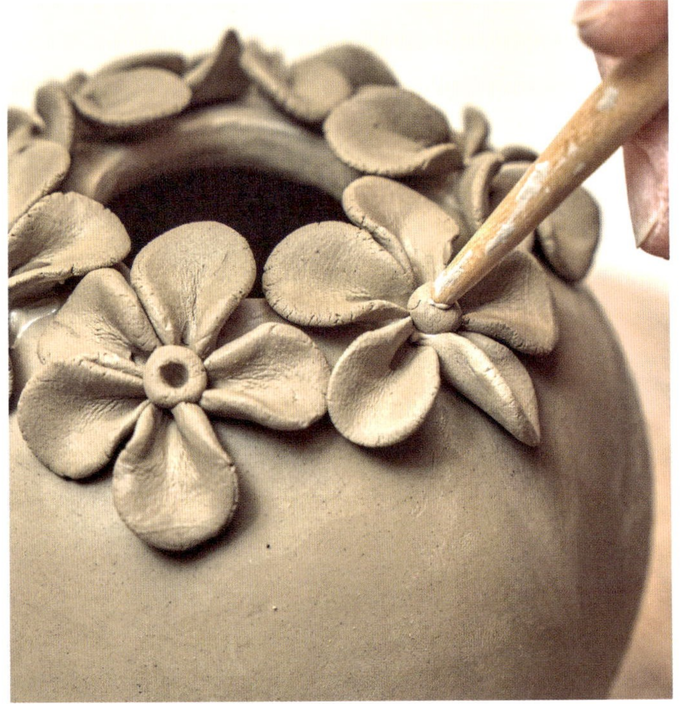

8 When all the flowers are in place, roll really tiny balls of clay and secure them at the center of each flower with a dab of slip. Impress the center of each one with a pointed tool to finish.

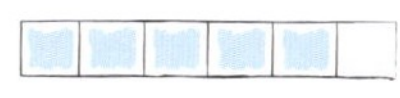

PORCELAIN TEA LIGHT

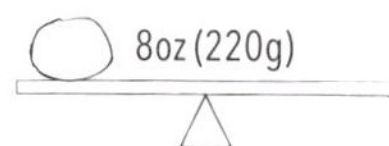

Width: 3in (8cm)
Height: 3in (8cm)

8oz (220g)

This is the most challenging of all the projects, not least because porcelain is a notoriously difficult clay to work with but also because the surface decoration requires a really delicate touch. The key to success is simply practice and patience, and not to be fearful of the technique. Once mastered, there is nothing to compare to porcelain for its beauty, plus it really makes glazes sing brightly so is worth experimenting with.

YOU WILL NEED

TOOLS
- Wooden bat
- Plastic or metal kidney or rib
- Banding wheel (turntable)
- Flexible circular protractor
- Pin
- Knife
- Sponge

CLAY
Porcelain (choose a really white firing type if possible)
- 4oz (110g) for each section

DESIGN NOTE
If you find porcelain difficult to work with, try a semi-porcelain instead; your clay supplier should be able to advise on the best to choose.

DECORATION
This surface technique stands alone and is difficult to achieve, so be warned: you may need several attempts before you are successful (see pages 130–131 for the decoration shown here). Alternatively, you could cut out a pattern in the wall for the candlelight to shine through.

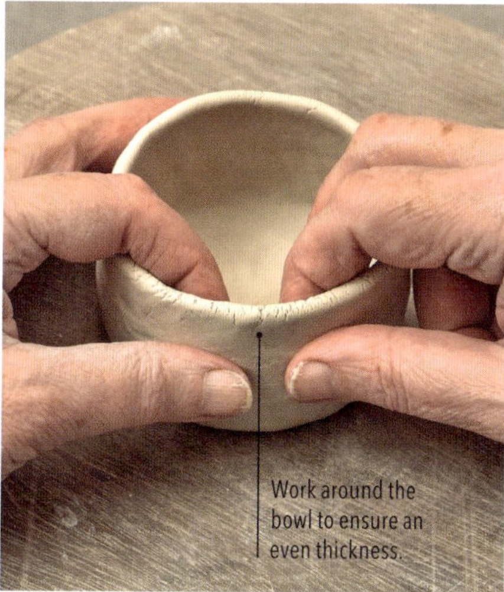

Work around the bowl to ensure an even thickness.

1 Taking the first 4oz (110g) of porcelain, carefully pinch a flat-bottomed bowl, about 2in (5cm) wide, with a vertical wall.

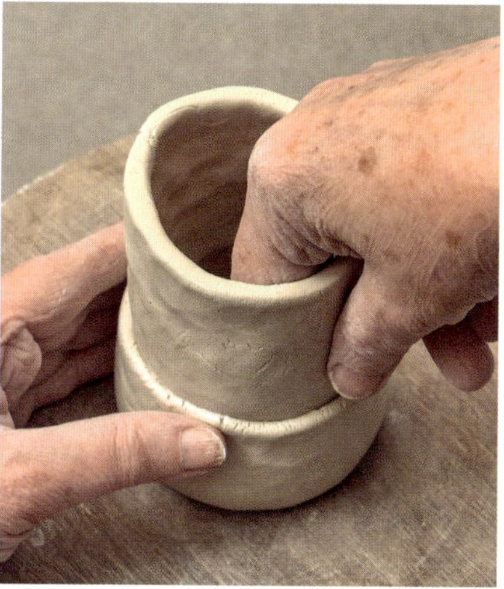

2 Pinch the second 4oz (110g) of clay to an open cylinder, fractionally narrower at the rim than the base. Apply slip to the interior rim of the base, then fix the extension just inside, pinching the rims together as you secure the position.

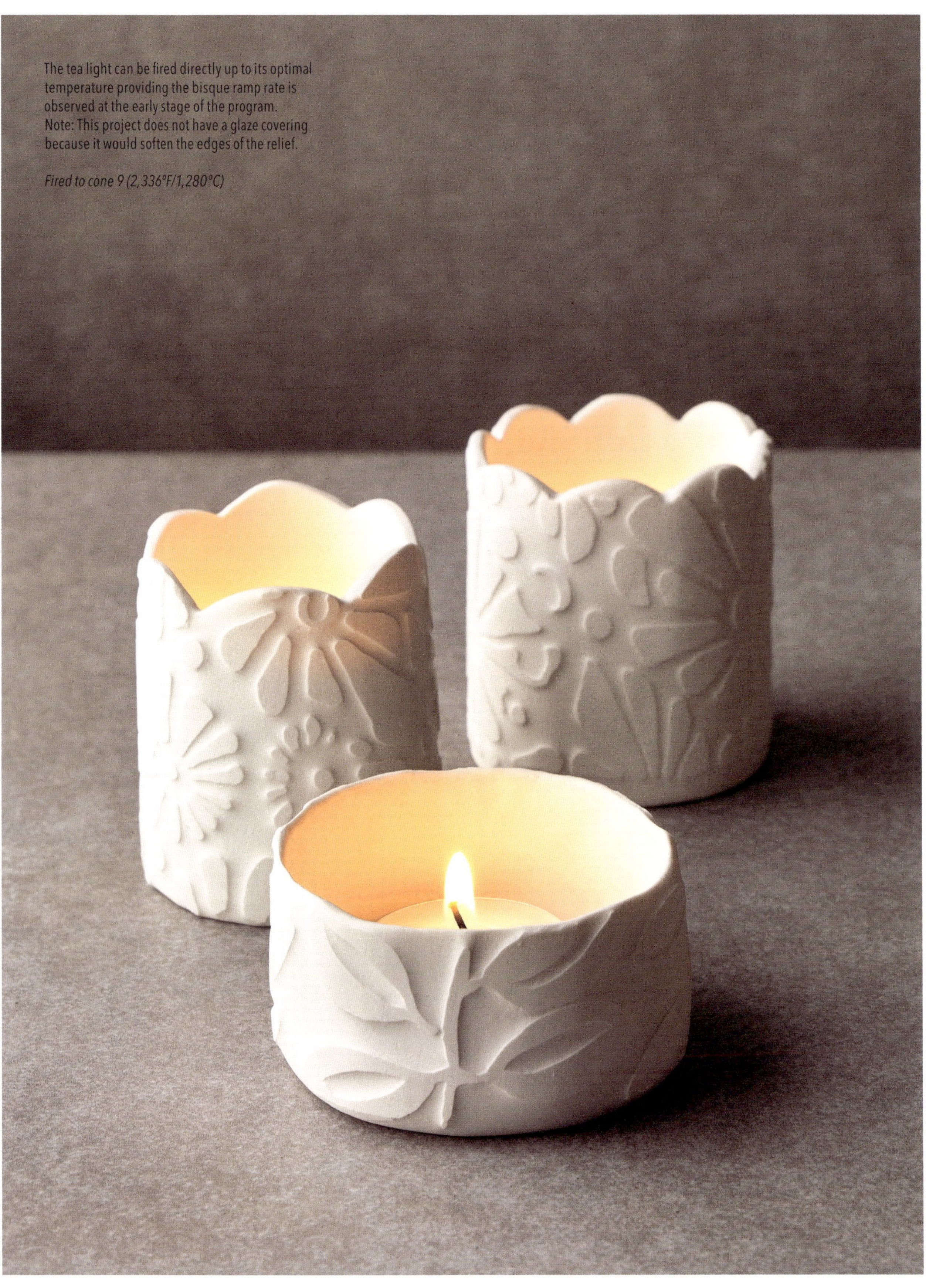

The tea light can be fired directly up to its optimal temperature providing the bisque ramp rate is observed at the early stage of the program. Note: This project does not have a glaze covering because it would soften the edges of the relief.

Fired to cone 9 (2,336°F/1,280°C)

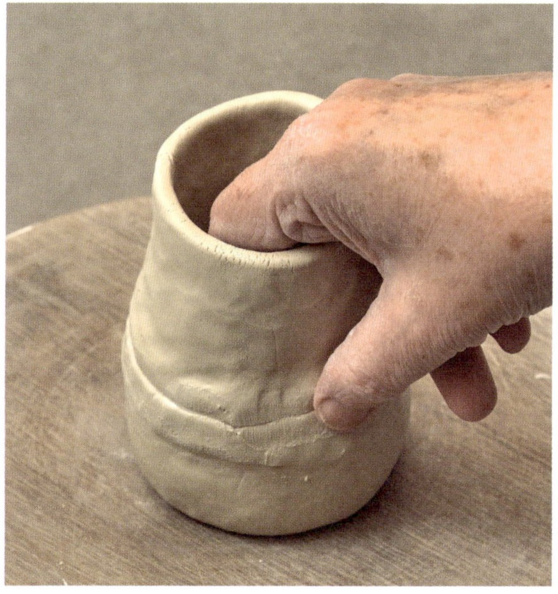

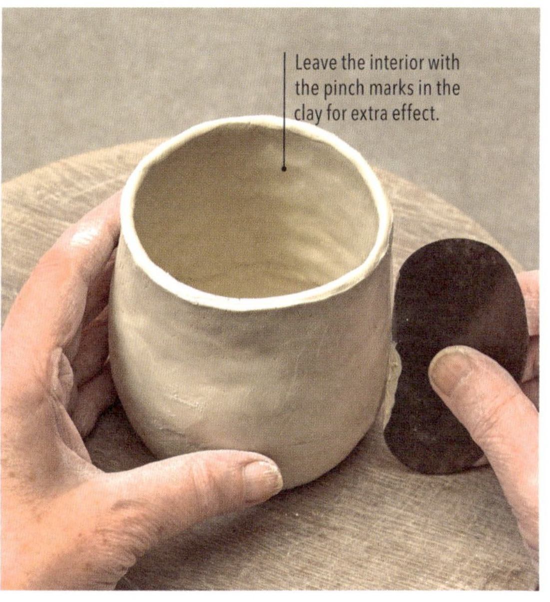

3 Continue to pinch the overlapping clay together, easing the base clay upward on the outside and the extension rim downward on the inside. Continue to work in this way until the join is no longer visible.

4 Work over the exterior wall of the tea light with a kidney to refine the surface, removing any bulk in the process and maintaining an even depth all round.

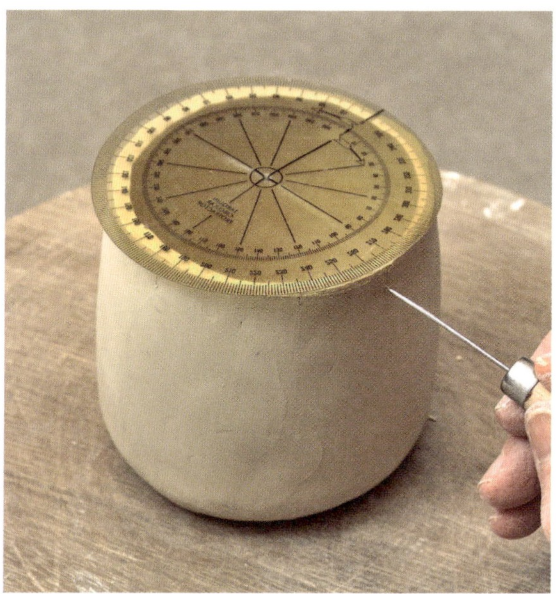

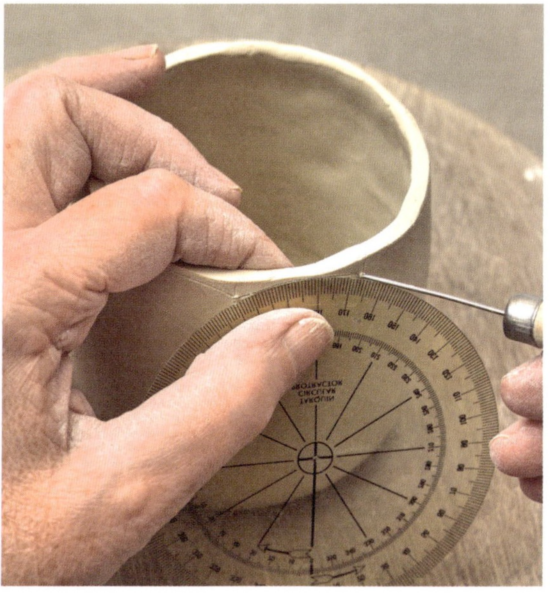

5 Place the protractor centrally on the rim of the form and divide the wall into eight equal sections, marking the positions with a pin.

6 Line the edge of the protractor up between the marked divisions and score around the curved edge to mark a scallop shape between them. Repeat around the rest of the rim to create a scalloped line.

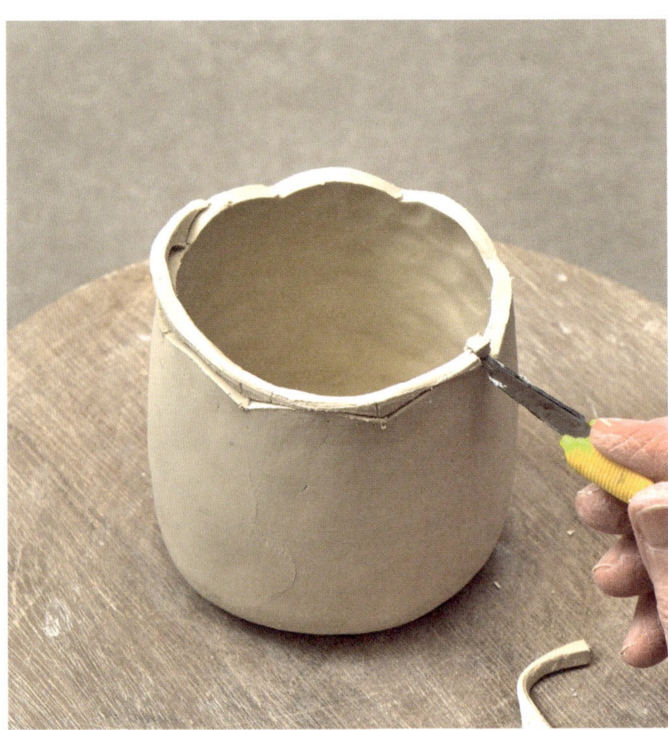

7 Carefully cut out the scalloped rim with a sharp knife. Be careful as you do this because the clay can tear—the knife must be really sharp!

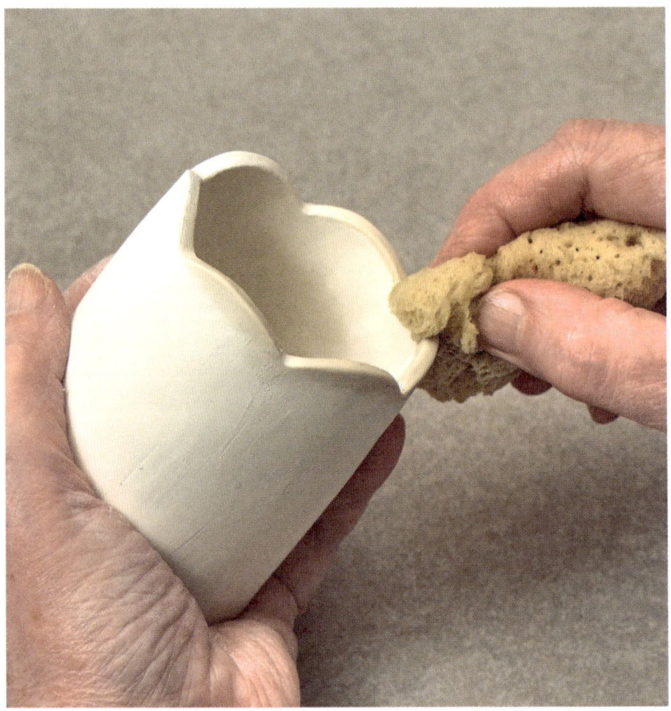

8 Allow the tea light to dry out completely, then very carefully fettle the scalloped rim by wiping around it with a damp (not soaking) sponge until any sharpness has been removed.

DECORATING THE TEA LIGHT

This wax resist method of decoration is applied to a dry clay surface. You can use a stencil, as shown here, to transfer a design, but a freehand drawing will work just as well.

YOU WILL NEED

- Stencil
- Pencil
- Wax emulsion
- Fine brush
- Sponge and water

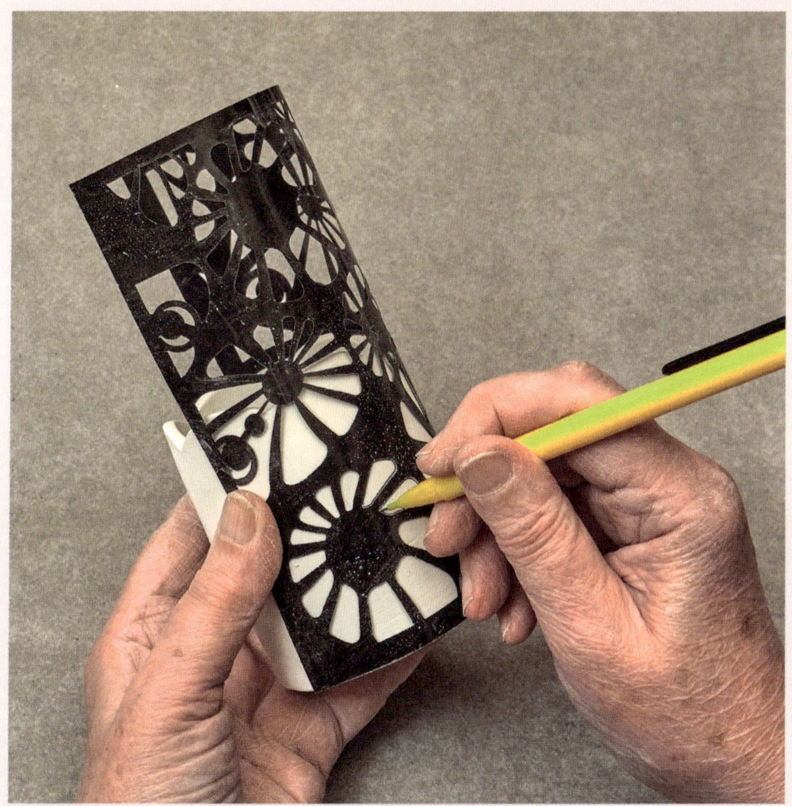

1 Place your stencil over the surface of the bone-dry tea light and transfer the outlines with a pencil, supporting the tea light with your other hand. Alternatively, draw a freehand design on the surface.

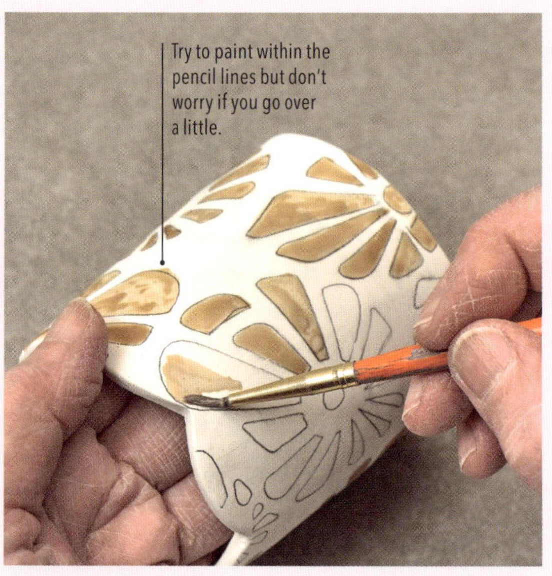

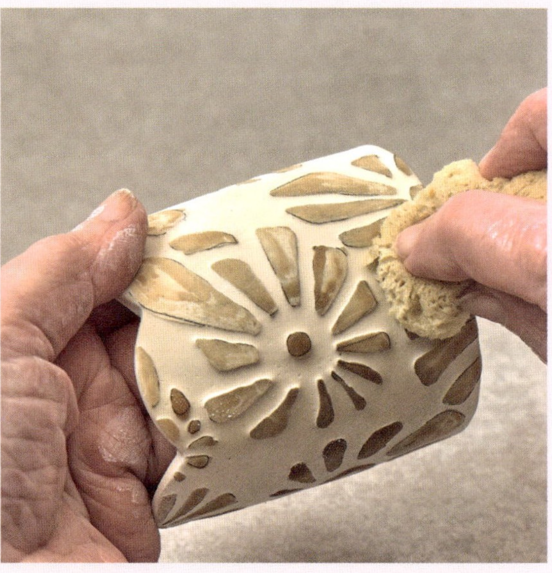

2 When all the design outlines have been drawn, paint in the design with wax emulsion, using a fine brush to stay within the lines as far as possible. Don't worry if you go over in places; it will not spoil the final effect.

3 When the wax is dry, begin to wipe away the clay around the design with a damp sponge. Refresh the sponge with clean water regularly. DO NOT saturate the clay! Work around the form in small stages, allowing the clay to dry out again before continuing.

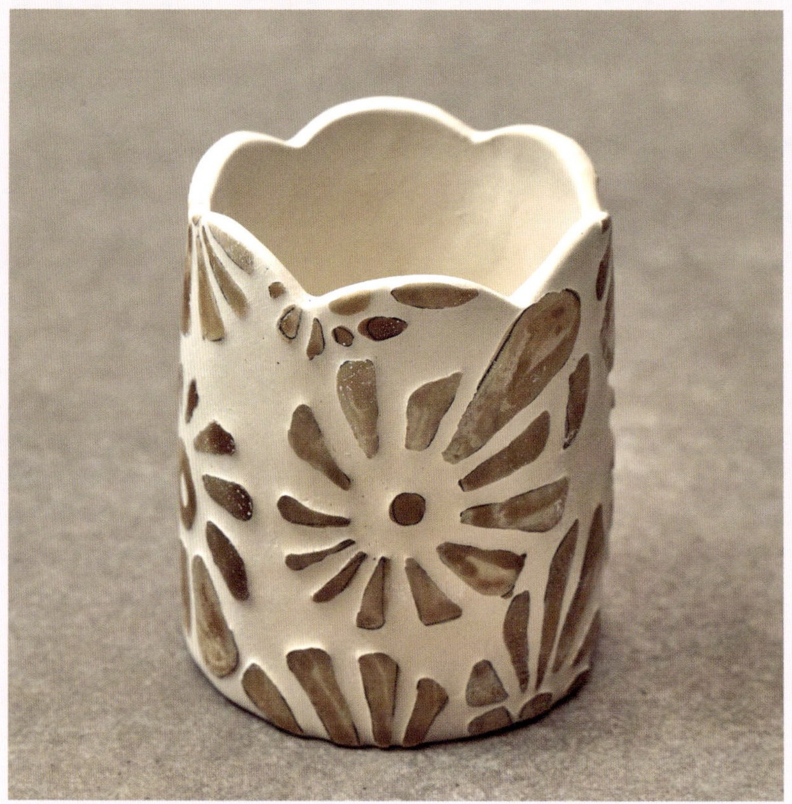

4 Continue to wipe away the surrounding clay until the design remains in raised relief. Allow the tea light to dry out again completely, then fire the form to its optimal temperature. The wax will burn away in firing.

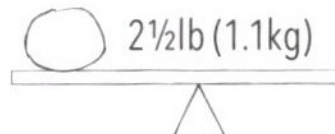

Total height: 6¼in (16cm)
Stem: 2in (5cm)
Base height: 9in (23cm)
Width: 3¼in (8cm)

2½lb (1.1kg)

SCULPTURAL FORM WITH PEARS

This simple sculptural form never ceases to impress with the lifelike pears balancing on their dramatic base, but to make it successfully there are several key things to get right that require precision and close attention to detail.

You could, of course, make another fruit if preferred—dark luscious plums, cherries, or peaches make wonderful alternatives to pears.

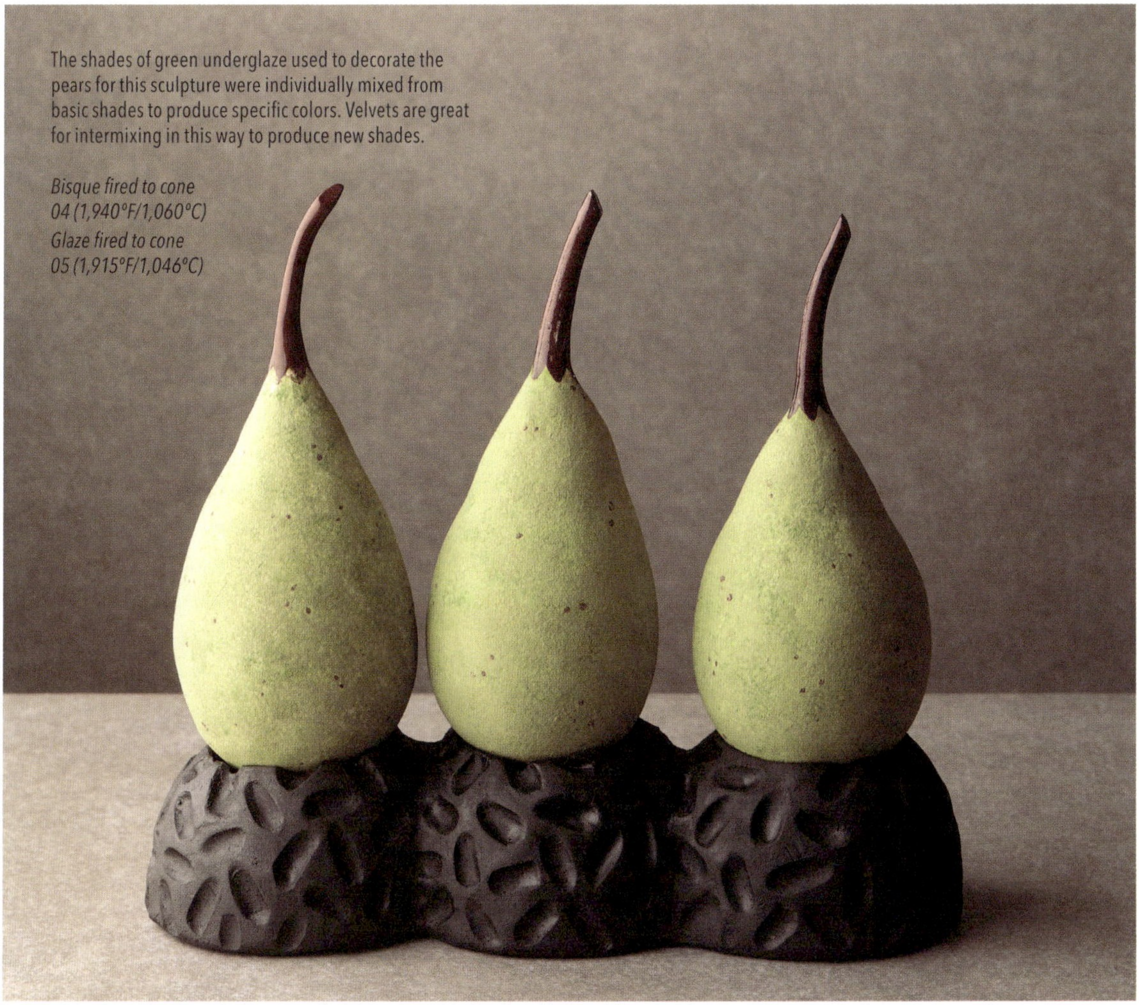

The shades of green underglaze used to decorate the pears for this sculpture were individually mixed from basic shades to produce specific colors. Velvets are great for intermixing in this way to produce new shades.

Bisque fired to cone 04 (1,940°F/1,060°C)
Glaze fired to cone 05 (1,915°F/1,046°C)

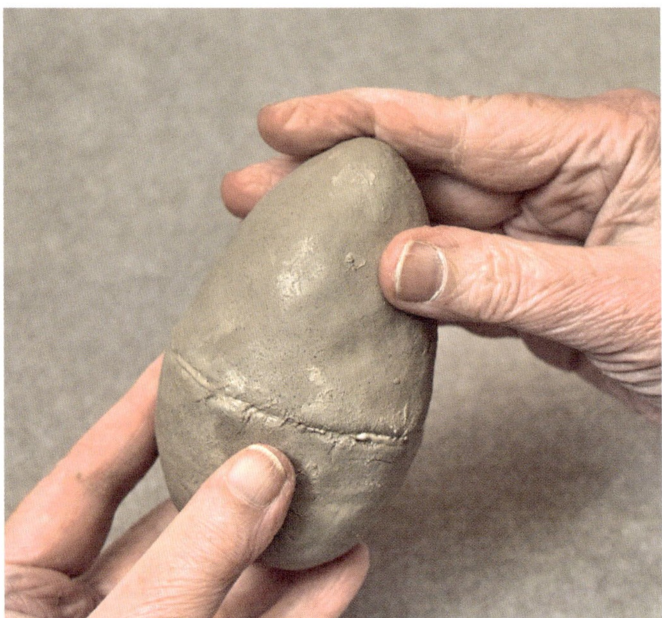

1 Using 4oz (115g) of clay for each half, pinch the two sections of the pear—one cup-shaped, the other conical, but each the same size at the rim. Join the halves together after scoring and slipping the rims, then reinforce the join with a coil of soft clay.

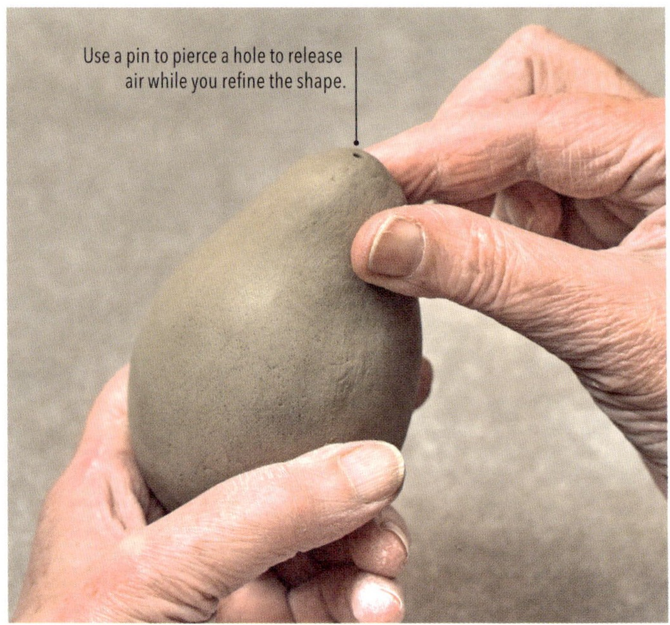

2 Refine the surface of the pear with a kidney, then pierce a hole at the narrow end to allow for the release of air as you manipulate the shape to make it more pear-like. Block the hole up again when happy with the shape.

YOU WILL NEED

TOOLS

- Metal kidney or rib
- Pin
- Tool for impressing (star-shaped pen top)
- Serrated kidney
- Wooden modeling tool
- Small, round-ended loop tool
- Small cookie cutter
- Knife (optional)

CLAY

White earthenware

- $8^{1}/_{4}$oz (230g) for each pear plus a little extra for the stalks
- 1lb (450g) for base

DESIGN NOTE

There are several ways in which this form can be altered: try squaring or triangulating the cup shapes for the base with a spatula before joining them together; or make different fruits in vibrant colors.

DECORATION

To make shiny fruit as opposed to the matte variety here, simply sponge the fruit in a low-fire glaze, building up a patina of color in layers. Mayco Foundations and Stroke & Coat glazes, used in combination, would work really well. See pages 136–137 for the decorative method shown here.

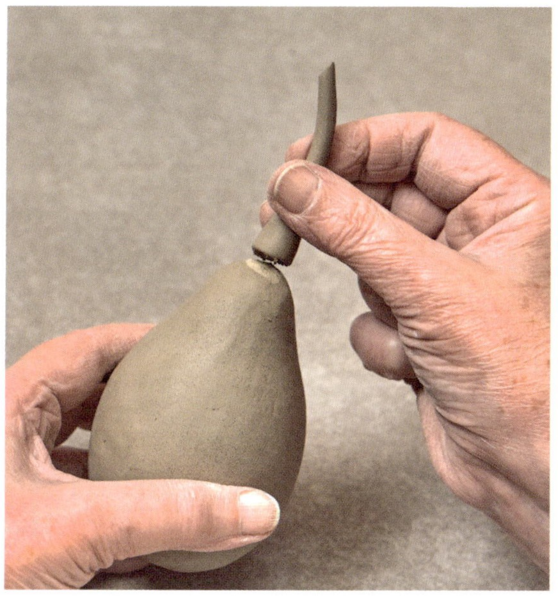

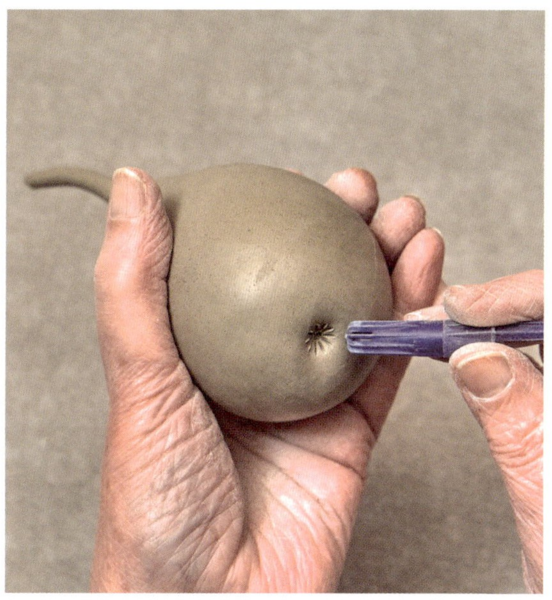

3 Roll a short, conical coil into a stalk, narrow at one end, fatter at the other. Cut it to a 2in (5cm) length. Fix the stalk onto the pear with a dab of slip and blend it onto the body neatly.

4 Impress the underside of the pear with the pen top stamp, then pierce the shape again with a pin at the center of the stamp mark to allow for the release of air in drying and firing. Make two more pears in exactly the same way.

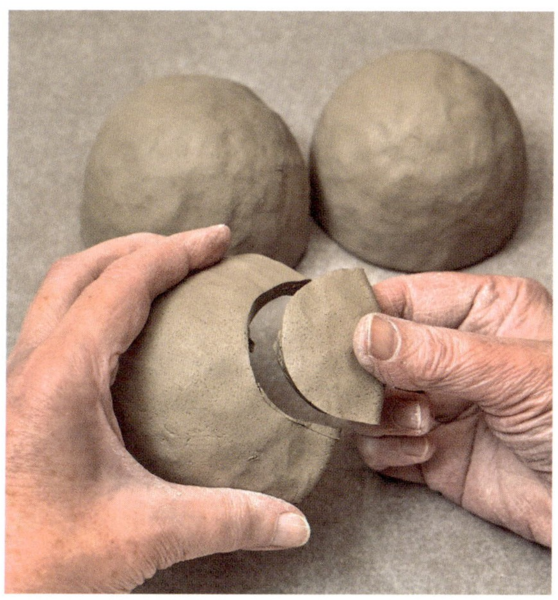

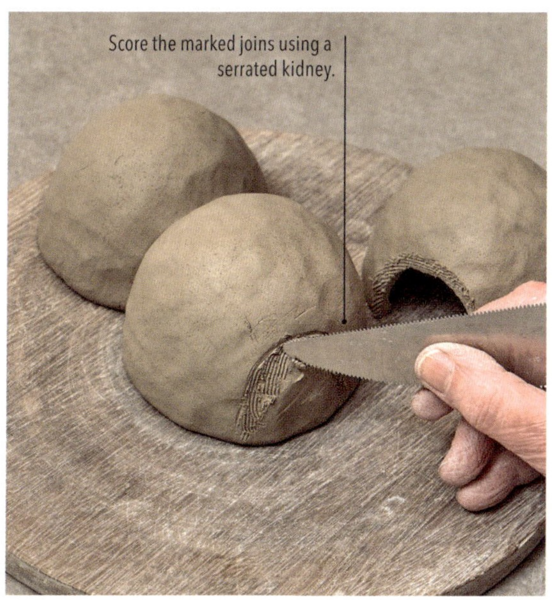

5 Divide the remaining clay into three equal amounts and pinch each one to a round-bottomed cup. Cut a semicircle from one side only of two of the cups—this will allow the side sections to butt up to the central one comfortably.

6 Working on the central section, mark the position for the end sections with a pin. Score and slip the marked areas on the central section, plus the surrounds of the semicircular cut-outs, on each of the side sections.

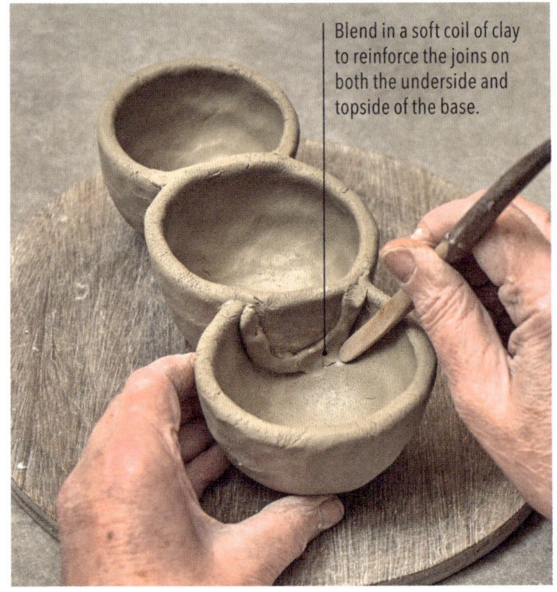

7 Fix the sections together and reinforce the joins on the underside with coils of soft clay. Blend these in with a wooden tool. Turn the base upright and work over the joins with a tool until they are no longer visible.

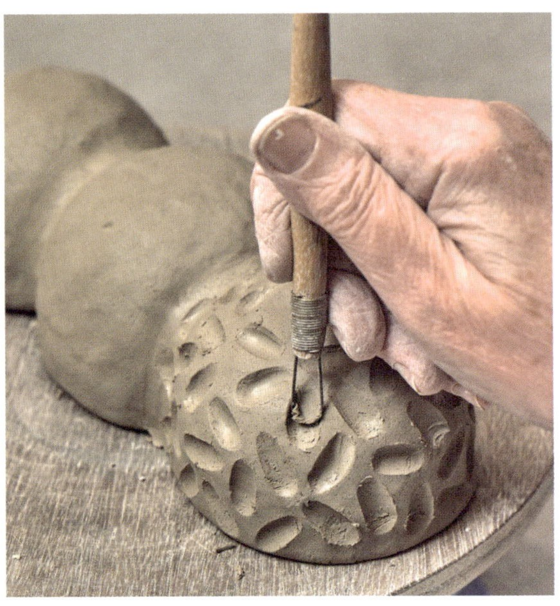

8 Using a loop tool, carve out a pattern across the outer surface of the base. Carve the clay at different angles for best effect. Alternatively, impress a design over the surface using a small stamp.

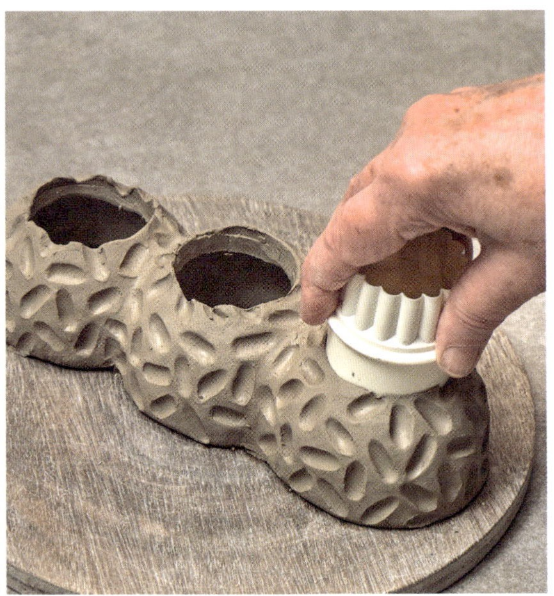

9 Using a small cookie cutter, cut a circle out from the top of each section of the base, making sure each is central. Use a knife if the clay has firmed up too much to use the cutter.

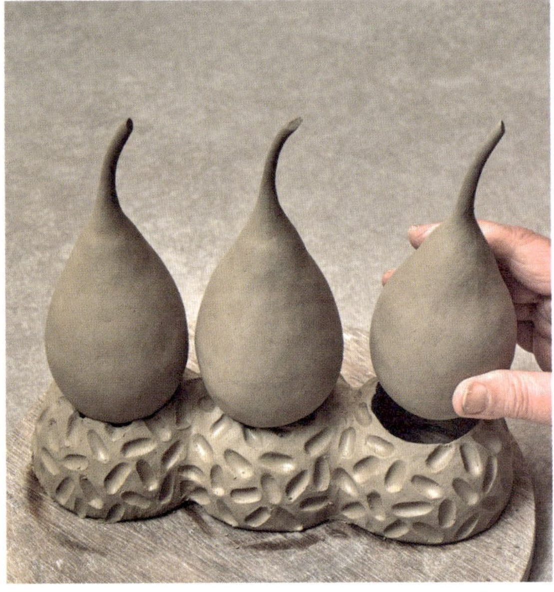

10 Check that the pears will sit comfortably on the base, lining the stems up in the same direction for best effect. Enlarge the openings the pears sit on slightly, if the balance seems too precarious.

DECORATING USING UNDERGLAZE

Velvet underglazes are the perfect coloring agents for this sculpture. They are, as the name suggests, velvet-like fired to low temperatures but because they contain some frit, they do fire to a semi-sheen at higher temperatures, giving the maker options according to preference and clay type used.

YOU WILL NEED

- Velvet underglazes in black, 2 or 3 shades of green, and brown
- Natural sponges for application
- Fan paintbrush
- Fine liner brush

FIRING DETAILS
The pears and base will need supporting on star props when fired to prevent the underglaze sticking to the kiln shelf.

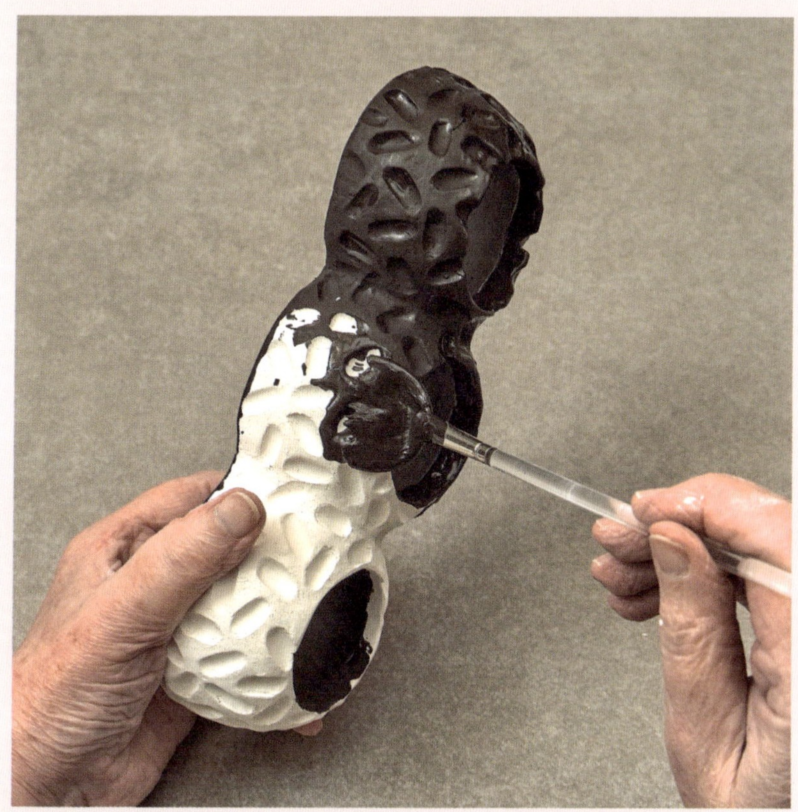

1 Using the fan brush, cover the entire surface of the sculpture base, inside and out, with black velvet underglaze, making sure to work it into the carved detail on the surface. Allow the underglaze to dry to the touch, then repeat.

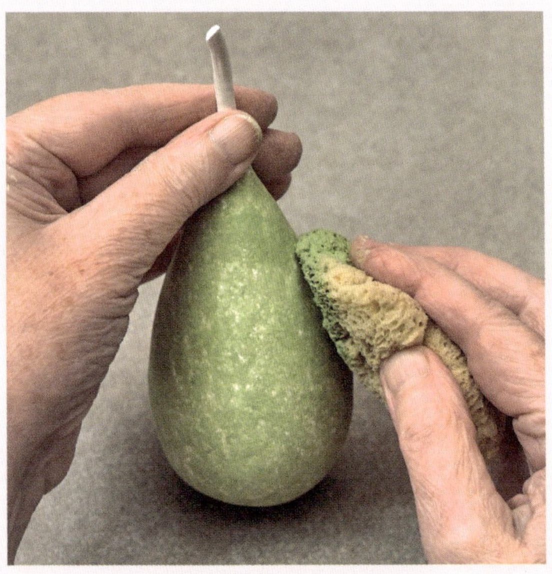

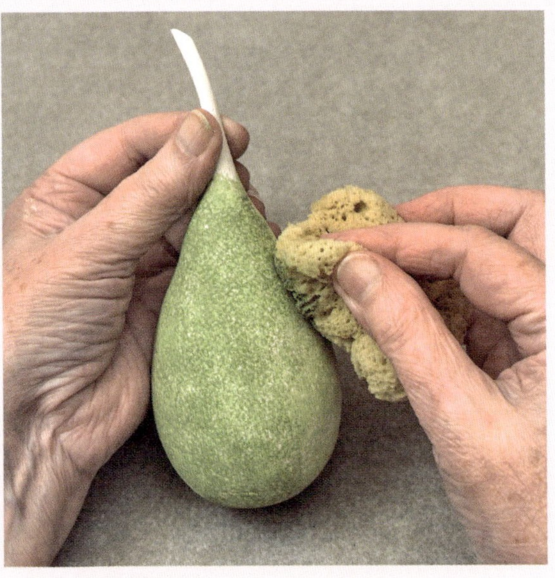

2 Using the lightest shade of green, sponge the color over the entire surface of the pear, omitting the stalk. Allow the color to dry to the touch.

3 Sponge a second, darker shade of green over the first color, using a slightly more open-textured sponge to allow the base color to show through.

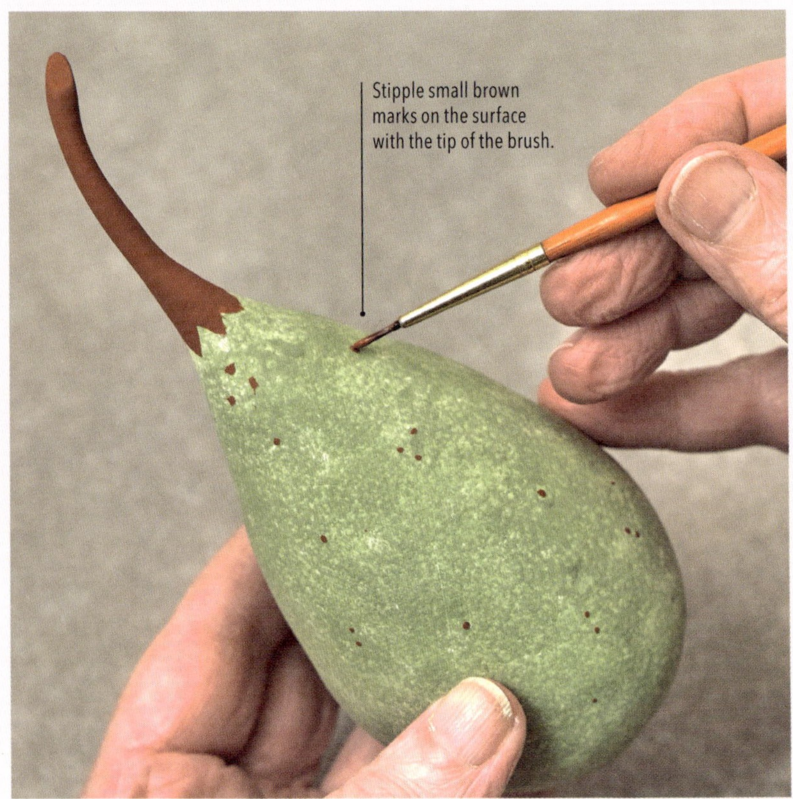
Stipple small brown marks on the surface with the tip of the brush.

4 Paint the stalk of the pear in brown, then, using the tip of a fine liner brush, dot a few little brown marks over the pear in order to give the finished surface depth.

PINE CONE

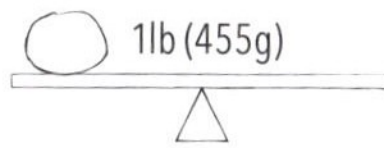

Height: 5½in (14cm)

1lb (455g)

This is a great project that requires almost no tools to complete. Make the cones in different sizes to use as paperweights, door stops, or simply something lovely to look at and handle. The only requirement to make these lovely items is patience—they are quite time-consuming to construct!

YOU WILL NEED

TOOLS
- Foam block to support the shape as it is constructed
- Paintbrush for slip
- Wooden spatula
- Pin

CLAY
Buff stoneware
- 12oz (340g) for cone body
- 4oz (115g) for scales

DESIGN NOTE
This is quite a large cone, which is why its construction is time-consuming. Scaling the weights down to make a smaller version will allow you to practice the technique before committing to a larger size.

DECORATION
There are several options for decorating the cone: try a heavy oxide wash, underglaze color, or a dark glaze. See pages 156–172 for other options.

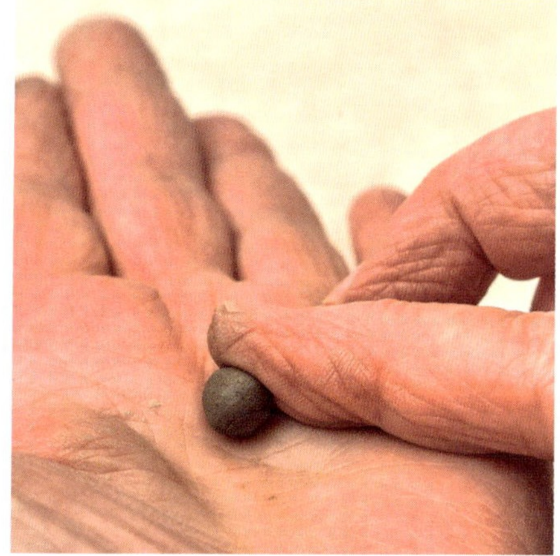

1 From two 6oz (170g) weights of clay, pinch the sections to form the basic cone—one cup-shaped, the other conical, and each the same size at the rim. Join the halves together and reinforce the join with a small coil of clay (see step 3, page 13, for a photograph). Roll a series of tiny balls of soft clay in the palm of your hand.

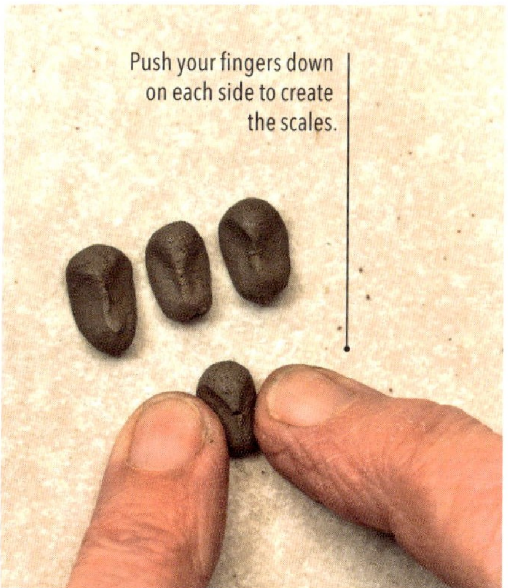

2 Place the balls on the work surface and press down on each side with your fingers to flatten the shape, as shown, leaving the top slightly fatter. This creates the basic shape of the scales. Make at least five to form the top row of the cone.

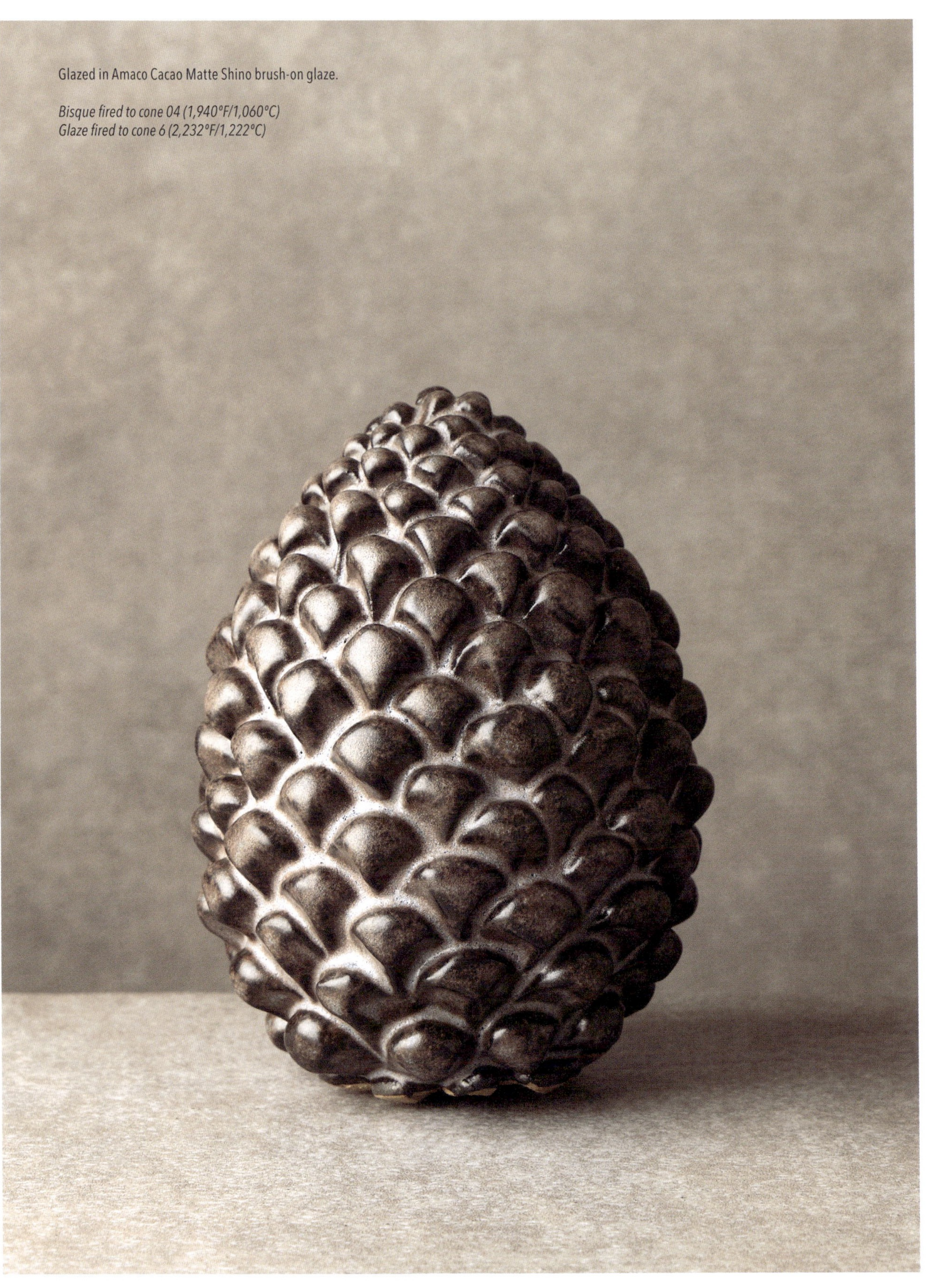

Glazed in Amaco Cacao Matte Shino brush-on glaze.

Bisque fired to cone 04 (1,940°F/1,060°C)
Glaze fired to cone 6 (2,232°F/1,222°C)

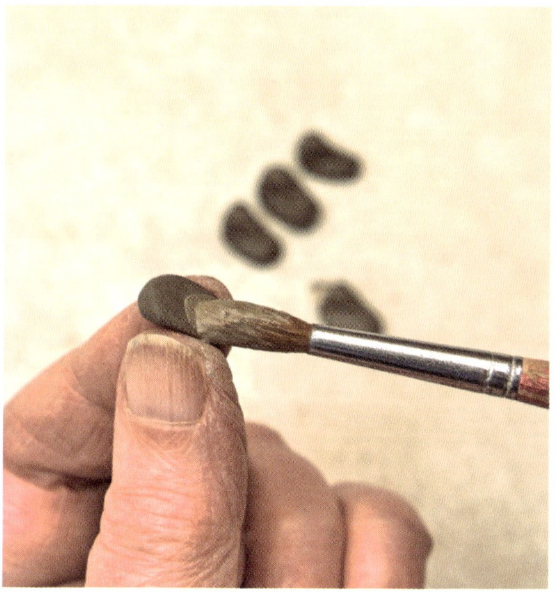

3 Apply a small dab of slip to the bottom end of the back of the scale. Do not slip the entire surface—the upper section needs to stand away from the body once applied and time will be wasted cleaning away excess slip if too much is used.

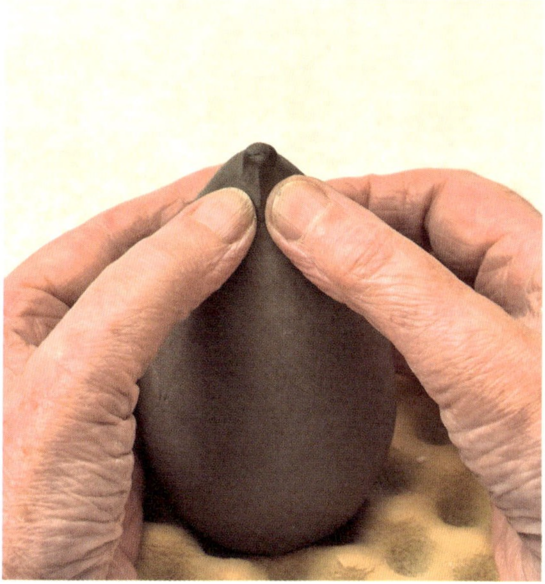

4 With the basic cone supported on a foam bed, fix the scale onto the body so that it rises just above the top. Smooth the base of the scale down onto the body, using your thumbs, which allows you to hold the shape in place with your fingers as you work.

5 Continue to apply the scales around the top of the cone in the same way, each one just touching the next. Three to five scales should form the first row—odd numbers always work better visually than even.

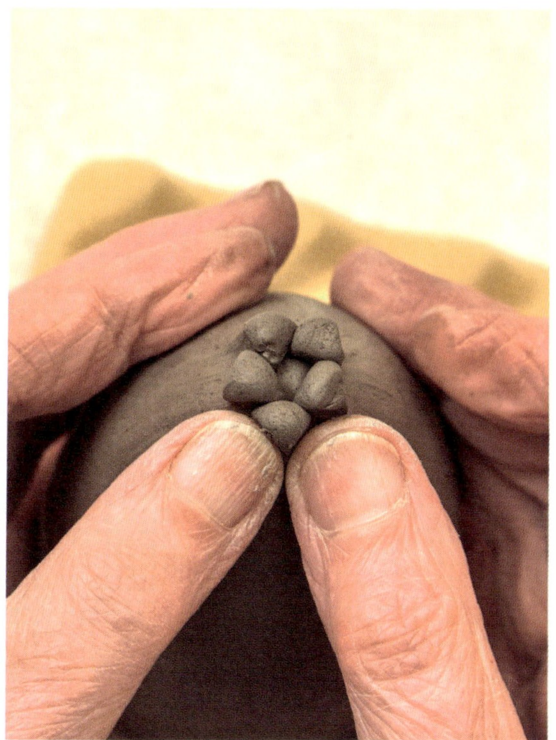

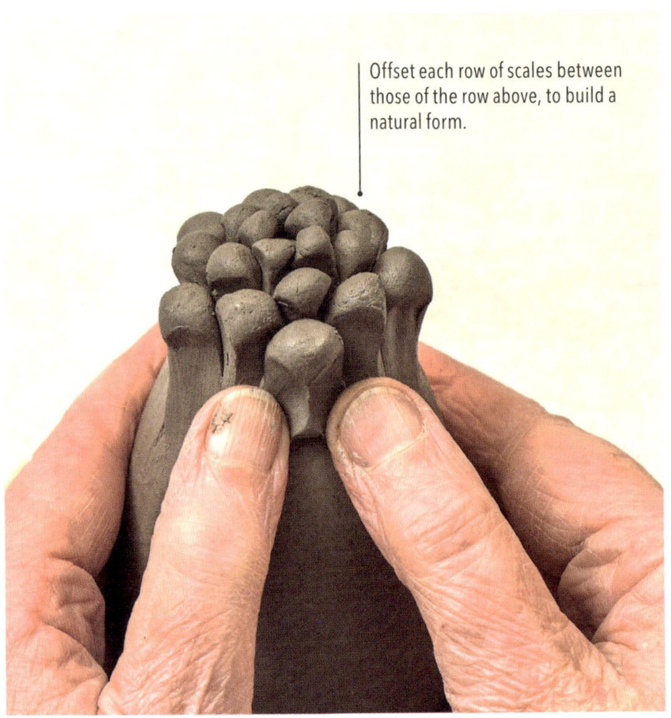

6 Attach a second row of scales below the first, working in the same way but this time offsetting the line by placing the scales between those on the previous row. As you apply each successive row, increase the size of the scales incrementally to fit the expanding shape of the cone.

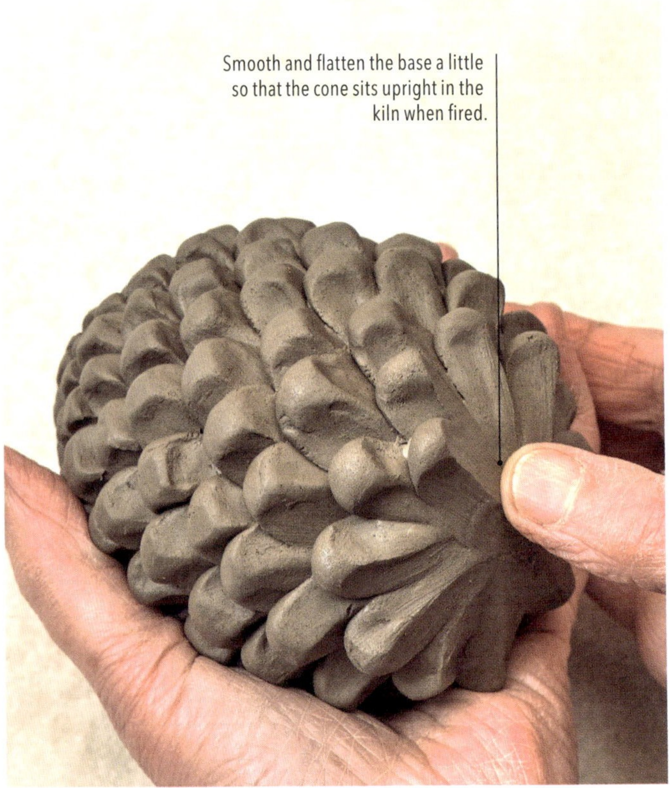

7 Continue to add rows of scales until you get to the bottom of the cone, finishing the last row in such a way as will allow the cone to sit upright on a surface for easy firing in the kiln. Make a discreet hole with a pin somewhere in the cone before allowing it to dry out.

Width: 3½in (9cm)
Length: 6¼in (16cm)

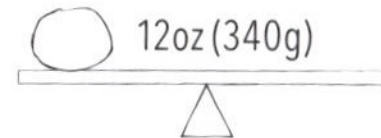

ARTICHOKE FORM

This form begins with the same basic shape as the pine cone made in the previous project. However, construction is a little more difficult because the component parts make it tricky to handle as the shape develops. You will definitely require a delicate touch to make this form successfully.

YOU WILL NEED

TOOLS

- Knife
- Foam block to support the shape in construction
- Paintbrush for slip
- Pin

CLAY

Buff stoneware

- 8oz (225g) for main body
- 4oz (115g) for leaves

DESIGN NOTE

If adding leaves seems too daunting, make the form a little thicker, then carve the leaves into the surface using a suitable tool. The effect will be more subtle but if the basic shape is thick enough, the leaves can still stand out from the body sufficiently for effect.

DECORATION

As with the pine cone, the artichoke looks best simply decorated with oxide, underglaze, or glaze. Choose a color that suits the form; see pages 156–172 for more decorating options.

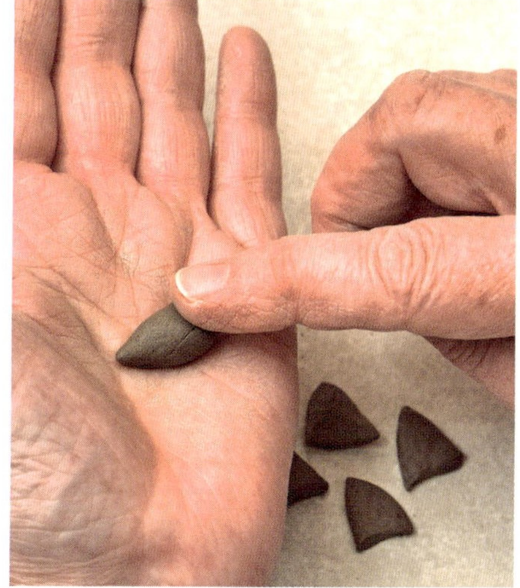

1 From two 4oz (115g) weights of clay, pinch the sections to form the basic cone—one cup-shaped, the other conical, and each the same size at the rim. Join the halves together and reinforce the join with a small coil of clay. Roll a series of five small, soft, clay teardrop shapes in the palm of your hand.

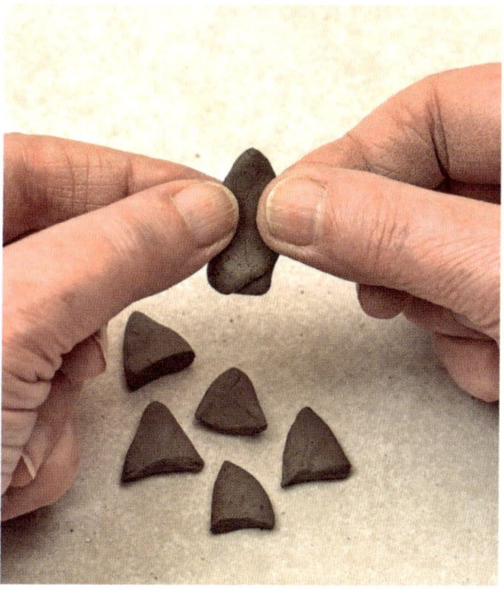

2 Pinch the teardrops to flatten them into thick leaf shapes, then cut the lower end of the shape level—you are aiming for half to three-quarters of a leaf shape with a straight lower edge.

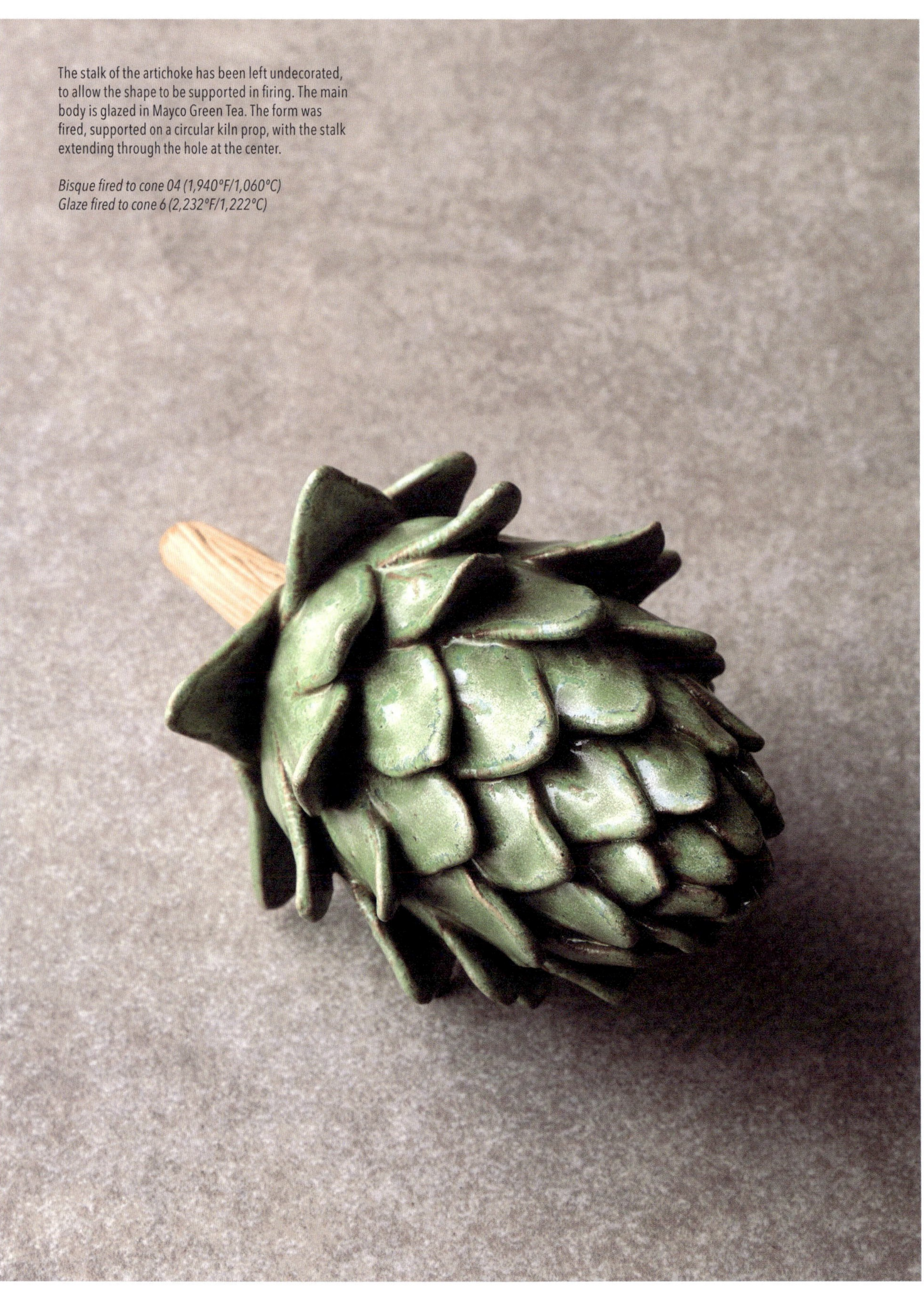

The stalk of the artichoke has been left undecorated, to allow the shape to be supported in firing. The main body is glazed in Mayco Green Tea. The form was fired, supported on a circular kiln prop, with the stalk extending through the hole at the center.

Bisque fired to cone 04 (1,940°F/1,060°C)
Glaze fired to cone 6 (2,232°F/1,222°C)

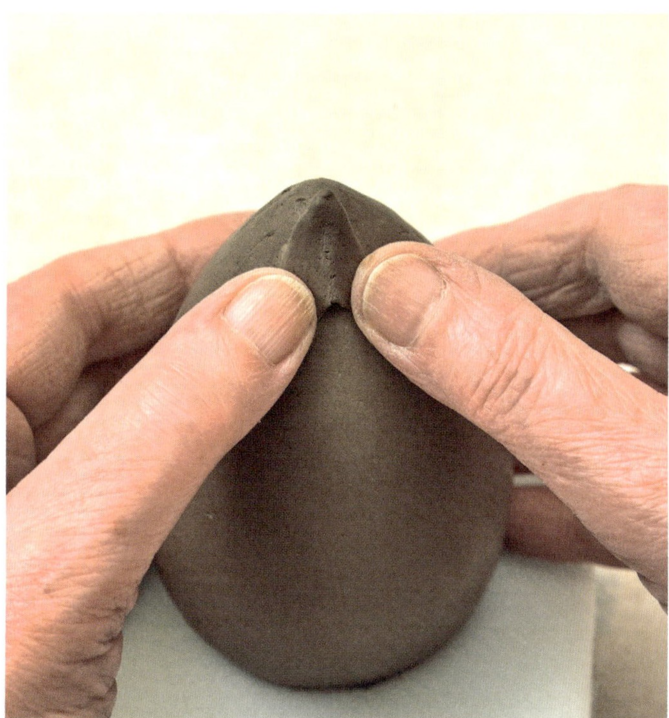

3 Apply a tiny amount of slip to the cut end of the leaf, then fix it onto the top of the body so the tip rises above it slightly. Blend the lower half of the shape onto the body with your thumbs.

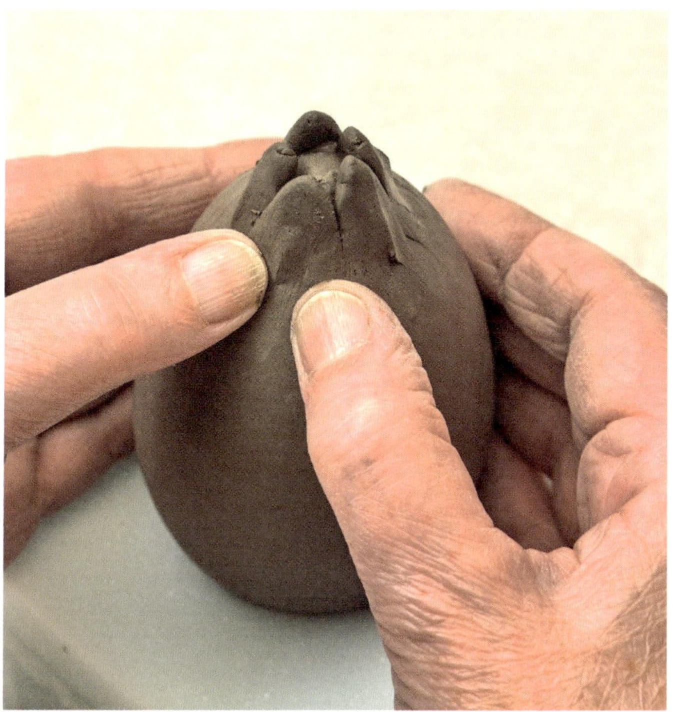

4 Attach four more leaves to the top of the basic shape. They should look as though they are just opening out from the bud underneath and, although each leaf does not need to be identical, they should fill approximately the same amount of space at each level.

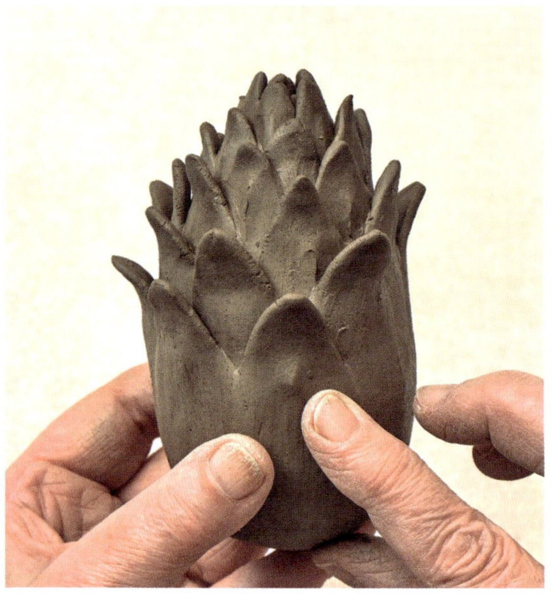

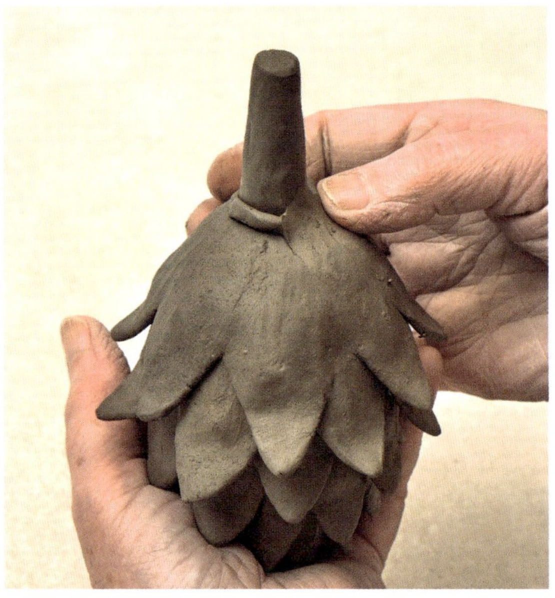

5 Continue to add rows of leaves in the same way, making them incrementally larger each time to fit around the form in the same number. You can add more leaves, but make sure they are offset to the row before. Position the tip of the leaf on each subsequent row between two leaves on the previous row for best spacing.

6 When you get close to the bottom of the form but not all the way there, roll a short coil of clay and, holding the artichoke carefully in one hand, attach the stalk to the base after scoring and slipping. Reinforce the join with a coil of clay.

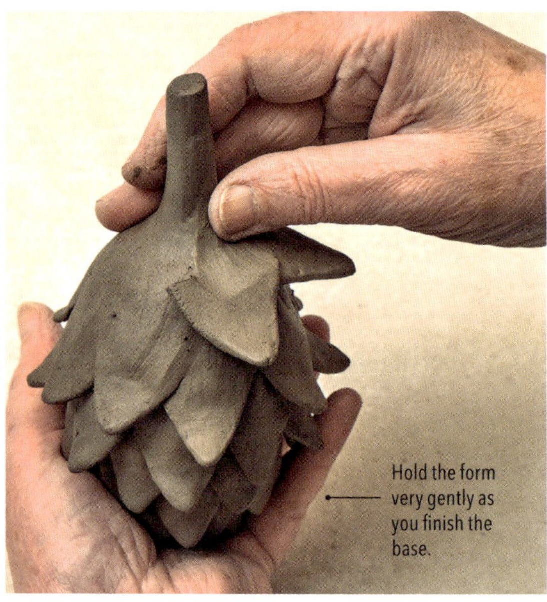

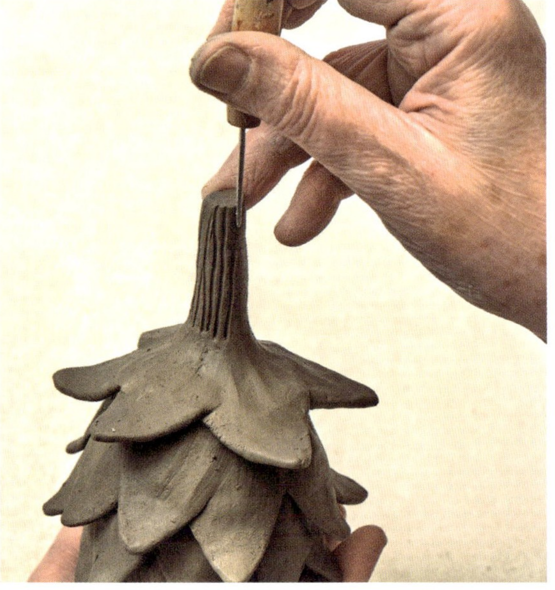

7 Now continue to attach as many more rows of leaves as required to cover the inner shape to the beginning of the stalk. NOTE: This is tricky because it requires holding the delicate form upside down as you work; a gentle touch is essential.

8 Still holding the artichoke upside down, finish off by scoring lines into the stalk with a pin or serrated edge tool. Finally, make a pin hole in the body in a discreet place to allow for the release of air in drying and firing.

PIGGY BANK

Width: 4in (10cm)
Height: 5in (12cm)
Length: 9in (22cm)

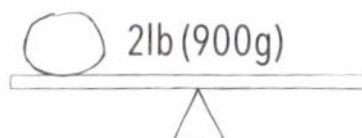

2lb (900g)

Animal money banks are always a good way of encouraging children to save and this little piggy is deliberately fat to contain a really good number of coins. The basic principles for building the money box would apply no matter what the animal, so it can easily be tailored to a child's preference.

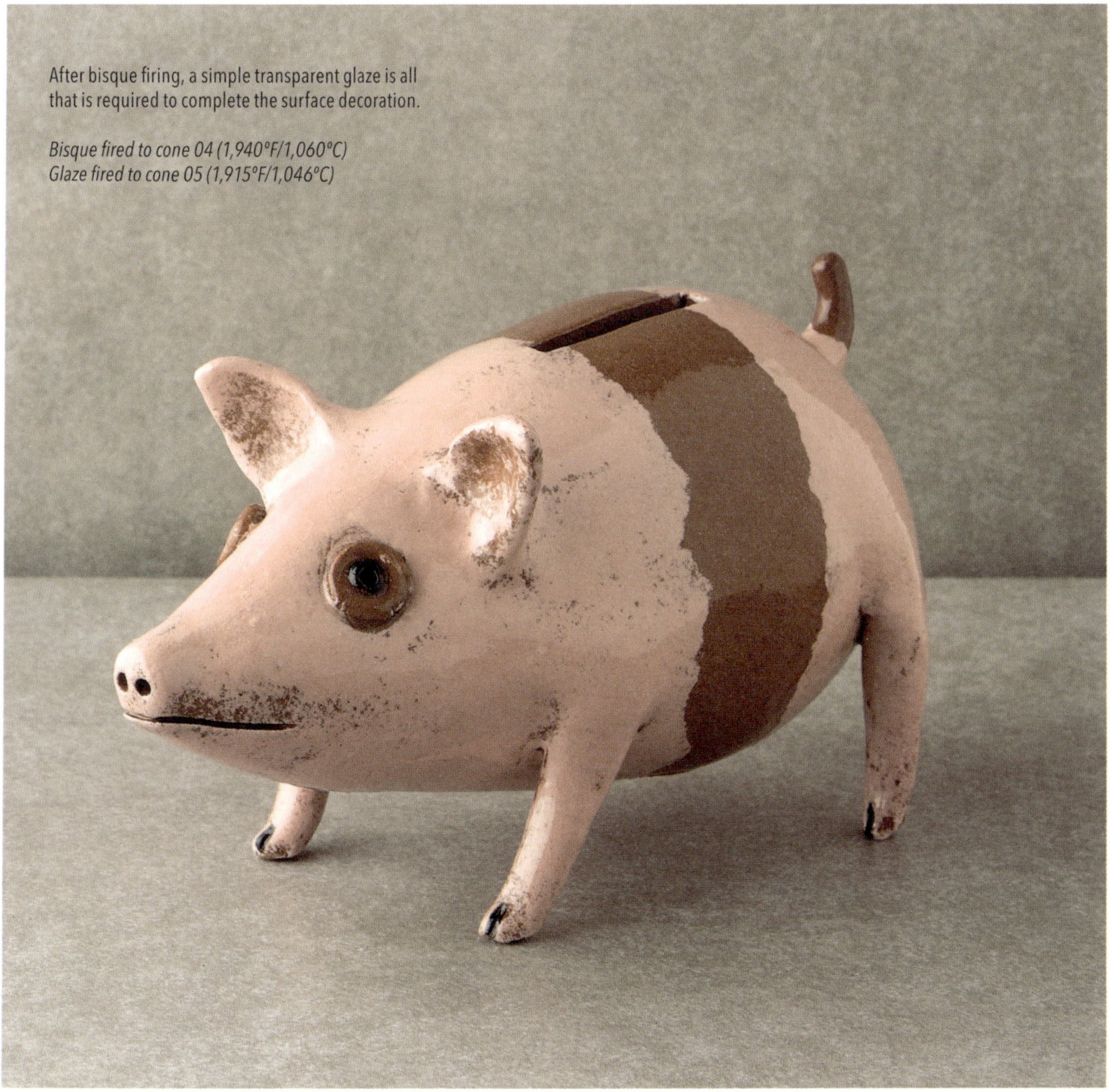

After bisque firing, a simple transparent glaze is all that is required to complete the surface decoration.

Bisque fired to cone 04 (1,940°F/1,060°C)
Glaze fired to cone 05 (1,915°F/1,046°C)

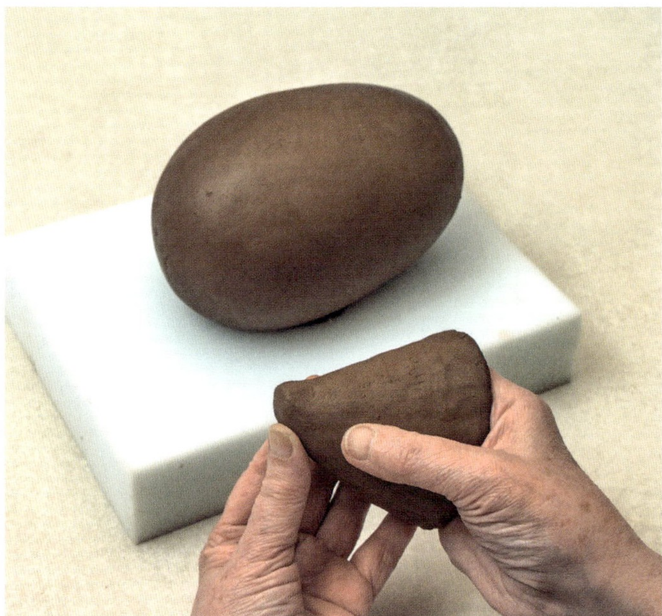

1 Begin by making the body from two pinched sections, both cup-shaped, each weighing 12oz (340g). Join the sections with a coil of soft clay and reinforce the join. Now pinch 4oz (115g) of clay into a cone, roughly manipulating the narrow end of the shape to a snout as you work.

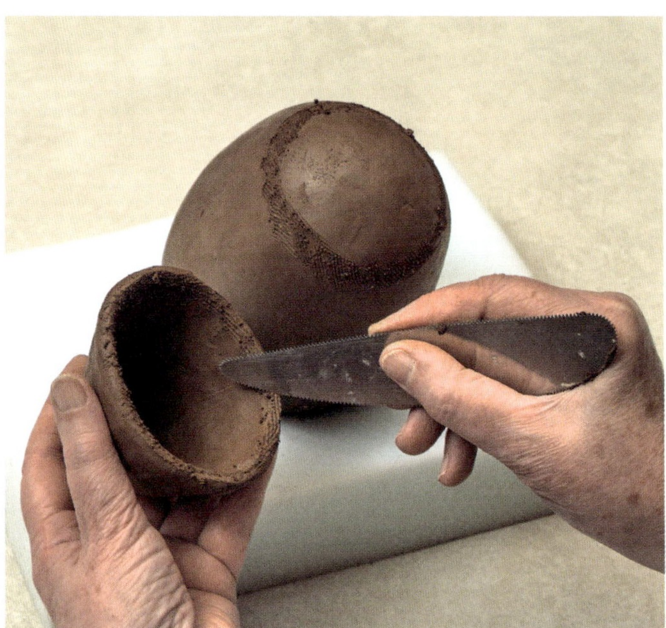

2 Position the head on the end of the body and mark the position with a pin. Remove the head and score around the rim and marked position on the body, with a serrated kidney.

YOU WILL NEED

TOOLS

- Foam block for supporting the shape
- Serrated kidney
- Pin
- Knife
- Plastic or metal kidney or rib
- Wooden modeling tools
- Rubber or cork stopper for the underside. Note: This must be large enough in diameter to allow for coins to be retrieved.

CLAY

Red earthenware

- 1½lb (680g) for main body
- 8oz (220g) for head and remaining parts

DESIGN NOTE

At the early stages of the build the pig could easily be adapted to make another animal, such as a hedgehog—just add shorter legs, smaller eyes, and some spiny body texture. The simple reshaping of parts is all that is required to make a different creature, while the principles of construction remain the same.

DECORATION

If you want a whacky, colorful pig, cover the body surface in a colorful glaze—try sponging a design similar to that used for the *Breakfast Cup and Saucer* (see page 62); it would work just as well on a pig. For the decorating method shown here, see pages 150–151.

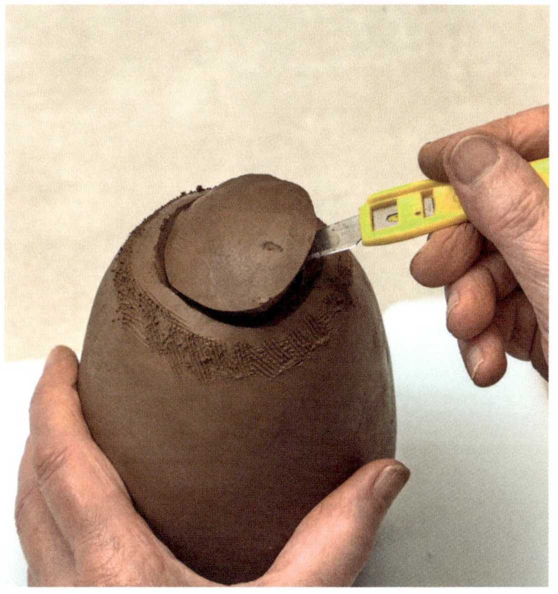

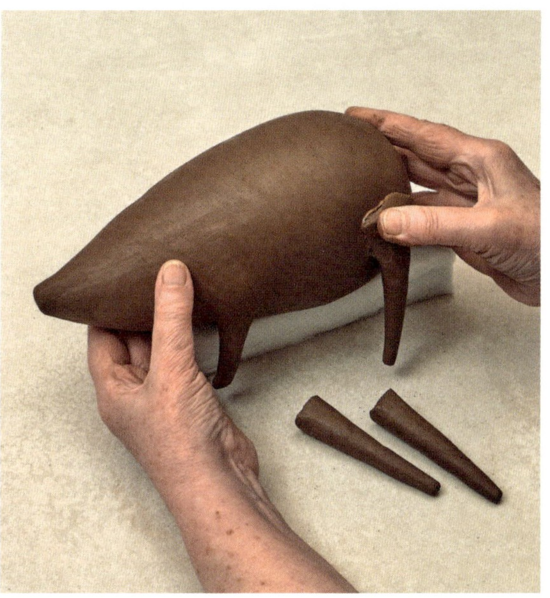

3 Working within the scored area on the body, cut out a circle, making sure there is still a good enough area for the head to fit onto. Apply slip to the adjoining areas, then fix the head in place, smoothing it onto the body with a finger before neatening up with a rib.

4 Roll four short, conically shaped coils to form the legs. Sit the pig on a strip of foam that elevates it to the correct height for the legs to actually touch the work surface without bearing any weight, then attach them after scoring and slipping the relevant areas.

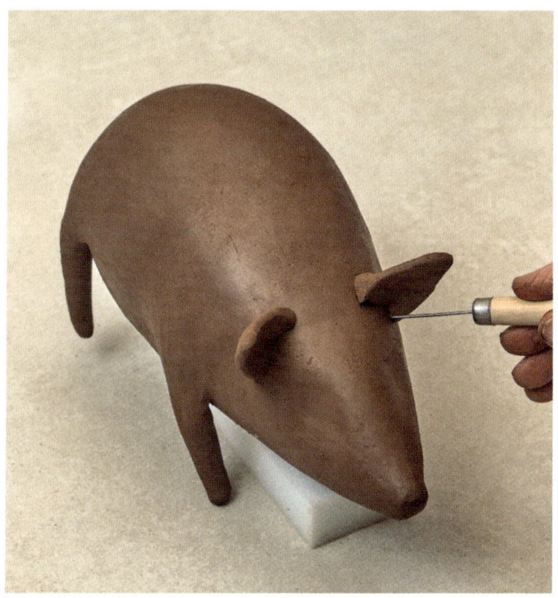

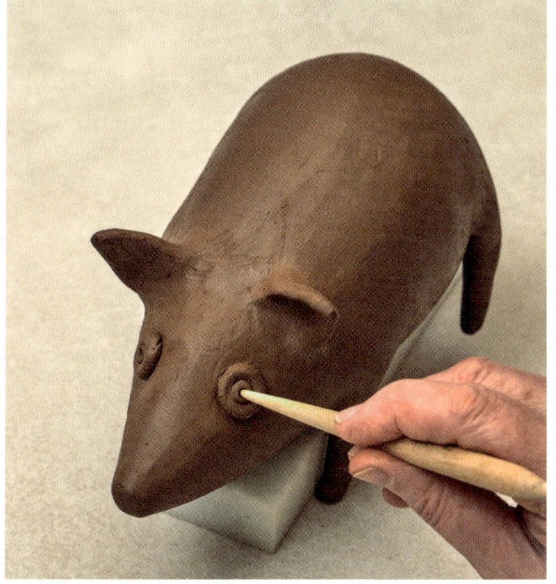

5 Pinch two equally sized, pointed ears and cut them to size to fit your pig. Sit them in place on the head and mark the position with a pin. Fix them onto the head and reinforce around the joins with tiny coils of soft clay.

6 Roll two small balls of clay, then flatten them between finger and thumb. Attach these to the head in the eye position. Form two more tiny balls and fix one at the center of each eye, then impress each with a pointed tool, such as the end of a paintbrush.

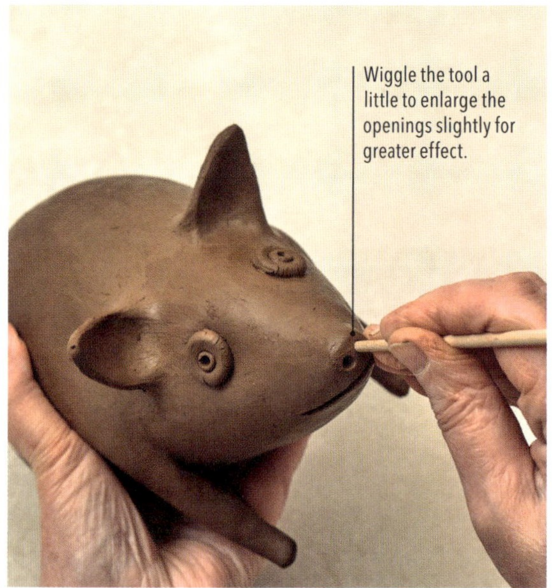

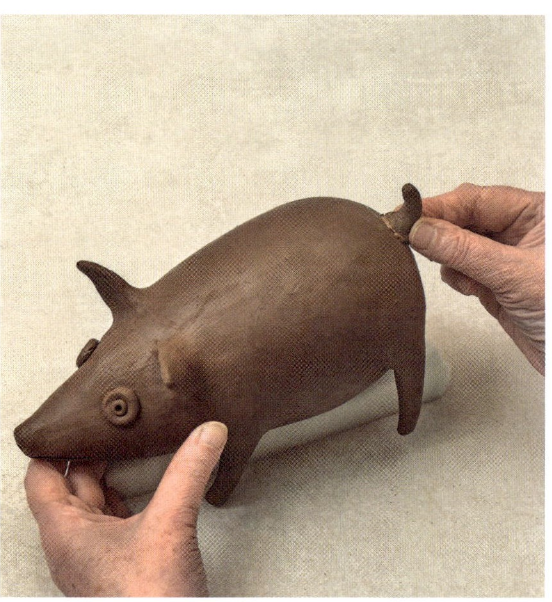

7 Using a pin, score a line for the pig's mouth under the nose, allowing for a little chin, then, using the same pointed tool as used for the eyes, impress the nostrils in the snout.

8 Form a tiny coil into a squiggly tail, then fix it onto the back end of the pig after scoring and slipping. Blend the tail onto the body with a finger or wooden tool until seamless.

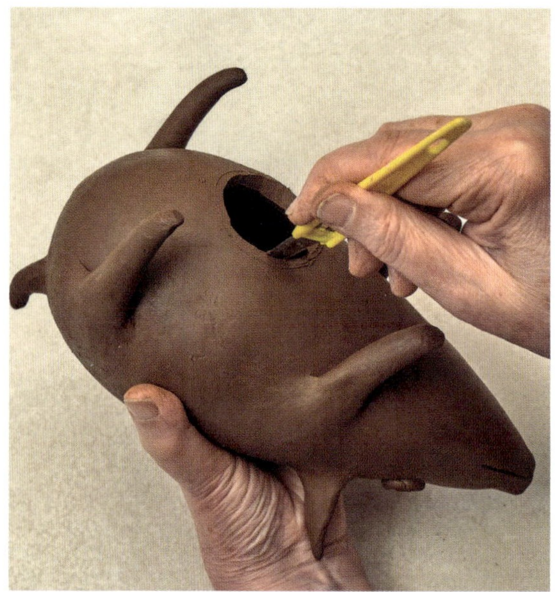

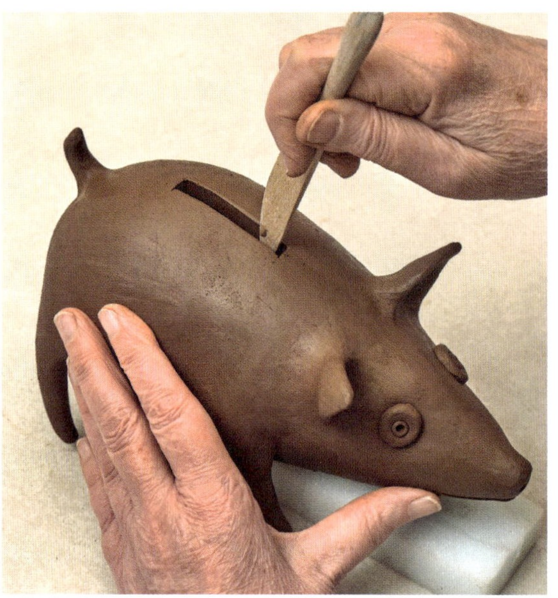

9 Determine the size of the hole required on the underside to match your chosen stopper, allowing a little extra for clay shrinkage. Mark the outline of the opening using a pin, then cut out the circle with a sharp knife. Neaten around the cut using a wooden tool.

10 Making sure it is large enough to accommodate the largest coin, score the outline for the money slot on the pig's back with a pin and then cut it out carefully with a sharp knife. Neaten around the slot with a wooden tool to finish.

DECORATING USING PAPER RESIST AND SLIP

Applying decoration to the piggy bank could not be easier as it only requires a single colored slip and some newspaper. The decoration is applied at the leather-hard stage of drying, so allow the pig to firm to this stage before beginning.

YOU WILL NEED

- Newspaper
- Close-textured natural sponge
- Pink slip
- Black slip or underglaze
- Fine liner brush

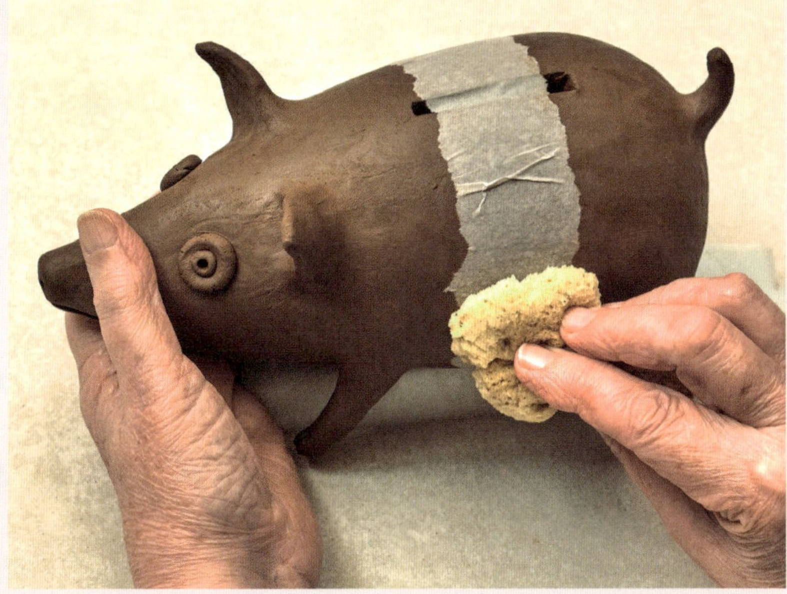

1 Roughly tear a strip of newspaper, long enough to fit around the pig at its fattest point. Fix the paper onto the surface of the clay with a damp sponge, pressing it down gently to seal it onto the surface so that slip cannot get underneath.

2 Using the same sponge, cover the entire surface of the pig, excluding the eyes, with pink slip. Work it over the edges of the paper carefully to avoid it lifting, but if it does, simply damp it back down into place again.

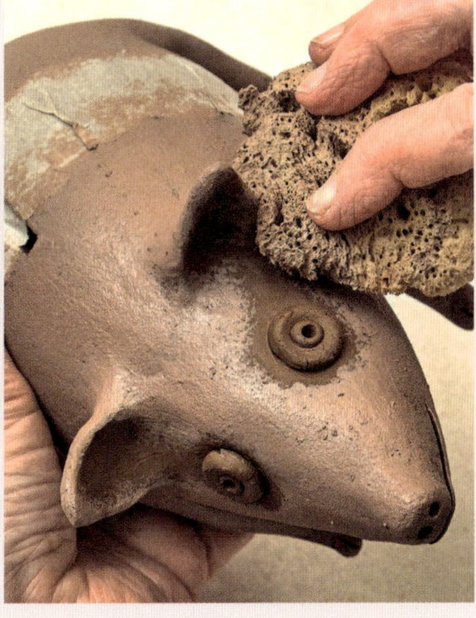

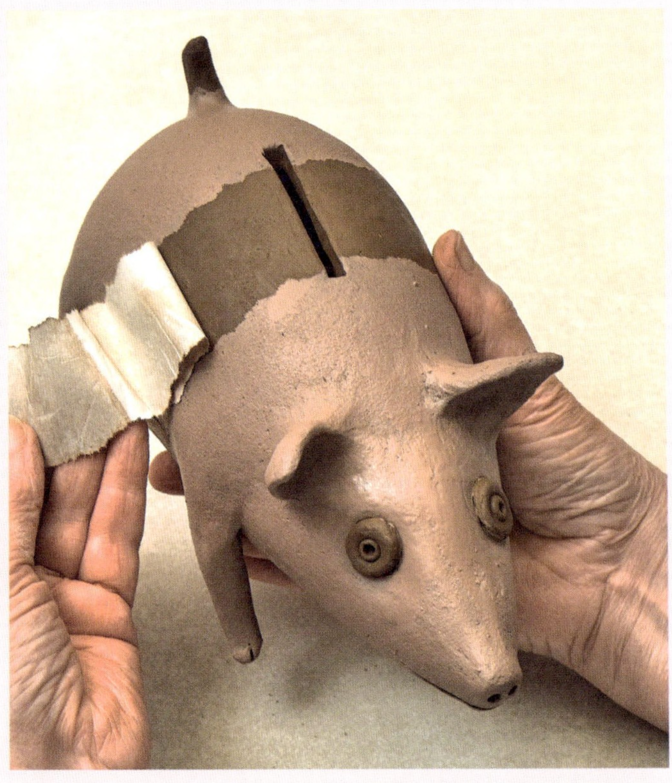

3 Sponge a second, darker shade of pink over the first color, using a slightly more open-textured sponge to allow the base color to show through.

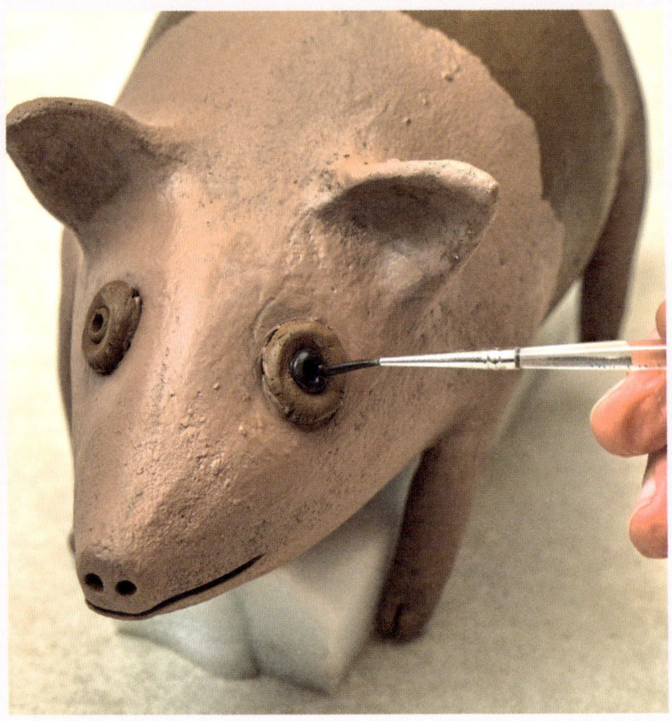

4 Finish up by painting the center of each eye in black slip or underglaze, using a fine liner brush. Allow the pig to dry out completely, supported on the foam block, until ready for bisque firing.

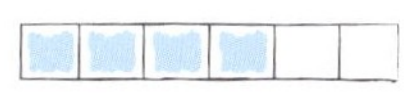

BLACKBIRD

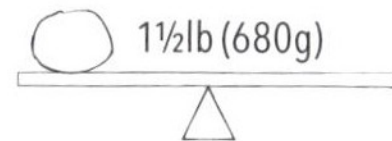

Height: 6in (15cm)
Length: 7in (18cm)

1½lb (680g)

Blackbirds are such a joy to watch, busily pecking away for grubs and other foods in the garden, and because of their coloring, they make the perfect subject for this sculptural project because little observational detail is required for the features—a touch of yellow underglaze, a black glaze, and another for the stone the bird sits on completes the decoration—simple!

YOU WILL NEED

TOOLS
- Metal or plastic rib or kidney
- Suitable tool to impress an eye (an old pen top)
- Knife
- Palette rib
- Wooden modeling tools
- Pin
- Wooden spatula

CLAY
Buff stoneware
- 10oz (280g) for body
- 6oz (175g) for wings and tail
- 8oz (225g) for base stone

DESIGN NOTE
You can make any bird following the basic making principles demonstrated in this project. Scale the weights up or down to make smaller or larger species of bird.

DECORATION
If underglaze colors are used instead of glaze, detail can be achieved for specific features and coloring of more ornate birds. Velvet underglazes can replace glaze for a matte effect if preferred, or transparent glaze can be applied over the top for a shiny surface.

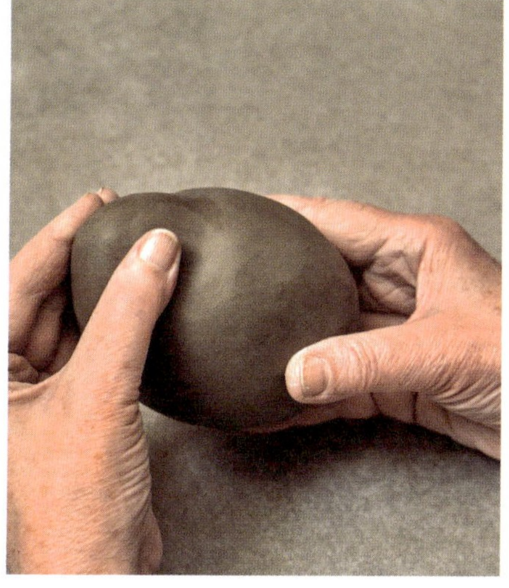

1 Pinch two 5oz (140g) weights of clay to make identical cup shapes. Join them together by scoring and slipping the rims and reinforce the join with a coil of soft clay. Make a hole in one end of the form, then manipulate the shape of the head by squeezing and smoothing the clay at the opposite end.

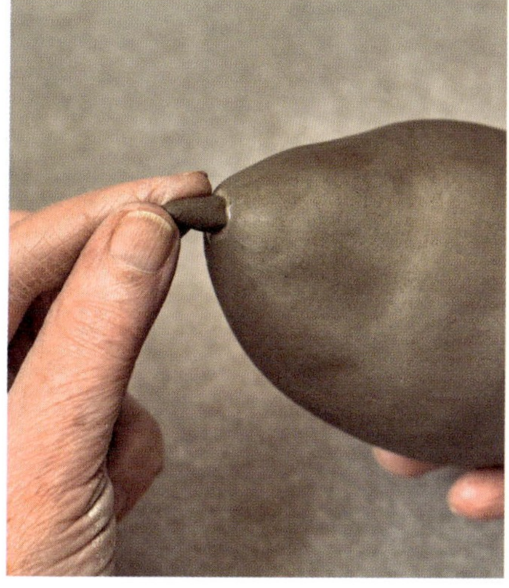

2 Plug the hole back up when the basic shape is correct, then form a beak from a small amount of clay and attach it to the head with a dab of slip. Secure the beak with a tiny coil of soft clay and blend it in until seamless.

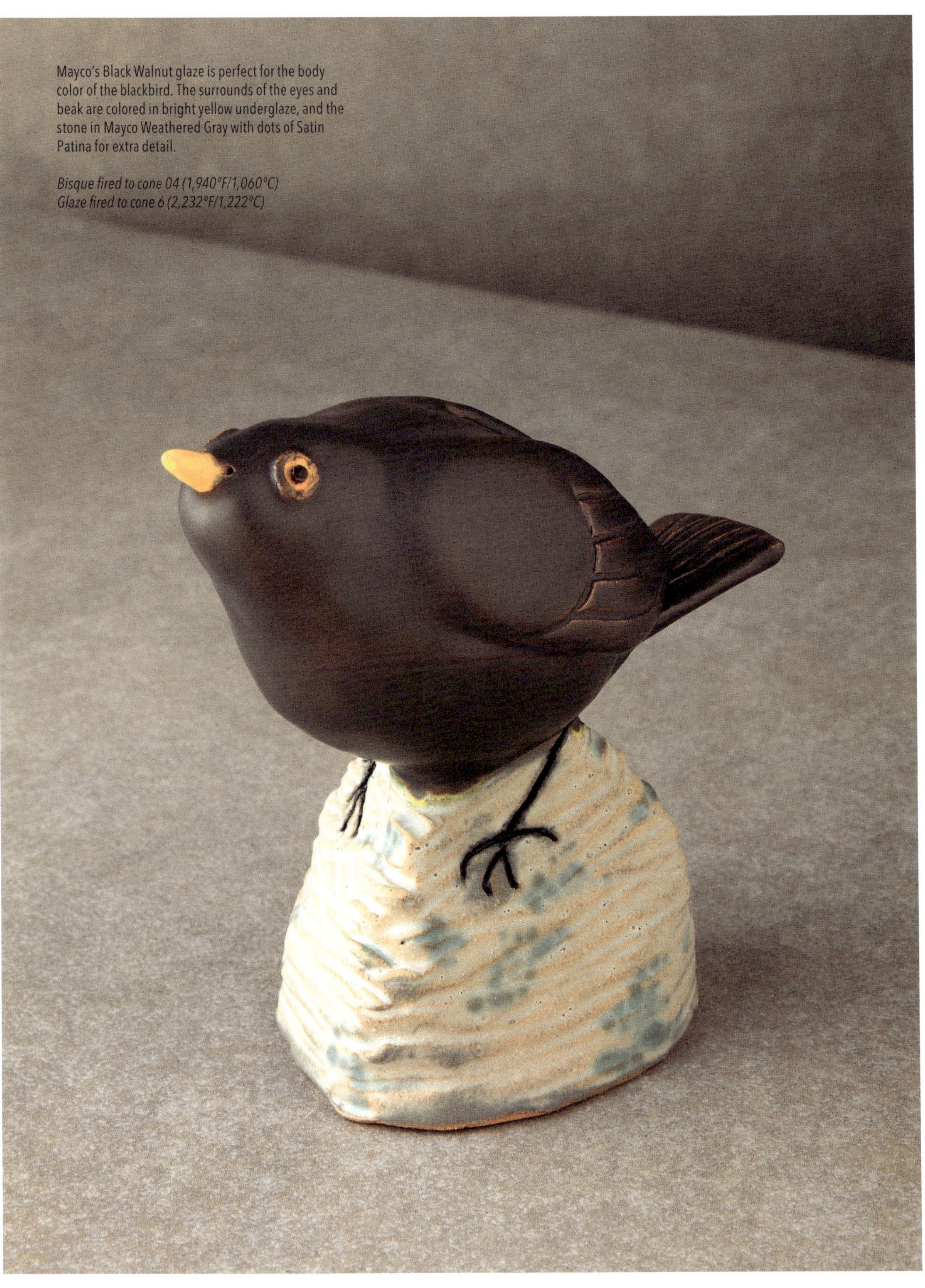

Mayco's Black Walnut glaze is perfect for the body color of the blackbird. The surrounds of the eyes and beak are colored in bright yellow underglaze, and the stone in Mayco Weathered Gray with dots of Satin Patina for extra detail.

Bisque fired to cone 04 (1,940°F/1,060°C)
Glaze fired to cone 6 (2,232°F/1,222°C)

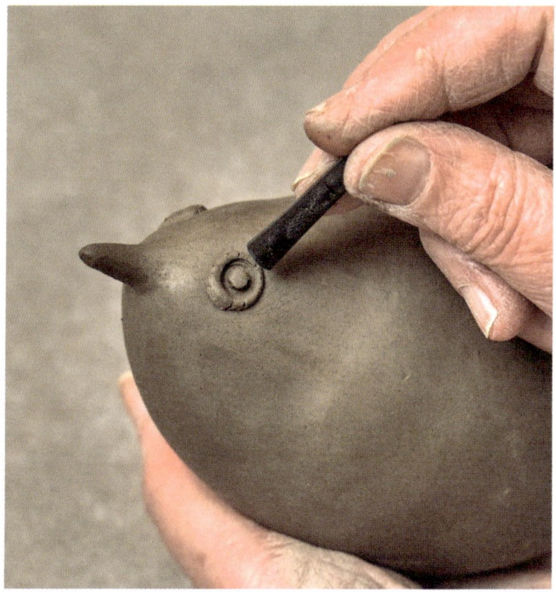

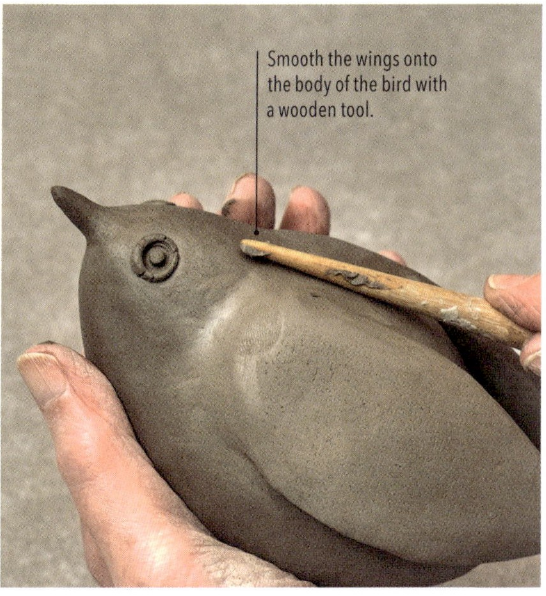

3 Attach two tiny balls of clay in the positions of the eyes with a dab of slip, then secure them to the head by impressing a suitable tool at their center. The clay around the impression may crack a little, but this all adds to the realism.

4 Pinch a flat slab from 6oz (175g) of clay and smooth over the surface with a palette rib. Cut out two identically sized wings to fit the scale of the bird, then attach them to the body after scoring and slipping adjoining areas.

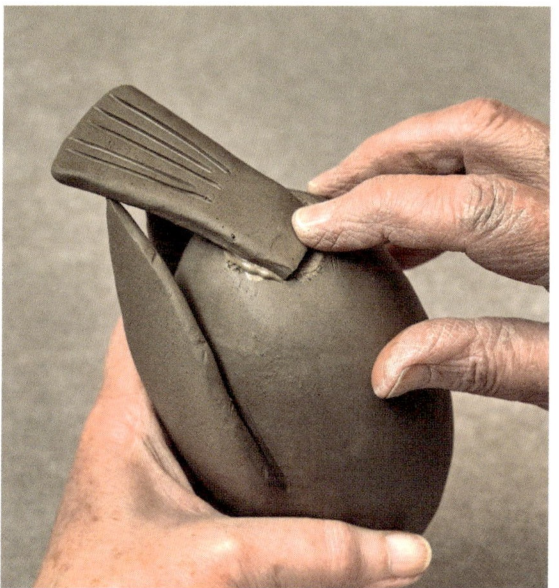

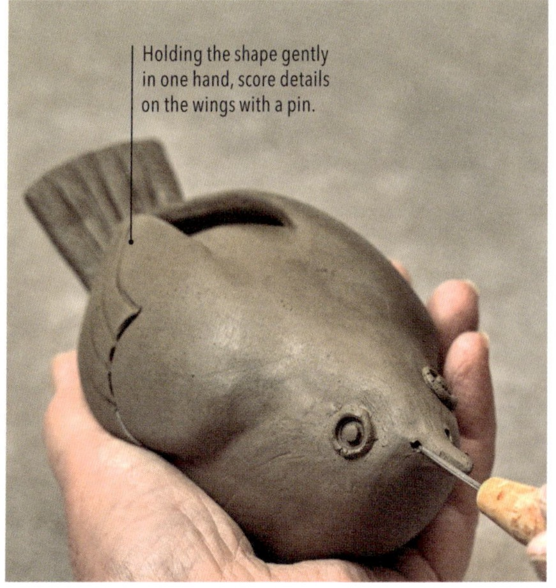

5 From the remaining slab, cut out a tail in a size to suit your bird. Score some feather lines into the tail, then fix it onto the back end of the bird. Blend the tail onto the body with a finger, then neaten up with the palette rib.

6 Draw in line detail to the wings using a pin, then pierce two nostril holes either side of the beak with a pin. This will allow for the release of air from the body as it dries and fires.

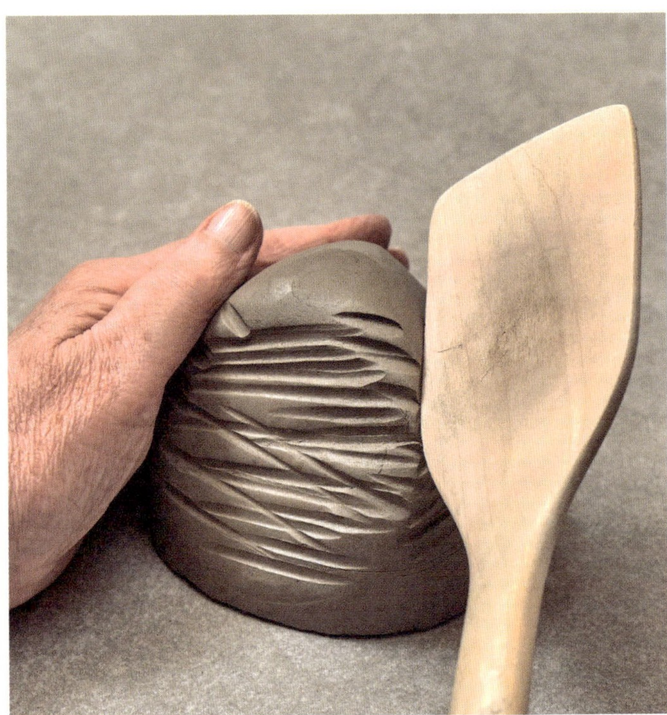

7 From the remaining clay, pinch a roughly shaped, thick-walled cup. Sit the cup on the work surface, rim down, and then beat it with the side of a spatula to texture the surface. Beat angles into the stone to make it more realistic.

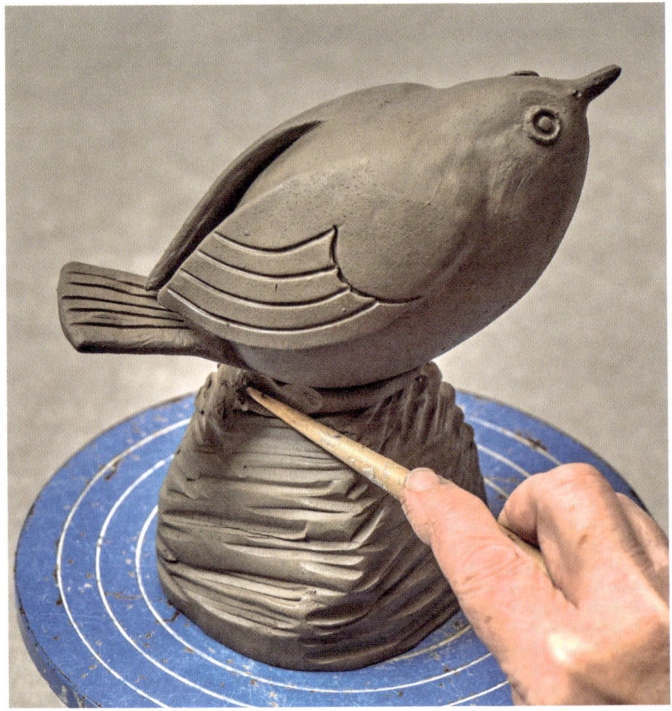

8 Fix the bird onto the stone after scoring and slipping adjoining areas, then reinforce the join with a soft coil of clay. Blend the coil onto both body and stone neatly, using a wooden modeling tool.

SLIP: MAKING AND COLORING

Slip is essentially liquid clay and its fundamental use is to glue composite parts of a form together. However, in refined, colored form, it is also used to decorate the surface of greenwares (pieces that have been formed but not fired). There are many slip decorating techniques, giving the maker a wide catalog of choice to produce unique and expressive surfaces—this chapter shows you some of the options.

DECORATING SLIP

The best slips are made from a clay body because this ensures the shrinkage rates of both will be the same or similar. If you like to work with a white firing clay, then you can do no better than to make your slip from this as it will provide the perfect fit.

JOINING SLIP

- Essential for all projects, this must always be made from the same clay body as the form you are working on.
- To make a joining slip, thoroughly dry out scraps of the clay and then place them in a container. Reconstitute the clay by just covering the scraps with warm water. When the clay has slaked down, mix it to a thick, yogurt-like consistency and it is ready to use.
- Slip can be applied with a brush to a scored surface and should, in most cases, be applied to both areas to be joined.
- Keep the slip in a sealed container for future use.

To make a basic white slip from a clay body

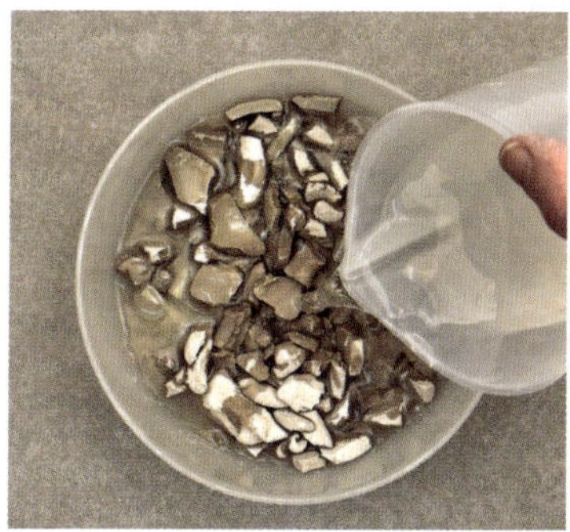

1 Dry out the clay body thoroughly in a bowl, then pour warm water over the mass, sufficient to just cover it.

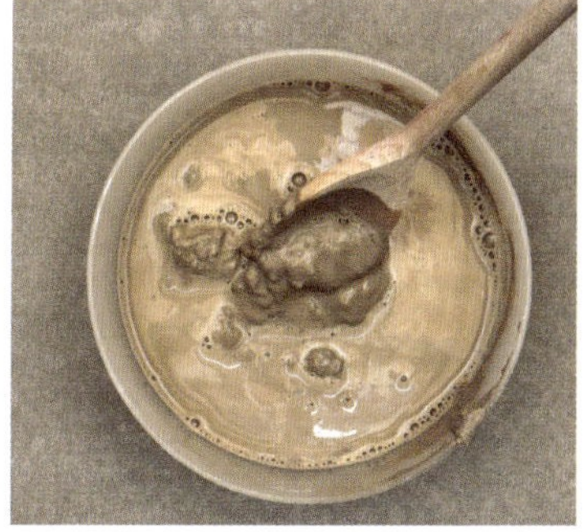

2 Allow the clay to slake down, then stir the mixture to a cream-like consistency.

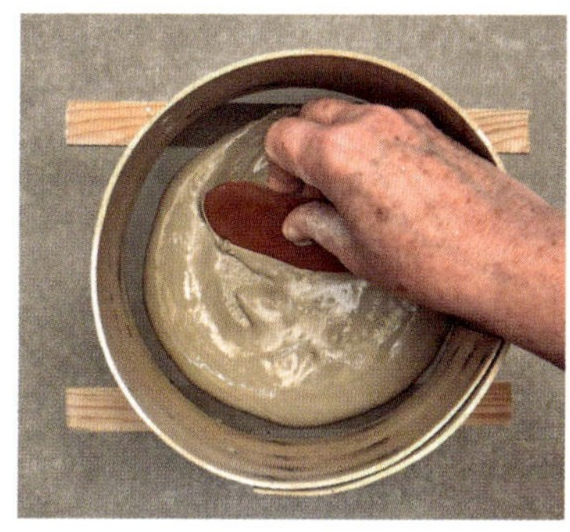

3 Put the mixture through an 80-mesh sieve using a rubber kidney, to remove large particles or grog content. Add more water to the slip until a thick consistency—more water can be added as required when using.

To make a colored slip from a clay body and stain

If this is something you are doing for the first time, make small amounts of slip to begin with and test fire them on tiles for color response. If unhappy with the outcome, scale the amount of stain or oxide up or down accordingly and test again.

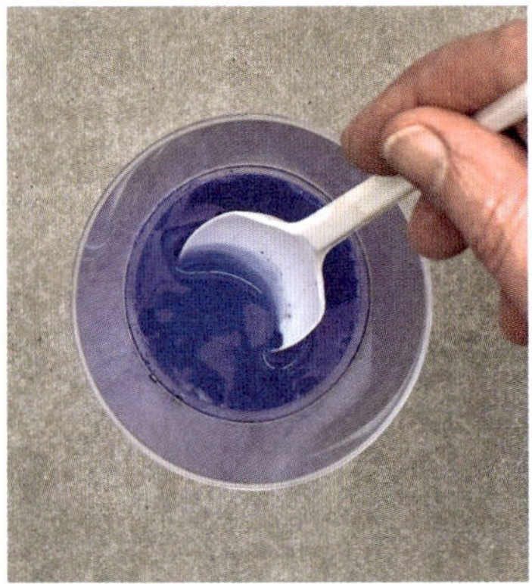

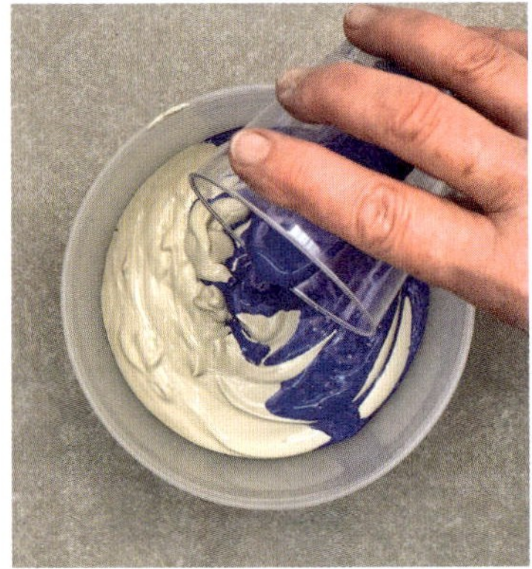

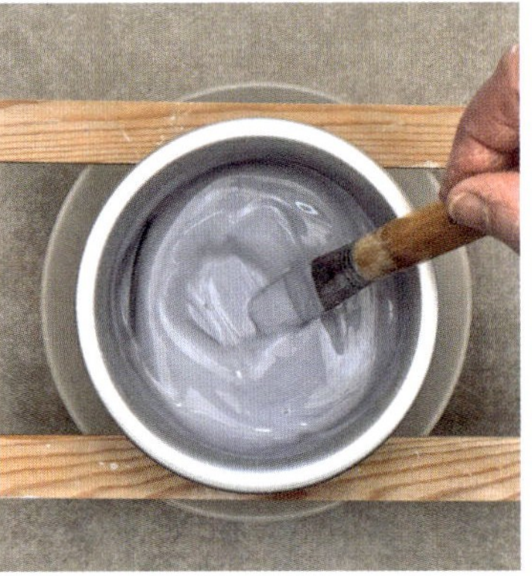

1 Follow step 1 of making a white slip. WEARING A DUST MASK, crush the clay to a powder in either a mortar and pestle or by placing it in a plastic bag and using a rolling pin. Carefully sieve out the grog content of the powdered clay. Weigh out the required amount of clay powder (a small amount for testing and a larger amount for greater quantity) and mix it with water to a thick cream consistency.

2 Body stain in the ratio of 5–15% of the clay weight will give a wide range of colors, the larger amount producing maximum color saturation. Weigh out the required amount of stain (proportionate to the clay weight) on a sheet of paper so that you can funnel it without mess into a container. Add a small amount of water and mix thoroughly to a paste to break down the color. If you don't do this certain stains will speckle when used.

3 Add the liquid stain to the clay mixture and stir well to a yogurt-like consistency and until the color is fully integrated.

4 Put the mixture through an 80–100-mesh sieve supported over a bowl on two wooden sticks. If the slip is very liquid, allow it to settle overnight, then syphon off sufficient water to reduce it to the correct consistency.

To use oxides instead of stains, see *Coloring slip using oxides, page 158.*

Ball clay slip

Slip can be mixed from ingredients other than white clay bodies for makers wanting to apply color to darker clays, like red earthenware. Ball clays form the base for most slip recipes, used by themselves or with the addition of other materials like china clay (kaolin). Sometimes a small amount of frit can be added to the slip but this is usually an addition to fit a specific clay, firing temperature, or technique.

RECIPES

Basic white, black, or brown decorating slips can be made using the recipes below. For different colors, oxides or stains give you more options. Apply before bisque firing for a matte color that can be enhanced further with glaze.

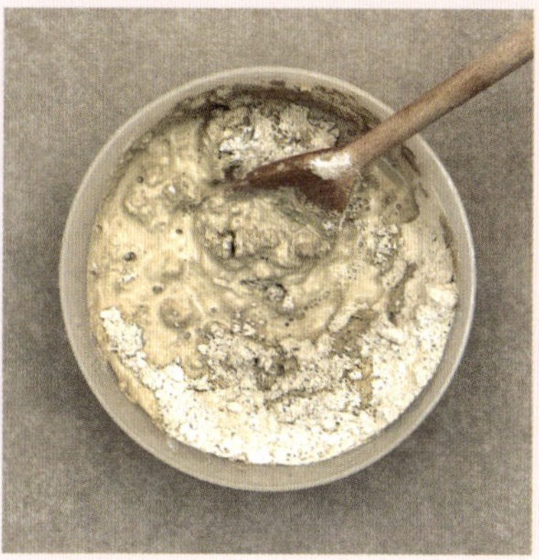

1 Mix the dry ingredients with water WEARING A DUST MASK and gloves.

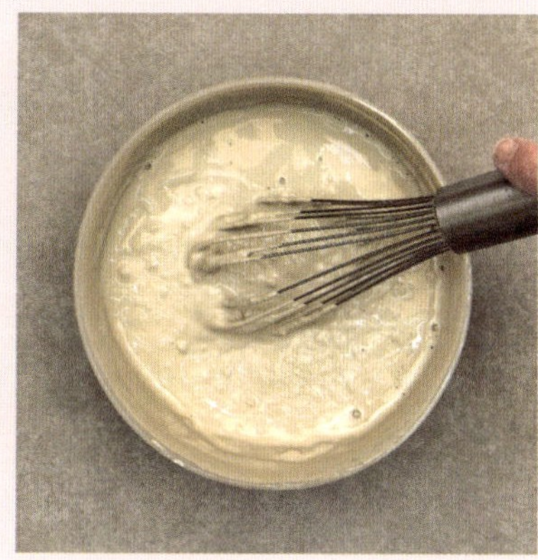

2 Whisk by hand or with an immersion blender until smooth. Press through an 80-mesh sieve to eliminate any lumps.

BASIC WHITE SLIP RECIPE

- 60% Ball clay
- 40% China clay

BLACK SLIP RECIPE

- 70% Powdered red clay
- 15% Manganese dioxide
- 15% Cobalt oxide

BROWN SLIP RECIPE

- 60% Powdered red clay
- 40% Ball clay

Varying shades can be achieved by adjusting the ratios of powdered red clay to ball clay.

Coloring slip using oxides

These quantities apply when coloring slips made from ball clay or a white clay body.

BLUE: Cobalt 1.5–2% (to intensify color, add oxide in increments of 0.5% to a maximum of 10%)

GREEN: Copper oxide 3% will give a good mid-green (to intensify color, add oxide in the same increments as for cobalt)

BLUE/PURPLE: Cobalt oxide 2%; Manganese dioxide 1%

Experiment and test oxide additions in the following percentages:

Light tones	0.2–2.5%
Medium tones	2.5–5%
Dark tones	5–10%

Body stains

These colors are powder pigments that provide a more extensive and brighter color palette than oxides.

Experiment and test body stains in the following percentages:

Light tones	2–5%
Medium tones	5–10%
Dark tones	10–15%

SLIP: METHODS OF APPLICATION

Only the slip application methods used in this book are included in this section; it is not a definitive list of approaches but will provide all you need to know to complete the projects.

Pouring

This is a good method for repeat production of items where speed and ease of application is critical. It forms a good base for further decoration like sgraffito or underglaze painting.

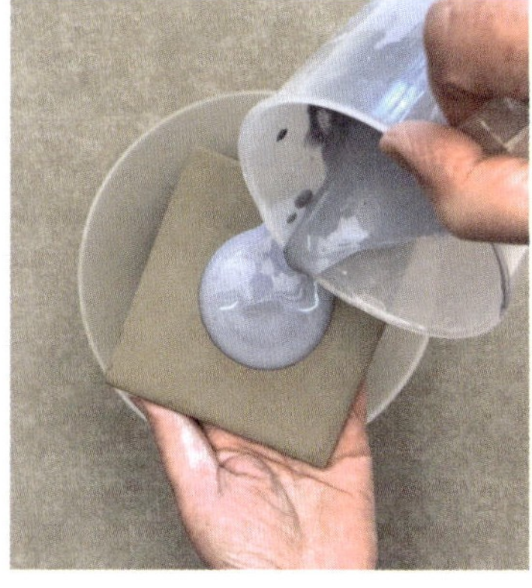

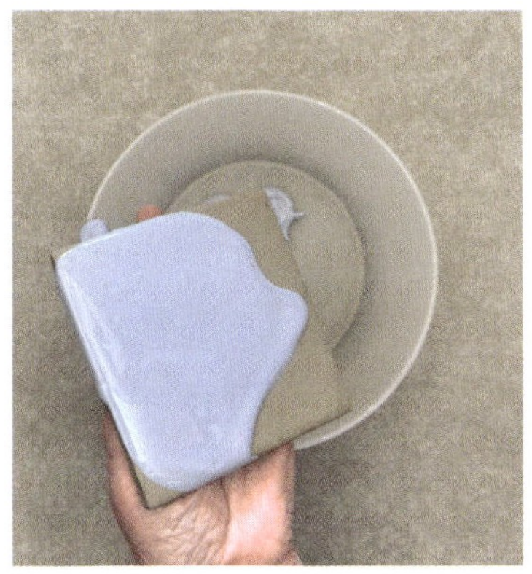

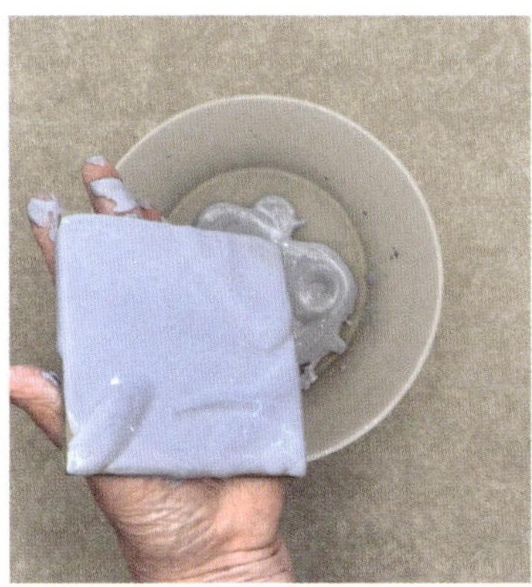

1 Pour slip from a pitcher to coat all or selected areas of a leather-hard piece.

2 Rotate the item to allow the slip to cover the entire surface.

3 Pour away the excess quickly to prevent saturation.

Brushing

Load a fan brush with slip and brush over the surface in even strokes. For best coverage, allow the first coat to dry to the touch, then apply a second coat.

This is an easy, standard method of application to form a base for further decorative techniques like paper resist, sgraffito, and slip trailing.

Slip can also be applied in a calligraphic way to create patterns using a liner brush.

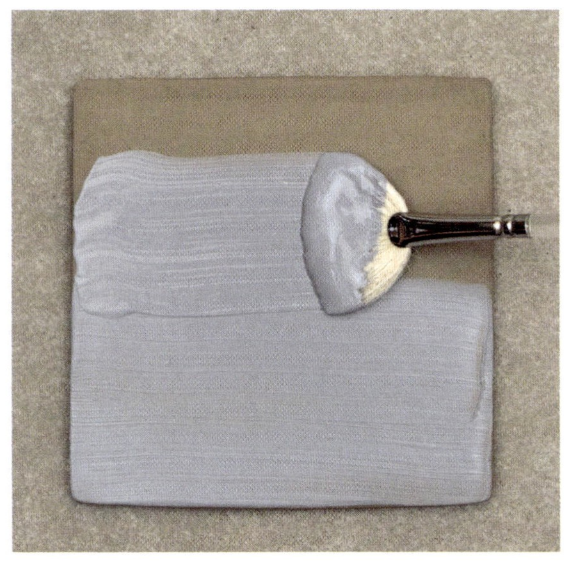

Sponging

Sponging slip over a surface is a good alternative to brushing.

NOTE: Sponging can also add texture to a surface if a thicker slip is used and synthetic, shaped sponges can be used to create surface designs.

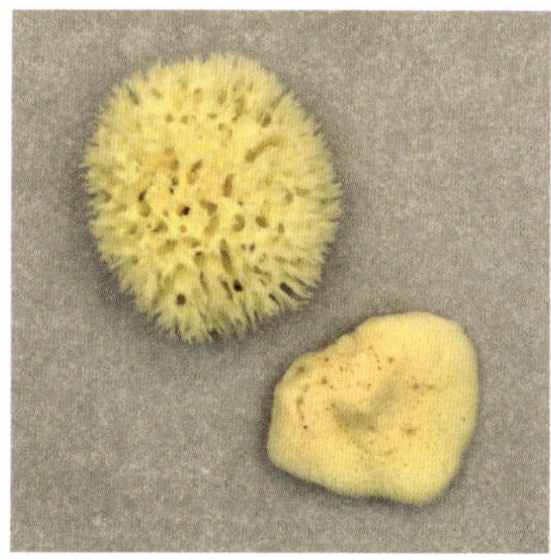

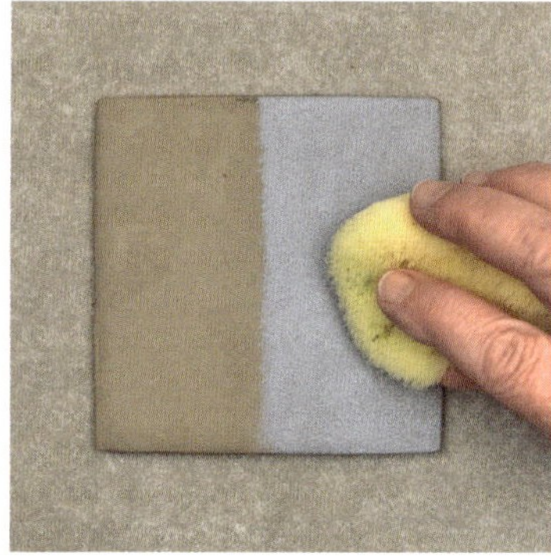

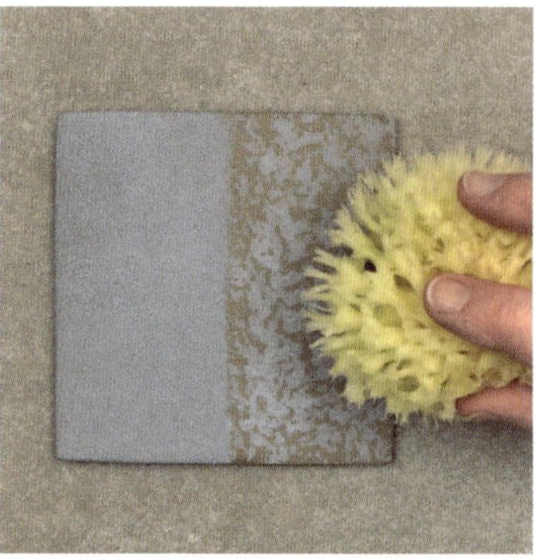

1 Different effects can be achieved with fine or open-textured natural sponges and it is useful to have a selection of different sorts to vary the quality of application.

2 Fine-textured sponges are best for all-over coverage: load the sponge and dab the color over the surface until covered. Build layers up gradually for even coverage.

3 Open-textured sponges produce a sparse covering and are most useful to overlay different colors so that the one below shows through.

DECORATIVE TECHNIQUES WITH SLIP

Slip is a very versatile decorating medium and can be applied in a variety of ways that give you more control over the pattern or design, with techniques similar to those used in painting and printing. Your decoration can also add texture with raised or scored surfaces.

Paper resist

This is a resist method that uses paper shapes to form a pattern on the surface of a slip or clay background. The paper forms a resist when other colors of slip are applied over the surface, leaving the design in sharp outline when the paper is removed.

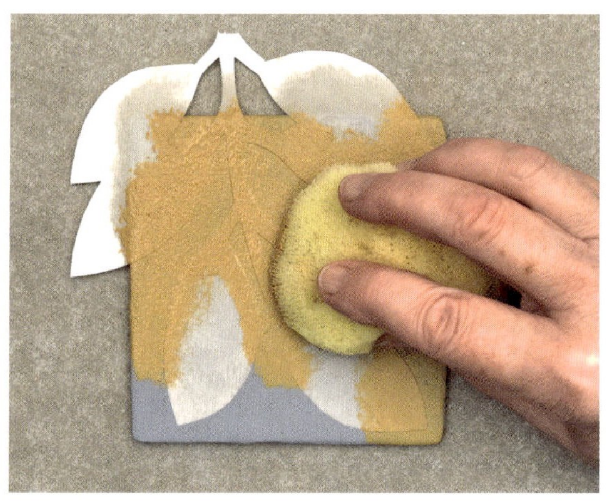

1. Cut out or tear your chosen paper shapes from newspaper. Place the paper cut-out over the clay form and dampen the surface with a wet sponge or paintbrush. This will seal it to the surface.
2. Carefully sponge a contrasting color of slip over the entire surface, including the paper resist. Remove the paper resist carefully with a pin when the slip is touch-dry.

Sgraffito

This is a technique that draws through a layer of slip or underglaze to the clay below to create a pattern in the surface of the pot. It is a form of incising which gives huge scope for artistic expression.

You can use any pointed tool for sgraffito—even a pencil—but mini loop tools are also useful because of the range of marks they produce. This is a technique that is suitable for all forms and the surface design can be a simple outline or specific areas carved away to create complex compositions.

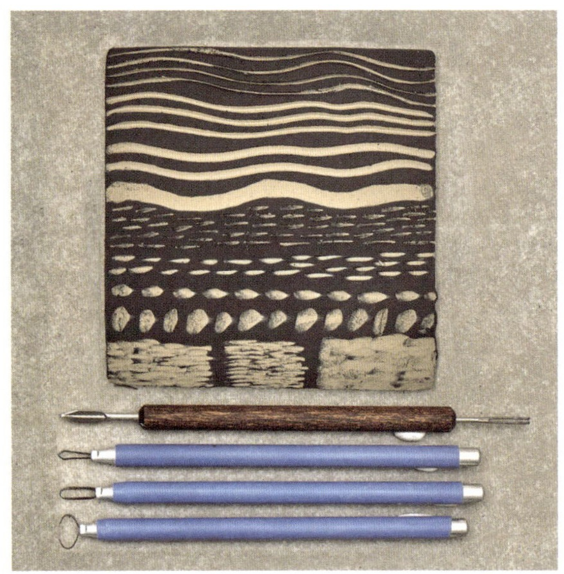

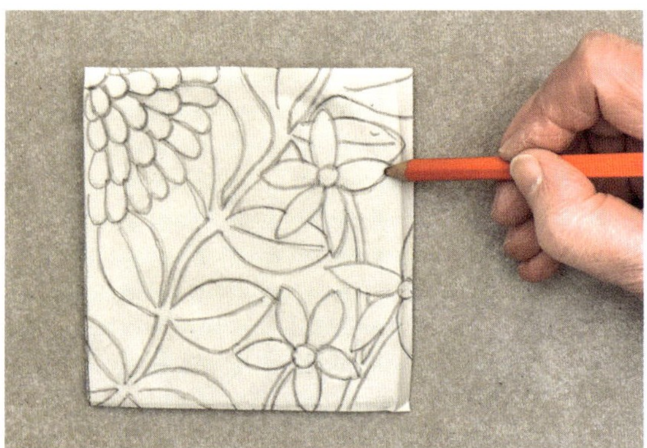

1 Apply a single base coat of slip or build up the surface by lightly overlaying more colors where required. Allow the slip to dry to the touch. Either draw the outline of your design freehand onto the surface of the pot or transfer the design through a paper drawing to impress the outline into the surface. Another alternative is to cut out a card template and use it to sgraffito around.

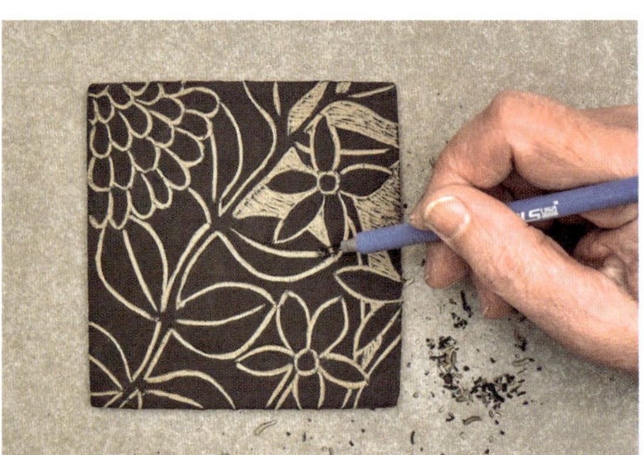

2 Sgraffito the outline of the design first, then remove the slip from the spaces between the image—either entirely or leaving traces of the slip to enliven the background as shown.

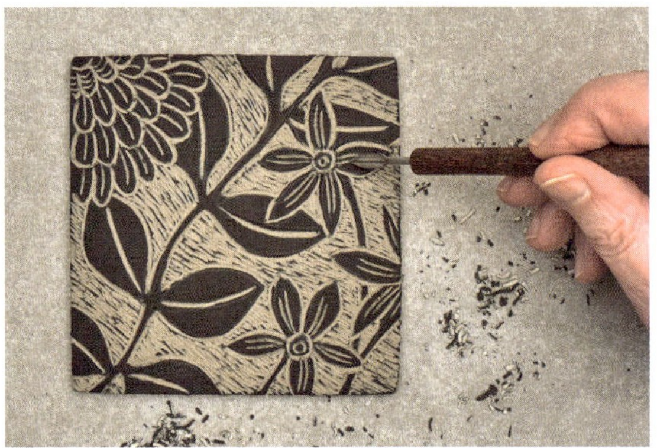

3 Add more features and finer detail as required to the image. Use a stiff brush to gently sweep away the clay scrapings and dust.

Slip trailing

Slip trailing requires a bold and confident hand to achieve good results. You will need a slip trailing bulb for this technique. There are many options available to buy in different sizes from ceramic suppliers, usually including a range of nozzles for different thicknesses of line, or you can use a bottle from a hair-dye kit for practice.

1. Apply to a leather-hard surface, either directly onto the clay or over a base layer of colored slip. The base layer can still be liquid, in which case the trailing pattern will meld into it, or the slip can be touch-dry and the slip pattern will remain in some relief when fired.

2. Fill the bulb with fairly thick slip—this is important because if too thin, the slip will run and spoil the surface.

3. Attach the chosen size of nozzle—practice trailing a few lines on paper or a test sample of clay to ensure the slip is moving well through the bulb before committing.

4. Squeeze the bulb steadily and evenly for continuous lines, and intermittently for dots and other small details.

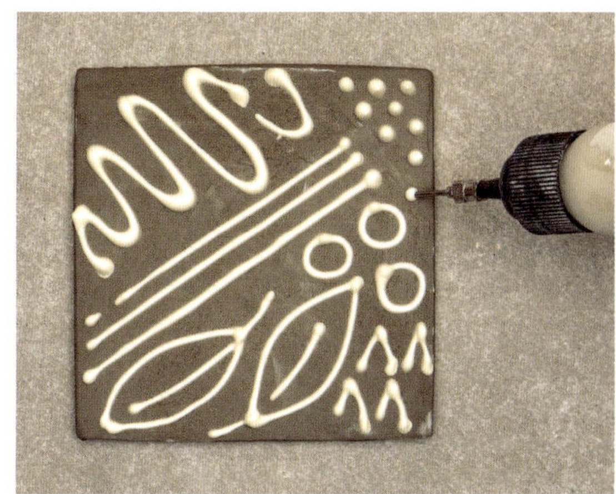

Tube lining

This is a variation of slip trailing where the slip stands in relief when fired. The lines are generally thin and depict fine detail, which, traditionally, is later filled with colored glazes. However, when used in the projects in this book it forms the base for other surface finishes. Slip for tube lining must be thickened so that it stays in relief on the surface of your work.

The best way to thicken slip is with Epsom salts, also known as magnesium sulphate. These act as a flocculent, to gel and thicken the slip and hold the constituent particles in suspension.

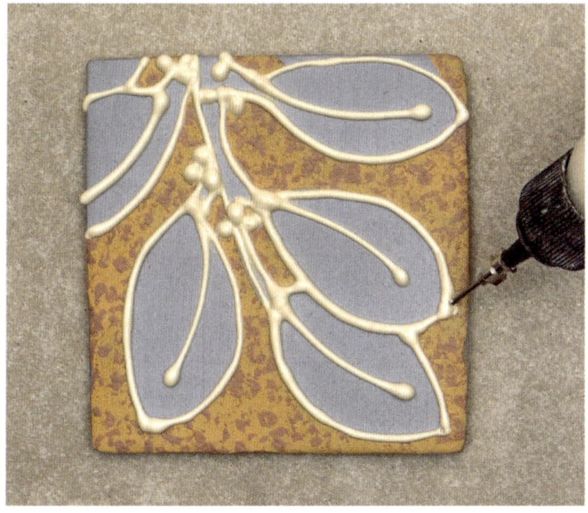

To make a slip for tube lining:
The most effective method of preparation is to make a saturated solution: dissolve 1oz (30g) Epsom salts in 3fl oz (100ml) water. Label the bottle and keep for future use. The slip should be made from the clay body for best fit.

Decant a small amount of slip to a separate container, add the Epsom salt solution a drop at a time, and mix thoroughly to a thick, yogurt-like consistency; continue to add more drops and mix until that is achieved.

1. Tube lining is usually applied directly onto the leather-hard clay but it can also be applied to surfaces decorated by other methods first, to enhance or outline a design.

2. Apply as you would for slip trailing if working directly on the clay surface. The outline can be drawn out in soft pencil first if the design is complicated.

3. To tube line a paper resist image, simply outline the design as shown.

GLAZE AND APPLICATION

Glazing is probably the most difficult element of working with clay for many makers, especially beginners—you need to choose the right glaze, mix it in the correct proportions, decide the best method of application, and, lastly, use it creatively. For some it is an amazing adventure; for others an epic disappointment. In this chapter we are going to dispel these anxieties and eliminate some of the challenges by using ready-made glazes for many of the projects, with a few mixed glazes added in.

PROS AND CONS: MAKING VERSUS READY-MADE

Ready-made: Pros

1. These glazes are tremendously convenient.

2. They are available in a huge range of finishes—from shiny to matte, opaque to crystalline, for earthenware, stoneware, and other firing methods. With specialty finishes like crackle or cobblestone which add texture, the list is endless and includes every finish you could wish for.

3. The results are reliable and consistent providing the firing guidelines are adhered to.

4. Application is easy—usually by brush or sponge in 2–3 layers—and drying time is very quick.

5. All you need to know about these glazes is printed on the container (firing range, food safety, etc.); therefore you don't need any prior glaze knowledge to use them.

6. They can be purchased in relatively small amounts for testing before committing to larger quantities.

7. None of the glaze is wasted because of the application method.

8. Many of these glazes can be used in combination with others for creative experimentation.

9. Application can be very specific for fine detail effects.

Ready-made: Cons

1. These glazes are not usually available in large enough quantities for dipping. However, dry versions of many glazes are available to mix larger amounts. It can be an expensive alternative, but at least the chemistry has already been done for you.

2. Application is more time-consuming because the glazes are brushed on in 2–3 coats. This can be tedious if you are glazing several large items.

3. Even with 3 coats, application can be streaky if insufficient care is taken. Practice will correct this.

Making your own: Pros

1. Although expensive to buy the raw ingredients to begin with, ultimately you will save money because they usually come in quantity, allowing the making of many glazes.

2. There are thousands of glaze recipes to choose from, giving great flexibility for experimentation.

3. Mixing your own glazes allows you to make bulk quantities suitable for your needs and chosen application methods, especially dipping.

Making your own: Cons

1. You will need some glaze chemistry knowledge to understand how to mix a compatible glaze for your work.

2. The cost of materials is initially considerable and includes equipment like sieves and tightly lidded containers.

3. Large containers of glaze take up space in the workshop.

4. Some of the materials are toxic, so great care must be taken when handling them.

5. Making glazes is a time-consuming and messy business. It will include weighing and measuring, mixing, sieving, then cleaning up. After which the glaze will need to be test fired before it can be used.

MIXING A GLAZE

Many glazes can be purchased in dry formulations, ready to mix with water. Whether using commercially bought glaze or developing your own, the principles for mixing them are the same. ALWAYS wear a mask.

1. You do not need to weigh commercially bought glaze, but if formulating your own you will need a good set of scales to weigh out the individual ingredients. Bathroom scales are good for weighing large amounts of glaze material.

2. Place the dry glaze ingredients in a clean, dry bowl, then cover with water and let soak for at least 30 minutes. Stir the glaze mixture thoroughly with a wooden spoon or stick.

3. Work the glaze through an 80–120-mesh sieve supported on sticks suspended over a large bowl using a stiff dishwashing brush.

4. The consistency of the sieved glaze should be like thick cream for most purposes.

About sieves: Sieves are available in several mesh sizes but for most purposes an 80–100-mesh sieve is adequate; use 120-mesh for finer particles.

TIPS

- Test the consistency of glaze by dipping your finger into the mixture—it is correct if it coats the finger but allows the creases to show through.
- If the glaze is too thick, thin it down with more water. If too thin, allow it to settle overnight, then decant some of the water off the top.

Keeping glaze in suspension

Glaze has a tendency to settle and harden in the bottom of the pail over time. Overcome this problem by adding 1–2% bentonite to the dry ingredients before adding water to mix. Do not add it after the glaze has been mixed because it will not disperse.

Epsom salts can be used as a good alternative to bentonite. Just mix a spoonful in water, then stir into the mix (see also page 162).

A WORD ABOUT PYROMETRIC CONES (ORTON)

Many potters use cones to measure temperature in their kilns as an alternative or in addition to a controller. Pyrometric cones are devised to measure "heatwork"—the increase of heat over time—and are graded according to the amount of heat they can withstand. Three cones which bend, or mature, at given temperatures are placed upright in holders in the kiln where they can be viewed from the spy hole. As each cone reaches temperature it will bend, indicating the temperature has risen to a given point.

Many glaze manufacturers give a cone temperature alongside the actual temperature in Fahrenheit (or Celsius) as a guide to the maturing temperature of the glaze. Maturing temperatures are never exact because all kilns fire slightly differently. Be prepared to experiment to find the best firing regime and final temperature for a glaze in your kiln.

Recipes for low-, mid-, and high-fire glossy transparent glaze

There are literally thousands of glaze recipes available from books, the internet, and various forums, for you to choose from.

Here are three "glossy transparent" recipes to experiment with. Add oxides or stains in the proportions suggested for mixing slips to find a color to suit (see pages 157–158). Be aware that some oxides added in larger quantities will flux a glaze (reduce its melting point) and make it more runny, so be sure to test all experiments on a vertical test piece before applying the glaze to your finished work.

Low-fire base glaze
Cone 03 (1,987°F/1,086°C)

Gerstly borate	55%
EPK kaolin	30
Silica	15
	100%

Experiment with stains and oxides as suggested on page 158 or try:

Blue: Cobalt oxide	2%
Rich yellow: Rutile	6–8%
Green: Copper carbonate	6–8%

Mid-range glossy transparent
Cone 05 (2,185°F/1,196°C)

Gillespie borate (Gerstly borate)	55%
Minspar 200 feldspar (Soda feldspar)	46
EPK kaolin	13
Silica	27
	100%

High-fire glossy transparent
Cone 8–10 (2,318– 2,377°F/1,270–1,303°C)

Gillespie borate	10%
Whiting	8
Nepheline syenite	55
Silica (flint)	27
	100%

GLAZING METHODS

Glaze can be applied to the surface of your pots in several ways:

Dipping

As the term suggests, pots dipped in glaze are quickly submerged in part

or whole into a pail of glaze.

1. Dip the form in the glaze to the desired height, then quickly lift it out again and shake off the surplus.

2. If dipping in two halves, turn the form around when it is dry to the touch, then dip the second half up to the line of the first dip.

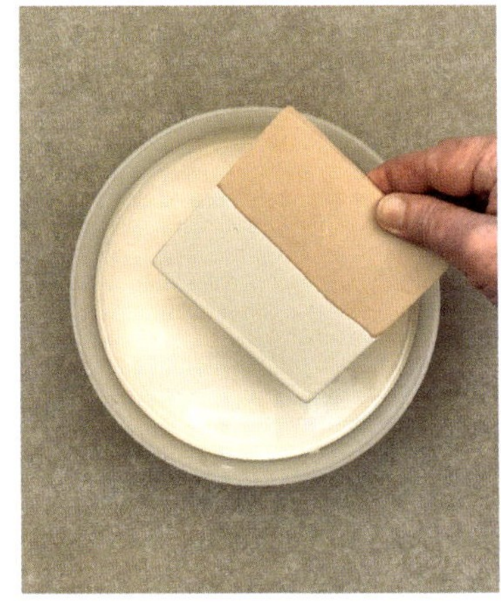

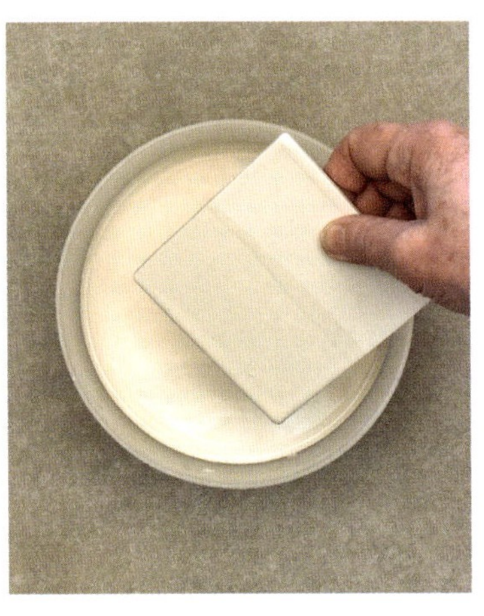

Pouring

If the pot is small enough, hold it in one hand over a container, then pour the glaze over the surface in one even coat.

Suspend larger forms, upside down, supported on two sticks suspended over a container that is large enough to catch the glaze as you pour.

Alternatively, try using a funnel as a chuck. Place the funnel inside a bowl with the pot inverted over the top. Place the bowl on a banding wheel to allow you to turn it as you pour the glaze for even coverage.

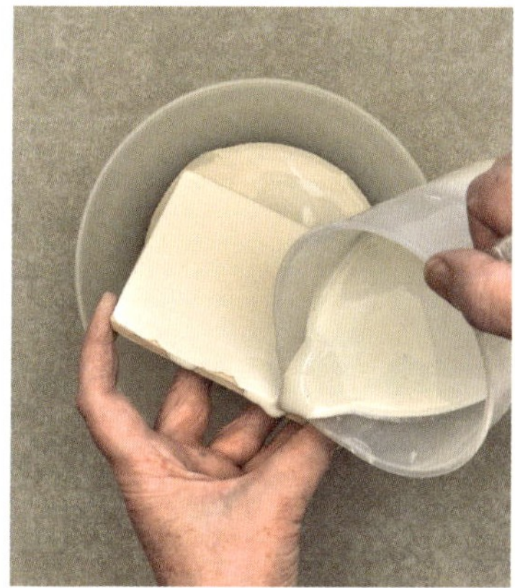

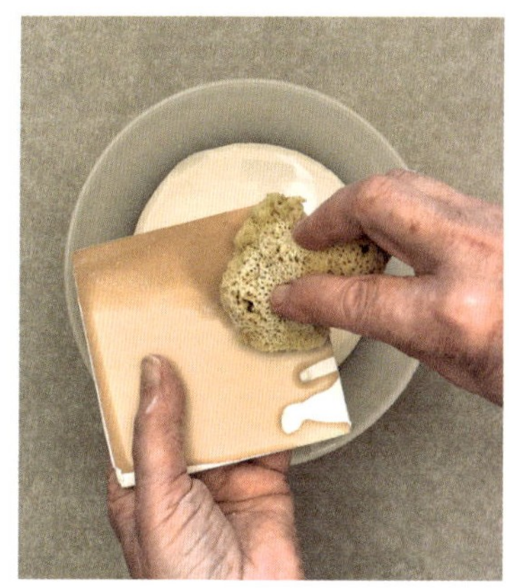

IMPORTANT Thoroughly wipe away any glaze which may have run onto the underside of the form with a damp sponge. Failure to do this will result in the pot sticking to the kiln shelf when the glaze melts in the kiln. However, the undersides of earthenware forms fired on star stilts can be glazed.

Sponging and decorative sponging

Entire surfaces can be sponged with glaze for special effects, or specific areas for detail.

To sponge all over in one glaze, simply load a close-textured natural sponge and dab it over the surface until evenly covered. Apply a second coat if the first looks patchy when dry.

Decorative sponging involves the use of specially shaped synthetic sponges to apply a surface design over a base layer of glaze. See pages 66–67 for an example of this technique.

Dotting and trailing

Depending on the size of brush used, dotty detail can be applied to a surface to enhance a design.

Glaze can be trailed in much the same way as slip (see page 162), using a slip trailing bulb. It is a technique that requires confidence as glaze is by nature runnier than slip. The technique is good for expressive lines, dots, and sweeps of contrasting color.

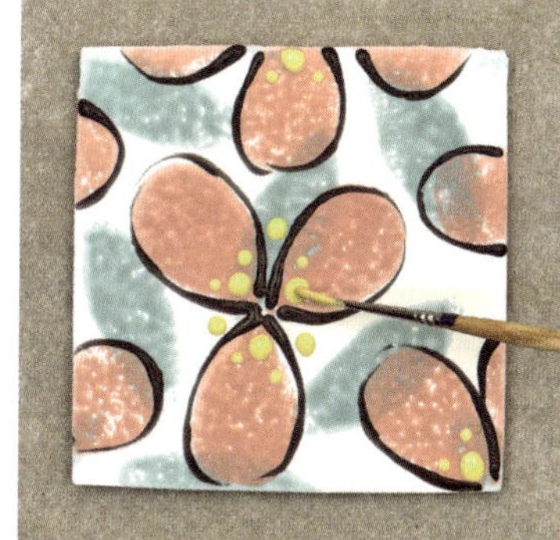

Dotting: Use a fine liner brush for small dots and a larger brush for more robust dots.

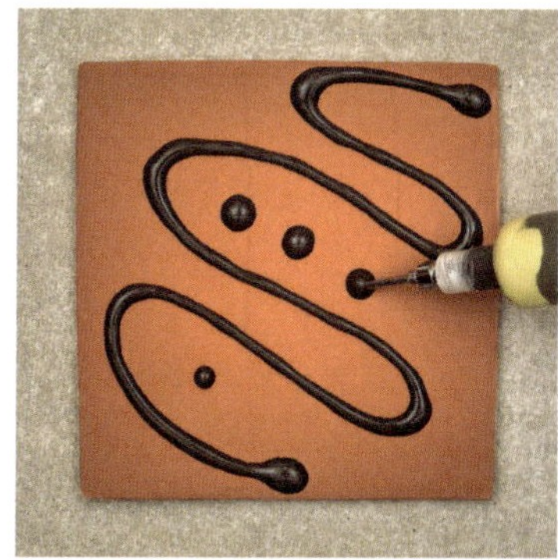

Trailing: Load the bulb with a contrasting color of glaze, then trail your chosen design on the surface. You can draw a design on lightly in pencil first as a guide.

Brushing

Many of the decorative surfaces in the projects make use of commercially prepared glazes, which are brushed on in two or three coats.

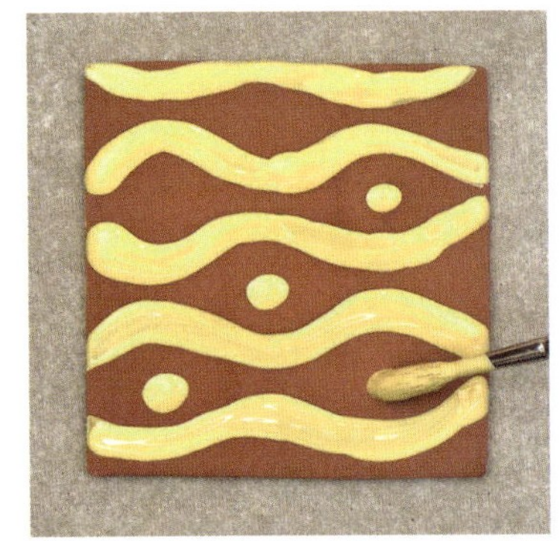

Method:
Load a fan-shaped, natural hair brush with glaze and paint over the surface of the pot in one direction. Reload the brush regularly for even coverage and don't overwork the application. Allow the first coat to dry to the touch before applying subsequent layers.

Glazes can be applied over one another for both earthenware and stoneware firings, but at higher temperatures the glazes melt into one another more freely and a reaction takes place as they mingle. Glazes can be randomly overlaid for a drippy, luscious mingling or you can apply them in a structured way by painting a specific design. To do this, make bold, sweeping, decorative marks in contrasting glaze with a single loaded brush, working quickly and confidently over the surface to produce lines, dots, or an outline.

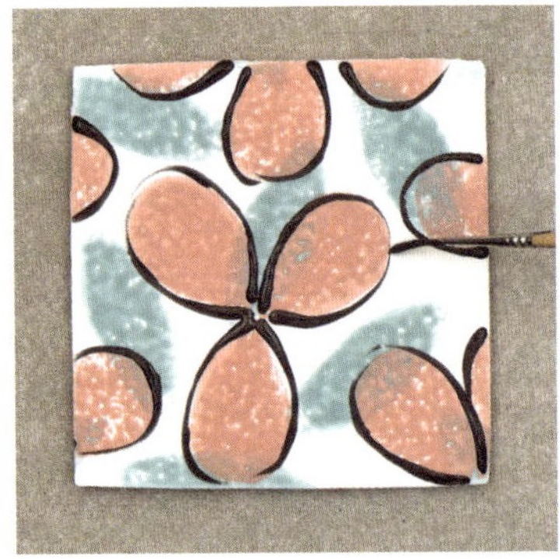

At lower firing temperatures, the brushing technique can be used to make secondary, expressive marks over a base glaze or to apply outline detail using a fine liner brush.

Majolica style

This is an adaptation of the majolica technique using brush-on glazes instead of the traditional tin glaze with underglaze colors. It is a much easier method of achieving a very similar effect if the recommended glazes are used, because they can be applied thickly for block color or in washes for watercolor effects.

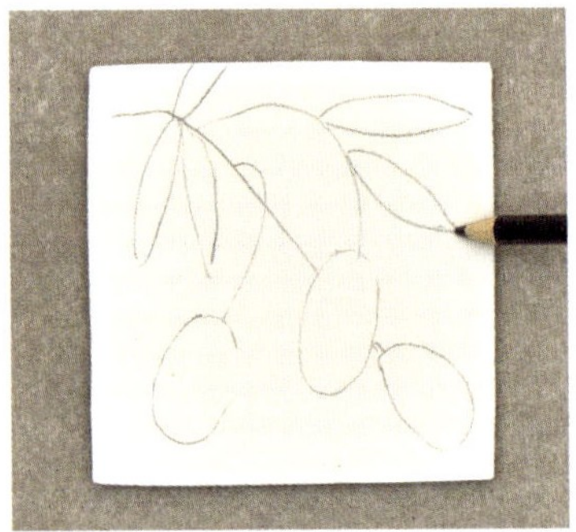

1 Apply two coats of base glaze; let dry between coats. Draw on the glaze surface in soft pencil.

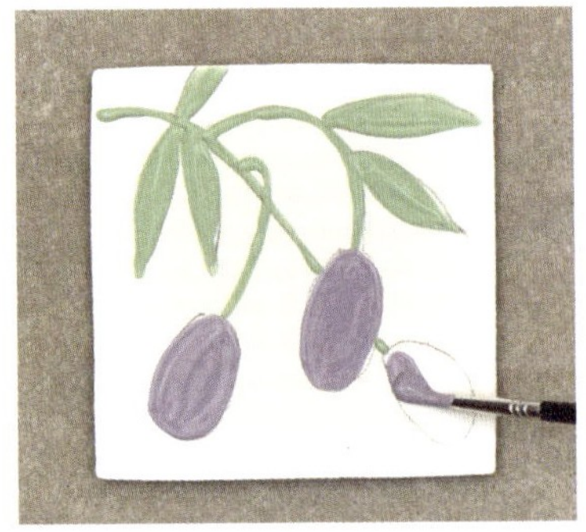

2 Paint in the detail of the design using a fine brush and your chosen glaze colors.

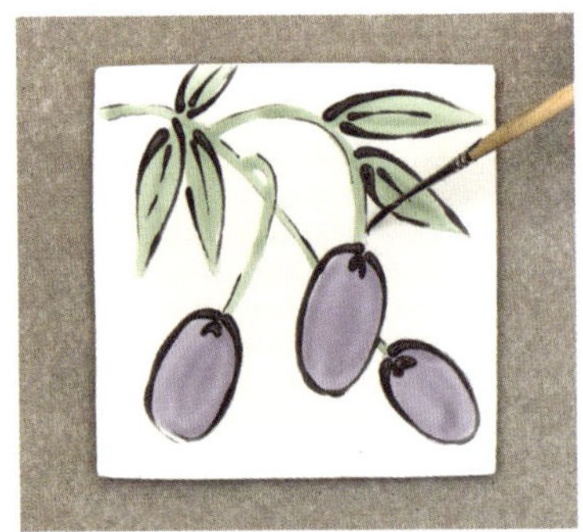

3 Outline the detail of the image in a bold color, using a fine liner brush.

Using resists

Resists are used to block out areas of a form that you don't want to glaze. This can be a blanket resist, covering specific areas, or the resist itself can be used to create a surface design.

There are generally three main resists used: paper tape, wax emulsion, or liquid latex.

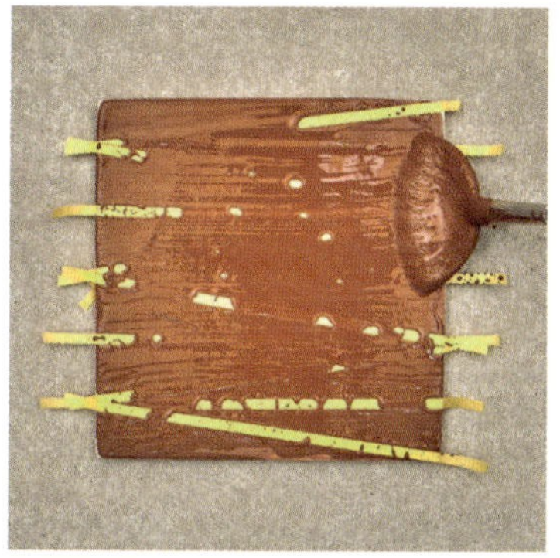

1 Apply a tape pattern to a bisque-fired surface, making sure it fully adheres by rubbing over it with a finger several times. Glaze over the tape using your chosen method: brushing, dipping, or pouring.

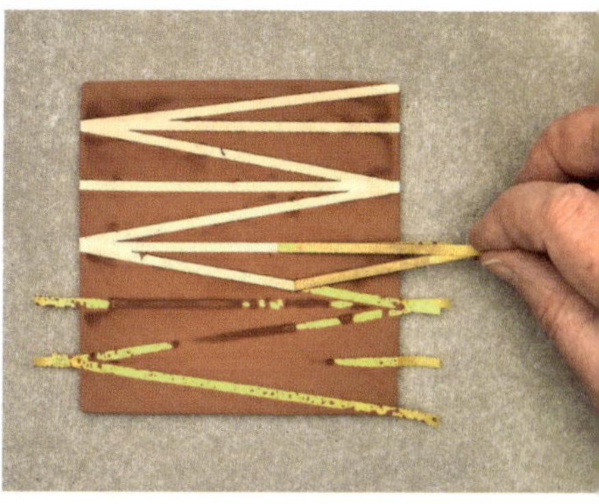

2 Remove the tape when the glaze has dried to the touch by lifting the corner with a pin and then carefully peeling away.

Wax emulsion and latex resist

The use of latex is not shown here because its application is the same as wax emulsion. However, unlike wax, which burns away in firing, the latex is removed before firing. It can be applied over or under glazes in the same way as wax.

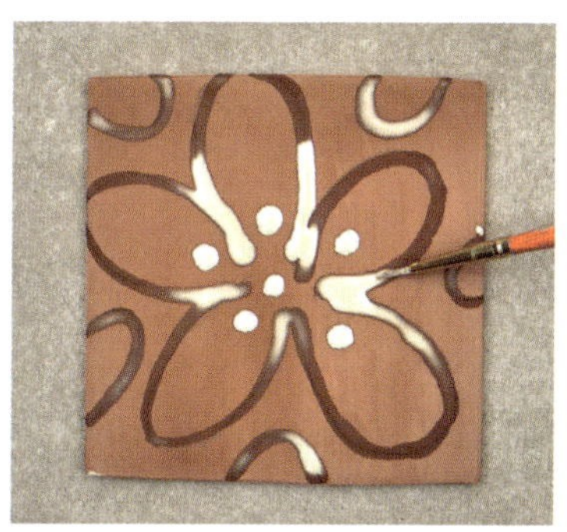

1 Apply a base glaze to the surface and let dry to the touch. Then draw a design over the glaze in soft pencil. Paint over the pencil lines in wax emulsion, and any further areas you want to resist the top glaze.

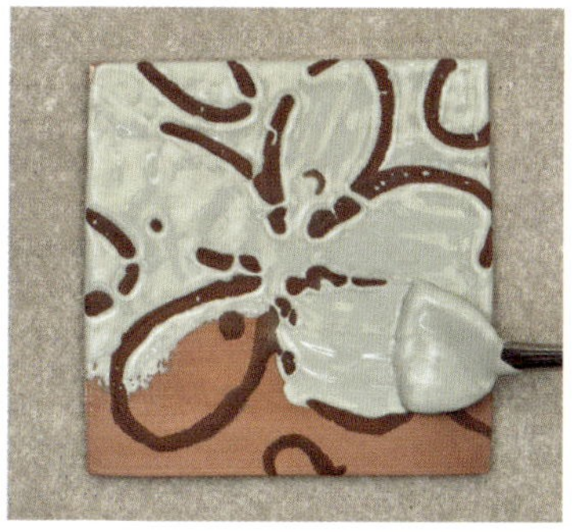

2 Cover the wax design in a contrasting glaze color.

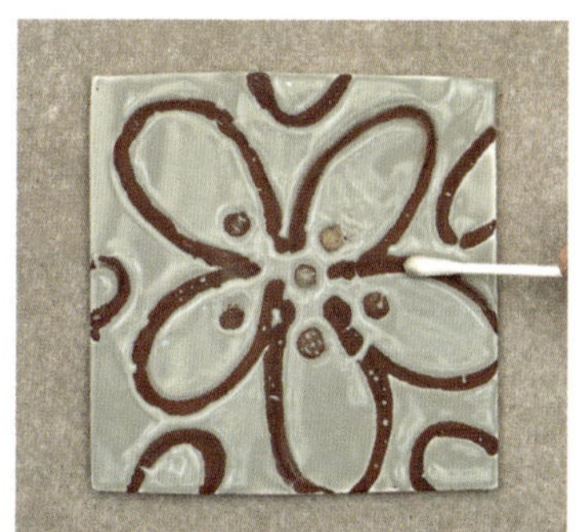

3 The wax will resist most of the top glaze but where it remains over the wax, simply remove it with a moist cotton bud. If latex was used instead of wax, peel it off the surface after the top glaze has dried to the touch.

UNDERGLAZE AND OTHER TECHNIQUES

The decorative techniques demonstrated in this section can be applied as finishes in their own right or in combination with others, including slip and glaze. They add to the arsenal of approaches to decorating and show the potential of combining techniques for unique expression.

WAYS TO USE UNDERGLAZES

- Underglaze is generally applied by brush to either a leather-hard surface (for sgraffito and other green-stage decorative methods), or a bisque-fired surface.
- It can also be sponged onto a surface in much the same way as slip.

UNDERGLAZES

As the name suggests, these are colored liquid pigments that are applied to a bisque-fired surface, under a glaze. They tend to be sold in small pots and are available in a huge range of colors, which can be mixed to create other shades. Generally applied with a brush or sponge, they can be used to create graphic design or in a looser, more painterly way for a freer effect.

Underglazes are usually applied in three coats for dense block color. They can be overlapped and intermixed to create exciting color combinations and in general are most vibrant when covered with a transparent glaze. But there are varieties of underglaze that are fluxed to fire with or without glaze; they are matte and velvety at low temperatures, but get shinier the higher they are fired. These underglazes are wonderful in combination with glaze where the two surfaces remain distinct from one another.

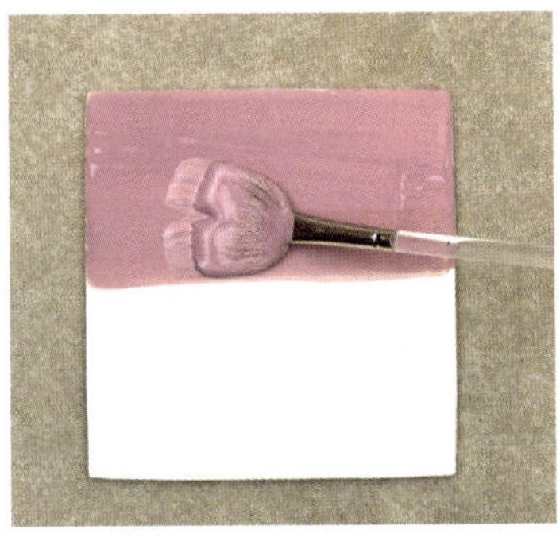

1 Load a fan brush with underglaze and paint over the surface of either a leather-hard or bisque-fired surface. One coat will give a wash of cover; two coats or more give a block color. Apply subsequent coats when the one before has dried to the touch.

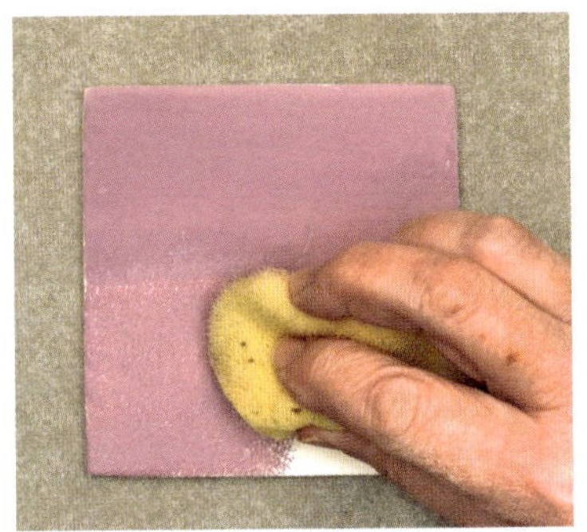

2 Use a close-textured natural sponge for even cover, again applying the color in layers depending on the depth of coverage that is required.

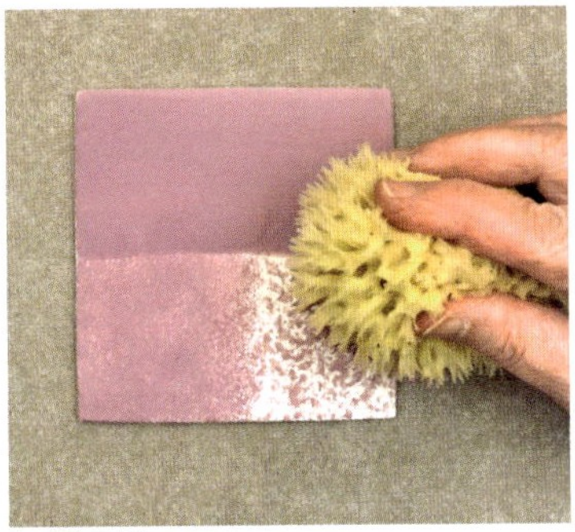

3 Open-textured natural sponges can be used for feature detail and overlaying color so that the one below clearly shows through.

Painting with underglaze

Underglaze colors can be used in a painterly way to produce imagery in the way an artist would use paint. Simply draw out a design on the surface of the clay in pencil (or paint freehand). Don't worry about pencil marks—they will burn away in firing. Fill in the design with underglaze colors of choice, applying one coat for watercolor-type washes and three coats for intense depth. Outline the design in a strong color to highlight.

Underglaze as inlay to outline a design

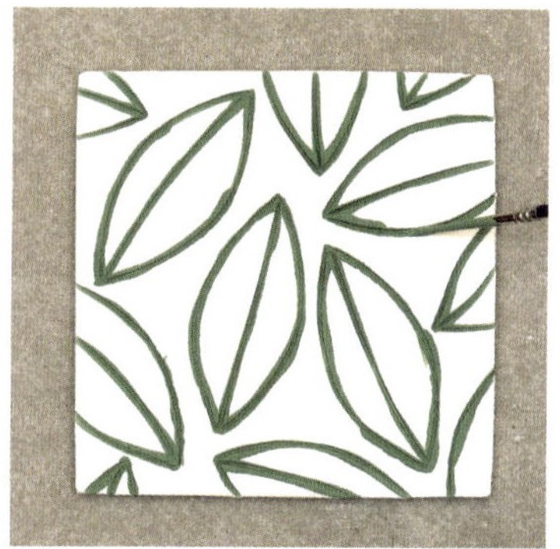

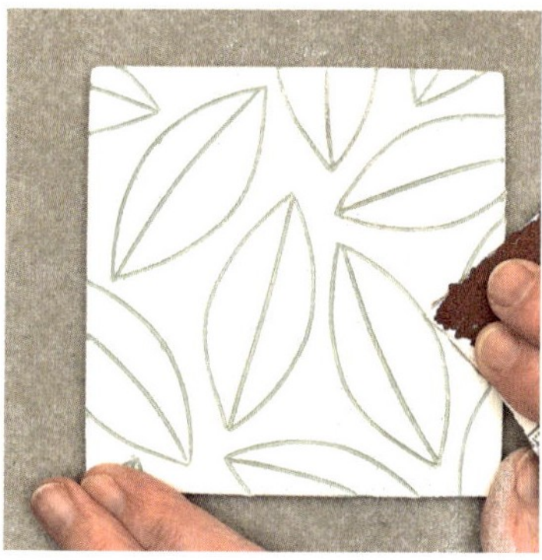

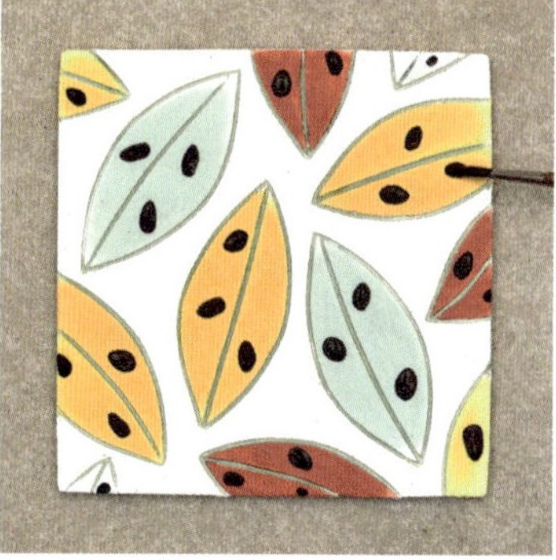

1 While at the green stage, score the outline of a design into the clay using a sgraffito tool, then dry and bisque fire the work. Once fired, fill in the lines with a bold color of underglaze, using a fine brush. Allow the underglaze to dry.

2 WEARING A DUST MASK and using sandpaper, work over the surface until the underglaze only remains in the line design and is crisp and sharp. Carefully brush away the excess dust before continuing.

3 Paint in extra detail freehand as required to enliven the design. Fill the outlined shapes with color as required.

Underglaze pencils or crayons

This technique is good for expressive lines, dots, and sweeps of contrasting color, as well as fine line drawing, script, and shading. Underglaze pencils are very useful as permanent markers on test items. Available in a variety of colors. NOTE: Reds and yellows generally only fire to 1,940°F (1,060°C).

Method:
Use the pencils to draw directly onto a bisque-fired surface, using them in the same way as artists' coloring pencils. Dust over the finished surface with a soft brush to remove excess particles but be careful, the pencil lines can smudge easily. Cover in transparent glaze for best color response.

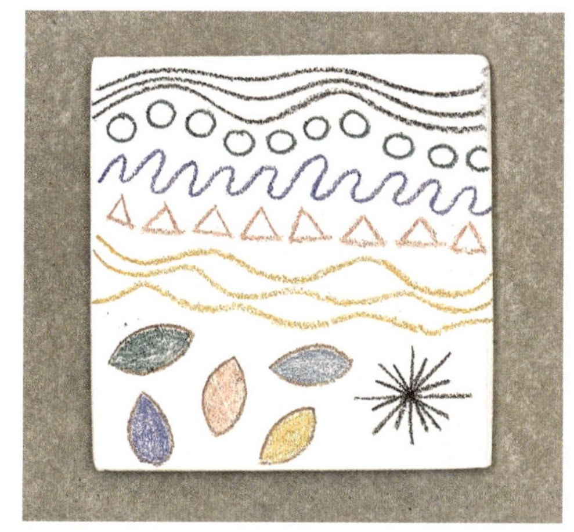

WATER ETCHING WITH WAX

This is a decorative technique that uses wax as a resist on bone-dry, but unfired clay (usually a fine clay like porcelain) to create a design that stands in relief when the area around it is water-etched. Let dry, then fire to your clay's given temperature; the wax will burn away in firing.

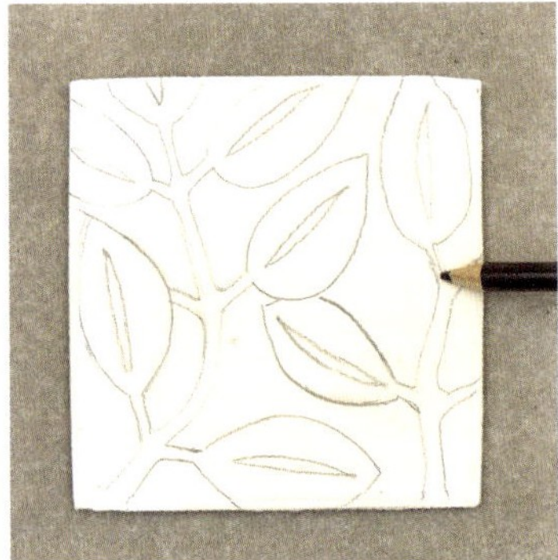

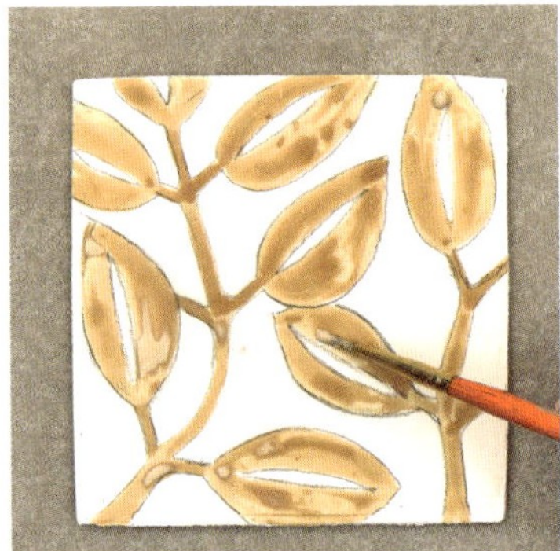

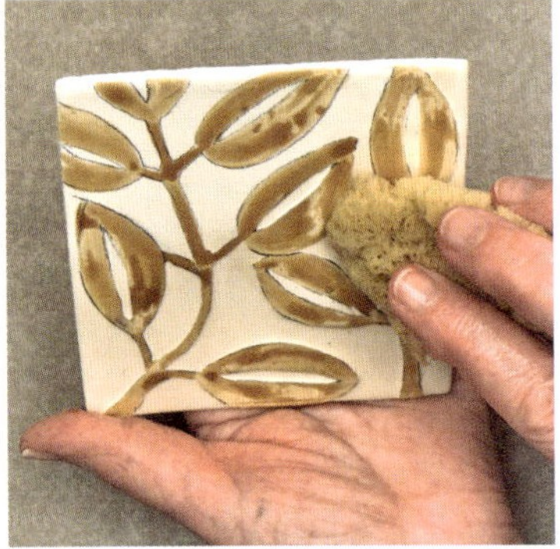

1 Transfer a design to the clay surface in pencil. If you make a mistake, just rub the pencil mark out and re-draw the shape in a better position. When you start to wipe away the clay some of the design will be positive and some negative, so think how you want the detail to look—it will be in relief if covered by wax or etched away otherwise.

2 Paint the design with wax emulsion and a fine brush, taking care to stay within the drawn lines as much as possible.

3 When the waxed area has dried completely, dampen a sponge and start to wash away the clay around the design. Rinse the sponge regularly and work over the whole surface systematically. If the clay starts to saturate and you are not yet happy with the surface, let dry completely, then etch again. You can do this as many times as you need.

CARVING AND TEXTURE

These are decorative techniques used at the green stage of making, that is, before the work is fired. Carved and textured surfaces require little in the way of additional decoration and can look most stunning simply decorated with a colored, transparent glaze that will pool in the detail to highlight it. However, stain or oxide washes can look equally stunning filling the textured surface.

Method:
Use a loop tool to carve leather-hard clay. You can make different marks depending on the size and shape of the loop; cut lines and ridges or make patterned arrangements of marks to suit the form being worked.

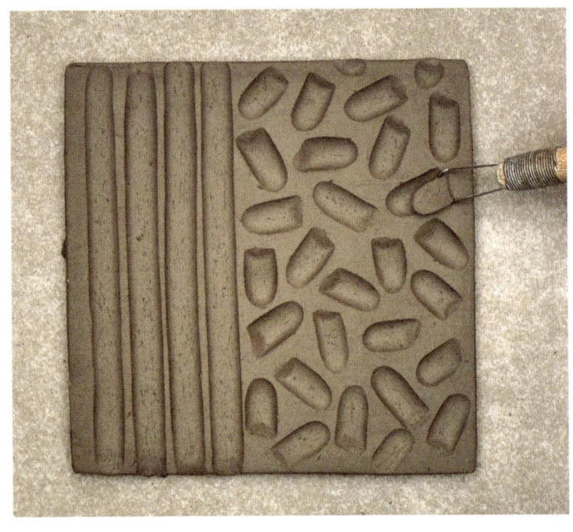

Texture: making marks

Almost anything will make a mark in clay. You do not need elaborate tools and equipment because found or re-purposed objects can create wonderful texture and pattern, and the beauty is that these will be unique to you.

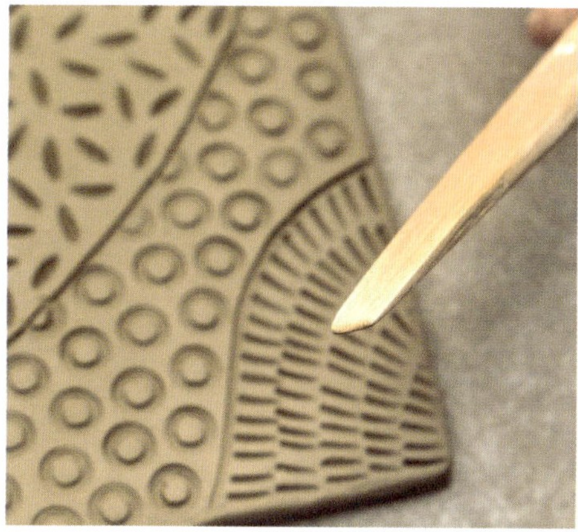

1 Impress boxwood or modeling tools in repeat to create simple designs. Practice on scraps of clay to see how many designs can be created from any given tool.

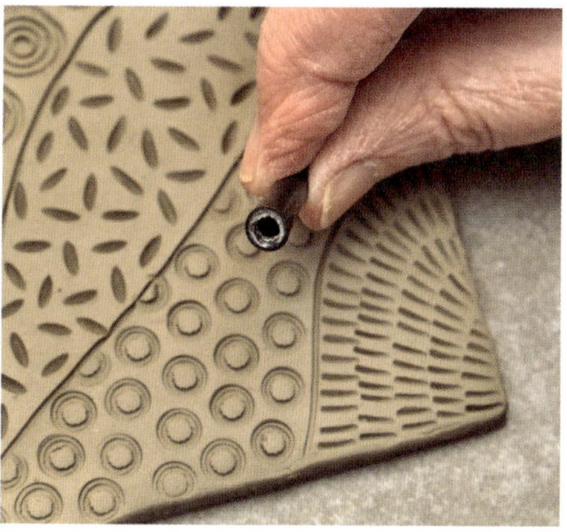

2 You can't beat old pen tops; they can be found in all sorts of patterns and shapes which make fabulous marks in clay.

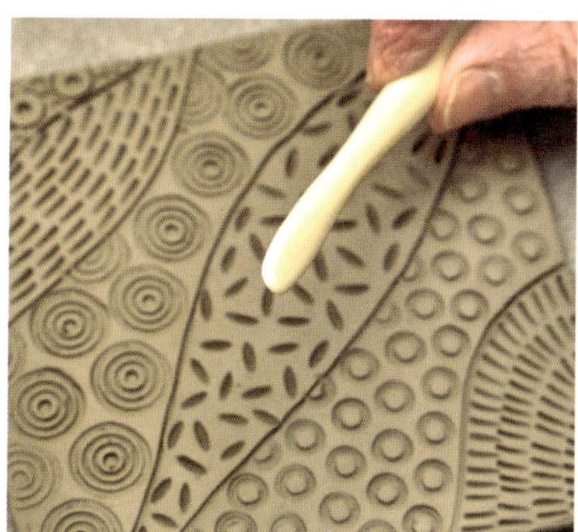

3 Plastic modeling tools, available from cut-price stores, are great for impressing seeding patterns.

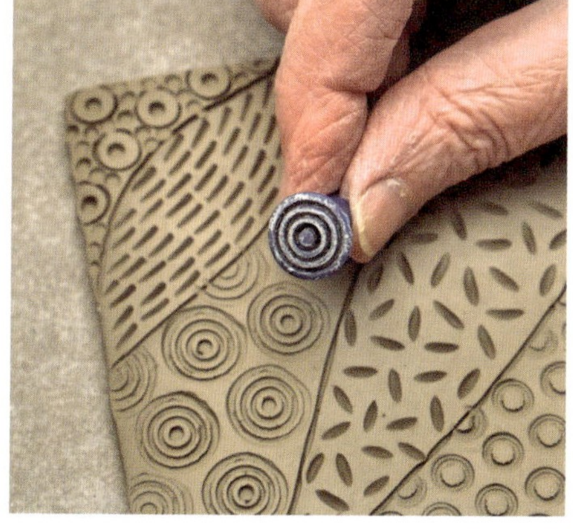

4 Often, dismembering pens will reveal some really original shapes. The key is to always be looking for interesting things to make marks in clay, but be warned—it can become quite compulsive!

FIRING: ELECTRIC KILNS

All the projects in this book have been fired in an electric kiln because this is the most common and accessible type of kiln, which can be accommodated in a home studio or in a workshop. For this reason it is the only kiln type covered here.

GUIDE TO ELECTRIC KILNS

- Electric kilns are generally the best choice for the beginner, especially those living in urban environments, because they burn cleanly, are safe, and easy to fire, with generally predictable outcomes.
- These kilns are available in many sizes, some small enough to fire in a domestic situation.
- Sophisticated programmers/controllers mean that you do not have to "kiln sit" to turn up the temperature and make sure electric kilns fire smoothly.
- Top-loading kilns are usually less expensive than front loaders. They suit small-scale workshops and are easy to install.
- Front-loading kilns have a solid metal framework with a more substantial firebrick wall, so are heavier and retain heat for much longer. They are more expensive to buy and install but much harder wearing than a top loader.

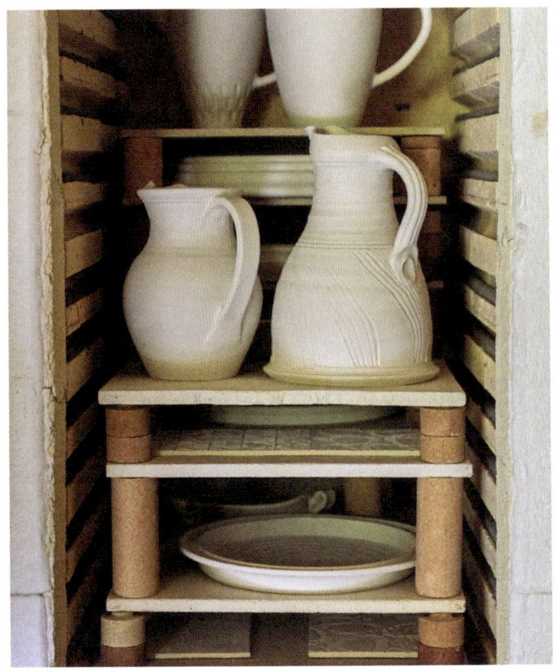

POINTS TO CONSIDER WHEN BUYING A KILN

SPACE: Where the kiln will be sited will dictate the possible size. Whether fitting into a studio or at home, a kiln needs space around it and a solid floor beneath it because it gets very hot.

POWER SUPPLY: Obviously an electric kiln needs an electricity supply and large kilns often need a larger supply than most domestic situations can provide. Make sure that your supply is adequate for the kiln's needs.

SCALE OF WORK: If you need to fire something in a hurry and your kiln is big, you will waste precious energy. It is far more economical to fire a small kiln more often.

ACCESSIBILITY TO THE KILN SITE: A large kiln will not fit through a small door and, importantly, electric kilns must be sited indoors. Similarly, moving a heavy kiln from the delivery vehicle to site can be a nightmare if you live on the side of a hill and it has to be moved some distance!

BUYING A KILN: NEW VERSUS OLD

If you can afford it, buy a new kiln because older kilns tend to be heavier, less efficient, and thus more expensive to fire. They can often be a false economy because they may need expensive overhauling. However, great bargains can be had from people who bought new kilns, then lost interest in pottery. Use the internet as a search engine for such bargains.

If you decide to buy new, most pottery suppliers will have a good range of kilns to choose from and be able to advise you on the best size and type to meet your needs. Shop around before committing to a purchase—often a supplier will do a deal if you say you have found something similar elsewhere that is cheaper!

KILN FURNITURE

Kilns are packed using shelves and supports. Tubular props are available in different sizes and are stackable to allow you to adjust the height of the shelves.

A standard set of kiln shelves and props in appropriate size usually comes with a kiln.

STAR STILTS—have short metal points which are used to raise earthenware glazed work off the kiln shelf. They are available from very small to large. The points leave tiny, barely noticeable marks in the glazed surface after firing which can be ground down with a carborundum if this is necessary.

SADDLES/PINS—are triangular bars that provide maximum support for large items in firing. They are also useful to support items with fine and detailed bases, or items with an odd shape that are otherwise difficult to position in the kiln.

SAFETY ASPECTS

The kiln should not be sited in the room where you work. If it has to be, fire it overnight so that you are not in the room at the same time.

The kiln should be sited away from flammable materials or structures, and have enough space to move around it easily.

Make sure the floor of your workshop or home can support the weight of the kiln and can tolerate heat.

VERY IMPORTANT: A top-loading kiln can be hazardous for people who suffer with back problems, especially when lifting large or heavy work up, then over, and down into the firing chamber. A front loader would be a safer choice.

Types of firings

All potters ultimately develop their own firing patterns, usually to accommodate the idiosyncrasies of their kiln or for particular effects. The key to success when firing in a new kiln is to keep records to compare to subsequent firings. It can be a slow learning curve, unfortunately, with many frustrations along the way, but with time you will come to understand and bond with your kiln and firing will become an exciting part of your production.

BISQUE

- The first firing is known as the bisque, or biscuit, firing and marks the point at which clay is changed into a hard and permanent material by an irreversible chemical process. The clay appears biscuit-like after the firing, as the name suggests, but although hard, remains very porous at this stage and ideal for glazing.
- Pots for bisque firing MUST be completely dry.
- When packing your kiln for bisque firing it does not matter if the pots touch one another. Bowls can be stacked rim to rim or base to base, as long as the weight is evenly distributed. Some pots can be fired inside others for economy, but they must fit freely and loosely; if they are wedged they will crack when the clay shrinks during firing.

Bisque firing schedule:
Bisque firing should start at a slow rate of 210°F (100°C) per hour to 930°F (500°C) with bungs and spy holes fully open to allow the escape of steam from the chemically held water in the clay. After this point it has mostly been driven out of the clay, so the bungs can be put in and the temperature can be raised to 300°F (150°C) per hour for the remainder of the firing. Most potters bisque fire to between 1,760–1,830°F (960–1,000°C) to ensure any carbon deposits in the clay have been burned out.

GLAZE FIRING

After bisque firing, pottery is usually glazed and returned to the kiln for a second firing. This firing will differ from the bisque firing, in that it will generally be to a higher temperature to melt the glaze.

Packing a kiln for glaze firing:
When packing a kiln for glaze firing it is essential that the pots do not touch one another and that the kiln shelf has been coated with bat wash to prevent glaze drips sealing the pot onto the shelf. This is especially important for high temperature firings. Bat wash can be bought from your supplier or made from a mix of two parts alumina and one part china clay, mixed with water to a brushable consistency.

General guide for glaze firing:

- Start the firing program slowly with the bungs out to ensure any water absorbed from glazing is driven out.
- At 840°F (450°C) the temperature can be accelerated to the optimal for the clay/glaze type and the bungs put in place.
- Many controllers will have a "FULL" setting and can be programmed to fire to the 840°F (450°C) temperature at a low ramp rate of 210°F (100°C) per hour, for example, then switch to FULL to complete the firing to the optimum temperature.

EARTHENWARE

Individual glazes will mature at different temperatures and earthenware's have a wide firing range, from 1,870–2,120°F (1,020–1,160°C).

Most earthenware clay bodies remain porous after firing. The solution to this problem is to glaze the entire form, including the underside, and fire the pot on stilts to raise the pieces off the kiln shelf (see *Kiln Furniture*, opposite). This seals the clay and is especially important for domestic wares, where hygiene is paramount.

STONEWARE

Mid-temperature stoneware glazes:
These fire from 2,134–2,219°F (1,164–1,215°C). Many potters are turning to a lower stoneware glaze firing as a way of reducing fuel costs and manufacturers now produce wonderful ranges of these glazes in a ready-to-use formula for brushing or dipping, for makers who don't have the time or means to make and test their own. Clay manufacturers have responded to the demand by producing clays that vitrify at lower temperatures to fit with these glazes. Make sure the two are compatible when buying clay and glaze.

High-temperature stoneware glazes:
These fire in the range 2,246–2,365°F (1,230–1,300°C) and include porcelains.

All work fired to these and the mid-fire temperatures must have all traces of glaze thoroughly removed from bases and foot rings. You cannot fire wares on stilts to these temperatures because the clay will slump over the stilt. They must be fired directly on the kiln shelf for stability. When using glazes that are known to be runny, remove the glaze ¼in (5mm) above the base for safety.

TIP

– Not all potters like to use bat wash on their kiln shelves but when firing to these high temperatures, stoneware clays can sometimes fuse to the kiln shelf even when glaze has been removed. A good alternative is to spread a thin layer of silica sand over the shelf. This acts like miniscule ball bearings, allowing the clay base to move as it shrinks and thus avoid sticking.

A WORD OF CAUTION: You must be very careful not to accidentally brush against the sand once in place. If it falls onto a glazed surface it will seal inside when it melts and create unsightly blemishes.

INDEX